Quest for Justice

Louis A. Bedford Jr. in his judicial robes in the 1970s. Dallas Municipal Archives, City Secretary's Office.

QUEST *for* JUSTICE

LOUIS A. BEDFORD JR. AND THE
STRUGGLE FOR EQUAL RIGHTS IN TEXAS

DARWIN PAYNE

Foreword by W. Marvin Dulaney
Afterword by Amilcar Shabazz

Southern Methodist University Press
Dallas

Copyright © 2009 by Darwin Payne
Foreword © 2009 by W. Marvin Dulaney
Afterword © 2009 by Amilcar Shabazz
First Edition, 2009
All rights reserved. No part of this book may be reproduced, stored in a retrieval program, or transmitted by any form or by any means, electronic, mechanical, photocopying, recording, or otherwise except as may be expressly permitted by the applicable copyright statutes or in writing by the author.

Requests for permission to reproduce material from this work should be sent to:
   Rights and Permissions
   Southern Methodist University Press
   PO Box 750415
   Dallas, Texas 75275-0415

Jacket and text design by Tom Dawson
Cover photo: "Cooksie's Café for Colored on Hall Street in Dallas, 1946," Marion Butts Collection, Texas/Dallas History and Archives Division, Dallas Public Library.

Library of Congress Cataloging-in-Publication Data

Payne, Darwin.
   Quest for justice : Louis A. Bedford Jr. and the struggle for equal rights in Texas / Darwin Payne ; foreword by W. Marvin Dulaney ; afterword by Amilcar Shabazz. — 1st ed.
      p. cm.
   Includes bibliographical references and index.
   ISBN 978-0-87074-552-2 (alk. paper)
   1. Bedford, Louis A. 2. Judges—Texas—Biography. 3. African American judges—Texas—Biography. 4. Lawyers—Texas—Dallas—Biography. 5. African American lawyers—Texas—Dallas—Biography. 6. African Americans—Civil rights—Texas. 7. Civil rights movements—Texas—History—20th century. 8. Practice of law—Texas—Dallas—History—20th century. I. Title.
   KF373.B355P39 2009
   347.73'14092--dc22
   [B]   2008055253

Printed in the United States of America on acid-free paper

10   9   8   7   6   5   4   3   2   1

For my sisters,

June Payne Marco and Sally Payne Estes

Also by Darwin Payne

Indomitable Sarah: The Life of Judge Sarah T. Hughes
Owen Wister: Chronicler of the West, Gentleman of the East
Big D: Triumphs and Troubles of an American Supercity in the 20th Century

CONTENTS

FOREWORD

Louis A. Bedford Jr.'s appointment as a municipal judge in 1966 shattered the racial ceiling that had prevented African Americans from holding public office in Dallas County. His appointment was a watershed in the city's history, and it helped to break the stranglehold that the white businessmen of the Citizens Charter Association had held over city government in Dallas since 1931. In March 1967, African Americans in Dallas recognized Bedford's achievement by presenting him a "Trailblazer" award at a special banquet. Joe Lockridge, the first black legislator from Dallas County, and C. A. Galloway, the first black city councilman, were also honored with "Trailblazer" awards at the event. The three men had blazed new paths for African American political participation in Dallas.

None of Bedford's trailblazing contemporaries, however, matched his longevity. None of them reached across subsequent generations to influence up-and-coming community organizers, politicians, and historians as much as Judge Bedford. I had the pleasure of meeting Louis A. Bedford Jr. over twenty years ago when I was curator for an exhibition on the history of African Americans in the Dallas political arena from 1936 to 1986. He was one of the consultants on the project, and I was very impressed by his knowledge of the topic. He knew everyone and had stories about every African American who had ever run for political office in Dallas County. In addition, Judge Bedford had not only run for political office himself on two occasions, but he had also been involved as an attorney in civil rights cases to desegregate the city's public schools. When the exhibition opened at the Dallas Public Library in 1988, it was one of the best ever assembled on the city's racial politics. Judge Bedford's knowledge and contribution were indispensable in making it a success.

Some fifteen years later I had the opportunity to work again with Judge Bedford while I was on a sabbatical to research on a book on Dallas's African American history. I spent three days interviewing him, learning about his family—especially his grandfather M. M. Rodgers—and his own long history of activism and contributions to the African American experience in Dallas. Subsequently, the Dallas African American Museum asked me to serve as curator for an exhibition on Judge Bedford's life and times. Entitled "Judge L. A. Bedford: A Life in Service," the exhibition was sponsored by the Dallas Bar Association (DBA) and the J. L. Turner Legal Association. It opened at the DBA's Belo Mansion offices on January 15, 2004, in celebration of Martin Luther King Jr. Day. It was an appropriate tribute to the life and contributions of Judge Bedford, one of many he has richly deserved.

The 2004 exhibition provided a mere snapshot of Judge Bedford's life and times. In no way could it convey to its viewers the grace, dignity, and tremendous courage that Judge Bedford's life represents. The exhibition outlined his many contributions to the Dallas community, but it did not and could not share with its viewers his warmth, his sense of justice, his commitment to community service, and how much of a difference he has made in people's lives in Dallas. Darwin Payne's *Quest for Justice* addresses much of what the exhibition failed to convey to its viewers about the life and times of Judge Louis A. Bedford Jr.

Payne has done a wonderful job of placing the life of Judge Bedford into the context of Dallas and Texas's history. By doing so he has achieved two things. First, he has highlighted the life of one of Dallas's African American professionals and described how he and his contemporaries fought for social and political justice for all Americans. Second, he has synthesized most of the scholarship on African American history in the region and made it accessible to a wider audience. Payne's work provides a good starting point for those of us interested in studying, researching, and writing the history of African Americans in Dallas and around the state. And he has done it by telling the story of Judge L. A. Bedford Jr., a role model for those who will follow him.

W. MARVIN DULANEY

W. Marvin Dulaney is associate professor of history at the University of Texas at Arlington and co-editor of *Essays on the American Civil Rights Movement.*

PREFACE

L ouis Arthur Bedford Jr. was born at a time and in a place where black people were reminded daily of their unfortunate status in life. The great majority accepted their lot with grim resolve and without protest. Achieving their rightful place in society, theoretically assured by the Constitution, seemed far away.

By the time Bedford reached middle age, dramatic changes were occurring across the nation and in his hometown to rectify the plight of African Americans; when he reached his later years, black leaders in Dallas, throughout Texas, and across the nation had achieved power and prominence. Past and present black officials in Dallas have included a mayor, a district attorney, a police chief, judges, school superintendents, county commissioners, and state senators. The nation had seen African Americans in national positions of high office—Supreme Court justices, secretaries of state, and a chairman of the Joint Chiefs of Staff—and in November 2008, voters chose by a wide margin a black man, Barack Obama, to be their president.

This remarkable transformation occurred in a single generation. Bedford, as one of the handful of black attorneys in Dallas in the 1950s and 1960s, participated in this transformation. He became the first black judge in Dallas County, he campaigned for city and county public offices, he managed the campaigns of other candidates, he represented and advised controversial activists and activist groups, and he was a pioneer black member of the Dallas Bar Association.

On the first day of January 2007, Bedford gave the oath of office to the first black district attorney elected in Dallas County, Craig Watkins. For symbolic reasons Watkins had asked this senior attorney and friend to swear him in, since Watkins's election was the culmination of a long journey that Bedford, perhaps more than anyone, appreciated.

As young men aspiring to be attorneys, Bedford and others like him were forced to leave the state to study law, because no law school in Texas then accepted black applicants. In 1950, after earning his law degree on the East Coast and enjoying the benefits of a desegregated society there, Bedford returned to his home city and state, where segregation remained as harsh as ever. He arrived in time to take part in the sweeping changes propelled by Supreme Court decisions, augmented by congressional civil rights legislation, and finally put into practice against fierce resistance through sheer grit and determination.

When the turmoil subsided, Bedford emerged as a figure beloved in both the black and the white communities. Young black lawyers, now too numerous for him to know each one personally, today revere him. Senior members of the Dallas Bar Association, who in the 1960s denied him membership because of his color, have bestowed awards and honors upon him.

Much has been written about the historic civil rights movement. Understandably, historians early on placed their emphasis on the national scene and on familiar individuals now ordained as national heroes. More recently, scholars have focused on Texas, a fertile ground where such cases as *Smith v. Allwright* (1944) and *Sweatt v. Painter* (1950) originated and marked key breakthroughs. As a result of these important studies, such Texas civil rights leaders as Lulu White, A. Maceo Smith, W. J. Durham, Juanita Craft, and Carter Wesley have become familiar figures.

This study of a less familiar leader, Louis Bedford, seeks to portray him in historical context as an individual and family man trying to overcome the inequities of a segregated society. In the course of detailing Bedford's legal career and social activism, this study also describes the struggles of other African Americans in the legal system, especially black attorneys in Texas, in overcoming inequities on an institutional level.

Bedford is the grandson of M. M. Rodgers, who, like his friend Norris Wright Cuney, gained considerable acceptance and power in Texas at the turn of the twentieth century as a prominent Republican. How strange it seems that in the next few years, a white majority was able to deprive men such as Rodgers and Cuney and all black citizens of so many of their basic rights as American citizens through such overtly hostile measures as the white primary, through segregated and inferior public schools, through denial of graduate and professional education, and through fear and intimidation. By examining his life, I hope to shed some light on Bedford's accomplishments and those of others that ended such injustices and brought greater freedom to all African Americans.

ACKNOWLEDGMENTS

This biography owes its origin to Elizabeth Lang-Miers, justice of the Court of Appeals for the Fifth District of Texas, who for many years has known and worked with L. A. Bedford Jr. in activities of the Dallas Bar Association. She saw his life as a story that deserved a broad audience, and she arranged for a grant from the Dallas Bar Foundation to help fund the work.

Mr. Bedford inspired a large number of the present generation of African American attorneys who encouraged this undertaking and assisted with their recollections. Among them were Paul Stafford, Joan Tarpley, Rhonda Hunter, DeMitris Sampson, and T. J. Johnson. Former Dallas Mayor Ron Kirk, State Senator Royce West, District Attorney Craig Watkins, and U.S. District Judge Sam Lindsay were among so many of those who offered their support. Al Ellis, former Dallas Bar Association president, enthusiastically lent his support, as did Harriet Miers, who before she went to the White House to be the president's counsel, was the first woman president of both the Dallas Bar Association and the State Bar of Texas.

The subject of this book submitted to numerous interviews and helped clarify certain events in which he was a participant. He opened up his office and collection of invaluable historical documents throughout the project. His assistant for many years, Carmena Adams, was a welcoming host in the office. Josephine Dye, who maintained a law office in the building, was equally helpful.

Mr. Bedford's wife Velma was a particularly valuable source who had excellent recall of events and dates. His sister, Deborah Bedford Fridia, described their early family life as children. Edward Harris and Peter Johnson gave important insights about their civil rights activism and Mr. Bedford's support.

I am especially grateful to those who read versions of the manuscript and offered their insights and suggestions: Michael V. Hazel, Michael L. Gillette, and Charles Martin.

W. Marvin Dulaney and Amilcar Shabazz, themselves noted scholars in the field of African American studies and especially concerning Texas, submitted to my requests to add their own perspectives to the manuscript, and I am indebted to them. Charles Vert Willy and Darlene Clark Hine were two other noted scholars who read the manuscript and offered encouragement.

As so often is the case, the Texas/Dallas History & Archives Division at the J. E. Jonsson Central Public Library in Dallas was a welcoming place where Carol Roark and her staff were essential to my research. So, too, were Southern Methodist University's Fondren Library and Underwood Law Library.

John Slate, City of Dallas archivist, found the portrait of Mr. Bedford that is the frontispiece. Linda Holmes of the Brooklyn Law School located and provided the photograph of the school at the time Bedford was a student there.

I am grateful to several copyeditors for their sharp eyes that saved me from embarrassing errors: Leah Hackleman, Katie Lanning, Peter Alan Nelson, Robert Fullilove, and Brooke Fugitt.

The fine people at the SMU Press—Keith Gregory, Kathryn Lang, and George Ann Ratchford—made this book possible. I am among the many authors who appreciate their knowledgeable guidance.

Quest for Justice

1

CONSTRICTED HORIZONS

In 1940 in Lansing, Michigan, a young African American named Malcolm Little was one of the brightest students in his integrated public school classroom. One day Malcolm's teacher, with whom he had developed a special relationship because of his academic prowess, spoke directly to his prize pupil: "Malcolm, you ought to be thinking about a career. Have you been giving it any thought?"

"Well, yes, sir," Malcolm replied. "I've been thinking I'd like to be a lawyer."

Mr. Ostrowski looked surprised. Malcolm would never forget this seminal moment in his life. Mr. Ostrowski leaned back in his chair, clasped his hands behind his head, and delivered in measured tones a response that was shocking to his impressionable student, who had not experienced the painful wounds of segregation: "Malcolm, one of life's first needs is for us to be realistic. Don't misunderstand me, now. We all here like you—you know that. But you've got to be realistic about being a nigger. You need to think about something you can be."

Mr. Ostrowski recommended that Malcolm Little—one day to be known to the world as Malcolm X—consider carpentry as his future occupation.[1]

In these same prewar years in Dallas, Texas, a city with a Southern heritage where state laws, municipal ordinances, and social custom enforced rigid segregation in every area of life, there lived another bright African American youth who was about the same age as Malcolm. Unlike Malcolm Little, Louis Arthur Bedford Jr. had never been in a classroom with a white student. Living in a strictly segregated society, he understood the limitations for a youth of his race. His own ambitions met Mr. Ostrowski's criterion for being realistic. Louis wanted to be a railroad mail clerk. Many blacks had found respectable careers in this occupation, just as they had found glamour in their work as Pullman porters.

Young Louis entertained no thoughts of a legal career. Not until his junior year at an all-black college would such an idea enter his mind. Louis Arthur Bedford Jr. did become one of his hometown's most recognized and honored attorneys, white or black, serving as a role model for other African Americans. He was not the first African American attorney in Texas or even in Dallas, but he was the first to be accepted on an equal basis by his local and state bar associations and the first to be appointed a judge in his home city.

But as Bedford later pointed out, he had stood on the shoulders of many early and courageous black attorneys. "When I become an old lawyer and can no longer stand before the bar," he declared in 1990 in an article in *Headnotes*, the Dallas Bar Association's official newsletter, "I will tell all who will listen of those Comets, dedicated, intense, and brilliant, who illuminated the legal sky for all seeking justice and equality from a hostile and racist legal system. . . . I will speak of men who maintained their dignity and never lost their pride, whose eloquence with words and knowledge of the law could never be denied." In affectionate terms he described those few African Americans in Dallas before him who had served as his role models—J. L. Turner Sr., W. J. Durham, and C. B. Bunkley Jr.—whose courage he would always remember as he tried to establish his own practice in a "sea of whiteness that covered the courthouse, except for janitors who were invisible."[2]

Bedford feared that the memory of these legal pioneers had already vanished by the 1990s. The young black attorneys in Dallas and in the state had little knowledge of the handful of brave African American pioneer lawyers who had provided those strong shoulders.

As a young man before the civil rights movement, Bedford did not have the advantage of their example. The few black lawyers who had broken barriers in the previous century were already almost lost to history. As late as 1973, a widely respected general history of American law by a prominent law professor made no mention of any of them.[3] For Bedford and the few others of his generation who became lawyers at midcentury, it was like Columbus and Magellan sailing into unchartered waters.

Being a lawyer in America has always been a lofty ambition favored by the privileged classes. The profession has been a ticket to broader success, to respectability, to leadership. With few exceptions, becoming an attorney has been a goal not easily achieved by anyone who lacked some means or a certain status in society.

One has only to look back on the nation's history to recognize the attraction of the profession. The democratic foundation of the nation relied heavily on lawyers. Of the fifty-two signers of the Declaration of Independence, twenty-five were lawyers. Thirty-one of the fifty-six members of the Continental Congress were lawyers. More than half of the nation's presidents have been lawyers, and between 1877 and 1934, 70 percent of the presidents, vice presidents, and cabinet members were lawyers. These facts reinforce Tocqueville's observation that lawyers "form the highest political class and the most cultivated portion of society."[4]

For those of the privileged classes with access to higher education, entry into the legal profession was not difficult. The difficulties increased as one went down the socioeconomic ladder. Stories of a few poor but ambitious frontier youths who studied hard and gained fame in the profession in the nineteenth century are common—Abraham Lincoln immediately comes to mind. Usually, such a tough-minded individual managed to make a fortunate connection, frequently with a town lawyer who permitted him to "read" law in his office as an apprentice. Following a respectable period of service, the apprentice might gain admission to the local bar after a brief and often cursory oral examination by his sponsor and the sponsor's friends.

If obstacles to entry into the profession were not absolutely insurmountable for African Americans, they were formidable enough that only the smallest fraction of blacks could overcome them. Very few considered the possibility of becoming lawyers even midway into the twentieth century.

Ironically, self-interest dictated that blacks *should* be entering the legal system, for here was the source of the laws that held them in a continuing form of bondage. If they wanted liberation, why not enter the fray? In school districts, city and county governments, state legislatures, and the halls of Congress, these same laws could be changed. But the world of the law was a white man's world. What difference could one black person hope to make?

Moreover, through emphasizing industrial education, such leaders as Booker T. Washington seemed willing to give up any possibility that blacks could have careers in intellectual activities. Washington's stance was an acknowledgment that African

Americans must start at the bottom and work their way up over several generations. "The opportunity to earn a dollar in a factory just now is worth infinitely more than the opportunity to spend a dollar in an opera house," he said.[5]

Despite the obstacles, a few intrepid blacks, whose stories were unknown to young Malcolm Little and Louis A. Bedford Jr., successfully defied the long odds and found their way into the legal profession. With a black population in Texas approaching 1 million in 1940—the year Louis turned fourteen—there were only twenty-two African American lawyers in the state. That figure paled in comparison to the 160 black physicians and surgeons and eighty-one dentists. The situation was hardly better anywhere else in the nation: of more than 12 million black Americans, just 1,052 were lawyers. The few young black Texans who aspired to be lawyers could not gain legal training in their own state. No law school in Texas—public or private—accepted black students.[6]

The nation's earliest known black attorney was Macon Bolling Allen, who became the first African American to gain admission to any state bar when in 1844, at the age of twenty-eight, he won authorization to practice law in Maine. Two influential men sponsored Allen: the fervent abolitionist Samuel C. Fessenden, a Congregationalist minister and general, and attorney Samuel E. Sewell. No racial restrictions existed in Maine. Any citizen of the state who produced a certificate of good moral character was eligible to be admitted to the bar. After it was determined that Allen, a native of Indiana, was not a Maine citizen and thus ineligible to be admitted merely by merit of his character, he took a second avenue—admission by examination, which he passed.[7]

Allen's entry into the learned profession of law did not go unnoticed. In an article evidently intended to counter possible criticism, the *Daily Eastern Argus* asked, "Is the practice of law so much more respectable than hoeing potatoes that a lawyer can be disgraced by contact with a black man, and not a farmer?"[8]

In sparsely populated Maine, there were few citizens of any race to sustain a law practice, let alone a sufficient number of African Americans who might be expected to be Allen's primary clients. Realizing this, Allen left Maine after a year for the more promising environs of Boston, a center of fervent abolitionist sentiment. Not for thirty-five years would another African American practice law in Maine.[9]

4

Allen was admitted to Boston's Suffolk County Bar on May 3, 1845, on a certificate of competency signed by a Judge Merrick. Allen thus gained the distinction of being Massachusetts's first black attorney, repeating the honor he had gained in Maine. News of Allen's admission again did not escape notice. Boston's sympathetic abolitionist newspaper the *Liberator* noted, with possible exaggeration, that Allen had benefited from a classical education. "Although a colored person, [he] is, we are informed, a young man of such character and deportment, gentle, unassuming and strictly upright."[10] Back in Maine the *Daily Eastern Argus* also took note with unusual candor. Describing Allen as a person whose "color and physiognomy" spoke of a mingled Indian and African extraction of about equal proportions, he was said to be "passably good looking" and of medium height and size. "He is indeed a better looking man than two or three white members of the Boston Bar, and it is hardly possible that he can be a worse lawyer than at least six of them, whom we could name."[11]

Allen encountered in Boston the same problem that confronted so many newcomers: the rigid social structure favored people with long family ties to the city. Even Boston's abolitionists were of little help, especially after he refused to sign a pledge protesting a possible war with Mexico, which abolitionists believed would extend slavery.

Allen persevered in Boston, though, and in 1847 Massachusetts Governor George N. Briggs, a Whig, appointed him justice of the peace, an appointment renewed in 1854 by Governor Emory Washburn. Allen thus became the first African American to be appointed to a judicial post.[12]

After the Civil War and at the advent of Reconstruction, Allen moved to Charleston, South Carolina, where he was admitted to the bar and began a law practice. On October 15, 1894, he died in Washington, D.C.[13]

The nation's second black lawyer also got his start in Boston. Robert Morris Sr. was sponsored for admission to the bar by abolitionist Ellis Gray Loring. Morris had begun working for Loring as a house servant at the age of fifteen. When his duties were expanded to copying documents in Loring's law office, his employer noted Morris's proficiency and encouraged him to study law. In 1847 Morris was admitted to practice in Suffolk County.

Later that year Morris became the first black lawyer in the nation's history to file a lawsuit on behalf of a client, and he won the case. "There was something in the courtroom that made me feel like a giant," Morris later wrote about his experience. "The courtroom was filled with colored people, and I could see, expressed on the faces of every one of them, a wish that I might win the first case that had ever been tried before a jury by a colored attorney in this country." When the verdict was returned in favor of Morris's client, the black observers in the courtroom "acted as if they would shout for joy."[14]

In 1849 Morris joined Charles Sumner, who two years later would become a passionately antislavery U.S. senator from Massachusetts, in representing a five-year-old black girl who had been excluded from a public school near her home and sent to a black school farther away. Morris and Sumner lost the case, *Roberts v. City of Boston*, and the U.S. Supreme Court cited it in 1896 in the regrettable *Plessy v. Ferguson* decision authorizing "separate but equal" facilities for blacks and whites.[15]

In the earliest years of the nation's history, few law schools existed for persons of any color, white or black. In about 1784 Judge Tapping Reeve founded in Litchfield, Connecticut, what has been recognized as the first law school. It developed out of Reeve's practice of permitting would-be attorneys to read law in his office. Reeve's "school" grew rapidly and gained a national reputation. It ceased to exist in 1833, but by then more formal law schools had arisen, many created as departments of colleges and universities. The College of William and Mary established the nation's first law professorship in 1779, and in 1816 Harvard began offering a specialized program of legal studies. In 1844 Harvard graduated 163 students with bachelor of laws degrees.[16]

The first black applicant at any of these American law schools was the extraordinary John Mercer Langston. In the early 1850s Langston, a twenty-one-year-old graduate of Oberlin College, tried to enroll for law courses in Ballston Spa, New York, a county seat twenty-five miles north of Albany. Langston, light complexioned, was told he would be admitted if he agreed to "pass" as white—as either a Frenchman or a Spaniard—and to sit separate from his white classmates. He would not be permitted to ask any questions. Langston refused these conditions and applied to a Cincinnati school, where he was also rejected. Langston finally secured an office apprenticeship with a sympathetic Ohio judge, Philemon Bliss, and in 1853 Langston was admitted to the Ohio bar.[17]

Langston was the freeborn son of a wealthy white planter, a Virginia slaveholder, Ralph Quarles, and an emancipated slave mother, Lucy Jane. When Langston's parents both died in 1834 from unrelated illnesses, they left Langston, then the age of five, a significant inheritance. He was subsequently reared in Ohio, and he earned bachelor's and master's degrees at Oberlin College, southwest of Cleveland. (Oberlin was established in 1833, and in 1835 it became the nation's first integrated college.) Langston became active in helping runaway slaves coming through the Underground Railroad, and he conspired with John Brown on his 1859 Harpers Ferry raid but declined to participate and was not prosecuted.

In 1868 the newly established Howard University in Washington, D.C., summoned Langston to organize a law department. He hired as law professors three white lawyers who liked the idea of educating former slaves in the law. Howard thus became the first university with a racially integrated faculty.

Howard's first law students were accepted in 1869, and for the initial graduation in February 1871, Langston invited Senator Charles Sumner of Massachusetts to give the commencement address. Sumner had the privilege of speaking to the world's first graduating class of black lawyers. He told the ten graduates that, being members of a race that for generations had been oppressed, they "should always be on the side of human rights."[18]

Langston served as the dean of the Howard University Law Department from 1868 to 1875. He became the second African American lawyer admitted to practice before the U.S. Supreme Court (the first was Dr. John Swett Rock, a physician and lawyer in Massachusetts). From 1875 to 1883 Langston served as U.S. minister to Haiti, and in 1889 he was the first black citizen elected to the U.S. Congress from Virginia. Langston University (north of Oklahoma City and founded in 1897 as Oklahoma Agricultural and Normal University) was renamed for him.[19]

Howard University had been founded by Congressional charter in 1867 to provide a college education for African Americans freed from slavery. Funds came from the Freedmen's Bureau; the name honored the chief of the bureau, General Oliver O. Howard. Howard University's graduates over the years have become some of the nation's most distinguished citizens. Edward Brooke, the first African American elected U.S. senator by popular vote, earned his undergraduate degree there in 1941. Thurgood Marshall, the first African American justice on the U.S. Supreme Court (1967–91), was first in his law school class of 1933.

In the seventy years following the establishment of Howard's law program, nineteen law schools were created specifically for black students. Almost all of them were short lived. During these years Howard's was the only major law school in the nation dedicated to educating African Americans in law.

The nation's primary professional organization for lawyers, the American Bar Association (ABA), refused for many years to admit African Americans. An incident in 1912 reflected its attitude. Without realizing the applicants' race, the ABA Executive Committee admitted to membership three black attorneys, William Henry Lewis and Butler Roland Wilson of Boston and William R. Morris of Minneapolis. Lewis was a Harvard Law School graduate and an assistant attorney general of the United States, the first person of his race to hold that position and the highest ranking black public official in the nation's history up to 1912.[20]

When the Executive Committee realized that these new members were black, it rescinded its action, explaining that "the settled practice of the Association has been to elect only white men to membership." When its statement was reported at the ABA's annual meeting in 1912, members recognized the unfairness of the retraction and passed a resolution declaring that it was too late to rescind the membership of the three black lawyers. However, their resolution also stated that no one had contemplated that "colored men" would be members of the American Bar Association. The members left that policy unchanged. One of the three black lawyers, Morris, tendered his resignation in disgust by telegram. Lewis and Wilson, despite pressures, refused to resign. At its next annual meeting, the ABA passed a resolution declaring that race and sex hereafter must be included in all future applications for membership.[21]

The resolution effectively blocked black lawyers from ABA membership. This gave the nation's black lawyers reason to form their own bar association. A handful of the nation's fewer than one thousand African American attorneys met in August 1925 in Des Moines, Iowa, to found the National Bar Association (NBA). Initial membership was about 120. (By 2007 the NBA, still predominantly African American, had eighty-four affiliate chapters throughout the United States, Canada, the United Kingdom, Africa, and the Caribbean, with more than twenty thousand lawyers, judges, educators, and law students as members.)[22]

Not until 1943 did the ABA change its restrictive policies, when it adopted a resolution stating that membership in the American Bar Association was "not dependent upon race, creed or color." In Texas, Louis A. Bedford Jr., who in 1943 was seventeen and a freshman at Prairie View College, had no knowledge of such events. Nor did he have a reason to care; the notion of becoming a lawyer had not occurred to him. But in his hometown, senior members of the Dallas Bar Association, objecting to the ABA removal prohibitions against black lawyers, passed their own resolution urging the organization to rescind its action. Admission of black members, they contended, would lower the dignity of the ABA. The full membership of the bar tabled the proposed resolution by a 33–31 vote, but it would be two decades before the local association would admit a black lawyer as a member.[23]

The identity of the first African American lawyer to practice law in Texas is uncertain. Perhaps the first was Allen W. Wilder, born a slave in North Carolina in about 1845 and elected from Washington County (seventy miles northwest of Houston) in 1873, during Reconstruction, to a single term in the Texas Legislature. After losing a Texas Senate race in 1878, he was by 1880 reported to be earning a living as a teacher and lawyer.[24] The precise date that Wilder was admitted to the bar is unknown. One who might have practiced law even earlier was W. A. Price of Fort Bend County, just southwest of Houston. Price was admitted to practice there in 1876 and in nearby Matagorda County in 1878.

Probably the first native-born black Texan to practice law in the state was Joseph Cuney, older brother of Norris Wright Cuney, the foremost black politician in the state in the last two decades of the 1800s. The Cuney brothers were two of eight children born to a white planter, Philip Minor Cuney, and a slave mother, Adeline Stuart, at Cuney's Sunnyville Plantation in Austin County (west of Houston). Joseph Cuney, born in 1840, was set free before the Civil War (as were his sisters and brothers) and sent to a private school in Pittsburgh, Pennsylvania. With the outbreak of the Civil War, he joined the Sixty-third Pennsylvania Volunteers as a Union soldier. When his mother, Adeline, learned at one point that he was in Virginia, she wrote to ask him to go and find her mother, Hester Neale Stuart of Centreville, west of Washington, D.C. Cuney located her, and he had the pleasure of liberating his own slave grandmother during the closing days of the war. Adeline, who had not seen her mother for forty years, was happily reunited with her. Cuney's grandmother, Hester, lived to be one hundred years old. After the war Cuney moved to Galveston, Texas, where his brother Norris soon would become a formidable figure, and started a law practice.

Norris Wright Cuney, who studied law but did not become a lawyer, achieved the greater recognition, becoming the Texas national committeeman of the Republican Party in 1886, the most important political position given to a Southern black man from that time to the end of the nineteenth century. He was a delegate to every national Republican convention from 1872 to 1892, a collector of customs for the port of Galveston, a labor organizer, a dispenser of patronage to both blacks and whites, and a proponent of education.[25]

In northeast Texas, Dallas was a newer city than Galveston, growing rapidly as a railroad center and attracting many new attorneys because of its commercial promise. Dallas's first African American lawyer was Sam H. Scott, who moved to the city in March 1881 from Memphis, Tennessee, where blacks had been practicing law since about 1868. He established an office and residence in Dallas at 301 Main Street, in the immediate area of the courthouse.

We know little about Scott's background. The 1880 Memphis census report shows him to be divorced, forty years of age, a lawyer, and a native of Massachusetts. In the space for the place of birth of Scott's parents, the census taker wrote "unknown." In the space for race, the enumerator recorded "mu" for "mulatto." A reference to Scott in the *Dallas Daily Herald* suggests that he had lived for a while in Oberlin, Ohio, where he likely was educated at Oberlin College.[26]

Scott's stay in Dallas was short lived. After just seven months, when the city's population of some ten thousand included about eighteen hundred African Americans, he left in October 1881 for Pine Bluff, Arkansas. His brief tenure in Dallas gained favorable notice in the *Dallas Weekly Herald*, though, which published a story about his departure under the headline "Our Colored Lawyer." The news story noted,

He came to this city highly endorsed by the bar of Memphis, and leaves here recommended by a number of the most prominent members of this bar, the judges of the courts, and some of our best citizens. He was the first and only colored lawyer who ever practiced his profession in this city, and at first there was perhaps a slight prejudice against him on account of his race, yet it must be said that he conducted himself with [such] propriety and discretion that he soon won the good will of all with whom he came in contact, and he leaves carrying with him the good wishes of those who knew him, both white and black.[27]

Pine Bluff, southeast of Little Rock, offered a better opportunity for Scott, for African Americans there outnumbered whites by two to one. In 1885 or 1886, a man from Pine Bluff named S. H. Scott—surely the same Sam H. Scott—served in the Arkansas General Assembly. In 1889 an African American attorney named S. H. Scott was admitted to the bar in Fort Smith, Arkansas. He was noted as one of the first persons of his race to be admitted to that city's bar.[28]

Despite his obvious role as a pioneer attorney in three states—Tennessee, Texas, and Arkansas—little else is known about Sam H. Scott. In Dallas he was forgotten until 120 years later, after the honor of first black lawyer had been given erroneously to Joseph E. Wiley. Scott was then identified as the true pioneer; Wiley followed Scott in Dallas by four years.[29]

One year after Scott departed Dallas, another African American, J. H. Williams—from the East Texas town of Mineola, about 80 miles east of Dallas—applied to the district court for admission to the bar. Judge George N. Aldredge appointed a four-man committee to review his qualifications and examine him. The committee failed to reach a conclusion, splitting in a 2-2 vote. Aldredge appointed a second committee of three, who voted unanimously that Williams was not qualified. Williams said he would continue his studies until he could pass the examination, but there is no record of his admission to the bar.[30]

The first black attorney to locate permanently in the city was Joseph Wiley, who came to Dallas from Chicago in 1885. He opened a downtown office in a building owned by A. B. Norton, a white Republican and former Reconstruction judge and postmaster in Dallas. Norton had quite likely encouraged Wiley to move to Dallas. The first reference in the newspapers concerning Wiley's work as an attorney came on October 6, 1885, when the *Dallas Morning News* published a routine item about a divorce petition he filed on behalf of a black client who accused her husband of "abusive, cruel and outrageous treatment."[31]

Wiley soon broadened his work, and his success as an entrepreneur overshadowed his career as a lawyer. He became involved in real estate and later owned the New Century Cotton Mill. In 1901 he organized a noted event in Dallas, the Colored Fair and Tri-Centennial Exposition.

The first African American attorney in Dallas whom Louis A. Bedford Jr. knew was John L. Turner Sr. A veteran attorney, Turner had arrived in the city in about 1898 at the age of twenty-nine. Born in Texas the son of a farmer, and a graduate of Kent College of Law in Chicago, Turner came to join Wiley in his law practice. The 1898 city directory lists him (with the letter "c" for "colored") as Wiley's partner, their office at 155 Main Street just across from the courthouse. Turner went on to practice law in Dallas for fifty-five years. Eventually, he was joined in his practice by his son J. L. Turner Jr. When the growing number of black lawyers in Dallas organized their own bar association in 1952, they named it the J. L. Turner Legal Society (later Association) because of Turner's lengthy practice.

Turner received a number of anonymous threats over his long career. As a result, he began arming himself. One night early in his career, while he was sleeping, his wife got up from bed. Turner heard a noise, saw a dark figure, and fired a shot, accidentally killing his own wife and leaving their son and daughter motherless. After this tragedy Turner never remarried.[32]

Later Bedford and others marveled at Turner's ability to absorb the personal insults and discrimination he faced as a black lawyer during his long career in Dallas. His cases were inevitably placed last on the court docket, heard only after all the white attorneys' cases. He was a diminutive man, but he had great courage.[33]

Another black lawyer, Ammon Scott Wells, is also listed in the 1898 Dallas city directory. He had appeared in the 1894–1895 directory, not as a lawyer but as an employee in the George W. Brooks carriage and wagon manufacturing shop. Four years later he appeared as a partner in the law firm of Henson & Wells, located at 790 Elm Street. (Henson was an early black attorney in Dallas who has not otherwise been identified or recognized.) Wells, born in 1876 in Collin County (immediately northeast of Dallas) and educated in the Dallas public schools, was a light-skinned black man noted by the 1910 census taker as a mulatto, as was his wife. His work at the carriage and wagon shop was short-lived, for Wells began teaching school in Kaufman County (immediately southeast of Dallas) and studying law at the same time under another African American lawyer in Dallas, D. M. Mason.[34] Wells became the first black citizen on record in Dallas to run for public office, seeking unsuccessfully in 1935 to become a state representative.

It might have been Wells's tutor, Mason, who was the second African American attorney after Wiley to establish a permanent practice in Dallas. Born in Dallas in 1872, Mason went to Howard University to study law and returned to his native city in the 1890s as an attorney. His office was at the downtown corner of Commerce and Market Streets.

Mason had two sons, Duane and Roger, who also earned law degrees from Howard University. Duane began his law career in Missouri, staying there for seven years before returning to Dallas in about 1930 to start a practice. Roger evidently had established his office in Dallas even earlier. For a while the two brothers practiced law together, but Roger eventually moved to California. When Duane died on December 10, 1978, he was recognized as one of Dallas's senior black attorneys, an indication of how few had preceded him.[35]

Even in the most law-abiding circles of the black community, there was general disapproval about the legal profession as a career. As Mark V. Tushnet has observed, as late as in the 1930s, black lawyers were not highly regarded as leaders of their communities. As sole practitioners, as they inevitably were, they were too busy with the fee-generating aspects of their profession to be involved in community work.[36]

To be an attorney was to enter a world dominated by the white man and all his prejudices. To work within this highly codified and white-dominated system, a black attorney was constantly forced to ingratiate himself. Gaining clients was a problem, too, for few if any white people would hire a black attorney. Even prospective black clients preferred a white attorney, recognizing the need for a lawyer who could work smoothly in the legal system. Law enforcement officers were white; judges were white; juries were white; court officials were white. There was little hope for a successful career in a legal system that had enacted laws to keep blacks in a position of inferiority. It seemed wisest to stay away from that profession, just as it was wise for a black person to avoid any entanglements at all in the legal system. A 1920s survey of black lawyers in seventeen Southern states found that at least half of them were not actively engaged in the practice of law, finding employment instead as mail carriers, real estate or insurance agents, ministers, and teachers.[37]

The choice of other professions immune to the prejudices of the white world was easier. To be a physician was a far more reasonable objective than being a lawyer. Indeed, black physicians in Dallas easily outnumbered black lawyers in the early twentieth century. A doctor had a ready pool of eager patients. To be a minister was another professional choice that met with approval. To be a teacher was fine, too. But not to be a lawyer.

The nation's legal system had authorized the strict segregationist social system under which young Louis grew to adulthood. The 1896 *Plessy* decision, which found separate facilities for blacks and whites to be constitutional, was not rejected for more than a half century. Meanwhile, the schools, restrooms, water fountains, hotels, theaters, waiting rooms, restaurants, and other features of daily life clearly demonstrated that the separate but equal doctrine promulgated separate and *inferior*, a gross injustice to black Americans especially evident in the South. As Bedford later said, the courts enforced the "separate" provision but not the "equal" one.[38]

If any African American youths had reason to aspire to a legal career and emulate these early black lawyers, it might have been Louis Arthur Bedford Jr., who came from a well-educated family with an illustrious maternal ancestor, M. M. Rodgers. Louis's parents were thoughtful, relatively prosperous individuals who provided a stable and happy home environment for him and his sister. A college education for Louis was expected.

Young Louis's father, Louis Sr., was from Weimar, Texas, a small town in Colorado County midway between Houston and San Antonio. Colorado County was part of Stephen F. Austin's original land grant from Mexico. Many of the first immigrants there were Southerners who arrived in the 1820s, and many of them were planters who brought their slaves with them. By 1860 Colorado County included some of the largest slave owners in Texas. John H. Crisp, a native of North Carolina, owned 146 slaves, and John Mathews, from Virginia, had 140.[39]

The Bedford ancestry grows dim just a few generations removed from his parents. The earliest family references are contained in a legal property description, and others are in the family Bible, with brief listings of Louis Jr.'s great-great-grandparents, Caesar and Nancy Bedford, both slaves. The 1880 census shows Caesar to have been born in Kentucky and Nancy in Georgia. Just how, when, or where they came together is unknown, but by 1853 they were in Texas, where in that year their son Jack, Louis A. Bedford Jr.'s great-grandfather, was born. Twenty-seven years later Jack was listed in the 1880 census as a farmer in Colorado County, married to a woman named Celia.[40]

One of Jack and Celia's five children was Will, Louis's grandfather, who with his wife, Emma, became the parents of six children. The eldest was Louis Arthur Bedford, given the nickname "Son," born in 1892.

Emma had witnessed a terrifying event in Weimar before her marriage to Will, one that typified the rough disdain some members of the white community showed to blacks, seemingly with little fear of legal consequences. One day a group of white men showed up unannounced at the house. They had noticed Emma's attractive sister, and they had come to take her and "break her in." Fortunately, Emma's sister was not home, but for months the family lived in fear they would return. The family managed to keep her hidden and safe, and the crisis passed. But the emotional scars, the impending threat, and the family's sense of helplessness were never forgotten, even one hundred years later.[41]

Such problems never seemed to be far away for a black family, even one as respected and stable as the Bedfords. Sometime after Will and Emma were married with a house full of children, their oldest boy, Louis—Son—got into a fight with a white boy. Son hit the boy on the head with a rock, drawing blood but not otherwise seriously injuring him. The boy happened to be the son of a prominent Weimar citizen, and for a black boy to injure a white youth—whatever the circumstances—could have serious and unfortunate consequences. The Bedfords were quietly advised that they should get their boy out of town before something bad happened. Although they had traveled very little, knew no other community, and had roots in the Weimar area going back to pre–Civil War days, Will and Emma Bedford quickly moved the entire family to San Antonio and never returned to their hometown.[42]

In 1910 the census taker visited the Bedford family in San Antonio and recorded a few facts. Will Bedford, thirty-nine years of age, was working with the Elsa Light Company. Son, now seventeen and with little more than a grade school education, was living at home and had a job as a porter in a saloon. Emma was taking in laundry at home, a job she continued with great success for half a century, until her death in 1958. (She was the only grandparent Louis Jr. knew; the others died before he was born.)[43]

When the First World War came along, Son, still a porter and with few prospects for anything better, joined the army. He was twenty-five. He became a cook, saw duty in Europe, and rose to the rank of sergeant at a time when the army was strictly segregated. During the war Son experienced a leg injury, the origin of which remained vague (his children did not think it was related to combat). In January 1920, Son was discharged from the military hospital at Fort Sam Houston in San Antonio, his last assignment having been with the 820th Company, Transportation Corps. His injured leg continued to plague him.[44]

After the war Son took advantage of a government-sponsored training program for veterans and underwent additional training in cooking at the all-black Prairie View State Normal and Industrial College fifty miles northwest of Houston (near Hempstead; now called Prairie View A&M University). After about a year at Prairie View, he found a job in Dallas at one of the city's biggest and finest hotels, the Oriental. He appears in the 1921 Dallas city directory as renting a room in the heart of the North Dallas black community, at 3313 Thomas Avenue. Next door was a young woman who quickly caught his eye, Callie Deborah Rodgers, who lived in a large house with her widowed father, M. M. Rodgers.[45]

M. M. Rodgers was one of several black Republicans in Texas who wielded political influence around the turn of the century but eventually saw their power disintegrate under the racist Lily-White movement.[46] Louis A. Bedford Jr. never knew his grandfather, but his mother's recollections of him were an inspiration to young Louis. The entry in the *New Handbook of Texas* describes Rodgers as a "black Republican politician and businessman." He was also involved in statewide church work, fraternal organizations, and education.[47]

Mack Matthew Rodgers was born a slave on July 13, 1859, in Wharton County, Texas, which—like Colorado County, adjacent to the northwest, where the Bedfords then lived—was populated by a number of planters who owned large numbers of slaves. In fact, there were more slaves than whites in Wharton County. The largest slaveholder, Albert C. Horton, had 167 slaves in 1860.[48]

The identity of Rodgers's owner is unknown, but Rodgers was said to be the son of a straw boss slave under orders to keep other slaves in line.[49] Six years old when the Civil War ended, Rodgers gained enough education to begin teaching school at the age of sixteen. He saved money to pay his way through Prairie View State Normal School (as it was then named), earning his degree in 1881. In 1887 he became principal of a public school in La Grange—just sixteen miles northwest of the Bedfords' Weimar—the beginning of a noted career that would bring him into contact with leading African Americans throughout the state and nation.

Rodgers served three terms as an alderman in La Grange. He came to know Booker T. Washington, and the two began a correspondence in which they discussed many mutual concerns. In 1887 Rodgers became the first black man in Texas to be named deputy collector of internal revenue, a position he held until 1909. From 1888 to 1912, he was a delegate to six of the seven Republican Party national conventions. As chairman of the four-county Eighteenth Senatorial District, he was a leader in the Black and Tan faction, which sought to prevent the Lily Whites from purging the Republican Party of African American influence.

Rodgers's business interests included a grocery store, an undertaking business, a real estate investment company, and a bank. He became president of the local chapter of the National Negro Business League, of which Washington was national president.

Ambitious black men, excluded from so many all-white civic and fraternal groups, began developing their own network of fraternal organizations. Rodgers was secretary of the State Grand Lodge of the Knights of Pythias, and in 1912 he became president of the first Fraternal Congress of Texas.

Rodgers was perhaps more dedicated to church work than to his other interests.

As longtime secretary of the Baptist Missionary and Education Convention of Texas, he dealt with African American Baptist churches throughout the state. In 1912 in Chicago, Rodgers made the successful motion that Negro Baptist churches across the nation be united through incorporation of the National Baptist Convention. Rodgers wrote the constitution for the organization.[50]

Rodgers and his wife, the former Caroline Jackson of Wharton (the Wharton County seat), had seven children. In 1900 all of them, ranging in age from nine to twenty-one, were living at home. The youngest, Callie Deborah, became Louis A. Bedford Jr.'s mother. The importance of education to the family was demonstrated by the fact that the two eldest daughters, Lucinda, nineteen, and Penda, seventeen, were already working as teachers in 1900. Also a part of the household was Mack Rodgers's father, George, seventy-six years old, who had been born in North Carolina as a slave and whose parents also had been born in that state.[51] (Nothing more is known about George or his wife, whose name has been lost.)

Every one of the Rodgers children had the advantage of some college education. They studied at all-black institutions, such as Prairie View and Tuskegee. The only boy, George, or "Bud," went to Tuskegee (Alabama) Normal and Industrial Institute and—despite his father's wishes that he become an attorney—learned to be a blacksmith. He settled in Phoenix, Arizona, and after the automobile took away the profits of blacksmithing, he established the first black-owned insurance agency in the state. He also taught himself the printing trade and began publishing a newspaper for African Americans, the *Arizona Gleam.*

M. M. Rodgers's wife, Caroline, died just a few years after the birth of their last child, Callie Deborah. Lucinda, Callie's oldest sister, took on the role of mother. A family photograph, taken sometime after Caroline Rodgers died, shows the Rodgerses in the yard in front of their house in La Grange. All are formally dressed, the women wearing white, long-sleeved blouses and long skirts.

Lucinda ultimately settled in Fort Worth and began a distinguished teaching career. Their second daughter, Penda, married a physician named Welch, probably from the family for which Welch Road in North Dallas was named. The couple settled in Wichita Falls, Texas.

In about 1912, motivated perhaps by the fact that the city was a more convenient location for his widespread church and lodge work, Rodgers moved to Dallas. With him came his youngest daughter, Callie. The other children had by now grown up and established their own households. Three or four years later, Rodgers purchased a ten-room house at 3317 Thomas Avenue, a block that in the prior half-dozen years had made a rapid transition from being white to black. It was in the largest and most prominent African American community in the city, originally known as Freedmantown because freed slaves had settled in the area. Most of the city's black professionals lived in the community north of downtown. Rogers maintained an office in the Pythian Temple on Elm Street, in the Deep Ellum portion of eastern downtown Dallas. From that office he conducted his work as secretary of the Knights of Pythias Lodge and secretary of the Baptist Missionary and Educational Convention of Texas. He also owned a barbershop in the building. Callie, having attended Samuel Huston College, worked for her father as his secretary and lived with him at the big house on Thomas Avenue.[52]

In May 1921 Rodgers was sixty-one years of age but already worn out, some observed, from his hectic pace. Despite advice that he needed a long rest, he went by train that month to Houston for a meeting of the Baptist Foreign Mission Board and commencement exercises of Houston College, where he was a trustee. Not long after arriving, he suffered an apparent heart attack, and he died in the early morning of May 18.[53]

News of Rodgers's death merited a page-one banner headline in the Dallas newspaper for African Americans, the *Dallas Express*. The news story described him as a "national figure of renown" who was one of Texas's "most brilliant sons, a scholar, diplomat and councellor [sic]." Distinguished African Americans from as far away as Arkansas, Nashville, Chicago, and Colorado, as well as cities across Texas, attended his funeral services at Macedonia Baptist Church. Many of them gave tributes from the podium.[54]

Rodgers left the house on Thomas Avenue to Callie. This was the same year that Louis A. "Son" Bedford rented a room in the house next door.

Son Bedford came from the same part of Texas as Callie Rodgers, but unlike the Rodgerses, his family had not enjoyed the benefits of higher education. They were, though, honest, hardworking, law-abiding, and intelligent people. To these family traits Son, a quiet, even-tempered man, added an element of worldly sophistication because of his time in Europe in the military.

Although Son and Callie married in Fort Worth—probably choosing that site because Callie's sister Lucinda was there—they returned to Dallas to live in Callie's large house. In addition to his regular job as a cook at the Oriental, Son began taking occasional cooking jobs across the street at the Adolphus Hotel, the city's newest and finest hotel. Soon, though, he found a new job as a Pullman porter on the Fort Worth and Denver Railway. On this job he traveled back and forth to Denver, interacting with well-heeled travelers and expanding his knowledge of the world around him.

On August 1, 1924, a daughter, Deborah Lucille, was born to Son and Callie. The birth took place at home with a black physician, Dr. R. E. L. Holland, in attendance. Dr. Holland lived down the street in a fine, Southern-style mansion with big white columns.

Two years later, on January 23, 1926, the Bedfords' second and last child, a boy, arrived. They named him Louis Arthur Bedford Jr., after his father. Once more, the birth occurred at home, and Dr. Holland again attended. Louis was a fine, healthy boy who weighed nine pounds at birth.[55]

Dallas, the place of Louis's birth, was experiencing rapid growth. Much of the population growth of Dallas was coming from sharecropping farmers, both black and white, who were abandoning the farm and moving to the city in hopes of a better future. Its white business and civic leaders, motivated by what they called the "Dallas spirit," aspired to even more growth and national recognition. The city's black population was just under 20 percent of the 1930 overall population of 260,475 and was not considered in the push for progress. Thus far, cotton brought prosperity, for Dallas was surrounded by some of the world's most fertile cotton fields, developed long after the Civil War without the benefit of slave labor. The city had become a huge inland cotton market.

In 1921, the same year M. M. Rodgers died, the new twenty-nine-story Magnolia Petroleum Building, the tallest building in town, was being completed at the corner of Akard and Commerce. Thirteen years later a double-sided "flying red horse" was placed atop the building and became a familiar icon, an indication of the city's transition from a cotton-based to an oil-based economy, for the red Pegasus was the symbol for an oil company.

The Thomas-Hall-State area had the largest concentration of black residents in Dallas, but rather than its being the single dominant black community, small African American enclaves were scattered throughout the city. They had colorful names, such as Bon Ton, Queen City, Mill City, and Little Egypt, and they usually had their own small business districts. To prevent residents from spilling into the white neighborhoods around them, Dallas by municipal ordinance designated all streets for either black people or white.

Schools, of course, were strictly segregated. Black students frequently had to walk past white schools to reach their own. They used old textbooks discarded by the white schools. Black teachers earned less than their white counterparts, sometimes considerably less, a common practice throughout the South. They were considered less qualified than their white counterparts, in disregard of the fact that black teachers had been prohibited from attending the state's all-white colleges and universities.

Even the city's ambulance services were segregated. The practice in Dallas was for funeral home ambulances to respond to emergencies, such as accidents, and to transport victims to hospitals. White funeral home ambulances picked up white victims; black funeral homes transported black victims. Zan W. Holmes recognized the absurdity of this system when he was a theology student at Southern Methodist University in the 1950s. Hearing a car crash outside his South Dallas apartment, Holmes went outside to investigate and saw two white ambulance attendants and two white police officers standing idly by while a black accident victim lay bleeding on the side of the road. "Why aren't you helping this man?" he demanded. They said they were waiting for a "black" ambulance to arrive to take the victim, who soon died from the accident, to the hospital.[56]

Strict separation of the races was the norm. Streetcars and buses were segregated by signs marked "Colored" that restricted African Americans to the rear. Even water fountains at public establishments were identified as "White" or "Colored." Most white-owned restaurants refused to serve black customers, although a few of them designated back rooms for them. In the various black business districts, black-owned restaurants catered to African Americans. Only a couple of movie theaters were designated for blacks, and at the city's finest first-run movie house, the Majestic, African Americans were permitted to sit in the second balcony but had to use a separate entrance. Other first-run movie theaters did not accept black customers at all. Hotels did not rent rooms to blacks.

Nowhere in Dallas was there a black police officer or judge. All public officials—city, county, and state—were white. Black citizens were virtually disfranchised in Dallas, the state, and throughout most of the South because, until the U.S. Supreme Court ruled the practice unconstitutional in 1944, Democratic Party primaries did not permit blacks to vote. Until this decision in *Smith v. Allwright*, African Americans could vote only in the general elections, a rather futile endeavor because it was the winner of the Democratic primary who without fail won the general election in the Solid South.

Not just in Dallas and in the South but throughout the nation, African Americans rarely if ever saw themselves reflected in the press in a positive way. Except for the comic characters of Amos 'n' Andy—portrayed on the radio by two white men, Freeman Gosden and Charles Correll—and Jack Benny's Rochester (black actor Eddie Anderson), they were not present on the radio. Not until 1947, when Jackie Robinson broke the color barrier, were there black baseball players in the major leagues of the twentieth century. (In the 1880s two black brothers, Moses Fleetwood Walker and Welday Walker, now all but forgotten, played for the Toledo Blue Stockings of the old American Association, which was a major league then.)

When Callie Rodgers and Louis A. Bedford married in 1921, Dallas was entering a particularly ugly period in race relations. The post–World War I phenomenon of the Ku Klux Klan had taken hold over much of the nation. A reign of terror having impact on Catholic, Jewish, and black citizens ensued. The KKK, which championed the superiority of white, native-born Protestant Americans and decried what it saw as a collapse in morals, often administered its own brand of justice with anonymous whipping parties—or worse.

A particularly egregious example of Klan cruelty occurred in Dallas in April 1921, when masked Klansmen kidnapped a black Adolphus Hotel elevator operator, drove him to a remote location, tied him to a fence post, flogged him with a whip, and then etched the initials "KKK" into the skin of his forehead with acid. His misdeed was an alleged liaison with a white woman at the hotel. Law enforcement officials declined to investigate the matter. "He no doubt deserved it," said Dallas County Sheriff Dan Harston, later revealed to be a Klansman himself.[57]

This event and others that followed sent a deadening chill throughout Dallas's black community. Son Bedford, who at one time worked at the Adolphus as a cook, could have known the victim, Alex Johnson. Perhaps it was the memory of this shocking deed that some years later prompted Callie Bedford to insist that her son, Louis Jr., give up his new summer job as a room service busboy at the Baker Hotel. The job, she believed, was too dangerous for a young black man, who could be accused of anything and considered guilty no matter what the facts might be.[58]

Dallas's Klan No. 66 claimed to be the largest in the nation. Its exalted cyclops (local chapter leader), a dentist named Hiram Wesley Evans, soon moved to the Klan's national headquarters in Atlanta to be the imperial wizard, the organization's highest position. Dallas Klan membership included many of the city's most prominent lawyers, ministers, public officials, and civic workers. In the 1922 Democratic primary, Klan-supported candidates won every office at the courthouse. The district attorney, the sheriff, and at least one district judge were avowed Klansmen. Klan-endorsed candidates swept city hall the next year, too. A struggle for control of the city ensued, but those opposed to the Klan did not prevail, despite a spirited anti-Klan campaign led by the *Dallas Morning News* and the *Dallas Dispatch*. So powerful and all encompassing was the Klan that in 1923 the State Fair of Texas sponsored a Ku Klux Klan Day, setting a record for attendance on any weekday in the fair's history. By the mid-1920s the Klan's power began to fade away. Its transgressions had gained too much notoriety by then, and internal squabbles proved disastrous.

This unhappy episode in Dallas history had largely passed by the time Louis Jr. and his sister, Deborah, were old enough to take note of such events. But many of the harsh feelings that had brought the Klan to prominence continued to exist. As late as 1929, the Klan maintained a full-time office at 101 Exposition Avenue, near Fair Park in South Dallas.

Classes at Booker T. Washington High School, from which both Louis and Deborah graduated, were so crowded that students had to attend in half-day shifts. In 1922 the old Colored High School, at Hall and Cochran Streets, was replaced by a new building on Flora Street with a new name: Booker T. Washington High School. It was new, but it still lacked amenities enjoyed by the white schools. For instance, it had no gymnasium. This was typical throughout the South. Despite the concept of separate but equal, huge disparities in per capita student expenditures existed between black and white schools.[59]

Three years after the new high school opened, the daughter of the late Booker T. Washington, Portia Washington Pittman, began teaching music there. In 1927 she directed the school choir in an appearance before the National Education Association's (NEA) national convention in Dallas, the first time ever that a black high school group had appeared on an NEA program. The result was an overwhelming success. Cries of "encore" resounded throughout the hall.[60]

How fitting this success would turn out to be. Decades later, after Dallas schools had been desegregated, Booker T. Washington High School was designated a special school for the performing arts in the Dallas Independent School District. High school students interested in the arts from throughout the city attended the specialized classes of the school, whose name was expanded to Booker T. Washington High School for the Performing and Visual Arts (1976). The school's location on Flora Street later became a part of the city's Arts District, which also includes the Morton H. Meyerson Symphony Center, the Dallas Museum of Art, and other important cultural institutions.

Yet another prominent black Dallas citizen in the 1920s was Portia Washington Pittman's husband, William Sydney Pittman, the architect who designed the prominent Knights of Pythias Temple, in which M. M. Rodgers had maintained his office. Pittman, a graduate of the architecture program at Philadelphia's Drexel Institute (now Drexel University), was the first African American architect awarded a federal contract to design a public building, the Negro Building at the Jamestown Tercentennial Exposition, held in 1907 in Norfolk County, Virginia. On moving to Texas in 1913, Pittman became the state's first African American architect. He designed major buildings not just in Dallas but also in Fort Worth, Houston, and San Antonio.[61]

At the pulpit of the oldest and one of the most prestigious black churches in town, New Hope Baptist (founded in 1873), was a distinguished minister and author named Alexander S. Jackson, so respected that he and the noted white preacher at First Baptist Church, George W. Truett, sometimes exchanged pulpits. In 1933, upon his retirement from New Hope Baptist, Jackson was succeeded by his energetic son, Maynard Holbrook Jackson, who became a prominent Dallas minister and activist and was the father of Atlanta's first African American mayor, Maynard Jackson Jr.[62]

A handful of African American attorneys were in town in the 1920s and 1930s: J. L. Turner Sr., Ammon S. Wells, D. B. Mason, and a few others. Far more numerous and visible were the town's black physicians, who numbered about a dozen. Most prominent was Dr. L. G. Pinkston, whose clinic on Thomas Avenue was just two doors from the Bedford house. Pinkston, who had graduated from Meharry Medical College in Nashville, Tennessee, moved to Dallas in 1921. He opened his Pinkston Clinic Hospital in 1927, the only such clinic in the city for black patients at the time.

Segregation cast an awful pall over the daily lives of the Bedford family and all these individuals. It was a social system based on a generally held belief, often expressed without challenge, that African Americans were inherently inferior and should be kept separate from the dominant white society. In general, the black community bore this burden stoically, without much hope for change. The National Association for the Advancement of Colored People (NAACP, founded in 1909) and some isolated voices already were fighting hard to claim the rights guaranteed by the Constitution, but progress was slow and often disheartening.

Louis Jr.'s parents began calling him "Brother" as soon as he was born, emphasizing for Deborah's sake that this newly arrived infant was indeed her brother. She in turn became "Sister." Louis's nickname endured for many years, and to his friends he was Brother.

By the time Louis Jr. was born in 1926, his father had given up his job as a hotel cook to be a porter on the Fort Worth and Denver Railway. This work took him away from the house for three or four days at a time as he traveled back and forth between the two cities. Being a porter required mobility, though, and the leg injuries he had suffered during the Great War worsened with time. Because the train regularly pulled into Denver, he became aware of the large Fitzsimmons Army Hospital there. Claiming his benefits as a veteran, he checked into the hospital in about 1931 to see what could be done. The "cure" was amputation. Son was outfitted with an artificial limb and soon resumed walking, with only a slight limp. Few people who met him were even aware that he had an artificial leg.

But his job as a railroad porter came to an end. Bedford was placed on disability at eighty-nine dollars a month, representing, as his son understood later, an 89 percent disability. It was a fair amount of money for the Depression years. There was no mortgage on the house, and the family earned extra money by renting out rooms.

Not long after the amputation, Louis—Brother, now about five years old—refused one day to come when his father called him to reprimand him for some minor transgression. "You can't catch me," the boy taunted. "You've only got one leg." Not many seconds passed before he learned his error, for his father did catch him and, on one of the few times in his life, administered a severe whipping to his son. Years later Bedford remembered his taunt with sadness.

Bedford recalled his youth as a happy, somewhat carefree time, though. "Money wasn't really the issue. The issue was whether you felt secure within your home. I never felt that I was going without food or proper shelter or clothing." Indeed, his parents not only encouraged him to do his best, they also paid for his education through college and law school.[63]

The house on Thomas Avenue was the only home the two children ever knew. By no means was it the only substantial, two-story house on Thomas. A few were grander, but its atmosphere was especially warming. The big front porch on the Bedford house was an attractive oasis for neighborhood children and adults. A number of narrow shotgun houses also dotted the area. Many of the residents did not have a telephone, and they knew they were welcome to use the Bedfords' telephone. The Bedfords had no automobile, but a streetcar line was one block away on State Street for transportation to all parts of town.

The Bedford children were fortunate. They had loving parents who had provided them a comfortable home; they lived in a stable community; they were well known by their neighbors; and schools and churches were nearby with caring principals, teachers, ministers, and Sunday school teachers. It was a time in America when black families were strong, melded close together, perhaps partially because of the inequities they faced outside. In this rather happy cocoon, the Bedford children—despite the strict segregationist policies and overwhelmingly racist attitudes of the day that surrounded them—had few complaints about their upbringing.

In the Bedfords' neighborhood, a small child could wander about without getting far from familiar eyes. A few blocks away from home stood the Moorland Branch of the YMCA, a prominent red-brick building with an indoor swimming pool, Ping-Pong tables, and other recreational facilities. Louis spent many happy afternoons there. The building was a community center for all sorts of activities. About the same distance away was the still-new Booker T. Washington High School, and just two blocks away on Hall Street was B. F. Darrell Elementary School. A few blocks from the Bedford house was the old Freedmantown Cemetery, forlorn and neglected but a good playground for young Louis and his friends.

The Thomas-Hall-State area had become the premiere black neighborhood in the city as well as the most extensive. Thomas and State were long, parallel streets, almost entirely residential, intersected by Central Avenue and the railroad tracks alongside it, by that time defunct, and by Hall Street, the lively retail and commercial center. The Paul Dunbar Public Library for blacks was an intellectual haven. Hall Street, only two houses from the Thomas Avenue residence, was a mecca for black Dallasites and others who visited from out of town. Here were Papa Dad's Barbeque, the State Theater, small restaurants catering to African Americans, barbershops, beauty shops, dry cleaners, and nightclubs, such as the Empire Room, where live entertainers—including Ray Charles some years later—could be found. The neighborhood was a center of activity that those days surpassed the Deep Ellum area, where black singers such as Huddie "Leadbelly" Ledbetter and Blind Lemon Jefferson had performed on the streets a few years earlier. Years later, part of the State-Thomas area was designated as a historical district. But a greater part of it was cleared for new development. The Bedford house was demolished in favor of a Wal-Mart store.

Neighborhood grocery stores were small, mom-and-pop operations. In the Bedfords' immediate neighborhood, the stores—unlike the other small businesses—inevitably seemed to be owned and operated by Italians. When other whites had departed as the neighborhood converted from white to black, the Italians remained with their stores, living in their back rooms. The Bedfords shopped with a corner grocer named Jim Degila. They and other customers were permitted to buy their groceries on credit; Degila kept the Bedfords' tab in a small book with the name "BEDFORD" on the spine. When Louis was old enough, he was permitted to go to the store himself to buy milk or bread. No cash was required; each purchase was put on the family tab.

· Almost all of Louis's playmates were black, but the Italians living behind their grocery stores in the neighborhood had children who played easily with the black youths. As Catholics, the Italians went to private Catholic schools.

In these years when the Dallas public school system had no kindergarten classes for children of any race, Louis's parents sent him to a private kindergarten, where Miss Hudson was his teacher. For elementary school he attended B. F. Darrell, a few blocks away, until it was time to go to Booker T. Washington High School.

Bedford's earliest memories include the family dog, a beautiful collie named Snookie, acquired from Callie's sister in Texarkana (on the Arkansas border). In the backyard an enticing barnlike structure, perhaps a carriage house in earlier days, attracted children for all sorts of games. Sometimes they would pop popcorn and eat it while they played dominoes.

One of the important outlets to the world was the radio. In the afternoons Louis and his sister could listen on the family's Philco to the serials that children of all colors enjoyed, and in the evening they would often be frightened by the macabre evil-doers on *The Shadow*. On Saturday mornings they enjoyed the children's show *Let's Pretend*. These radio shows triggered the imagination in ways that television could not. Neighborhood people of all ages sometimes would congregate on the Bedfords' big front porch to listen to radio broadcasts of the boxing matches of Joe Louis, who rose to meteoric success in the mid-1930s and whom the black community adopted as its special hero. Louis Bedford so treasured his memories of these hours around the radio that as an adult he purchased the same model as the family's Philco and placed it prominently in his office.

Callie Bedford devoted her full energies to her children's upbringing. It was a job she loved. She was the primary disciplinarian in the family. Son Bedford, although more easygoing, was no less ambitious for his children. It was understood that both children would have college educations.

Callie was a mother figure for many of Louis's and Deborah's friends, as well. Her network of friends permitted her to keep up with their activities—good and bad—and she could be penetrating with her questions and her advice for them.

She was, in Louis's words, "the queen of the house." Anyone who played in her yard had to obey her rules, and they did so willingly.

Sometimes on Sundays when there was nothing much for Bedford and his friends to do, someone might exclaim, "Let's go streetcar riding!" They would simply board the State streetcar one block away, pay the three-cent fare, sit in the back "colored" section, ride to the end of the line, then turn around in the same car and come back home.

A year or so before Deborah graduated from Darrell Elementary School, she was diagnosed with rheumatic fever. Recovery was slow, and when she was able to return to her classes, she was still weak. Louis began meeting her every afternoon after school so he could carry her books home. He did so without complaint for the entire semester, a kindness his sister remembered fondly nearly seventy years later.[64]

Church was important to the Bedfords, as it was to most of the families in the neighborhood. The family first attended Macedonia Baptist Church, where M. M. Rodgers had been a member. When internal dissension led to a split in the church, the Bedfords joined New Hope Baptist Church, where in 1933 a young, charismatic pastor, Maynard Holbrook Jackson, took over for his illustrious father. The new pastor soon baptized young Louis.

Louis was then only vaguely aware that the young preacher who dipped him beneath the holy waters was one of several aggressive members of the Dallas black community who in the 1930s were beginning to push for greater equality and opportunity. Jackson, so light-skinned that he might have passed for white, possessed a fine education—a bachelor's degree from Morehouse College in Atlanta and a bachelor of divinity degree from Garrett Biblical Institute on the Northwestern University campus in Evanston, Illinois. Jackson had worked in Philadelphia for the Foreign Missionary Board of the Baptist Church, and he had spent time in Africa overseeing missionaries before returning to Dallas. Shortly after his return, Jackson became president of a new organization that continues to the present day, the Progressive Voters League, dedicated to making the black population a political force in the city. Jackson also affiliated with the Negro Chamber of Commerce, which only recently had been energized under the direction of another new arrival, A. Maceo Smith.

Jackson and Smith, accustomed to the relative freedoms they had enjoyed on the East Coast, struck up a strong partnership in their endeavors to transform Dallas.

Smith, born in 1903 in Texarkana, Texas, was his family's fourteenth child. He graduated from Fisk University in Nashville and earned a master of business administration in 1928 from New York University in Manhattan. He stayed in New York City to begin his business career. He moved to Dallas in January 1933 to help manage an undertaking business and to organize a new insurance company. He immediately joined the nearly moribund Negro Chamber of Commerce, became its executive director, and transformed it into a vital force for promoting increased economic opportunities for blacks. He also became secretary of the Dallas branch of the energized NAACP and, with Jackson as president, became secretary of the newly formed Progressive Voters League. Soon Smith became executive secretary of the NAACP's Texas Conference of Branches. In 1939 he became the regional racial relations adviser for a six-state area for the U.S. Housing Authority.

Less visible but almost equally involved in these activities was Dr. Pinkston, whose clinic was two doors from the Bedfords' house. Pinkston enthusiastically supported the work of Smith and Jackson and with them founded the Progressive Voters League. He served on its executive committee and eventually became its president.

As a result of the enthusiasm of Smith and Jackson, the African American community in Dallas awakened to new possibilities. The organizing activities of these two men went largely unnoticed in the city's four daily newspapers, but they made big news in the weekly newspaper that served the black community, the *Dallas Express*.

As late as 1935 no black person had ever run for public office in Dallas or in Dallas County. To seek office was simply asking for unwanted trouble with no chance of winning. But in this year Smith and Jackson, as co–campaign managers, promoted the candidacy of one of the handful of black attorneys in town, Ammon Scott Wells, for the state legislature. A vacancy was created when Governor Jimmy Allred appointed State Representative Sarah T. Hughes judge of the 14th District Court.

Wells was no stranger to activism or to its consequences. In 1918 he and a local teacher named George F. Foster organized the first Dallas chapter of the NAACP; Wells was elected president. The chapter was one of four local branches formed that year following national board member Mary B. Talbert's visit to Dallas, her tour part of an aggressive campaign that resulted in a jump in national membership from ten thousand in 1917 to almost eighty thousand in 1919.[65] The Dallas chapter's initial membership roll of 138 included, as Wells wrote to the national headquarters in New York City, men and women "from all walks of life." Maynard Jackson's father, the Reverend A. S. Jackson, was on the executive committee, which included some of the city's most respected African American citizens: Dr. B. R. Bluitt, physician and surgeon; Mrs. J. L. Frazier, teacher; and J. P. Starks, principal of Douglass School.[66]

The chapter did not prosper, though, nor did the other thirty-one chapters that existed in Texas by 1919. A number of racially motivated violent incidents occurred in the state. When the Texas attorney general challenged the NAACP's right to conduct business in the state, national secretary John R. Shillady, a white man, came to Austin to talk to the attorney general. His efforts were met with verbal abuse. Afterward, in front of the Driskill Hotel in downtown Austin, Shillady was severely beaten by County Judge Dave J. Pickle, Constable Charles Hamby, and a third man. The constable escorted Shillady to the train station, put him on a train for St. Louis, and warned him not to return.[67] When the NAACP's national vice president demanded an investigation and punishment, Governor William P. Hobby blamed Shillady, calling him a troublemaker who should be sent back North where he came from, "with a broken jaw if necessary." The governor told the NAACP to stay out of Texas.[68]

The Dallas chapter was hampered by the fact that the police department ordered an officer to attend each of its meetings. The threatening presence rendered the organization ineffective.[69] One Dallas member, George F. Porter, reported in 1923 to the NAACP national office that the local chapter's officers were "afraid to death" to hold meetings because of the Ku Klux Klan. Another member wrote that the Dallas chapter was "run by cowards." Somehow the Dallas chapter managed to survive, but by 1923 only five of the original nineteen chapters in Texas still existed.[70]

Wells, perhaps more than anyone else, knew of the dangers of his candidacy for the vacant legislative seat. He was one of an unusually large field of sixty-five candidates who filed for the vacant position. Leading Dallas business and civic leaders viewed the presence of a black candidate as disruptive to the social order. Smith and

Jackson, seen as the real powers behind Wells, found themselves summoned before two or three well-known city leaders and presented with a not-so-veiled threat. Wells's candidacy, these leaders argued, would only stir up trouble and threaten to disrupt race relations. If Wells would withdraw, they said, a one-hundred-thousand-dollar appropriation expected from the Texas Legislature to build a Hall of Negro Life for the upcoming 1936 Texas Centennial Exposition would be secure. If not, the appropriation would be in jeopardy. In an earlier day such a threat likely would have ended Wells's candidacy at once. Now, though, Smith and Jackson refused to bow down. Wells stayed in the race.[71]

One anonymous political observer quoted in the *Dallas Morning News* said that Wells had a good chance to win, evidently noting the recent aggressive voter registration drives in the black community. Texas Speaker of the House Coke Stevenson said, however, that even if Wells were elected, he would not be seated, noting that the state constitution gave each branch of the legislature the right to determine the qualifications of its own members. A general opinion existed, he said, that the House would hold any Negro to be unqualified.[72]

Wells, who proclaimed himself a supporter of President Franklin Roosevelt and his policies, finished sixth in the large field of candidates, with 998 votes to winner Sam Hanna's 1,862. As had been strongly hinted, because he had declined to withdraw, the anticipated one-hundred-thousand-dollar appropriation for the Hall of Negro Life was denied. Later the federal government awarded the money, and the Hall of Negro Life was constructed for the Texas Centennial as a celebration and documentation of black achievements.[73] (The next year, when the Greater Texas and Pan American Exposition was about to be held—at Fair Park, like the Texas Centennial Exposition—complaints were made that the Hall of Negro Life would be out of harmony with this event. To the dismay of not just the black community but Mayor George Sergeant, the Centennial Commission dismantled the building.)

In 1935 Louis A. Bedford Jr. was nine years old. He was dimly aware of Wells's candidacy; it was a subject of some discussion around the Bedford dinner table. Even at his age Bedford glanced occasionally at the headlines in the *Dallas Express*, for he was a young salesman for the weekly newspaper. Each week he delivered it and other newspapers to regular customers. The other papers included the *Pittsburgh*

Courier, the *Kansas City Call*, the *Chicago Defender*, and the *Baltimore Afro-American*. These newspapers had found a nationwide market by devoting special sections or pages to regional news about blacks, whose activities were virtually ignored by the white daily newspapers.

As he grew older and learned more about the community around him, Bedford became aware of the discrimination awaiting him as an adult. The movie that left a deep impression on him as a boy, *Imitation of Life*, was a Hollywood rarity in that it had a racial theme. In the 1934 movie starring Claudette Colbert, the light-skinned daughter of Colbert's black housekeeper seeks to pass for white. Another movie that left a lasting impression on him was *Gunga Din* (1939), based on the Rudyard Kipling poem about British soldiers in colonial India. Less directly, the film also dealt with race. Then, of course, there were the Saturday cowboy movies Louis saw at the nearby State Theater on Hall Street, starring such heroes as Buck Jones, Hopalong Cassidy, Tim McCoy, and Bob Steele. He and most of his friends thought nothing of the fact that these heroes were all white and that during the Tarzan movies they cheered for Tarzan in his hostile encounters with African natives.[74]

Louis enjoyed going to the movies, and his parents knew it. Here, they realized, was an incentive they could use to encourage good grades. The school issued individual grade reports every six weeks, and if Louis's report was not satisfactory, his parents punished him by removing his movie privileges for the next six weeks. This was necessary only a few times, but Louis was always mindful of this possible punishment.[75]

Louis A. Bedford Jr.'s thoughts about his future career as a railroad mail clerk continued into his college years. It was a realistic and exciting possibility for an African American. Many in the black community thought being a railroad mail clerk was a carryover from Pony Express days, when many of the brave riders carrying the mail across the frontier were black. Railroad mail clerks could see even broader swaths of the nation by riding the rails from city to city. So precious was the cargo under their supervision that they were even permitted to be armed.

This early ambition changed, of course, but only gradually. Perhaps the idea of a possible legal career occurred when Louis was about twelve years old. For the first time he became specifically aware that in downtown Dallas, the distinctive old red courthouse, a building so familiar to him, was a place where lawyers argued cases before judges and oftentimes juries. Supposedly composed of ordinary citizens, juries heard the facts and then rendered decisions based on the law as presented by the attorneys.

In Dallas County, however, African Americans did not serve on juries. Custom forbade it, even in instances when the accused or a party in a civil suit was black. Potential jury members were selected from among citizens who paid their poll taxes. Citizens were not identified by race on the tax lists, so when a black citizen happened to be called, the practice was to pay him the normal three-dollar daily rate for jury service and just send him home. (Women of any race were not eligible to serve on a jury in Texas until 1954.)

In 1938 a small, bespectacled, scholarly man named George F. Porter, the man who had complained in 1923 that the Dallas branch of the NAACP was "run by cowards," dramatically challenged the exclusion of blacks from juries. Porter was the fifty-five-year-old president of Wiley College's local junior college branch, located down Thomas Avenue from the Bedford house (the college's main campus was about 150 miles east in Marshall, Texas). When summoned for jury duty, Porter refused to accept the proffered payment and dismissal by District Judge Paine L. Bush. He insisted on his right to serve on a jury. The four other black men called that day accepted their three-dollar payments and went home, but Porter continued to sit quietly in the central jury room along with some 150 white men.

This was not the first time Porter had challenged the system. In 1921 he made a similar protest but was attacked and thrown out of the jury room. In 1936 he again tried to remain in the central jury room but left after threats of violence.

Now, in 1938, flanked at first by three NAACP observers, he was determined to stay. As the day wore on, Porter quietly ignored the muttered threats of white men, who warned the deputy sheriff in charge of the jury room that they would resort to drastic action unless Porter left.[76] On Tuesday, the second day of his protest, Porter, dressed neatly in suit and tie, sat in a corner away from the hostile glares of other potential jurors. He was sent to District Judge John Rawlins's courtroom to be on a jury panel for a damage suit, but both attorneys struck him from the list.[77]

On the third day he received a call to come to Judge Sarah T. Hughes's court for possible service, but before he could go, two unidentified white men approached him and, in full view of court officials and deputy sheriffs, forcibly grabbed him and threw him headfirst down the concrete steps of the courthouse. After glaring at him for a few moments, they dusted their hands in approval and strolled casually up Main Street.

Porter managed to get up from the sidewalk and make his way to the court-room. There he was separated from the white potential jurors and placed in a sec-tion of the courtroom reserved for black spectators. Sheriff Smoot Schmid and three deputies now protected him from further violence. When attorneys for both sides scratched his name from their lists of preferred jurors, Judge Hughes dismissed him. Porter collected the nine dollars to which he was entitled for his three days and then was escorted out of the courthouse by the sheriff.[78]

Although Porter had been able to make his way to Judge Hughes's courtroom, he evidently had been seriously injured by the brutal action. Sometime later he became blind, and many in Dallas's black community believed that the attack had caused his blindness. Bedford himself remembers having seen Porter as a blind man a few years after the incident, his career with the college ended, selling the same African American newspapers that Bedford had sold.[79] Residents of Dallas's black neighborhoods believed that the two men who had thrown Porter down the steps were sheriff's deputies. Such could be the serious consequences, the young Bed-ford now saw and believed, of challenging the dominant white establishment. The perpetrators of the assault had gone unpunished. Porter was now blind. Bedford recognized, more than ever, the unfairness of the judicial system.

A number of protests from the white community arose concerning Porter's harsh treatment, along with laudatory comments about his courage. *Dallas Morn-ing News* columnist Lynn Landrum said that what happened to Porter was "on a par for ruthlessness, for cruelty and for lawlessness, with what is happening to members of the Jewish minority in Germany."[80]

The incident attracted the attention of the NAACP's national office in Washing-ton. Thurgood Marshall, the organization's counsel, came to Dallas on October 8, 1938, to meet with local NAACP officials and to conduct his own investigation into the incident. It was likely his encouragement that prompted other black Dallasites to follow Porter's example and challenge the system, for two days later W. L. Dickson, a shoe repairman, sat for three days unmolested in the central jury room before accepting his dismissal. In December three other men refused to leave the central jury room when they were excused and ordered brusquely to leave by District Judge Claude McCallum. By then the Texas Rangers had been ordered by Governor James Allred to protect all jurors, white or black. Five sturdy Rangers stood around the courtroom to protect the three men.[81]

Gradually, in the years that followed, barriers against blacks on Dallas juries were removed. Not until about three decades later would blacks be routinely accepted in numbers that represented their proportion of the population.

A pervasive fear existed in the black community about the helplessness of any African American in the presence of the law. Especially feared were those in uniform who represented the judicial system at its first level: police officers. They alone had daily contact with the black community. Apprehension toward the police and their often-unbridled exercise of power existed even in a law-abiding family such as the Bedfords. Louis heard his parents and other adults talk about how a police officer might beat a suspect or slap a black person who had done nothing wrong, about how a black person who approached an officer without removing his hat and speaking carefully and deferentially could expect a sharp reprimand, and about how a black person must step off the sidewalk to make room for an officer. Police officers generally accepted—if they did not insist on—deference, for it was a time when educational requirements for the job of police officer were minimal and sensitivity concerns were not emphasized in their training.

In later years, long after the worst days of discrimination had passed, long after black police officers in Dallas had become common, and long after concerns for minority rights were ingrained, these memories remained with Bedford. Fear of the police and the vulnerability of black citizens to their arbitrary powers were the worst aspects of growing up in a segregated society. "It was the arrogance and mistreatment of citizens by the police who say 'I am the law,'" Bedford recalled years later. "Whatever they decided to do, they would do, and you were helpless."[82]

The campaign by the Progressive Voters League and the Negro Chamber of Commerce to have black citizens pay their poll taxes, vote, and become a political force began to pay off in the late 1930s. To gain the support of these newly registered voters who suddenly had power to sway an election if the white vote was divided, city council candidates in 1937 made several promises. Among them were to hire black police officers and to construct a second high school to relieve overcrowded conditions at Booker T. Washington.

In January 1939 the new Lincoln High School for black students was completed in South Dallas. Threats of bombings and violence delayed its opening, for many residents resented having the school in their predominantly white area. They held meetings and discussed ways to stop black students from passing through their neighborhoods on their way to school. One city councilman seriously suggested prohibiting blacks from walking on certain city streets. A series of bombings, fires, hangings in effigy, and throwing of stones and bricks rocked the area in 1940 and early 1941.

Louis was personally unaffected, but he and other black residents heard of these and other incidents, for such news circulated rapidly throughout the black community. At least one racial disturbance, unrelated to the school opening, occurred not far from his house. In September 1940, when Louis was fourteen, hundreds of white residents, many of them housewives, bombarded with rocks two adjoining houses purchased by blacks in a previously all-white block on Howell Street. The ugly scene lasted all day. Not until after midnight did police persuade the mob to disperse. Bedford, at home, heard a loud explosion. Later he learned that a black-occupied house on Howell had been struck by dynamite. News reports described only a probable shot by a firearm.[83]

Housing for the growing black population was severely limited in segregated Dallas. With no new housing developments for African Americans, encroachment into white neighborhoods was inevitable, and white residents resisted on many fronts. A federally funded low-cost housing project, Roseland Homes, was completed in 1942 for some 650 Negro families at Hall and Central, just a few blocks from the Bedford home. But the huge project required the destruction of about five hundred low-cost homes where black families already resided. Since these families were forced to find housing in other parts of the city while the Roseland Homes were being built, racial tension only increased. For Louis and several of his friends, though, the massive Roseland construction project presented an opportunity. They set up a soda pop stand—a washtub filled with ice and soft drinks—and sold drinks to the workers.[84]

Black students found a strong support system in their teachers, who knew all too well about the financial hardships of so many of their students. Not only did the teachers encourage the students to be prepared through their studies for any opportunities that might arise; they often brought clothing they had purchased themselves to pass out to needy students. The teachers themselves suffered in comparison with white teachers in the Dallas school system because their salaries were lower.

"Our teachers, as far as I'm concerned, were tremendous," Bedford said years later. He remembered that one of his teachers, Miss Richardson, seeing that he was not feeling well one day, had him accompany her to her house after school to give him some Black Draught, a popular remedy for many ailments. Such care was not unusual.[85]

Louis became a freshman at Booker T. Washington High School in 1937 at the age of eleven, having completed the seven years of public elementary school allotted to black students. (White elementary schools had eight years.) Booker T. was familiar to him; he had come to know it well because of his sister, Deborah. He had attended school functions and had even escorted his sister to some of the school dances, usually held in the ballroom on the top floor of the Pythian Temple in Deep Ellum.

Classrooms were so crowded during Louis's freshman year that students attended school in two shifts, the first from 8 AM to noon and the second from 1 to 5 PM. Ninth- and tenth-grade students attended in the mornings, juniors and seniors in the afternoons. The opening of Lincoln High School in 1939 relieved the pressure and permitted all students to go for a full day, a fact that signaled a new era for black high school students in Dallas.

Booker T.'s principal, T. D. Marshall, transferred to Lincoln and was replaced by a teacher named John Leslie Patton Jr., who had been in Booker T.'s first graduating class in 1922. After graduating from Prairie View College, Patton returned to Dallas, taught for two years at an elementary school, then taught history at Booker T., starting in 1928. Patton, a familiar and beloved figure in the black community, went on to serve as principal for forty-one years. As a history teacher, he had been far ahead of his time, in 1933 offering a unique elective course in black history resulting in the publication of *A Student's Outline Guide for the Study of Negro History.*[86] It was about this time, perhaps coincidentally and perhaps not, that Louis became interested in history.

During Louis's junior year in high school, he suffered a serious illness, bronchial pneumonia, which kept him out of school for some weeks. His parents insisted that he stay home for the rest of the school year to recuperate and wait until the fall of 1940 to reenroll. This meant he would graduate in 1942 instead of 1941, at the age of sixteen instead of fifteen. There was not much for Louis to do during the rest of the semester but rest, read, and listen to his favorite afternoon radio serials. He could not avoid hearing the news about the war in Europe and Hitler's march toward supremacy over the Continent. The voices of such broadcasters as Gabriel Heatter, Edward R. Murrow, and Walter Winchell became familiar.

One of the defining moments in American history, December 7, 1941, occurred with the surprise Japanese attack on the U.S. naval base at Pearl Harbor, Hawaii. As did almost all Americans, Louis and his parents heard the news on the radio that Sunday. The surge of patriotism that swept across the nation, Louis remembers clearly, included the black community in Dallas. African Americans across the nation announced they were ready to support the war effort in any way they could.

But the volunteers learned that they were not universally welcomed. "There are more Negroes on the lists than the Government knows what to do with," wrote the *Dallas Express*. The newspaper lamented the fact that "we can't get into the defense jobs to make guns and ammunition and planes and ships for national defense; we can't get decent places in the Navy to help fight the enemy; and now it develops that even the Army is placing a limitation upon the number of Negroes who can prepare to spill their blood to save the nation." The army and navy remained strictly segregated, and the Marine Corps accepted no blacks for any type of service.[87]

The *Express* lost patience. "This situation ought to make the white people of Dallas hang their heads in shame; but that would perhaps be expecting too much, for so many of the people who ought to be ashamed do not have the heart."[88]

The *Express* offered some hope two weeks later in an editorial with the headline "No Time for Racial Trouble in Dallas Now." Since Pearl Harbor, the newspaper noted, there had been no further outbursts of racial strife in South Dallas. The city, it summarized, was "too busy now getting ready to send young men white and colored—to the war."[89]

In the first month of the war, when the Red Cross called for blood donations for the army and navy, African Americans across the nation soon realized that things had not changed all that much: their blood was not wanted. The army and navy asked the Red Cross to supply blood plasma only from white donors, not black ones. As for blacks serving in the nation's military forces who might need transfusions, they were to be given blood from white donors unless they specifically asked for black donor blood. No such restrictions existed in Great Britain, a fact ruefully noted in the black community.[90]

Blatant rejection of black employees in the burgeoning defense industry, whether in the North or South, brought a radical change in thinking for some leading African Americans that would have profound consequences. A. Philip Randolph, a labor organizer who had founded the Brotherhood of Sleeping Car Porters (1925), took the lead, having concluded that only intense pressure from masses of black citizens could have an effect. "We ought to get 10,000 Negroes and march down Pennsylvania Avenue and protest against the discriminatory practices in this rapidly expanding economy," he declared in 1941.[91]

Randolph began organizing such a march, and President Roosevelt was worried. In a meeting with Randolph and Walter White, executive director of the NAACP, Roosevelt was stunned to hear that not ten thousand but a hundred thousand were anticipated to take part in the march on Washington. Not long afterward Roosevelt signed an executive order that called upon employers and labor unions to provide for "full and equitable participation of all workers in defense industries, without discrimination because of race, creed, color or national origin." Randolph called off the march as unnecessary.[92]

Randolph's strategy wasn't forgotten in the years ahead. The hypocrisy of a nation claiming to fight for the democratic freedoms it denied to its own African American citizens was all too evident. Blacks began pushing harder for their rights. Racial tensions were heightened, marked by street fighting and numerous deaths, such as occurred in Detroit in 1943, when thirty-four people died, twenty-five of them black. Dallas was not immune. In January 1943 a riot in Louis's immediate neighborhood involved black soldiers, civilians, and police officers. Fighting went on for some three hours before order could be restored. Only minor injuries occurred, but the army briefly declared Dallas off-limits for black military personnel.[93]

Conflict surrounded Louis A. Bedford Jr. as he and his classmates approached graduation from high school in spring 1942, but their primary concerns lay elsewhere. Their senior prom was held at the familiar Pythian Temple in Deep Ellum. Louis and his date took a taxicab there. The gangly and rapidly growing Louis, approaching his full height of six feet two inches but weighing about 130 pounds, enjoyed himself at the prom.

Louis and his fellow students could look back on a truly extraordinary year. Booker T. had won state championships in football, basketball, and track. The Parent-Teacher Association treated the seniors to a program of music that spring, most of it by famous classical composers, such as Schubert and Sibelius. Concluding the program, though, were piano renditions of four of the popular songs of the time: "Body and Soul," "I Surrender, Dear," "The Very Thought of You," and "In a Sentimental Mood."[94]

Commencement and baccalaureate services were held in the neighborhood's St. Paul Methodist Church on May 29, 1942. The class commencement had a patriotic theme, "America Calling," and opened with "The Star-Spangled Banner."[95]

Robert Prince, a graduate of Booker T. Washington, wrote in a memoir about his life in Dallas, "My black teachers cared for all of us. They taught us survival tactics for black people. . . . We were taught that the white man would never give us our rights without a fight. . . . This was a good education. Education should teach one to survive in one's own environment. Our environment was hostile."[96]

The students' futures were especially uncertain in times that were perilous for all Americans. The teachers at Booker T. and other institutions for black students were realistic about future opportunities for their graduates, but they had cheered them on in their studies as best they could. The students had to prepare themselves to be ready for a future in which all doors of opportunity would come ajar. One day, the teachers believed, that would come. Only a handful of Booker T. grads would go to college, though. Although there were a few underfunded black colleges, no white institution of higher education in the state—public or private—enrolled black students.

Louis knew what he would do. He would enroll at Prairie View College that fall. He had seen the smartly dressed Prairie View cadets in their military outfits at Negro Day at the State Fair of Texas, and now he would be one of them.

1. *The Autobiography of Malcolm X*, with the assistance of Alex Haley (New York: Grove Press, 1966 paperback ed.), 36.
2. L. A. Bedford Jr., "When I Become an Old Lawyer and Can No Longer Stand before the Bar," *Dallas Bar Association Headnotes*, Nov. 19, 1990, 1.
3. Lawrence M. Friedman, *A History of American Law* (New York: Simon and Schuster, 1973).
4. Geraldine R. Segal, *Blacks in the Law: Philadelphia and the Nation* (Philadelphia: University of Pennsylvania Press, 1983), xiv; Alexis de Tocqueville, *Democracy in America*, ed. Richard D. Heffner (New York: New America Library, 1956), 125.
5. August Meier, *Negro Thought in America, 1880–1915* (Ann Arbor: University of Michigan Press, 1968), 101.
6. Amilcar Shabazz, *Advancing Democracy: African Americans and the Struggle for Access and Equity in Higher Education in Texas* (Chapel Hill: University of North Carolina Press, 2004), 42; U.S. Census figures cited in J. Clay Smith Jr., *Emancipation: The Making of the Black Lawyer, 1844–1944* (Philadelphia: University of Pennsylvania Press, 1993), 634, 637.
7. Smith, *Emancipation*, 93.
8. Ibid.
9. Ibid., 94.
10. Ibid., 95.
11. Ibid.
12. Ibid., 96.
13. Ibid., and 115n19. See Charles S. Brown, "The Genesis of the Negro Lawyer in New England," pt. 1, *Negro History Bulletin* 22, no. 7 (Apr. 1959): 147–52. See also Clarence G. Contee, "Macon B. Allen: 'First' Black in the Legal Profession," *Crisis* 83, no. 2 (Feb. 1976): 67–69.
14. John Daniels, *In Freedom's Birthplace: A Study of the Boston Negroes* (Boston: Houghton Mifflin, 1914), 451, cited in Smith, *Emancipation*, 96.
15. Segal, *Blacks in the Law*, 126.
16. Friedman, *History of American Law*, 279–80.
17. Smith, *Emancipation*, 34; Segal, *Blacks in the Law*, 208.
18. Smith, *Emancipation*, 44.
19. Langston's autobiography is titled *From the Virginia Plantation to the National Capitol, or The First and Only Negro Representative in Congress from the Old Dominion* (Hartford: American Publishing, 1894). An excellent biography is by William Cheek and Aimee Lee Cheek, *John Mercer Langston and the Fight for Black Freedom, 1829–65* (Urbana: University of Illinois Press, 1989). See also Oberlin Electronic Group, "John Mercer Langston (1829–1897)," c. 1998, in "Oberlin

and the Struggle for Black Freedom" exhibit, at *Oberlin through History*, http://www.oberlin. edu/external/EOG/OYTT-images/JMLangston.html.

20. Smith, *Emancipation*, 542.
21. Segal, *Blacks in the Law*, 18.
22. National Bar Association, "The Association: The NBA Perspective," at *National Bar Association*, Washington, D.C., http://www.nationalbar.org/about/#history.
23. Smith, *Emancipation*, 545; "Bar Tables Issue of Negro Membership," *Dallas Morning News*, Sept. 12, 1943; Darwin Payne, *As Old as Dallas Itself: A History of the Lawyers of Dallas, the Dallas Bar Associations, and the City They Helped Build* (Dallas: Three Forks Press, 1999), 233.
24. S.v. "Allen W. Wilder," in *The New Handbook of Texas* (Austin: Texas State Historical Association, 1996), 6:968.
25. The remarkable Cuney family is portrayed by Douglas Hales in *A Southern Family in Black and White: The Cuneys of Texas* (College Station: Texas A&M University Press, 2003). See also s.v. "Norris Wright Cuney," in *New Handbook of Texas*, 2:446.
26. Payne, *As Old as Dallas Itself*, 57–58.
27. *Dallas Weekly Herald*, Oct. 6, 1881.
28. Scott's stay in Dallas went unnoticed until publication in 1999 of the author's history of lawyers in Dallas, *As Old as Dallas Itself*, 56–58; Smith, *Emancipation*, 327.
29. Payne, *As Old as Dallas Itself*, 56–58.
30. Ibid., 58.
31. "Divorce Suits," *Dallas Morning News*, Oct. 6, 1885.
32. Louis A. Bedford Jr., interview by Darwin Payne, Aug. 11, 2005.
33. L. A. Bedford Jr., interview in *J. L. Turner Legal Association: Over Fifty Years of Service in Dallas*, DVD (Dallas: J. L. Turner Legal Association).
34. "Memorial Record" of Wells funeral, Feb. 1936, "Memorials for Attorneys" binder, Louis A. Bedford Papers, Dallas. (These papers are in Bedford's law office in three-ring binders. Bedford gave the author full access to these papers.)
35. Duane Mason funeral program, Dec. 1978, "Memorials for Attorneys" binder, Bedford Papers.
36. Mark V. Tushnet, *The NAACP's Legal Strategy against Segregated Education, 1925–1950* (Chapel Hill: University of North Carolina Press, 1987), 30.
37. Darlene Clark Hine, *Black Victory: The Rise and Fall of the White Primary in Texas* (Columbia: University of Missouri Press, 2003), 175.
38. Louis A. Bedford Jr., interview by Darwin Payne, Sept. 20, 2005.
39. The number of slaves in Texas counties in 1860 is reported by Randolph B. Campbell in *An Empire for Slavery: The Peculiar Institution in Texas, 1821–1865* (Baton Rouge: Louisiana State University Press, 1989), 274–76.
40. Caesar and Nancy Bedford's places of birth are listed in the 1880 U.S. Census entry for their son, Jack, Series T9, Roll 1297, p. 323.
41. Deborah Bedford Fridia, interview by Darwin Payne, July 27, 2005.
42. Louis A. Bedford Jr., interview by Darwin Payne, July 10, 2005.
43. 1910 U.S. Census, Bexar County, Texas, Series T624, Roll 1532, p. 136.
44. "Honorable Discharge from the U.S. Army, L. A. Bedford," Jan. 30, 1920, L. A. Bedford Jr. personal files.

45. Bedford interview, July 10, 2005; *Worley's Dallas City Directory* (Dallas: John F. Worley Directory Co., 1920).

46. During and after Reconstruction, politically minded black citizens naturally gravitated to the Republican Party because of its policies and were accepted as equals by sympathetic members of the party. The Lily-White movement arose as some Republicans, in an effort to win approval from Southern whites, began to purge black Republicans, eventually ridding the party of their influence.

47. S.v. "M. M. Rodgers," in *New Handbook of Texas*, 5:650.

48. Campbell, *Empire for Slavery*, 58, 276.

49. Fridia, interview, July 27, 2005. A straw boss is a worker who also supervises his peers.

50. These details come from a paper written by L. A. Bedford Jr. as a history student at Prairie View College in 1946, titled "M. M. Rodgers: A Study of a Negro in the Age of Transition" and based on original sources, including documents held by his mother.

51. U.S. Census, 1900, Fayette County, Texas, Series T623, Roll 1634, p. 84. Caroline is listed as "Ida" in this census.

52. City of Dallas directories, 1916–21 (published with various title changes by John F. Worley Directory Co., Dallas); Bedford, interview, July 10, 2005.

53. "Texas Looses [*sic*] an Illustrious Son, State and Nation Mourn the Loss," *Dallas Express*, May 21, 1921.

54. Ibid.; M. M. Rodgers funeral program, May 1921, L. A. Bedford Jr. personal files.

55. Standard Certificate of Birth, Bureau of Vital Statistics, Texas State Board of Health, Register No. 374, and family baby book, L. A. Bedford Jr. personal files.

56. Paul McKay, "Dallas Pastor Looks Back: Rev. Zan Holmes Retires," at *BlackandChristian*, Aug. 2002, http://www.Blackandchristian.com/articles/pulpit/umns-08-02.shtml.

57. Darwin Payne, *Big D: Triumphs and Troubles of an American Supercity in the 20th Century* (Dallas: Three Forks Press, 2000), 84–85. Extensive local coverage of the event appeared in the *Dallas Daily Times Herald*, Apr. 2–4, 1921. Payne provides good details of the Klan in Dallas. Overviews are found in Kenneth T. Jackson, *The Ku Klux Klan in the City, 1915–1930* (New York: Oxford University Press, 1967); Charles C. Alexander, *The Ku Klux Klan in the Southwest* (Lexington: University of Kentucky Press, 1965).

58. Louis A. Bedford Jr., interview by Darwin Payne, July 19, 2005.

59. Tushnet, *NAACP's Legal Strategy*, 5.

60. Payne, *Big D*, 83.

61. Ibid., 82.

62. Ibid., 45–46.

63. Louis A. Bedford Jr., *L. A. Bedford, Jr.: Oral History Interview* (Austin: Texas Bar Foundation, 2002), 2.

64. Fridia, interview, July 22, 2005.

65. Michael L. Gillette, "The NAACP in Texas, 1937–1957" (PhD diss., University of Texas at Austin, Dec. 1984), 1.

66. Wells et al. to NAACP, Oct. 7, 1918, "J. L. Turner Legal Society" binder, Bedford Papers.

67. "Judge Thrashes Man Organizing Negroes," *Dallas Morning News*, Aug. 23, 1919; Carl T. Rowan, *Dream Makers, Dream Breakers: The World of Justice Thurgood Marshall* (Boston: Little, Brown, 1993), 32.

68. Gillette, "NAACP in Texas," 2; Hine, *Black Victory*, 90.
69. W. Marvin Dulaney, "Whatever Happened to the Civil Rights Movement in Dallas, Texas?" in *Essays on the American Civil Rights Movement,* ed. John Dittmer, George C. Wright, and W. Marvin Dulaney (College Station: Texas A&M Press, 1993), 69.
70. Gillette, "NAACP in Texas," 3.
71. Payne, *Big D*, 206.
72. "Philp to Enter Race as G.O.P. Candidate; Aspirant List," *Dallas Morning News*, Feb. 24, 1935.
73. "Hanna Wins Legislature Seat from Field of 60 Candidates," *Dallas Morning News*, Mar. 17, 1935.
74. Bedford, interview, July 19, 2005.
75. Ibid., Sept. 20, 2005.
76. "Negro Dismissed as Juror Demands Right to Serve and Stays," *Dallas Daily Times Herald*, Sept. 27, 1938; "Negro Tries to Get on Jury," *Dallas Morning News*, Sept. 27, 1938.
77. "Negro Accepted on Jury Panel but Name Stricken from List by Attorneys," *Dallas Daily Times Herald*, Sept. 28, 1938.
78. "Tossed Out Negro Ends His Jury Vigil," *Dallas Morning News*, Sept. 29, 1938.
79. Bedford, interview, July 19, 2005.
80. Lynn Landrum, "Thinking Out Loud," *Dallas Morning News*, Sept. 30, 1938.
81. "Rangers Guard Negro Jurors; Judge Objects," *Dallas Morning News*, Dec. 13, 1938.
82. Bedford, interview, July 10, 2005.
83. Payne, *Big D*, 231; Louis A. Bedford Jr., interview by Darwin Payne, Sept. 1, 2005.
84. Bedford, interview, July 10, 2005.
85. *Bedford Oral History Interview*, 4.
86. Dallas Historical Society, "John Leslie Patton, Jr.: Portrait of an Educator," in "Dallas History: Archived Items," at *Dallas Historical Society*, 2002, http://www.dallashistory.org/history/dallas/portrait.htm.
87. "Negroes Anxious to Serve the Country," *Dallas Express*, Dec. 13, 1941.
88. Ibid.
89. "No Time for Racial Trouble in Dallas Now," *Dallas Express*, Dec. 20, 1941.
90. "Negro Blood O.K. for British; Refused by U.S. Navy, Army," *Dallas Express*, Dec. 27, 1941.
91. Quoted by Doris Kearns Goodwin in *No Ordinary Time: Franklin and Eleanor Roosevelt; The Home Front in World War II* (New York: Simon and Schuster, 1994), 247.
92. Ibid., 252.
93. Payne, *Big D*, 236–37.
94. Spring music program, 1942, "L. A. Bedford Jr. Personal" binder, Bedford Papers.
95. Booker T. Washington High School Commencement program, May 29, 1942, "L. A. Bedford Jr. Personal" binder, Bedford Papers.
96. Robert Prince, *A History of Dallas from a Different Perspective* (Dallas: Nortex, 1993), 95; quoted in Michael Phillips, *White Metropolis: Race, Ethnicity, and Religion in Dallas, 1841–2001* (Austin: University of Texas Press, 2006), 110.

2

PRAIRIE VIEW AND BEYOND

L ouis—Brother—was only sixteen when he began his freshman year at Prairie
View College. That was young for college, but he would have been even
younger—fifteen—if he hadn't contracted bronchial pneumonia when he was
fourteen. Although located more than two hundred miles from home, much nearer
to Houston, Prairie View was familiar to him, for just as with Booker T. Washington
High School, his sister, Deborah, had preceded him there. She was now entering
her third year. Just after the First World War, Louis's father had attended chef classes
there, and Louis's noted grandfather M. M. Rodgers was a Prairie View graduate.
Despite so many family ties, Louis had no sense of being pressured to attend the
institution. He realized, though, his parents were pleased with his choice.

He could have chosen any number of all-black colleges in the state. Much nearer
to Dallas, the small town of Marshall in East Texas boasted two colleges for African
Americans, Wiley and Bishop. Wiley College was the state's oldest college for blacks,
founded in 1873 by the Freedman's Aid Society of the Methodist Episcopal Church.
The Baptist Home Mission Society founded Bishop College in 1881. In Tyler was
Texas College, started in 1894 by the Colored Methodist Episcopal Church. In the
state capital of Austin were two other black colleges, Samuel Huston College (1900)
and Tillotson College (1881). (In 1952 these two merged into a single college.) Louis
had not considered any college possibilities besides Prairie View. His vision of the
Prairie View cadets marching in their high boots and khaki uniforms at Negro Day at
the State Fair of Texas remained powerful. He wanted to be a proud cadet.

Louis also had emotional support from some of his best friends in high school—
Harold M. Harden Jr., William Wakefield, Marvin Brotherton, Robert Maxwell,
Alfred Bowens, and A. J. Anderson—all of whom also chose Prairie View. Some of
the girls from Booker T. Washington High were also going there. Louis had never
been farther away from home than San Antonio, where he visited his grandmother,

but his youthful exuberance could not be denied. He was so eager to get to Prairie View that he went there in the early summer, long before classes would begin, to earn extra money.

Through his sister, Louis had learned of a special program that would permit him to work on campus for the summer and use the money toward his tuition. As he soon learned to his dismay, he was assigned to be a dishwasher in the faculty dining hall. He arrived for work each morning at 5:30 AM and worked through the entire day. Four weeks of that was enough. He returned home for what was left of the summer.[1]

In September 1942 Louis returned to Prairie View to begin his studies as a freshman. He joined a large number of students from Dallas and boarded the Southern Pacific's "Owl" train, so named because it made its run in the middle of the night, departing Dallas at about 11:00 PM and arriving at the Prairie View depot shortly before dawn. The train, segregated by race, had two or three coaches designated for the eager black students. The campus was about a mile from the depot, and Louis walked there with other students, leaving their luggage and trunks to be delivered by truck to their dormitories.

Such services were often provided by the college's night watchman and sometimes "cab" driver, a popular character nicknamed "Buck Mix," whose real name was George Pitkins. Because he wore a ten-gallon cowboy hat, students had combined for him the names of the Western movie stars Buck Jones and Tom Mix.

Louis's assigned dormitory, Lucky Hall, was a three-story brick building designated for freshmen. Constructed in 1909, it provided minimal amenities. Four students were assigned to each room. Showers and bathrooms were in the basement. Louis's three roommates included two friends from Dallas, Harold M. Harden Jr. and William Wakefield. Louis stayed in a campus dormitory all four years, moving on to Foster Hall for his sophomore year, Woodruff for his junior year, and Shoemake for his senior year.

Throughout his college days, Louis's parents paid for his tuition, $25 each semester, and his room and board, $18 a month at first and $22 by the time he graduated. His parents also sent him and his sister monthly allowances of $2 each. Movies on campus on Fridays and Saturdays cost just a dime or fifteen cents, so the $2 monthly allowance went a long way. After his freshman year, Louis found part-time work on campus for extra spending money.

He didn't have much money, certainly, but it was more than many students had. Sometimes those who lacked money to pay for their room and board resorted to a practice called "catting." They would float from room to room, counting on the goodwill of their friends to put them up and to sneak food to them from the dining hall. Such students were said to be just "catting around."[2]

Prairie View State Normal and Industrial College, the only state-supported college for black students, had been founded in 1876 as a part of the Texas A&M system. When Louis enrolled, the total student population was about twelve hundred. The campus, half a dozen miles from Hempstead and about fifty miles northwest of Houston, consisted of a large number of buildings in the middle of a huge, rolling, treeless plain once cultivated as a part of the Alta Vista plantation of Colonel Jared Ellison Kirby. In that same region of the state, Louis's parents had grown up and his ancestors had been slaves.

An emphasis on practical studies predominated at Prairie View, following Booker T. Washington's model at Tuskegee. In the Mechanic Arts Department, students studied auto mechanics, broom and mattress making, cabinetmaking, carpentry, dyeing and dry cleaning, electrical maintenance and repair, laundering, shoemaking and repairing, and tailoring. The Division of Agriculture offered a bachelor of science degree in agriculture. Many agriculture students aspired to be county agricultural agents.

In the Division of Arts and Sciences, one could study biology, business administration, chemistry, economics, English, history, math, music, philosophy, and modern foreign languages. Forty-eight faculty members were assigned to this division, which offered bachelor of arts, bachelor of music, bachelor of science, and bachelor of science in education degrees.

If the prevailing "separate but equal" doctrine had held true, Prairie View would have been a far better place. In fact, it was impoverished. State appropriations to Prairie View lagged behind, by a considerable margin, the funds other Southern states gave their all-black state colleges. Faculty salaries were woefully inadequate, and the proportion of overall operating costs borne by the students was considerably higher than in Texas's all-white institutions of higher education.[3] Yet, as the only state-supported African American college in Texas, Prairie View was for black students the state's leading institution of higher education. Its students seemed to hold in their hands the future progress of their race.[4]

Prairie View's official philosophy was realistically understated: "The education of Negroes must have for its objectives the making of a worthwhile life and respectable living." To those ends, the institution had two specific goals: "(1) To serve the colored citizens of Texas at the point of their greatest need. (2) To bring the students' training into closer relationship with life's occupations and problems."[5]

The administrative head of the college was the long-suffering Willette Rutherford Banks, born in Georgia in 1881 as the second of thirteen children. The Texas A&M board had given Banks and his predecessors the diminished title of "principal" rather than the more appropriate title of "president." Since coming to Prairie View in 1926 from Texas College in Tyler, Banks had fought a valiant battle to raise standards, increase salaries, and win accreditation from the Southern Association of Colleges. He had gained accreditation, but his struggle for increased resources from the Texas A&M board was never ending. Once he bitterly complained, "We have men at Prairie View who find it difficult to meet their grocery bill." In 1941 Prairie View was the only state-supported college in Texas to have its funding reduced; in response Banks cautiously described the situation as one "of such gravity that it precipitates an emergency."[6]

In photographs Banks is seen as a stern, slender man always standing at attention. In one picture in Prairie View's 1946 *Purple and Gold* yearbook, though, he is in overalls and pushing a plow. Banks planted and worked his own garden, sharing vegetables with local families.[7]

In the first full year of World War II, 1942, enrollment in the Reserve Officers Training Corps (ROTC) was mandatory for male students. Louis signed up with some excitement, donning the woolen uniform that he so admired. Soon he began drilling with the other cadets, using wooden rifles. Prairie View officials were pleased that in 1942 the ROTC program had achieved "senior" status, having been accepted as an official training site for future officers.

War news in the fall of 1942 was all encompassing. German troops had reached

Stalingrad and were fighting street by bombed-out street with Russian defenders, with fearful losses on both sides. U.S. Marines were on Guadalcanal. On the home front, scrap metal drives were being held, and victory gardens were springing up.

Prairie View offered enthusiastic support for the war effort. Principal Banks signed a message rededicating the college's available resources to the government in the "gigantic struggle to Win this War and also to Win the Peace."[8]

Louis shared in the patriotic fervor, never doubting the need to defend democracy, even one that failed to recognize equality for all its citizens. Still as thin as he was in high school, he is depicted in uniform in the freshman section of the yearbook, the 1943 *Panther*, gazing solemnly into the camera lens. The yearbook has a full-page photograph showing a soldier in shadow, with the American flag highlighted in the background. At the bottom of the page is a pledge with space for student signatures, duly signed by Louis and his sister: "We, <u>Deborah & Louis Bedford</u>, pledge allegiance to the Flag of the United States of America and to the Republic for which it stands."[9]

Throughout Louis's college days, male students—including most of his best friends, such as Marvin Brotherton, Alvin Gosey, Alfred Bowens, Robert Maxwell, and George H. Stafford—were eventually drafted into military service. Very few of them remained at Prairie View through their senior years. Louis, so young when he enrolled, had no concerns for a while about being drafted, but when he turned eighteen, he went to Dallas to be classified by the draft board. The examining doctor determined that he had a weak heart, and he was declared 4-F, ineligible for military service. Louis's parents, alarmed, took him to the family doctor, who could find nothing irregular. The doctor's only explanation, he laughed, was that maybe Louis was "nearly scared to death." Never again did Louis ever have such a diagnosis, and he never had heart problems as an adult.[10]

In Louis's sophomore year, a number of U.S. Army soldiers already on active duty were assigned to campus as part of the Army Specialized Training Program. Because these new soldiers wore their army uniforms every day, got up early each morning for reveille, and followed other military protocol, it was decided that ROTC students, including Louis, should do the same. Thus, five days a week, Louis fell out for early morning reveille and calisthenics, then marched in formation with his company to the dining hall. His enthusiasm for the military began to wane.

Louis was beginning to develop an independent mind. While it seemed fair enough for actual soldiers to have to follow this strict morning routine, it was another matter for students who were not yet in the army. As a college student with course-work as his major concern, Louis could not rationalize the need to rise before sunup every day or follow other military procedures. In March 1943, in Louis's freshman year, the ROTC director sent him a warning letter listing ten demerits. His violations included failure to turn out his lights at 11:00 PM, being absent from reveille, being absent from chapel, going to the canteen during study hour, and being absent from guard duty.[11]

The letter occasioned a meeting with Principal Banks. Louis and a few other offending cadets were summoned to Banks's office, where the ROTC officer, Captain Reeves, advised the principal that these students were failing to make reveille. Louis would never forget Banks's exclamation: "Great God Almighty—the world's on fire, and you can't get up in the morning!" If he heard of these transgressions again, Banks warned, he would send the young men packing.[12]

As it happened, reveille was not the only thing Louis was missing. In that same month a Prairie View official advised Louis's parents by letter that their son had already been absent eleven times from mandatory Sunday morning chapel and Sunday evening vestry services. This would cease to be a problem, for during his junior and senior years Louis became a member of the Ushers Board, responsible for ushering and taking up collections at the Sunday morning services. On the other hand, his compliance with military regimentation, although briefly improved after his session with Banks, was not long standing. In his junior year Louis was warned again by letter that he had another ten demerits for being out of uniform and being absent from reveille and retreat. Luckily, Banks did not follow through with his previous threat.[13]

Louis was drifting without much purpose. By his own admission, he had been little more than an average student in high school, and up to this point he had been no more than that at Prairie View. As he completed his second year, he had not decided upon a major course of study. He still intended to be a railroad mail clerk, but there was no specific major to prepare him for that.

As Louis neared his junior year, he made a fortunate acquaintance. His promise, unfulfilled to this point, somehow attracted the attention of a young history professor, George Ruble Woolfolk, who had come to Prairie View in 1943 after completing coursework toward his PhD at the University of Wisconsin. Woolfolk recognized in Louis a potential that Louis himself had not seen. Flattered by Woolfolk's attention as well as intrigued with his field, Louis told Woolfolk that he had decided upon history as his major. "All right," Woolfolk responded, "but now you've got to get on the ball." Woolfolk pulled Louis and a few others closer into his circle of influence, trying to awaken in them an awareness of their possibilities. They became known as "Woolfolk's boys."[14]

Woolfolk had an inspiring message for his disciples. He, a black man, had earned his bachelor's degree at Louisville (Kentucky) Municipal College and his master's degree at the Ohio State University, and he was still working toward his PhD. He had been doing his graduate work at two of the finest state universities in the nation, both essentially all-white establishments. Louis and his Prairie View classmates, educated in all-black public schools, had subconsciously been imbued with the common notion that their intellectual capabilities were unequal to those of white students in established universities. They had no way to test this assumption, nor could they be certain such assumptions were wrong. Now came their professor, a man who had entered the white man's world of higher education and who was completing his doctorate, assuring these Prairie View students they were fully capable of doing the same. They must elevate the level of their ambitions.

Louis believed a history major would open doors to other careers. Almost inexplicably, Louis decided at about the same time that after earning his undergraduate degree in history, he would go to law school. Woolfolk encouraged this decision, although they both knew there were no law schools in Texas that would accept black students. Years later Louis could not remember precisely why he decided upon a legal career. Perhaps it was because he was told that his grandfather, M. M. Rodgers, had wanted to be a lawyer. Perhaps he was influenced by his awareness of the Bedford family friend J. L. Turner Sr., whom he knew to be making a good living in Dallas. Gradually, Louis was becoming aware of the significance of a legal career and what it could do not just for him but also for other people of color: laws could be changed.

Bedford, future attorney and jurist, would not be the only one of Woolfolk's boys to go far in life. Otto Fridia (who later would marry Louis's sister, Deborah), the first history major to graduate under Woolfolk, became an educator and the super-intendent for the Dallas Independent School District. Bedford would be the second graduate. William Downing had a career in the army and retired as a colonel.

Neither Louis nor his compatriots at Prairie View exhibited intense feelings over the social injustices thrust upon them by segregation. That would come later. Louis remembered that as an undergraduate, he was more resentful about the injustice of the discrimination against Prairie View as an institution than about segregation. It was his understanding that despite the meager resources it was allotted, Prairie View still had to squeeze its budget so that at the end of each fiscal year, Principal Banks could send back 10 percent to Texas A&M.[15]

Also vivid in Louis's memory were the deliberations that occurred just before crusty Texas Governor Coke R. Stevenson, a conservative rancher from central Texas, visited Prairie View to meet with administrators and tour the campus. School officials pondered whether they should ask the governor, well known for his seg-regationist commitments, to address the student body. The concern was that he would mispronounce "Negro" (at best as "nigra"), and if he did, the students would likely make an unpleasant scene, at least booing him. The officials finally decided Stevenson should not speak to the student body. Certainly, a proper greeting had to be ensured for the governor, though, so when he arrived, Louis and all ROTC cadets were posted along the road standing at the present arms position, holding their wooden rifles.[16]

As Louis was becoming more knowledgeable about the world around him, he was increasingly aware that the constraints on the lives of African Americans in Dallas and elsewhere were being chipped away. The process was slow, and it required sup-port from sponsoring organizations, lawyers who were working in an all-white legal system, and brave individuals willing to accept possible retribution. George Porter's heroic efforts at the courthouse in Dallas were not forgotten, but the refusal to per-mit African Americans to serve on juries continued. The fact that this was not proper or even constitutional was apparent, but social customs changed at a snail's pace.

An example of the system's continued racial bias against blacks came in 1940 after a black man named Henry Allen Hill was found guilty of raping a white woman. Hill was charged with knocking the woman's twenty-five-year-old male companion unconscious with a rock, then raping her. In the struggle the attacker's pocket, which contained identification papers, was torn from his coat. The papers left behind easily identified Hill as the attacker. A jury sentenced Hill to death in the electric chair.

As usual, there had been no black men on the jury that convicted him, nor had they been present on the grand jury that indicted him. In fact, no black men had served on a Dallas County grand jury since Reconstruction. Hill's attorney, J. Forest McCutcheon, chose to appeal the conviction on the failure to have African Americans on the grand jury, and in May 1942 the U.S. Supreme Court heard McCutcheon's arguments, overturned the conviction, and ordered a new trial.[17]

Dallas County officials now placed an African American named John King, owner of a thirty-acre farm between Irving and Grand Prairie, on the next grand jury. Hill was promptly reindicted, and on October 30, 1942, a petit jury found him guilty and sentenced him to death. Once again his attorney appealed the conviction, arguing that the presence of a single black man on the grand jury was insufficient. Before this appeal could be exhausted, Hill died in 1943 of a ruptured appendix.[18]

An important principle was won, but it was short lived. There was no follow-through. Not until five years later, in 1947, did the next African American, Samuel William Hudson Jr., serve on a Dallas County grand jury. Memories were short, for it was believed at the time that Hudson was the first black man to have done so.[19]

In the same year that the U.S. Supreme Court reversed Hill's conviction, another legal victory was won in Dallas, this one on behalf of black public school teachers. African American teachers in Dallas, and throughout the state and the South, were paid significantly less than their white counterparts. This inequity was widely recognized and lamented in the black community, and Louis and others were well aware of it.

The Negro Teachers' Alliance of Dallas, encouraged by successful equalization suits in Maryland by the NAACP's Thurgood Marshall, decided to pursue the matter. A prominent black attorney from Sherman (sixty miles north of Dallas), William J. Durham, was hired to represent Thelma E. Page, a Spanish and French teacher at the new Lincoln High School. Louis Bedford later understood that Ms. Page had been chosen as the plaintiff because she was young, single, and from Colorado, and she had earned her bachelor's degree at the nonsegregated University of Denver, where her education was the same as that of white teachers. If the Dallas school district fired her because of her challenge—a very realistic possibility—it was reasoned that as a young single woman, she could return to Colorado and find a new job.[20]

Ms. Page was being paid $1,260 annually. White teachers with the same qualifications and experience were earning $1,800. Dallas's discrimination in salary, Durham alleged in the suit, filed in federal district court, was based solely on race and color, a denial of equal protection under the law as guaranteed by the Fourteenth Amendment.[21]

In response, the Dallas Board of Education argued that differences in salary were based on educational qualifications, ability, merit, experience, or performance, and on the nature of duties performed. There was no fixed teacher or principal salary based on "individual worth," the board said in its reply. Moreover, the district said, it had no funds to increase the pay of black teachers without breaking the contracts of white teachers by lowering their salaries. "The remedy sought by the plaintiffs . . . will tend to disrupt the entire public school system of Dallas," it was argued.[22]

At a court hearing, Durham was accompanied to the federal building, as the *Dallas Morning News* reported, by a "Negro attorney from New York, said to be a consultant on the case." This attorney was otherwise unidentified in the story, but he was none other than future U.S. Supreme Court justice Thurgood Marshall, counsel for the NAACP.[23]

Once again, appealing to the legal system for rights guaranteed by the Constitution was successful. The Dallas school board agreed to a consent decree that would bring the salaries of 235 African American teachers in the system to the same level as whites' salaries over a three-year period of adjustments. The Dallas teachers' action was the first in the state, but within two months the Houston school board, faced with a similar suit, agreed to equalize the pay for its black teachers.[24]

Over the next three decades, W. J. Durham was the outstanding African American lawyer in Dallas and in Texas, said by one scholar to be "virtually indispensable to the Civil Rights Movement in Texas."[25] If Maceo Smith and Maynard Jackson energized the city's black community beginning in the 1930s with their organizing abilities, in the 1940s and 1950s it was Durham—acting in conjunction with the local and national chapters of the NAACP—who carried the battle for equality into the courts with great success.

When Durham died in 1970, his obituary in the *Dallas Morning News* listed his age as sixty, off the mark by some fifteen years. According to the 1900 U.S. Census for Hopkins County (seventy-five miles northeast of Dallas), he was five years old when the census taker visited the home of his parents, Henry and Mary Smith Durham, in the little community of Sandfield. Henry Durham was forty-six and described by the census taker as a farm laborer, but he also worked as a barber in the nearby settlement of Reilly Springs. Henry was unusually light-skinned, and in interviews area residents said they believed he was the son of Zack Durham, a white man, and a mulatto slave, Daisy, whom Zack married and with whom he had a large family.[26]

Henry Durham was born somewhere in Texas, presumably southeast Texas, in 1853, and at the age of twenty he married Mary Smith, a native of Missouri. Their son William (who used the initial "J" for his middle name, although there is no record of what it stood for) was born in April 1895, the sixth of eight children. According to the 1900 census, the Durham children, in addition to five-year-old William, included three daughters (Daisy, seventeen years old; Pauline, six; and Mary, two) and four other sons (Marion, fourteen; Bruce, twelve; Albert, ten; and Fred, three months). Unfortunately, the family did not appear in the 1910 and 1920 censuses.[27]

The Durhams were pioneer members of the Independence Baptist Church in the freedman settlement of Sandfield. The children attended Sandfield School, and at an early age Willie, as he was called, developed an ambition to become a lawyer. When he was seventeen years old, it is said, he moved to Dallas for a while to further his education. Sometime afterward he took the train to Kansas Normal School (today Emporia State University) in Emporia, enrolling for classes and working odd jobs to pay his way. That institution's records show he was enrolled for one semester in fall 1917 and that he had graduated from high school in 1915. After that semester Durham was inducted into the army and served in France during World War I.

Later in life Durham would say he was born in 1904 and graduated from the law school at the University of Kansas. That birth date was certainly wrong, and the University of Kansas School of Law has no record that Durham ever studied there. Even Durham's official death certificate states erroneously that he was born April 6, 1904. That information, of course, was provided by survivors who themselves must not have been certain of Durham's true birth date.[28]

According to a historian of the NAACP in Texas, Durham entered the legal profession after studying law in the office of Ben F. Gafford, a white attorney in Sherman. After several attempts to pass an admissions examination, he succeeded in 1926 and established a law practice in Sherman, primarily as legal counsel to an insurance company.[29]

Sherman was a small town with a population of about ten thousand, located north of Dallas in the same northeast portion of the state where Durham had been born. In 1930, not long after Durham began his practice there, a lynch-minded mob, attempting to seize an accused black rapist, set the courthouse on fire and cut the firemen's hoses, but they didn't get their man until after the fire was out. They found the suspect dead in the vault of the devastated courthouse, where he had tried to hide from the mob, which now proceeded to mutilate the corpse. In the widespread disturbances that followed, the town's black business district was set afire. Durham's law office was one of those burned down. It was one of the worst racial riots in the nation's history.

Perhaps these shocking events provided Durham the motivation to begin to take on civil rights cases. By 1940 he was recognized as the leading African American lawyer in Texas. Before his death in 1970, Durham had participated in more than forty civil rights cases.

In his history of outstanding Dallas lawyers, veteran Dallas attorney John L. "Jack" Hauer called Durham one of the most memorable of the city's lawyers of the first half of the twentieth century. He described Durham as having an encyclopedic knowledge of the law, being an expert cross-examiner, and possessing a temperament that was "unfailingly courteous, patient, and understanding."[30] Another historian noted, however, that outside the courtroom Durham's "irritable temperament and tough money-making instincts made him difficult to get along with."[31]

Durham told Louis Bedford that he had once walked into the courtroom of a small Texas town and informed the judge that he was an attorney representing the client in the case before him. "Well, you can't practice in my court," the judge said. Durham said, "Fine, Judge, that's all right. All I want to do is dictate something into the record." The judge told him to go ahead. Durham told the court reporter, "My name is W. J. Durham. I am licensed to practice law in the State of Texas. I am appearing in this District Court, and I have been denied the right to do this."

The judge suddenly reconsidered: "Wait a minute." He then allowed Durham to represent his client.[32]

In 1943, after practicing law in Sherman for thirteen years, Durham moved to Dallas, where his career continued an additional twenty-seven years. His increasing activism as counsel to the Texas NAACP made Dallas a more logical base, and the wartime shortage of gasoline made the expense of frequent automobile trips between Dallas and Sherman prohibitive.[33]

The seeds of Durham's involvement in one of the nation's most important civil rights cases had already been planted by the time he moved to Dallas. This case challenged the outrageous practice in the Solid South of excluding African Americans from voting in Democratic primaries. The "white primary," the most important of all the disfranchisement devices, was introduced in Texas in 1903 with the Terrell Election Law, which gave Democratic county committees the right to exclude blacks from voting in their primaries. This law was followed more definitively by a 1923 legislative act stating that "in no event shall a negro be eligible to participate in a Democratic Party primary election."[34] Since the Democratic primary winners, without exception, won the general elections, a vote in the general election was meaningless. The rationale for allowing such laws, however, was that the Democratic Party, as a private organization separate from the state government, could deny participation in its primary without violating the Fourteenth Amendment.

Reaction to the 1923 act was immediate from African American leaders. Overturning the white primary became the principal target of the NAACP in Texas for two decades, beginning in 1924 after a black physician, Lawrence A. Nixon of El Paso, presented his paid poll tax receipt at the primary voting place, only to have the election judges deny him a ballot. While the U.S. Supreme Court ruled in his favor in *Nixon v. Herndon* (1927), its opinion was not definitive and was easily circumvented. Other similar cases that followed also yielded unsatisfactory results but with occasional glimmers of hope.[35]

In January 1940, with a presidential election coming up, the NAACP's executive secretary, Walter White, suggested that the national organization concentrate on Texas in seeking to overturn the white primary. The Texas NAACP would play the lead role. In March 1940 a number of African American leaders of Texas met in Houston and organized a statewide fund-raising effort to finance the next legal challenge. Two months later Thurgood Marshall met in Dallas with the State Legal Redress Committee to discuss the suit. At that meeting, Durham, still living in Sherman, was appointed resident counsel for the anticipated lawsuit. Durham was to be paid $2,500 plus expenses.[36]

Although a suit had yet to be filed, delegates to the Texas NAACP conference in Corpus Christi that same month were optimistic about its prospects. A. Maceo Smith called the session the "greatest in the history of our State Conference." He wrote to Walter White in New York that "we laid plans that will realize for the Negroes of Texas a new era in the fight for civil rights." They had determined not only to challenge the white primary but afterward to break down the state's segregated educational system.[37]

Thurgood Marshall was no less excited. "This Texas group will really go down in history and they are not afraid to fight for their rights," he told White.[38]

A favorable Supreme Court ruling in a Louisiana case, *United States v. Classic*, 313 U.S. 299 (1941), provided further hope. The court held that the primary was an integral part of a state's election machinery and thus subject to federal authority. As Durham observed, the Supreme Court was now "on our side of the question."[39]

The Texas NAACP's first choice for a plaintiff was a Houston mail carrier named Sidney Hasgett, an active NAACP member who had been denied the right to vote in the August 1940 Democratic Party runoff. When the case went to federal court in April 1941, it was determined that because Hasgett had not tried to vote in the primary itself, he lacked proper standing. The case was dismissed. This failure was devastating. Marshall especially faced severe criticism. Members of the Dallas NAACP accused him of "messing up the case." One of the Houston NAACP members advised him he had better win the next case or not return to Texas. Durham, who had played second fiddle to Marshall, seemed to escape similar criticism.[40]

Durham, A. Maceo Smith, and Marshall went to work again, beating the drums to raise enough money for the next court challenge. This time a plaintiff with better standing was located, a dentist named Lonnie E. Smith, who was an NAACP member. Smith had been rejected as a voter in both the Democratic primary election on July 27, 1940, and in the runoff that followed on August 24. He was tough-minded, willing to withstand the pressures and criticisms that inevitably awaited him as the plaintiff.

In their suit in U.S. District Court for the Southern District of Texas, Marshall and Durham contended that refusal to give a ballot to Smith was a denial of his rights under the Fourteenth and Fifteenth Amendments. The Fourteenth Amendment forbade states from making or enforcing any law abridging the privileges or immunities of citizens of the United States, and the Fifteenth Amendment specifically prohibited any denial or abridgement by a state of the right of citizens to vote because of color. The court denied their petition, concluding the primary was a "mere party procedure" that could be controlled by the party, a voluntary organization. Marshall and Durham appealed, and together they argued the case before the U.S. Court of Appeals for the Fifth Circuit. Again their argument was rejected.

Then came their appeal to the U.S. Supreme Court. Durham, who had not argued before this highest court, stayed behind. Marshall recruited his former law school professor, William H. Hastie—a Harvard Law School graduate, now dean of Howard University School of Law, and famous for his unflappable manner—to join him. (Nearly two decades later, both President Kennedy and President Johnson considered Hastie for an appointment to the U.S. Supreme Court. If he had been appointed, Hastie and not Marshall would have been the Supreme Court's first African American justice.) Marshall and Hastie's presentation before the Supreme Court was persuasive, and now came a favorable decision that was final: the highest court in the land declared the white primary unconstitutional. As the executive director of Houston's NAACP branch, Lulu B. White, jubilantly declared, the victory in this case, *Smith v. Allwright* (1944), represented "the second emancipation of the Negro."[41]

Here was a legal victory, some thirty years in the making, that not only opened up Democratic primaries to African American voters throughout the South but also energized NAACP branches in their activities and inspired the creation of new chapters. White in Houston and Juanita Craft in Dallas directed massive membership campaigns in Texas, venturing outside their home cities to smaller towns throughout the state. By 1946 the Dallas branch had approximately 7,000 members. National NAACP membership grew from 50,556 in 1940 to just under 450,000 in 1946, and the number of branches jumped from 355 to 1,073.

Registration of black voters in Texas more than tripled between 1940 and 1947, climbing from 30,000 to 100,000.[42] The impact of black voters' participation in the

1948 Texas Democratic primary, the first such primary for which they were eligible, was apparent in the senatorial contest. Notwithstanding the Duval County dispute, Lyndon B. Johnson's margin of victory over Coke Stevenson was attributed to the support for him by a majority of the black voters.[43]

In the flush of the *Smith v. Allwright* decision and with more legal challenges on the horizon, Durham now was placed on a monthly retainer of twenty-five dollars as resident counsel of the Texas NAACP. The governing State Conference also gave him oversight for all civil rights cases filed by local branches.

In this era three figures emerged as the most powerful in Texas's NAACP. Although Houston had taken the initiative in the fight against the white primary, two of the three leaders were from Dallas: Durham as legal counsel and A. Maceo Smith as executive secretary. Lulu B. White of Houston was the third.

L. A. Bedford Jr., concluding his junior year at Prairie View and having decided by now to become a lawyer, was beginning to pay attention to these people and events. Lulu White, a Prairie View graduate and officer of the Prairie View Alumni and Ex-Student Association, was a frequent visitor to the campus, and her presence and comments on civil rights always stirred interest.

The long struggle to obtain a meaningful ballot for blacks was not nearly over, despite the abolition of the white primary. There were other barriers to be overcome. Durham now began researching a lawsuit for what already had been decided would be the next battleground in Texas—the segregated system of higher education. A successful court challenge might permit Louis to stay in Texas to earn his law degree, a decided advantage for anyone who wanted to pass the state's bar exam and practice law in the state.

Durham sent his research to Thurgood Marshall, requesting, in conjunction with Smith, that Marshall return to Texas to discuss handling the challenge. "We want to go about it in the same manner that we handled the Texas Primary Case," Smith told Marshall.[44]

In Dallas on June 2, 1945, Durham, Marshall, Smith, Carter Wesley (the activist publisher of the *Houston Informer* and a lawyer himself), and John J. Jones, president of the Texas NAACP State Conference, met and made plans for the new legal assault. They determined the specific target would be the University of Texas graduate and professional schools, and they announced a fund-raising drive for ten thousand dollars to finance the case.[45]

An immediate feeble response by the legislature was to change the name of Prairie View State Normal and Industrial College to Prairie View University. This had no impact on the NAACP's goals. Durham, already on retainer, was now contracted by the NAACP State Conference to take the lead role in the case for a one-thousand-dollar fee, plus expenses and five hundred dollars for appellate work. While the State Conference would assume financial responsibilities, the suit would be coordinated with the national NAACP "in conformity with its policies and procedures." Thurgood Marshall, therefore, would continue to be involved. Carter Wesley, whose *Houston Informer* had a statewide circulation, would head the publicity effort to raise the money.[46]

The first order of the legal battle was once more to find a proper plaintiff, and again the best candidate emerged in Houston. He was a slight, balding, thirty-three-year-old mail carrier named Heman Marion Sweatt, who some time before had been urged by Durham to seek admission to the University of Texas Law School. Sweatt, like Sidney Hasgett, was a member of the Good Hope Missionary Baptist Church, whose pastor, Rev. Albert A. Lucas, was a leader in the NAACP battle against the white primary. As local secretary of the National Alliance of Postal Employees, Sweatt had worked with an attorney in documenting a case of discrimination against blacks in the post office. This work had created in him an interest in the law as a means of challenging discrimination, and he had decided in 1945 to go to law school.

His background made him comfortable with being the plaintiff in a case certain to raise controversy and bring personal anguish. Sweatt's father, James Sweatt, had provided an example of social activism to his six children. After a career as a teacher and principal at a small school in Beaumont, James had become a postal clerk in Houston. There he helped organize the National Alliance of Postal Employees and became a charter member of the Houston NAACP branch. As a boy, Heman had attended NAACP meetings with his father. One of the family's friends was Lulu B. White, and Heman Sweatt's dentist was none other than Lonnie Smith. In fact, Sweatt had helped raise money for *Smith v. Allwright.*

Heman Sweatt had graduated in 1934 from Wiley College, where an atmosphere of agitation for racial equality already existed. Sweatt studied under two out-spoken African American activists, James H. Morton and Melvin Beaunorus Tolson. He was a classmate of James L. Farmer Jr. Morton later became president of the Austin NAACP branch. Tolson was a poet and inspired speaker against racial discrimination. Farmer founded the Congress of Racial Equality in 1942.

(Farmer gained national recognition for his civil rights activism, which included organizing the Freedom Rides throughout the South in 1961. He was awarded a Presidential Medal of Freedom in 1998. Tolson gained the nation's attention much later. First, his collection of poetry, *Harlem Gallery*, won high praise when it was published in 1965.[47] But even greater recognition came through a 2007 film, *The Great Debaters*, which depicted the Wiley campus atmosphere in 1935. The film told the story of how Tolson, portrayed by Denzel Washington, led his Wiley debate team, of which Farmer was a member, to an upset victory over the reigning national debate champions, the University of Southern California [changed to Harvard for the film].)

Sweatt, after graduation and a period of time working at various jobs, went to the University of Michigan School of Public Health. The state's cold weather persuaded him to return to Houston, where he took his post office job and joined the Houston branch of the NAACP.[48]

There was one potentially damaging aspect to Sweatt as a plaintiff. In a long letter to the NAACP's Walter White, he had declared he was a Communist sympathizer. If such sentiments were revealed, the results could be a devastating publicity setback in these early days of the Cold War. But after serious internal deliberations, it was decided that the suit must go forward, and it must go forward with Sweatt as plaintiff.[49]

Sweatt signed a contract in which the state NAACP would assume responsibility for all legal fees and underwrite his travel expenses. For several months Durham, NAACP leaders, and Sweatt made preparations for the legal challenge, studying Sweatt's transcript and the law school's admission requirements and making certain all details had been covered.

For several years prior to this, the State of Texas had avoided desegregating its graduate programs by offering scholarships that sent qualified black students to out-of-state schools. A black Dallas physician, Richard T. Hamilton, concerned about the absence in Texas of graduate and professional schools for African Americans, had begun campaigning in 1934 for a scholarship program, but by 1938 enacting legislation stalled.[50]

As a result, leaders of the student aid effort decided to try another approach: they would seek to integrate the University of Texas. They expected failure, but the effort would prompt legislative approval of the scholarship program. Thus, in 1938 the Dallas branch of the NAACP sponsored a black insurance salesman, George L. Allen, to enroll in an extension course in business psychology and salesmanship. Allen, who later was the first elected black Dallas city councilman, was surprised when officials accepted his registration without comment. Ten days later, realizing the significance of this act, the university cancelled his enrollment.

Allen's rejection, anticipated and planned for by the NAACP, prompted the legislature, nine months later, to provide twenty-five thousand dollars annually for out-of-state scholarships for black graduate and professional students. Within a month black students had submitted sixty applications for these funds, and forty-five awards, ranging from two hundred dollars to three hundred dollars, had been granted. Soon, though, black students realized that these scholarships failed to compensate for the added expenses of moving out of state and the distress of being far from their families.[51]

The goal now was different. In February 1946, accompanied by an NAACP delegation, Sweatt met in Austin with the University of Texas's registrar and its president, Virginia-born Theophilus Shickel Painter, whose PhD was in zoology with a specialty in genetics. Painter, who became president in 1944 after the Board of Regents had fired Homer Rainey for supporting faculty members who favored the New Deal, tried to discourage Sweatt, pointing to the availability of out-of-state scholarships for African American students who wanted graduate study. Sweatt, undaunted, insisted the only thing he wanted was to occupy a single seat in a law classroom and ultimately to practice law in Texas. He was applying as an individual, he said, seeking to head off criticisms that he was a pawn of the NAACP.[52]

Painter forwarded the question to the Texas attorney general, Grover Sellers, who announced he would uphold Texas's "wise and long-continued policy of segregation." He advised Sweatt to apply for legal training at Prairie View, where a suitable law curriculum could be set up for him under the auspices of Texas A&M.[53]

As Durham prepared the lawsuit, he recommended to A. Maceo Smith that the NAACP have African Americans apply for admission to every one of the University of Texas's professional schools. In 1947, before the *Sweatt* case was finished, a series of applications were made. Two months after Sweatt's rejection, Durham filed suit in a state district court, demanding Sweatt's admission to the law school. District Judge Roy C. Archer ruled the state must provide a "substantially equal" course in legal instruction for Sweatt in six months. Durham immediately expressed his gratification for a decision that was "extremely fair and impartial," although in truth what he wanted was integration of the existing law school at the University of Texas.[54]

Attorney General Grover Sellers, a candidate for governor, began making political capital out of Sweatt's attempt to enter the law school, winning applause by declaring that as long as he held the office of attorney general or governor, Sweatt would "never darken a door of the University of Texas." Sweatt's application, he said, was just "another instance of the attempt of highbrow whites and highbrow Negroes . . . to stir up racial unrest in Texas."[55]

At the end of Judge Archer's six-month deadline, the Texas A&M regents had done nothing but offer a last-minute declaration of intentions for a Prairie View law school, now projected as a branch in Houston. The judge was not ready to order Sweatt's admission, though. "I am compelled to assume," he declared from the bench, "and I do assume, that the regents will put into operation a first-class university teaching a first-class law school in February." If such did not happen, he said, "the matter is then squarely open, on proper application, for an admission to the law school at the University of Texas."[56] Durham and Marshall, disappointed at the judge's backtracking, made plans for an appeal.

Creation of a separate law school for African Americans was not what Sweatt, Durham, Marshall, or the NAACP had in mind. Moreover, their suit had prompted important support from students and faculty at the University of Texas who rallied to the cause. A number of UT students and organizations demonstrated on Sweatt's behalf. At least ten campus organizations—including Baptist, Methodist, Lutheran, and Episcopalian student groups and the president of the student council—urged his admission. Many faculty members also spoke in Sweatt's favor, including prominent professors J. Frank Dobie of the English Department and Dr. Frederick Eby of the Education Department.[57]

The chairman of the Board of Regents and other university officials favored the creation of a separate school for African Americans that would not drain any funds from the university's endowment. The legislature voted to create a new Texas State University for Negroes in Houston (since 1951 known as Texas Southern University) as well as a law school for blacks at a temporary Austin facility. Space for the Austin law school was leased in the basement of a building next to the Capitol Grounds, and with an emergency appropriation of one hundred thousand dollars, a library began to be assembled. University of Texas Law School officials and faculty members would devote part of their time to the new school. The basement school opened for registration in March 1947; although Sweatt was sent a personal invitation, neither he nor anyone else applied that spring.[58]

In the many proceedings that followed in the *Sweatt* case, it became apparent that its real target was the segregated school system. Segregated schools were inherently unequal, it was argued in *Sweatt*, in terms that foreshadowed the landmark 1954 *Brown v. Board of Education* decision.

When the U.S. Supreme Court finally heard the *Sweatt* case in April 1950, this time W. J. Durham made the opening remarks. Thurgood Marshall followed. (William Hastie was now governor of the U.S. Virgin Islands, and he did not participate in the case.) Durham and Marshall argued that the State of Texas had failed to provide an equal education for Sweatt and it could not do so by providing a separate law school. Texas Attorney General (and future governor) Price Daniel and Joe R. Greenhill, a future Texas Supreme Court justice, represented the state, but their arguments for the first time failed to persuade.

As the Supreme Court opinion, delivered by Chief Justice Fred Vinson, stated, "The law school for Negroes which was to have opened in February 1947, would have had no independent faculty or library. The teaching was to be carried on by four members of the University of Texas Law School faculty, who were to maintain their offices at the University of Texas while teaching at both institutions. Few of the ten thousand volumes ordered for the library had arrived; nor was there any full-time librarian. The school lacked accreditation."[59] In short, the State of Texas had failed to provide an equal alternative to Sweatt under the "separate but equal" doctrine.

Heman Marion Sweatt must be admitted to the law school under the Equal Protection Clause of the Fourteenth Amendment. For the first time in history, an all-white school was ordered to admit a black student despite the separate but equal doctrine. The Texas Council of Negro Organizations held a victory dinner in Dallas's Moorland YMCA.[60]

The day after the *Sweatt* decision, a number of blacks applied for admission to the University of Texas, and two were accepted. Between June and October 1950, thirty-two blacks applied for various programs at the university, and twenty-two were accepted for graduate training. Five of these entered the law school in September 1950 along with Sweatt.[61]

Sweatt was now thirty-seven years old; his health had declined; his wife soon divorced him. He was distracted by such things as being greeted by a burning cross one night as he left the law library and, when he reached his car, finding all four tires slashed. His grades suffered. After a year and a half, he dropped out, moved to Atlanta, earned a graduate degree in social work, and found employment with the Urban League.[62]

Fellow law students, though, had shown kindness to Sweatt, which he acknowledged in a letter to Thurgood Marshall. And a black law student, George Washington Jr. of Dallas, who entered law school with Sweatt but without the headlines, had a more positive experience and earned his degree in 1954.[63] Just on the horizon was another case that could have been predicted by the court's findings in *Sweatt v. Painter*: the monumental *Brown v. Board of Education* decision in 1954.

Texas newspapers, both the metropolitan dailies and the weeklies with predominantly black readership, gave wide publicity to both *Smith v. Allwright* and *Sweatt v. Painter*. Louis A. Bedford Jr. was surely aware of their significance. However, activities on the Prairie View campus did not include agitation for equality as a primary focus. Student activities during the war years included such things as Armistice Day programs and homecomings replete with floats.

Bedford, after his initial anonymity, gradually became prominent on the campus. He was president of the Prairie View–Dallas Club, a social organization for students from Dallas. He served on the Ushers Board during his last two years. He was a member of the Dramatic Club; the Grandchildren's Club, for students whose parents or grandparents had also attended Prairie View; and the History, Philosophy, and Political Science Club. He was also one of five seniors who served on the staff of the school newspaper, the *Panther*. He did not, however, rise in the ranks of the ROTC program.[64]

During his senior year, Louis had more money, too. When Otto Fridia, Deborah Bedford's boyfriend and future husband, graduated, he turned over to his friend Louis his lucrative part-time work, making special mail deliveries on campus. Louis was able to earn between fifty and seventy dollars a month, depending on the amount of mail to deliver.

Louis also set up movies every Friday and Saturday night on campus, earning five dollars for each showing. For this job he obtained the film, set up the equipment, pulled the curtains, turned down the house lights, and afterward took everything down.[65]

As one of Woolfolk's boys, he was doing well academically, too. A particular accomplishment during Louis's senior year was researching and writing a term paper on his grandfather M. M. Rodgers. Though his mother always had been proud of her father and made Louis and Deborah aware of his accomplishments, now, for the first time, Louis recognized his grandfather's important role in statewide and national affairs. Woolfolk was pleased to approve the project, for he understood his student would have access to original sources—letters and documents his mother had saved.

Bedford dedicated his paper, "M. M. Rodgers: A Study of a Negro in the Age of Transition," to his "family and especially to my mother, Callie Rodgers Bedford." The purpose of his study, he wrote in his introduction, was "to relate how Negroes strived to make progress in politics, business, religion, education, and fraternal organizations during the closing years of the 19th and the dawn of the 20th century." He expressed a hope that "we, the younger generation," would receive inspiration from the lives of "our foreparents who advanced under greater hardships than we are encountering."[66]

It was a project that excited Bedford in at least three ways: it related to his new interest in history, it dealt with his own grandfather, and it described an individual who was a major figure not only in his family but also in the state. Louis's mother was rightfully proud of her father's accomplishments, and even though he had died before Louis was born, she wanted her son to be mindful of him, so she often spoke of him. M. M. Rodgers provided an increasingly important role model for Louis, for his grandfather, born a slave, had succeeded despite social, economic, and political limitations. Louis always revered him.

Louis's research for his paper was far more ambitious than that of the typical undergraduate and more sophisticated. It more closely resembled a master's thesis than an undergraduate's term paper. Forty-one pages long, it contained footnotes and a bibliography, and it summarized Rodgers's career in four sections: "The Politician," "The Business Man," "Rodgers and the Church," and "The Man and the School." The paper was an early example of the high standards Louis established and maintained throughout his academic and professional careers.[67]

During the summers and the Christmas holidays, Louis always returned from Prairie View to the comfort of his parents' home on Thomas Avenue. Like most of his friends, he found temporary jobs that were unusually varied. One summer he worked as a porter at a prominent downtown clothing store, Dreyfuss & Sons. He would remember polishing the brass handles on the front door. Another summer he worked a physically demanding job at the Swiss Packing Company, unloading sacks containing the leftovers from processing cattle—horns, teeth, hooves, and the like—which were put in a press to squeeze the oil out of them. The remaining material was sold for chicken feed, concentrated into something about the size of a manhole cover an inch or two thick and weighing about twenty-five pounds. Louis loaded these into railroad boxcars for shipping. "That's when I found out how big a boxcar was," Louis later said.[68]

Far less onerous was a summer job at Film Row just off Harwood Street on the south edge of downtown Dallas. Louis's job was sending out films with accompanying advertising posters to movie theaters. When the movies were returned, he filed them in their proper places.

Another job, more short lived, was at the Baker Hotel as a busboy for room service. Louis's mother, Callie, was worried, though, because the 1943 Detroit race riots had just occurred, and she no doubt remembered the incident in which the young elevator operator at the Adolphus Hotel across the street from the Baker was beaten by the Ku Klux Klan after being accused of a dalliance with a white woman. She finally forbade Louis from keeping the job. She felt it was too risky for a young black man who might find himself accused of anything, and he would have little recourse with white officers. Louis's father had found this job for his son because he knew the man who headed room service, but his wife trumped him, so Louis found a new summer job as a shipping clerk at Purse Furniture Company, across the street from the courthouse.

Through it all Louis retained his easygoing personality. In Prairie View's 1946 yearbook, the descriptive caption placed under his name was "lackadaisical, droll." Even so, he was named one of five orators for the senior class. The class prophecy for the 110 seniors, published in the school newspaper, *The Panther*, predicted that Louis would earn his law degree from Harvard and win cases before the U.S. Supreme Court.[69] "I guess deep down there was a dream in 1946 that maybe someday an African American could be on the United States Supreme Court," Bedford later said. Improbable though the goal may have been, the dream had inspired him.[70]

The war years took a serious toll on the men in Louis's class. There had been sixty-three men and ninety-nine women in his freshman class. At graduation the sixty-three men had declined to just fifteen. The number of women had held pretty steady; ninety-one of the original ninety-nine graduated.[71]

By the time Louis received his degree in 1946, Prairie View State Normal and Industrial College had its grander name, Prairie View University, given by act of the Texas Legislature on June 1, 1945, in its effort to forestall the integration of the state's white graduate schools. The act authorized Prairie View to establish courses in law, medicine, engineering, pharmacy, journalism, "or any other generally recognized college course taught at the University of Texas." But little contained in the act, aside from the name, came into being. Engineering and journalism (communications) ultimately were added to the curriculum, but none of the other courses were. By 1947 the university designation didn't seem realistic, and the school was renamed Prairie View Agricultural and Mechanical College of Texas. (In 1973 Prairie View became Prairie View A&M University.)[72]

On the morning of May 19, 1946, to the tune of Mendelssohn's "War March of the Priests," Louis and his classmates proudly walked into the auditorium-gymnasium for Prairie View's seventy-sixth convocation. They and the congregation sang "God of Our Fathers" and listened to the commencement speech of Dr. Mordecai Wyatt Johnson, president of Howard University. Louis was one of eighteen students awarded bachelor of arts degrees. By far the largest group of graduates consisted of women receiving bachelor of science degrees in home economics, thirty of them in all.[73]

Louis A. Bedford Jr. was ready for another forward step—the study of law—but the situation in Texas was uncertain. It was not for another year that the legislature would establish even the faux law school in a basement across from the state Capitol. The program still existed to provide legal aid for African Americans so they could pursue their legal studies in other states and not upset Texas's segregated system of higher education. The uncertainty of what might become available worried Bedford. He concluded that his best course was to stay out of this complicated situation. He did not want to study law in an improvised school, and he feared that if he applied for out-of-state tuition benefits, he might be forced to enter it instead. Thus, while this situation remained uncertain, he delayed. He would wait a year to enter law school. Meanwhile, he would find temporary jobs in Dallas and save money.

His first job as a college graduate was at the Park Cities Packing House, but it did not last beyond October. One day that month, two plainclothes police officers arrived at the Bedford house and told Louis's mother that they were looking for her son. Alarmed, she summoned him from inside. Yes, he acknowledged, he worked at the packinghouse. Then you're coming with us, they told him. Some meat had been reported missing, and he was needed for questioning.

"My mother almost had a stroke," Bedford recalled painfully years later. The son of whom she was so proud was about to be hauled down to the police station. "I know what you're going to do," she told the officers. "You're going to take him down there and beat him."

More than half a century later, the memory of that day remained vivid in Bedford's mind. "I never will forget that," he said. "It is still painful for me to remember hearing my mother, because that was the thing she feared was going to happen: they would just beat a confession out of me for a crime I didn't commit. My mother just cried and cried, and she was totally distraught as the officers put me in the car. It just about killed her, because everybody felt that when you got into a police car, you were going to be whipped."[74]

Callie Bedford's alarm was well founded. Probably fresh in her mind was the well-known story circulating in the community about the severe beating that young George Flanagan Jr. had received. Flanagan's father was in charge of the locker room at the Dallas Country Club, and he owned a late-model Cadillac, which he occasionally let his son drive. One day police stopped George Jr., questioning how he could be driving such a fancy car. The young man's responses didn't please them, so they beat him so severely that for a while it was not known whether he would even survive. Louis himself remembered the time when his father was dressed in a suit and a police officer mockingly wanted to know what sort of work he did. To be hauled off to the police station for any reason was indeed alarming.[75]

Bedford knew he had nothing to do with anything missing at the meatpacking plant. Never before had the police questioned him. But he climbed fearfully into the police car as ordered, the sound of his mother's frightened wails ringing in his ears as he departed with the officers. An unexpected thing happened, though. The officers drove around the corner, stopped at Rain's Grocery Store, and went inside, leaving Louis alone in the car. When they returned, they did not say a word but circled the block and let Louis out in front of his house. He never heard from the officers again, but his memory of the terror of those moments never subsided.[76]

It was time for a new job. Louis found one close to his original ambition to be a railroad mail clerk, except that he would not be traveling. The job was unloading mail from, and loading mail onto, railroad cars at Union Terminal on Houston Street, just down from the courthouse.

At the same time that Louis had his encounter with the two detectives, a successful effort was already under way to break the Dallas Police Department's color barrier. To this point it had been impenetrable. As early as 1888, African Americans in Dallas had petitioned the city council to hire black officers to patrol their neighborhoods. Their request was rejected, but six years later another petition succeeded. The council hired a black officer, William McDuff, to work in African American neighborhoods. Two months later he was shot and killed while attempting to arrest two juveniles. The city council chose not to replace him.[77]

From time to time in the ensuing years, more requests were made, to no avail. By the 1930s, Houston, Austin, Galveston, and San Antonio had African American police officers, but Dallas did not. A. Maceo Smith and Rev. Maynard Jackson, through the Progressive Voters League, renewed the effort to desegregate the force in the 1930s. A turning point came in early 1937, when they pledged the support of their organization to an independent-minded city council slate of candidates in return for promises that included hiring black officers.

That slate won, and after these council members took office, they honored the commitment, voting 5–2 to hire black police officers. A former Ku Klux Klan official then mounted an opposition drive, and he gained broad support. Intimidated by growing pressures, the council members rescinded their action.[78]

In October 1946 three African Americans, accompanied by the executive director of the Negro Chamber of Commerce, showed up at an announced qualifying examination for officers. The City Civil Commission turned them away because of their color. Before the month was over, the Dallas city manager, supported by the police chief, recommended—and the city council approved—the hiring of fourteen "apprentice" black officers for service in African American neighborhoods.[79]

Forty-nine black applicants took the exam; four passed.[80] One of the first two officers hired was Lee G. Brotherton, the older brother of Marvin Brotherton, Louis's close friend in high school and at Prairie View. Lee Brotherton, also a graduate of Prairie View, had served as an officer in an army chemical warfare division in World War II.

On March 25, 1947, Brotherton and the other African American officer first hired, Benjamin Thomas, began patrolling the State-Thomas-Hall neighborhood on foot. The appearance of African American officers was so surprising that Louis later remembered their first days well. He and others, though grateful for the breakthrough, noted ruefully how the two officers were required to dress at the nearby Roseland Homes housing project rather than at the downtown station with other officers. They observed, too, that the officers had been assigned to walk their beats rather than permitted to drive patrol cars. Their work, though, was hailed as very successful. "Negro Police Given Praise" was the headline that appeared in the *Dallas Morning News* after they had been on duty for six weeks.[81] (Before the end of the century, the city had African American police chiefs, assistant chiefs, and a large percentage of police officers.)

Meanwhile, Bedford was ready to pursue studies that would lead to becoming a lawyer. He sent off applications to the only two law schools he knew of that would accept African Americans, Howard University School of Law in Washington, D.C., and Lincoln University in St. Louis, Missouri. Then he heard from Marvin Brotherton, who was by then living in Brooklyn, New York, with another friend, Alvin Gosey. Brotherton was studying at the RCA Radio and Television School, and Gosey was a student at Brooklyn's Long Island University. They had a room at the Carlton YMCA, and not far from them was the Brooklyn Law School. Why, Brotherton asked, didn't Bedford apply there?

Bedford had never been east of Texarkana. Brooklyn? Why not? He sent his application to Brooklyn Law School.

---

1. Bedford, interview, July 19, 2005.
2. Louis A. Bedford Jr., interview by Darwin Payne, Dec. 9, 2005.
3. George Ruble Woolfolk, *Prairie View: A Study in Public Conscience, 1878–1946* (New York: Pageant Press, 1962), 352, 359.
4. Amilcar Shabazz provides a good profile of Prairie View in *Advancing Democracy: African Americans and the Struggle for Access and Equity in Higher Education in Texas.*
5. Prairie View University, *Purple and Gold* yearbook (Prairie View, TX: Prairie View University, 1946), 33.
6. George Ruble Woolfolk, "W. R. Banks: Public College Educator," in *Black Leaders: Texans for Their Times*, ed. Alwyn Barr and Robert A. Calvert (Austin: Texas State Historical Association, 1981), 142, 147.
7. Prairie View University, *Purple and Gold*, 10.
8. Prairie View State College, *Panther* yearbook (Prairie View, TX: Prairie View State College, 1943), Banks message dated Jan. 6. 1943 [6]. (By 1946 the yearbook had been renamed *Purple and Gold*, and the college had become Prairie View University.)
9. Prairie View State College, *Panther*, 1943 [4].
10. Bedford, interview, Dec. 9, 2005.
11. Letter from Reserve Officers Training Corps program to L. A. Bedford Jr., Mar. 17, 1943, "L. A. Bedford Jr. Personal" binder, Bedford Papers.
12. Louis A. Bedford Jr., interview by Darwin Payne, Nov. 9, 2005.
13. Letter from Prairie View State College to L. A. Bedford Sr., Mar. 20, 1943, and Nov. 8, 1945, "L. A. Bedford Jr. Personal" binder, Bedford Papers.
14. Bedford, interview, Nov. 9, 2005.
15. Ibid., Sept. 8, 2005.
16. Ibid.
17. "Supreme Court to Hear Death Penalty Case," *Dallas Morning News*, May 1, 1942; "Negroes on Texas Juries May Follow Case Reversal," *Dallas Morning News*, June 2, 1942; *Hill v. State of Texas*, 316 U.S. 400 (1942).

18. "Convicted Negro's Death Ends Appeal to Supreme Court," *Dallas Morning News*, Sept. 22, 1943.
19. "Samuel William Hudson Jr.: Longtime Civil Servant, Civil Rights Leader, 94," *Dallas Morning News*, June 21, 2005; "Commission Names Grand Jury Panel," *Dallas Morning News*, June 14, 1947.
20. Bedford, interview, July 19, 2005.
21. "City School Heads Deny Discrimination in Negro Salaries," *Dallas Daily Times Herald*, Dec. 24, 1942; "Negroes Ask Equal Wage as Teachers," *Dallas Morning News*, Dec. 24, 1942.
22. "Board Answers Negro Teacher Pay Hike Suit," *Dallas Morning News*, Jan. 23, 1943.
23. "Negroes Ask Equal Wage," *Dallas Morning News*. For a general discussion on salary equalization cases, see Tushnet, *NAACP's Legal Strategy*, 49–69.
24. Gillette, "NAACP in Texas," 14–15; "Pay Hike of Negro Teachers Will Cost $200,000 a Year," *Dallas Morning News*, Feb. 25, 1943; Merline Pitre, *In Struggle against Jim Crow: Lulu B. White and the NAACP, 1900–1957* (College Station: Texas A&M University Press, 1999), 58.
25. Michael L. Gillette, quoted in Bobby McDonald, *Out of Darkness: The Black Face of Hopkins County* (n.p.: Author, c. 2002), 3:110.
26. McDonald, *Out of Darkness*, 106; U.S. Bureau of the Census, "Hopkins County, District No. 260, Enumeration District 52" (Washington, 1900), 130.
27. "W. J. Durham, Leader in Integration, Dies," *Dallas Morning News*, Dec. 26, 1970; U.S. Bureau of the Census, "Hopkins County," 130.
28. Gillette, "NAACP in Texas," 35; Bureau of Vital Statistics, "Texas Death Records" (Austin: Texas Department of Health, 1970), no. 93178.
29. W. J. Durham to the Board of Legal Examiners, Dec. 1, 1924, State Bar of Texas Files, State Bar of Texas, Austin, cited in Gillette, "NAACP in Texas," 35.
30. John L. "Jack" Hauer, *Finest Kind! A Memorable Half Century of Dallas Lawyers (plus a few from out-of-town)* (Dallas: Dallas Bar Foundation, 1992n.d.), 148.
31. Gillette, "NAACP in Texas," 20.
32. *Bedford Oral History Interview*, 19.
33. Gillette, "NAACP in Texas," 19.
34. General Laws of Texas, *38th Legislature Journal*, 2nd called sess. (Austin, 1921), 74, cited in Hine, *Black Victory*, 94.
35. A comprehensive study of the white primary in Texas and the struggle to have it declared unconstitutional is Hine's *Black Victory*; *Nixon v. Herndon*, 273 U.S. 538 (1927).
36. Gillette, "NAACP in Texas," 18–19.
37. Ibid., 21.
38. Pitre, *In Struggle against Jim Crow*, 34.
39. Hine, *Black Victory*, 228.
40. Gillette, "NAACP in Texas," 24–25.
41. Gillette, "NAACP in Texas," 25; *Smith v. Allwright*, 321 U.S. 649 (1944). S. E. Allwright was the election judge who denied the ballot to Smith. Juan Williams, *Thurgood Marshall: American Revolutionary* (New York: Times Books, 1998), 307, 330.
42. Hine, *Black Victory*, 242, 254.
43. Pitre, *In Struggle against Jim Crow*, 53. In the closely contested election, the lead shifted dramatically in the last hours as returns were reported. Johnson won at the last minute when Duval

County reported a late tally from a box that had been held up, which gave Johnson the margin he needed. More than two hundred names had been added in alphabetical order, a strong indication of fraud.

44. Smith to Marshall, Apr. 9, 1945, NAACP Files, Library of Congress, Washington, cited in Gillette, "NAACP in Texas," 45.

45. Gillette, "NAACP in Texas," 46.

46. Ibid., 47.

47. Melvin Beaunorus Tolson, *Harlem Gallery and Other Poems* (New York: Twayne, 1965).

48. Vivé Griffith, "'Courage and the Refusal to Be Swayed': Heman Marion Sweatt's Legal Challenge That Integrated the University of Texas," in *TxTell: UT Stories* (Austin: University of Texas Library, n.d.), http://txtell.lib.utexas.edu/stories/s0010-full.html.

49. Sweatt to White, Nov. 8, 1946, NAACP Papers, Library of Congress, Washington, cited in Williams, *Thurgood Marshall*, 176.

50. Michael L. Gillette, "Blacks Challenge the White University," *Southwestern Historical Quarterly* 86, no. 2 (Oct. 1982): passim. This article offers a full account of the effort to desegregate the law school. See also Shabazz, *Advancing Democracy*, 25–29, concerning Richard T. Hamilton and George L. Allen.

51. Gillette, "Blacks Challenge the White University," 321–22; Shabazz, *Advancing Democracy*, 31.

52. Shabazz, *Advancing Democracy*, 67–68.

53. Gillette, "NAACP in Texas," 64.

54. "Negro School Seen as Result of UT Ruling," *Dallas Daily Times Herald*, June 18, 1946; "Court Orders UT to Admit Negro," *Dallas Morning News*, June 18, 1946; Gillette, "NAACP in Texas," 63.

55. "Sellers Defies Negro Move," *Dallas Morning News*, June 18, 1946.

56. "Sweatt Loses Court Round," *Dallas Morning News*, Dec. 18, 1946.

57. "UT Students Group Would Admit Negro," *Dallas Morning News*, Nov. 20, 1946; "Sweatt Loses Court Round," *Dallas Morning News*, Dec. 18, 1946.

58. "Negro Law School to Open March 10," *Dallas Morning News*, Mar. 5, 1947; "No Negroes Show Up for New Law Course," *Dallas Morning News*, Mar. 11, 1947.

59. *Sweatt v. Painter et al.*, 339 U.S. 629 (1950).

60. Shabazz, *Advancing Democracy*, 105.

61. Ibid., 109, 115–16.

62. Ibid., 116–17.

63. Ibid., 116.

64. Prairie View University, *Purple and Gold*, 75, 136.

65. Bedford, interview, July 19, 2005.

66. L. A. Bedford, Jr., "M. M. Rodgers: A Study of a Negro in the Age of Transition" paper submitted for bachelor of arts degree, Prairie View University, Division of Arts and Sciences, 1946), 1, Bedford Papers.

67. Ibid., 2.

68. Bedford, interview, July 19, 2005.

69. "Class Prophecy," *Panther*, undated clipping [1946], 4. The *Panther* was the name of the Prairie View University newspaper, though by now the yearbook name had been changed from *The Panther* to *Purple and Gold*.

70. *Bedford Oral History Interview*, 6.

71. Prairie View University, *Purple and Gold*, Prairie View.

72. Forty-ninth Legislature, reg. sess., 1945, General and Special Laws of Texas, Chapter 308, Senate Bill No. 226, cited in Woolfolk, *Prairie View*, 326.

73. Commencement program, May 19, 1946, "L. A. Bedford Jr. Personal" binder, Bedford Papers.

74. Bedford, interview, July 10, 2005.

75. Ibid., Dec. 9, 2005, and July 10, 2005.

76. Ibid., July 10, 2005.

77. W. Marvin Dulaney, *Black Police in America* (Bloomington: Indiana University Press, 1996), 34.

78. Dulaney, *Black Police in America*, 36–37.

79. Payne, *Big D*, 290.

80. "Negroes Take Tests for Jobs as Police," *Dallas Morning News*, Nov. 16, 1946.

81. Louis A. Bedford Jr., interview by Darwin Payne, Nov. 10, 2005; "Negro Police Given Praise," *Dallas Morning News*, May 4, 1947.

3

A TEXAN IN BROOKLYN

Bedford chose Brooklyn Law School. If he was going to be so far from home, he reasoned, he might as well be with friends. At Howard or Lincoln, he would be surrounded by strangers; although there would be few if any Texans in his classes at Brooklyn, he could share a room at the Carlton YMCA with Brotherton and Gosey, his good friends from Prairie View. Money would be tight wherever he went, but with three in a room he could economize.

Other factors were important in his decision. In Texas, Sweatt's lawsuit was still unresolved. Both Howard and Lincoln were schools for African Americans; Brooklyn's student body was predominantly Jewish. Attending classes with white students for the first time was intriguing to him, and the many attractions of New York City for a young man like Bedford were undeniable.

Bedford's decision to choose Brooklyn had been one of happenstance. Although he had escaped military conscription while at Prairie View, Brotherton and Gosey had not. Brotherton served with the U.S. Navy at the Brooklyn Navy Yard. He liked the area enough to come back and enroll in classes at the RCA Radio and Television School in Manhattan, and he persuaded Gosey to come east and join him. Gosey enrolled as an undergraduate at Long Island University, whose classes were offered in the Brooklyn Law School building and across the street in the Consolidated Edison building. Knowing of Bedford's intention to study law, they persuaded their pal to join them.

First, of course, he had to be admitted. He filed credentials—primarily his transcript from Prairie View—with the State of New York and obtained the requisite law-qualifying certificate. Soon came the good news of his acceptance at a law school that he had never seen and about which he knew almost nothing.

Going to Brooklyn from Texas was an enormous step for a young man who had hardly set foot outside his home state. The only out-of-state experience he had had was when he visited his mother's sister in Texarkana on the Texas-Arkansas border.

His great adventure began in September 1947, at the same time the makeshift Texas law school for blacks opened in Austin with a single student. His parents, proud and concerned, accompanied their son to the downtown Union Terminal, traveling in a taxi because they still had no car of their own. A wardrobe trunk filled with Bedford's belongings had already been sent by rail. Bedford boarded the segregated Texas & Pacific passenger train for New York City, via St. Louis and Cleveland. He remained in the same chair car (a nonsleeper) for the entire two-day journey, not even venturing into the dining car. He relied on snacks his mother had prepared and packed for him and on items he bought from "butcher boys," who went from car to car selling sandwiches.

In St. Louis, Bedford's car was switched to an eastbound line. When the train was halfway across the Mississippi, it entered Illinois, the home state of Abraham Lincoln. Here segregated seating officially ended. Such a change was monumental in principle, but Bedford could hardly discern it. There was no sudden dramatic shift in seating patterns.

On the second morning, the train stopped briefly in Cleveland. That evening it pulled into Grand Central Station in the heart of Manhattan, fully integrated by now in its seating pattern. Bedford timorously found his way into the great open terminal, uncertain of how he would get to Brooklyn.

Passersby were glad to help, and following their directions, he boarded a subway train for the first time in his life. The law school, he knew, was located on Pearl Street, and as the train made its way underground, he saw a sign on the wall indicating Pearl Street. He hurried off at the next stop, found his way upstairs to the city streets, looked around—and saw nothing resembling the law school he had expected to see. He asked a man if he knew where the Brooklyn Law School might be. "You're in Manhattan," the man replied. "Maybe the Brooklyn Law School is in Brooklyn." Bedford had gotten off too early; the sign he had seen referred to the Pearl Street on Manhattan Island, not in Brooklyn.

With clearer directions from this passerby, he returned to the subway and soon arrived in downtown Brooklyn. There at 375 Pearl Street was Richardson Hall, the law school building, a tall structure of a dozen or so floors that appeared to be more of an office building than a school. After briefly satisfying his curiosity by looking at the outside of the building, Bedford caught a taxicab for the Carlton YMCA, where he would be living. The Y was at 405 Carlton Avenue, about a mile and a quarter southeast of the law school, a distance he would normally walk when classes began.

Brotherton and Gosey gleefully introduced him to the place that would be his home for the next three years. Bedford's share of the rent was about thirty dollars a month, an amount he was able to cover with the one hundred dollars or so his parents sent him each month. The Carlton Y was a residential facility with few amenities. It had a gymnasium but no restaurant or swimming pool. Three half-beds were squeezed into the small room that Bedford shared with his friends on the top floor of the four-story building. A communal bathroom with showers was located down the hall. Probably twenty-five or thirty persons lived inexpensively at the Y. All were stretching their dollars. Some were retirees, a few were students, a couple were lawyers, and a handful were basketball players on the Long Island University team.

"Everybody said there was no segregation in New York," Bedford later recalled. But this, he saw, was not true. In fact, only African Americans stayed at the Carlton Y. The nearby Brooklyn Central YMCA was the place for whites. Still, for the first time he could sit where he pleased while using public transportation, go into any restaurant, and attend any theater with no limitations. Furthermore, he was attending a law school whose student body was almost entirely white.

Gosey and Brotherton were better off financially than Bedford, for they were getting monthly stipends courtesy of the G.I. Bill, which subsidized education for veterans. They too needed to economize, however, and with food as their biggest living expense, the three roommates did everything they could to save money. Cooking in their room was prohibited, but the three managed to conceal a hot plate for heating the canned foods they purchased at a nearby A&P supermarket. Since their room was on the top floor, they had convenient access to the roof, and during cold weather they stored bottles of milk there to use with cereal. (Bedford regularly ate

Raisin Bran, theorizing that the combination of bran and raisins had to be healthy.) For lunch he frequently bought a couple of franks and a big orange drink at a hot dog stand called Nedicks.

Some meals they took down the street at a little place called Nick's, the only nearby short-order restaurant. "Nick the Greek" himself worked behind the counter, and as time went by, he and Bedford worked out an agreement: Bedford would clean up Nick's place on weekends for a few dollars and free breakfast on weekdays.

Brooklyn Law School was founded in 1901 in the basement of a business school on Ryerson Street. It became affiliated two years later with St. Lawrence University of Canton, New York, but remained in Brooklyn. The high-rise Richardson Hall on Pearl Street opened in 1928 when the school had outgrown its former home, the old *Brooklyn Eagle* newspaper's building. There were other law schools in the area: Columbia, in upper Manhattan, was the most prestigious, with admission strictly limited; Fordham University School of Law and St. John's University School of Law were Catholic institutions. Brooklyn Law School, as Bedford soon learned, catered to Jewish students. It had a reputation for accepting students who could not afford to attend more elite schools or who were denied admission because of discriminatory policies.

The affiliation with St. Lawrence had ended in the early 1940s. That institution decided to close Brooklyn Law School, whose demise seemed certain, but distressed faculty and alumni raised money to buy it and operate it as an independent law school, beginning in 1943. Enrollment was dangerously low at first, but an onslaught of veterans returning from the war brought a dramatic increase in enrollment, compliments of the G.I. Bill, and the school's viability was ensured.

The law school offered students three separate shifts of classes: morning, afternoon, and evening. Bedford registered for the afternoon program.

Bedford's entering class had fewer than three hundred students. He soon realized that classmates with names like Brodsky, Cohen, Dreyfuss, Edelman, Goldstein, Klein, and Rosenberg were Jewish. They seemed to represent about 90 percent of the student body. The same was true of the faculty. In Bedford's world in Texas, people had fallen into two categories: they were white or they were black. Now his consciousness about the complexity of the world around him expanded almost daily.

On his first visit to the registrar's office, Bedford encountered two fellow students on the elevator. One expressed his unhappiness at being given a B for a course instead of an A. Bedford listened with a bit of awe. Without knowing anything at all about the course, he told himself that he would have been happy if he had earned a B.

Having come from a segregated system of education, from a school with limited resources, he wondered if he would be able to keep up with white students who had enjoyed advantages. Woolfolk's assurances that he was capable of academic work were helpful in this respect, but only actual experience would prove it. Soon Bedford realized that being white did not automatically make a person smart, but at this moment he was not entirely convinced of that.

He discovered immediately that as an African American, he was in a distinct minority. Out of nearly three hundred students in his class, there was only a handful of other blacks: Hugo Madison, Tim Mathis, Helen Gardner, J. E. Smith, L. A. Tobias, and Nathan Mitchell. As far as he knew, he was also the only Texan in the entire law school.[1]

Most important to Bedford, certainly in his first months, was whether he would be able to keep up with the challenging law school curriculum. Never before had he been forced to deal with courses as demanding as contracts, property, taxation, and evidence.

He had to be well prepared for each class, for the professors regularly quizzed individual students to see how well they knew the day's assigned cases. Some professors called on students in alphabetical order. In other classes students never knew when they might be called upon to summarize a complicated case or expound on a point of law.

Performing well was a matter of pride. "I didn't want to be lacking," Bedford later recalled. "You were a black, and the majority were whites, and you had a feeling that, 'Hey, I'm not going to let anybody tell me I can't do this or that.'" In the classroom with him were students from Harvard, New York University, Notre Dame, and even Oxford and Eton. None of them had ever heard of Prairie View, and

Bedford saw raised eyebrows when students or professors heard of his undergraduate preparation there.[2]

Bedford was studying harder than ever before. He had not developed good study habits at Prairie View; they had not been necessary. Now he had to read, comprehend, summarize key points, and answer hypothetical questions. Frequently, there was no single right answer. Even learned jurists often disagree in interpreting the law. The four dissents in a 5-4 U.S. Supreme Court decision might, after the replacement of a single justice, become the basis of a very different decision on a similar issue.

Study groups emerged, and Bedford's was entirely African American, consisting of himself; two other students who lived at the Carlton Y, Tim Mathis and Hugo Madison; and a New Yorker, Nathan Mitchell, who joined them at the Y for study sessions. The fact that Bedford had to prove his ability in the classroom to compete on an equal basis was always on his mind. He was fearful, but he was desperate to succeed. He could not return home to his parents a failure after all the sacrifices they had made and the hopes they held for him.

There was not enough money that first Christmas for a trip back home to Dallas, nor would there be at other Christmases. He returned to Dallas only briefly during summers. At Thanksgiving and Christmas, he called home long-distance, curious about what the family was eating for the holiday meal. Sometimes his mother would send him a box filled with canned foods.

Word somehow reached Woolfolk at Prairie View that his prize pupil had quit law school. When he learned that the report was false, he wrote to Bedford to say he had not written sooner because he had heard the rumor and thought Bedford was back in Dallas doing nothing. "I was heart-broken for a while," Woolfolk wrote. "I was even afraid to ask anyone for fear that it might be true. So I am really glad that you are still there, and will be glad to get a letter [from you] . . . as often as I can."[3]

Woolfolk's letter, which Bedford saved, was a strong encouragement to persevere. Warm and personal, it reminded Bedford of the close relationship he and Woolfolk had enjoyed. "How is my little ugly boy doing?" Woolfolk asked. "My heart is really with you son, even when I don't write. I think of you often and wonder how you are getting along. I do hope it is good, because I want you to do well, Bedford—more than some I have here with me. You know I consider you my greatest undergraduate."[4]

Brooklyn for many years had exerted a powerful and colorful hold on the American imagination. Settled on the southwestern end of Long Island by the Dutch in 1636, and ten years later given the name of Breuckelen, it was the site in 1776 of the great Battle of Long Island (sometimes known as the Battle of Brooklyn), in which George Washington's tattered Revolutionary forces were defeated by the British. Before complete disaster could occur, though, the surviving American troops managed on a foggy night to escape on small boats across the East River to Manhattan. More than a hundred years later, in 1883, the Brooklyn Bridge, then the largest suspension bridge in the world, connected the highly urbanized city of Brooklyn with Manhattan. In 1894 Brooklyn gave up its independent status to become one of the five boroughs consolidated into modern New York City.

When the naïve young Bedford emerged from the subway station in September 1947 to see Brooklyn for the first time, the nation's fascination with the famous borough was at its peak. Much of the country and virtually all of Brooklyn were infatuated with the Brooklyn Dodgers baseball team. Not only was the team engaged in an exciting pennant race, but one of its stars was Jackie Robinson, who that year had become the first African American to play modern major league baseball and had already become a national hero. Just after Bedford arrived, the Dodgers clinched the National League pennant, but then in October they lost to the New York Yankees in a memorable seven-game World Series regarded as one of the most exciting in baseball's history. Bedford did not get to see the Dodgers that fall, but he would see them and revel in their glory during the next two seasons.

A fellow resident at the Y introduced Bedford to the Concord Baptist Church of Christ in Brooklyn. The church, predominantly African American, had an outstanding young pastor named Gardner C. Taylor, who was attracting wide attention with his provocative sermons. Concord was in walking distance east of the Y, and attendance there on Sundays became a habit for Louis.

Bedford was fortunate in his choice of churches, and especially in its pastor. Taylor, in only his second year at Concord Baptist Church, was eventually hailed as the "dean of American preachers" and in 1993 cited by *Ebony* magazine as the nation's greatest African American preacher. Born in Baton Rouge, Louisiana, he was an agnostic until 1937, when he was involved in a car accident in which a man died. Taylor enrolled in the Oberlin Graduate School of Theology and soon began a career that has continued into 2008. He became a civil rights activist, a mentor to Martin Luther King Jr., a Presidential Medal of Freedom honoree in the year 2000, recipient of more than a hundred honorary degrees, and an occasional teacher at some of the nation's most prestigious theological schools.[5]

Other attractions, when they could be afforded, were of a different nature. Across the East River, Manhattan offered a wide variety of amusements, ranging from museums to—especially—music, and it didn't take long for Bedford to take advantage of them. Brotherton and Gosey introduced him to clubs and theaters where the nation's most famous jazz musicians played. Bedford had known well the clubs at Hall Street so near his house, especially the Empire Room, but nothing could match the excitement he now found. Harlem was just a subway ride away, and here—when he had the money—he could go to places like the Savoy Ballroom, where he listened to Duke Ellington and Count Basie in a huge room that accommodated hundreds of people. What he especially liked about the Savoy was its continuous music. While one band was finishing up its set, another band would get set up with its instruments on a second stage, ready to begin playing as soon as the first band stopped. "The home of happy feet, where the music never stops" was the Savoy's slogan. Small's Paradise and especially the Apollo Theater were frequent destinations. Bedford saw Billy Eckstein, Ella Fitzgerald, Pearl Bailey, Nat "King" Cole, the great tenor saxophonist Illinois Jacquet, and the guitar player T-Bone Walker, who himself had grown up in Dallas a few years earlier than Bedford in an area known as the Bottoms, on the opposite side of town.

About once a month, when money arrived from his parents, Bedford enjoyed going to Frank's Restaurant in Harlem, where his favorite dish was lamb chops. The restaurant was now open to all races, but Bedford understood that before World War II it had exclusively served white patrons who came to Harlem for entertainment.

Bedford did not limit his forays to Harlem. One of his favorite sites was the 845 Club in the Bronx. In midtown Manhattan he sometimes went to the legendary Bop City on 52nd Street, where patrons could pay a dollar to stand at the bar rather than sit at a table, and hear such musicians as Dizzy Gillespie and Charlie Parker. Bedford remembered one evening when the charismatic New York congressman Adam Clayton Powell Jr. and his wife, the famous pianist-actress Hazel Scott, made the crowd buzz when they showed up, both of them beautifully attired in white suits. Powell, who in 1937 had succeeded his father as pastor at Harlem's huge Abyssinian Baptist Church, had been elected in 1944 to Congress, where he was continuing his vigorous crusade for civil rights and attracting attention because of his extravagant lifestyle.[6]

Bedford's social life, constricted in Brooklyn because of an expensive new environment and a tight budget, soon expanded. He made a connection with a young woman he had known at Prairie View, Marguerite Bradshaw of Denison, Texas, who had graduated a year before Bedford and was now teaching school in New York. She began taking Bedford to social affairs, such as one for African American firefighters and the Urban League's Harvest Moon Ball, often held at the Savoy Club. Once someone got on the list of invitees for such affairs, more invitations inevitably followed.[7]

Another old friend from Dallas emerged. Charles Vert Willie, son of a Pullman porter, was one year younger than Bedford and had attended the new Lincoln High School in South Dallas and then Morehouse College. Willie was now in graduate school at Syracuse University working on his doctorate, and about once a month he would come to New York City. On such occasions he and Bedford would visit Bop City and listen to music. Willie became one of the nation's leading sociologists, a prolific writer of scholarly books, and holder of the Charles William Eliot Professor of Education Chair at Harvard University's Graduate School of Education. He served as a consultant, expert witness, and court-appointed master in many school desegregation cases in the 1970s.[8]

Another social event that broadened his circle of acquaintances came when a young merchant marine from Duluth, Minnesota, moved temporarily into the Carlton Y prior to getting married at Concord Baptist Church of Christ. He needed groomsmen for his wedding, and Bedford still had the formal wear he had found necessary at Prairie View. Bedford thus became one of the groomsmen. The reception afterward gave him an opportunity to meet more people, and he enjoyed further social occasions as a result.[9]

Fascinated with his new environment, Bedford wrote to his father that for the first time he was feeling like a man. The safety net—except for his monthly stipend from home—was gone. He was making his own decisions. One of those decisions his first year was not to spend money on an overcoat. He had not counted on the severity of New York winters, though, and suffered through the cold months with just a light topcoat. The next year he was wiser—he bought a heavy woolen overcoat.[10]

Marvin Brotherton was first to return to Dallas that summer of 1948, and the stringent diet he and his roommates had to endure in Brooklyn was apparent. The last time he had been home, Brotherton, whose nickname was "Big Boy," weighed more than 200 pounds. Now he was down to a trim 160 pounds. Callie Bedford was shocked at what she saw. If Big Boy had lost that much weight, what had happened to her slender Louis, who had started out weighing only 140 or so pounds?[11]

Louis's return home for a brief few weeks that first summer was a triumphant event. His mother need not have worried. He had not lost weight. Bedford was obviously happy in his new life at law school and in New York City, and his parents were pleased. During those few weeks in Dallas, he worked as the cook for the YWCA at Camp Pinkston, responsible for three meals a day for the girls in the summer session. After this brief visit home, it was back to Brooklyn, where he and his roommates had maintained their fourth-floor room at the Carlton YMCA.

In his second summer, Bedford's stay in Dallas was even shorter. He and Gosey had found jobs as janitors in Brooklyn at one of the nation's pioneering department stores, Abraham & Straus, and they couldn't be gone long. They reported for work after the store closed each day and cleaned up until midnight.[12]

Current events were making an impact on Bedford in this postwar era. Law school and the media hotbed of New York City brought the political scene much closer than it had seemed in Dallas. As summer 1948 gave way to the start of the school year, not only was the nation facing a presidential election that might return the Republicans to the White House after a sixteen-year absence, but it was in the grips of fears about Communist infiltration into the highest ranks of the federal government. In August, Whittaker Chambers, a former Communist spy and an editor at *Time* magazine, had testified before the House Un-American Activities Committee that Alger Hiss, a former top official at the State Department, was a contact from whom he accepted secret government papers.

For the first time, Bedford, now twenty-two and of voting age, was able to vote in a presidential election. Harry S. Truman, Roosevelt's successor in 1945, had won the Democratic nomination, but he was not highly regarded, and it seemed certain he would not be elected to a full term. The Republican Party's dapper Thomas Dewey, governor of New York, was an overwhelming favorite.

It was a third-party candidate, though, who caught Bedford's early attention, as he did for so many African Americans. Henry Wallace, former secretary of agriculture (1932–40) and vice president under Roosevelt before Truman, had won the NAACP's praise for his stance on racism, poll taxes, and Jim Crowism. Now the Progressive Party had nominated him for president. The Progressive convention in Philadelphia included a large number of African Americans as delegates, including the prominent actor and singer Paul Robeson. Much criticized because of his sympathetic views toward Communism, Robeson was nonetheless a hero to many in the black community as he decried racism and questioned why African Americans should support a government that did not treat them as equals. Bedford's first thought was to vote for Wallace in November.

When it became apparent that a vote for Wallace would improve the Republican Party's chances for victory, many African Americans turned to Truman. Bedford's allegiance changed late in summer 1948 when Truman launched his aggressive whistle-stop campaign. Bedford stood in the huge crowds that gathered on the sidewalks in Brooklyn one day to cheer the embattled president as his motorcade passed en route to a speaking engagement. Truman, Bedford concluded, was a man of conviction who was unafraid to speak the truth, no matter the consequences. Truman propounded a liberal program that included a strong civil rights effort, calling for a federal law against lynching, eliminating the poll tax as a requirement for voting (which Texas still had), and ending racial segregation in the military. He also urged a national health insurance program, a massive public housing program, increased support for education, conservation of natural resources, and an increase in the minimum wage from forty to seventy-five cents an hour. "I went all out for Truman," Bedford later recalled.

He didn't regret his decision.[13] Truman's upset victory over Dewey was a happy moment for Bedford. Years later he considered Truman to be one of the nation's great presidents. Bedford's prominent grandfather M. M. Rodgers had been a Republican, his parents had switched over to the Democratic Party under Roosevelt, and now Bedford was starting out as a Democrat, where he would remain.

Bedford's expanding circle of friends continued to bring new experiences. One important new acquaintance was a family friend from Dallas, Hattie Faye Lowe (later Long), who was at this time a domestic worker for a wealthy family living on Great Neck, Long Island (fifteen miles northeast of Brooklyn). Hattie would entertain Bedford, Gosey, and Brotherton at her employers' huge house on weekends, and with her employers' permission, the young men would load up on groceries and other essentials from their shelves before returning to Brooklyn on the Long Island Railroad.

Hattie took Bedford to his first Broadway musical, *Lost in the Stars*. With its setting in South Africa, it was memorable. The musical, based on Alan Paton's novel *Cry, the Beloved Country* (1948), starred Todd Duncan, with music by Kurt Weill and lyrics by Maxwell Anderson. Seeing it represented still another forward step in Bedford's growing consciousness of social injustice.

A new friend who lived at the YMCA was Hugo Madison, a gregarious fellow student at Brooklyn Law School. Hugo learned that the famed minister Father Divine had a huge house for his followers and guests in the Bedford-Stuyvesant area about eight blocks away, and he persuaded Bedford and Tim Mathis to accompany him there to investigate the inexpensive meals regularly offered as part of Father Divine's ministry.

Father Divine, born about 1882 near Savannah, Georgia, as George Baker, was one of the nation's most fascinating and charismatic religious leaders, a striking contrast in his theology to Gardner C. Taylor, although both were staunch advocates of civil rights. As a young preacher in Georgia, Baker declared himself the only true expression of God's spirit, adopted the name "the Messenger," and preached the virtues of celibacy; equality for women; and abstention from vices, such as alcohol, tobacco, and gambling. His sixty-day sentence to a chain gang in Georgia, after conflicts with local ministers, only increased his popularity.

In 1914, after being arrested for lunacy but found sane, Baker and a number of followers moved to Brooklyn and formed a commune. Expansion into other New York City neighborhoods, especially Harlem, followed, and he began calling himself simply Father Divine. His movement soon extended through New York and New Jersey and even to the West Coast, where most of his followers were middle-class whites. His ministry, which he called the International Peace Mission Movement, was dedicated to ending poverty and racial discrimination. His heyday came during the Depression, by which time he had gained wide publicity and criticism as the hypnotic leader of a huge cult. Divine was eventually accused of engaging in sexual improprieties with many of his young female followers, and occasional run-ins with the law occurred. When in 1932 Divine was found guilty of disturbing the peace and given the maximum sentence of one year in prison, the judge declared him a menace to society. A few days later the judge died of a heart attack, and Father Divine famously took credit for his death. "I hated to do it," he said.[14]

What Bedford, Mathis, and Madison wanted in their journey to Divine's Brooklyn facility had nothing to do with spiritual redemption—they were in search of the bargain meals they had heard about. They were getting tired of a constant diet of beans. Inside the mansion they made their way upstairs, not realizing that uninitiated visitors ate their meals in the basement. They found themselves seated at a long table with Divine's followers. Realizing their mistake, Madison, utilizing his ability to speak extemporaneously, got up and made expansive apologies, saying the three of them, poor students at Brooklyn Law School, had not intended to infringe, but to be sitting with Father Divine's followers was like being at the Holy Communion table. Observing that both whites and African Americans were at the table, Madison said that this was very democratic and pleasing to three young men who had never been part of such an integrated gathering.

Madison's oratorical skills paid off, Bedford said later, because Father Divine's followers adopted the three students—one of them a Texan—as their "schoolboys." Thereafter, the three of them, joined by other hungry students from the Y, ate with Father Divine's followers most evenings for the rest of that year and the next, always sitting with Divine's followers at the "Holy Communion" table and enjoying excellent home-style meals with an unusually large array of selections for just fifteen cents, or twenty-five cents if they wanted salad and dessert. Meals began with "Thank Father," and before eating, someone would read from Father Divine's newspaper, *New Day*, which glorified his work and put his special interpretations on current events. Women, who had prepared the meals, would sit on one side of the table, and men on the other side, women always outnumbering men. They had special "inspired" names such as Sister Hope, Sister Joy, Sister Mary, and Sister Gable. Frequently, Bedford and his friends were expected to testify, which they readily did. Sometimes, when they were late, Divine's followers would delay the beginning of the meal, looking for their "schoolboys."[15]

Before the meal, they would thank Father Divine for his goodness and his deeds and sing hymns in which the word "Father" was often substituted for Jesus. "Father's on the main line, tell him what you want; / Father's on the main line now" was a ditty often repeated before going to the serving table for seconds. When they wanted more of a certain dish, they were expected to say, "Thank Father, I want some more potatoes."

A place was always set at the head of the long table for Father Divine and his "virgin bride." They were never there, but the followers would pour a glass of water to symbolize their presence. In fact, Bedford never saw Father Divine, who was living in Philadelphia and coming to his main Harlem temple only on Sundays. He was avoiding a subpoena, taking advantage of the fact that New York law prohibited the serving of subpoenas on Sundays.

Word reached Father Divine of these young law students who were regular visitors to his Brooklyn facility, however, and, evidently, he was intrigued. He sent word that he would like to meet them some Sunday at his Harlem temple. Bedford and the others considered it and decided they should avoid getting personally involved with Father Divine. Still, they continued to enjoy evening meals at his Brooklyn facility as well as an occasional hearty breakfast.

The young men were strongly tempted to attend Sunday services at the Brooklyn temple and to enjoy the bountiful spread of food available on those special days. Bedford and Madison went once, and the astonishing amounts tempted them to return. By this time, though, they were regulars at Gardner C. Taylor's Concord Baptist Church. "We'd be torn between whether we should go to Father Divine's and eat or to go to our own church. We finally decided to stay at our own church." But the decision was not easy.[16]

Father Divine lived until 1965, by which time he had become an object of great skepticism. The cultist Jim Jones tried to take over the movement in 1972 from Father Divine's widow, a white woman named Edna Rose Ritchings, but failed. Jones claimed to be a reincarnation of Father Divine and incorporated the doctrines of the International Peace Mission Movement in his own movement, which ended in 1978 in the mass suicide he led at Jonestown, Guyana. (In the 1980 made-for-TV movie *Guyana Tragedy: The Story of Jim Jones*, James Earl Jones portrayed Father Divine.)[17]

Bedford said years later that to Father Divine's faithful followers, he truly gave off a feeling of divinity. Bedford knew better, but the fellowship, the camaraderie, and the good meals he enjoyed made the experience one that he would neither forget nor regret.

Despite the many pleasant attractions he was enjoying in New York, Bedford's first priority remained law school. There was no specializing at Brooklyn Law School; his degree would be a general one, from a curriculum that, except for one or two electives, was the same for all students. His first year had been difficult ("I was scared to death," Bedford later confessed), and his grades were undistinguished. As time went by, they improved. Bedford's second year, his January 1949 midyear grade report showed an A in Business Organizations and Cs in Administrative Law, Equity, and Taxation. At the end of the next semester, he had three Bs and two As—Bs in Property, Criminal Law, and Labor Law; and As in Domestic Relations and Bills & Notes.[18] He sent his grade reports home, where his mother happily showed them to Dr. Green's wife, her next-door neighbor. "Look here," she said, very proud of her far-off son. "I got Brother's grades."[19]

Classes were large, and there was little chance to get to know any of the professors. Certainly no faculty-student relationship developed that resembled his association with Woolfolk. To his recollection, Bedford never had the same professor for any two classes.

It might have been tempting to remain after graduation in the New York City area, where opportunities for an African American lawyer were far more promising than in Texas. Even if New York was still segregated by custom, it was not segregated by law, and restaurants, theaters, and other public facilities were open to all races.

But Bedford was never tempted to stay. He had determined from the first that he would return to Dallas to establish his practice, and nothing had changed his mind.

The presence of his parents and friends in Dallas was important. "I felt that in order to stay in New York and be successful, you had to have strong political connections. Otherwise, you weren't going to get too far," Bedford later said. That lesson was reinforced one Christmas in Brooklyn when he was desperately seeking holiday work with no luck. A fellow student heard about his search. "You want a job?" he asked. He advised Bedford to go to a certain post office and give them his name. Bedford was hired immediately. Such connections might work for a holiday season, but he knew they were unlikely to help a young lawyer succeed.[20]

In Dallas he certainly knew about Durham and his good work, he knew about the Masons, and he and his family were good friends with the pioneer lawyer J. L. Turner and his attorney son, J. L. Turner Jr. All these men, especially the Turners, might be helpful. It would be hard, and he would have to pass the state bar exam without having taken a single course in Texas law, but he was determined to do it.[21]

His interests, though, had broadened, now including sports, as well as religion and the progressive music he was hearing in Harlem. He followed the Brooklyn Dodgers closely and enjoyed seeing the great Jackie Robinson play at Ebbets Field, as well as the two African American stars who joined him in spring 1949, Roy Campanella and Don Newcombe. His favorite professional football team was the Cleveland Browns, whose two African American players, fullback Marion Motley and Bill Willis, who had both signed in 1946, were achieving stardom and breaking color barriers in that sport.

He personally knew two prominent basketball players for the powerhouse Long Island University (LIU) team, Sherman White and LeRoy Smith. They also lived at the Carlton YMCA, convenient because it was near the ConEd building, where LIU was offering classes. White, who nearly set an all-time collegiate scoring record in his career, was en route to being named player of the year in 1951 by the *Sporting News*.

As players on the Long Island team, White and Smith were given "food books," good for free meals at a certain restaurant. "If they had a wonderful game, the coaches might give them several of those food books," Bedford recalled. "If they didn't play too well, they would get just one." Sometimes when they were tired from workouts or games, Bedford would go to the restaurant for them and bring back food for all three to share at the Y.[22] On one occasion Bedford accompanied one of them on a clothes-buying spree. Where they got their money for clothing was a mystery to him.

Unfortunately, the answer materialized. The year after Bedford graduated, both players were caught up in a point-shaving scheme that scandalized college basketball. (In point-shaving, the outcome of a game, win or lose, might not be altered, but the margin of victory would be diminished so gamblers could beat the point spread.) Both White and Smith were among more than two dozen college players convicted, including some of the most famous players in the nation at such basketball powerhouses as Kentucky, City College of New York (CCNY), and Bradley. Between 1947 and 1951, eighty-six games had been fixed. White, who had stashed $5,500 in an envelope taped to the back of a dresser drawer in his room at the Carlton YMCA, was given a one-year sentence and served nine months on Rikers Island. Smith and five others on the team were given suspended sentences. Bedford had not had the slightest inkling of their involvement. "I hated what happened," Bedford said, for they had been fine friends. Sherman White would have had an outstanding professional career, but his conviction ruined his chances for that. He was banned for life from the National Basketball Association.[23]

On June 7, 1950, Louis Arthur Bedford Jr. of Dallas, Texas, was one of 245 Brooklyn Law School students who walked across the stage at Brooklyn's Academy of Music on Lafayette Avenue. The diploma handed to him by Dean William B. Carswell certified that he had been conferred the degree of bachelor of law. Of those 245 students, 57 were in Bedford's afternoon shift of classes. Rabbi Max Schenk gave both the invocation and the benediction, and the Honorable John MacCrate, justice of New York's Supreme Court Appellate Division, delivered the commencement address.[24]

For the first time in her life, Callie Bedford went to New York, proud to see her son graduate with his bachelor of law degree. With her on the train came Deborah, now married to Otto Fridia, who was teaching in Dallas, and Deborah's friend Willie

Pearl Chambers. Louis Sr. stayed behind on Thomas Avenue. In New York, Deborah and Willie Pearl struck out on their own as sightseers, and Bedford took over the pleasant duty as his mother's guide.

Callie wanted to see the Brooklyn Dodgers play. She had become fascinated with Roy Campanella. Ebbets Field, then, was one of their first destinations, and although the Dodgers lost that day, being there was a special thrill. Mother and son also visited various museums in the area, including the Museum of Natural History and Hayden Planetarium.[25]

When Bedford's mother, sister, and their family friend returned to Dallas, the young law school graduate stayed behind for the rest of the summer. He had a temporary job as a shipping clerk at the New York City distribution center owned by Hattie Faye Long's employer. Bedford unloaded materials arriving from a textile manufacturing plant somewhere in the Carolinas and shipped them out to customers. The position required no legal skills, but it was certain money.[26]

Brotherton by now was gone, having returned a year earlier to Dallas, where he soon opened a radio and television repair shop. Later he went back to Prairie View, earned a degree in electrical engineering, and enjoyed a career at the White Sands Proving Grounds in New Mexico. Gosey remained in the area, completed his degree at Long Island University, and worked with the City of New York.

In August, Bedford gave his farewells, a fond one to Gladys Webster, a YMCA secretary with whom he had recently developed a special relationship. He pulled up his meager stakes—clothes and books—and returned to Dallas, not to come back to New York until the New York World's Fair in 1964.

1. Louis A. Bedford Jr., interview by Darwin Payne, Dec. 15, 2005; class photo of 1950 Brooklyn Law School graduating class, Bedford Papers.
2. Ibid.
3. George Ruble Woolfolk to Louis Bedford, Mar. 8, 1948, Bedford Papers.
4. Ibid.
5. *The HistoryMakers*, "Rev. Gardner Taylor Biography," in "The ReligionMakers" (Chicago: History-Makers, 2002), http://www.thehistorymakers.com/biography/biography.asp?bioindex=175&category=ReligionMakers.
6. Louis A. Bedford Jr., interview by Darwin Payne, Sept. 8, 2005.

7. Ibid.

8. Louis A. Bedford Jr., interview by Darwin Payne, Dec. 22, 2005; *The History Makers*, "Rev. Gardner Taylor."

9. Bedford, interview, Sept. 8, 2005.

10. Ibid.

11. Ibid.

12. Louis A. Bedford Jr., interview by Darwin Payne, Dec. 20, 2005.

13. Ibid., Sept. 8, 2005.

14. S.v. "Father Divine," Wikipedia, the Free Encyclopedia, http://en.wikipedia.org/wiki/Father_Divine; s.v. "Father Divine," infoplease, http://www.infoplease.com/ce6/people/A0815667.html.

15. Bedford, interview, Sept. 8, 2005.

16. Ibid.

17. "Father Divine," Wikipedia.

18. Brooklyn Law School Report Card, Spring Semester, 1949, "L. A. Bedford Jr. Personal" binder, Bedford Papers.

19. Bedford, interview, Sept. 8, 2005.

20. Ibid.

21. Ibid.

22. Ibid.

23. Dave Anderson, "College Basketball; When Sherman White Threw It All Away," *New York Times*, Mar. 22, 1998; Bedford, interview, Sept. 8, 2005.

24. Brooklyn Law School graduation program, June 7, 1950, "L. A. Bedford Jr. Personal" binder, Bedford Papers.

25. Bedford, interview, Dec. 15, 2005.

26. Ibid., Sept. 8, 2005.

4

A TIMOROUS BEGINNING

I
n September 1950 the young law school graduate, his head filled with contracts, torts, and criminal procedures, wound up his summer job as a shipping clerk in Manhattan and returned by train to Dallas. He had sent ahead his meager belongings, some clothing, books, and linens. A small accumulation indeed for a three-year stay, but the most important part of his time in Brooklyn had been the classroom lessons—his key to a fruitful future.

There was much to think about on the long journey home. Despite the obstacles he had already overcome, the most daunting one lay ahead: to find out whether he could make a living as a lawyer.

First he had to pass the state bar exam, no mean feat, since his New York professors had understandably paid no attention to Texas law. Then he needed to find clients with confidence in his ability—clients with enough money to pay reasonable legal fees. The possibility of finding a position at an established law firm where he would be surrounded by helpful veteran attorneys did not occur to him. Law firms in Dallas did not hire African American attorneys. The few black attorneys in the city were sole practitioners.

A less serious obstacle but still an important one was emotional: adjusting from the freer, fast-paced life he had enjoyed in New York City to life in a hometown that still reflected the racial prejudices of the Old South. Dallas, booming in commerce and ambitious to be recognized for its successes, liked to think of itself as something other than a Southern city, but insofar as race relations were concerned, it was steeped in Southern prejudice.

For years Dallas's African American citizens accommodated themselves to white society, believing that the way to win expanded opportunities was to prove themselves worthy. Dallas blacks still desired to reflect Caucasian characteristics in their appearance, an unthinking rejection of their African ancestry. Advertisements in the *Dallas Express* promoted products that promised to straighten hair and lighten complexions. "Too Dark to Be Loved?" was the not-so-subtle message for a skin whitener guaranteeing "lighter, lovelier skin," which would bring new possibilities for romance.[1]

Attitudes had been changing, however, in Dallas among African Americans ever since A. Maceo Smith and Rev. Maynard Jackson organized the Progressive Voters League and galvanized the Negro Chamber of Commerce in the 1930s. Jackson by now had moved to Atlanta after his failure to be elected in 1944 to the Dallas school board, a campaign marred by anonymous threats to his personal safety. He had accepted a pastorate in Atlanta, where his son, Maynard Jackson Jr., would in 1974 be elected the first black mayor in the city's history. The relentless push for advancing opportunities for African Americans in Dallas and the state had continued, in 1950 especially through local leaders of the NAACP and the energy and fortitude of attorney W. J. Durham. Equal pay for schoolteachers, African Americans on grand juries, the elimination of the all-white Democratic primaries, and Heman Sweatt's admission to the University of Texas Law School were signs of the steady progress being made.

By this time, too, an African American Dallasite had been seated on a courtroom jury: in 1949 in Judge Sarah T. Hughes's 14th District Court, NAACP member Edgar Washington served on an otherwise all-white jury to determine a child custody case. Washington, a federal government employee, was well-known in the community and active at the Moorland Branch of the YMCA, as well as with the NAACP.[2]

Yet, even as Louis Bedford returned to his hometown, a familiar crisis had resurfaced: bombings of black-owned residences and businesses in South Dallas. A decade after the unsolved bombings accompanying the opening of Lincoln High School, the same thing was happening again as African Americans gingerly spilled out of the crowded black communities into white neighborhoods. The postwar boom and population explosion was affecting all citizens in their search for adequate housing, but it was worse for African Americans because strictly segregated housing severely limited their options. The African American population in Dallas had grown from 50,407 in 1940 to 83,352 in 1950. A report in 1950 revealed that for 21,568 black households only 14,850 housing units were available.[3] Between February and mid-July 1950, six bombings had occurred in South Dallas. The African American community was demanding that something be done. (A year later a blue-ribbon grand jury—which included NAACP counsel W. J. Durham; Rev. Bezeleel R. Riley, president of the local NAACP chapter; and Rev. Robert L. Parish, pastor of a black church—was formed to investigate. Ten men were indicted. The jury returned a not-guilty verdict for the first man tried, despite evidence incriminating him. Jury trials for the nine other men appeared to be a waste of time, according to the district attorney, and no more trials took place. Nevertheless, the bombings ceased.)[4]

Meanwhile, the housing shortage did not improve. When public housing developments were proposed to alleviate the critical situation, opponents shouted the proponents down at city council meetings as "socialistic" and "communistic." A plan for a $14 million project to build houses for two thousand black families in the Oak Cliff section of town was stymied because nearby white residents lodged loud protests.[5] Such projects could best be achieved away from the gaze and authority of the city council. Just outside the southern city limits, a new development, Carver Heights, was offering ten houses as the beginning of a "complete Negro community" that ultimately had eight hundred houses.[6]

Obviously, something had to be done. A Dallas businessman, Roland Pelt, proposed a huge new development that would have provided low-cost housing for some thirty-five thousand to forty thousand black residents in single-family residences, duplexes, and apartments. The development would have schools, a business district, several shopping centers, parks, and paved streets. Its location was unfortunate, though: adjacent to a levee in the Trinity River bottoms. Black communities spurned the plan, and many in the white community understood why.[7]

Soon, though, with the cooperation of leading African Americans—including A. Maceo Smith and C. B. Bunkley Jr., an attorney who was president of the Negro Chamber of Commerce—Dallas business and civic leaders created a nonprofit organization to develop a community for more than seven hundred African American families just north of the Dallas city limits. Bunkley praised the site as "high, beautiful and well situated." The development, he said, would be a place "from which future citizens will come to help and to make possible a type of progress that Dallas, our city, has never known before." It was called Hamilton Park—named after black Dallas physician Richard T. Hamilton, who had worked so hard for the scholarship program for Texas black students seeking graduate study—and became known as a model community for African Americans. As the city limits extended northward, Hamilton Park eventually would be annexed into Dallas.[8]

Implicit in Hamilton Park's creation as a special community for African Americans was the belief that segregated housing patterns would continue indefinitely. Little did the white or black civic leaders realize that a sea change lay just ahead, bringing an end to the "separate but equal" doctrine.

In the *Dallas Express* a series of articles highlighted the feud between black publishing magnate Carter Wesley of Houston and NAACP counsel Thurgood Marshall. Wesley, a lawyer himself and a leading civil rights figure in Texas, insisted on enforcing the equalization of segregated public facilities, such as schools, libraries, and transportation. He agreed that direct attacks on segregation were appropriate, but success likely was years away—meanwhile, black schoolchildren were suffering unfairly from schools that in no way were equal to those provided for white children. Marshall and the national NAACP had concluded that efforts to achieve equalization were a distraction. Their strategy was to attack all separate facilities as inherently unequal.[9]

In 1950 whites and African Americans alike were flocking to see a new movie, *The Jackie Robinson Story*, in which the baseball player portrayed himself. Despite the black community's keen interest in the movie, they could see it only at the downtown Majestic Theater, where African Americans were relegated to the second balcony after they entered through a separate box office and used a separate elevator. In the movie's advertisements, the Majestic announced that extra seats had been made available for them in the colored balcony. Bedford was proud of the fact that he had actually seen Robinson play at Ebbets Field.[10]

Bedford also was proud to have enjoyed firsthand in New York the nation's most acclaimed African American entertainers. In comparison, the fare he found on his return to Dallas seemed lackluster. Yet, in Bedford's first months back home, the sensational electric guitarist Aaron Thibeaux "T-Bone" Walker, a Dallas native who now could be seen more frequently in New York, and the soon-to-be-famous Ray Charles, who would move to Dallas in 1953 for a few years, performed at the nearby Empire Room on Hall Street.

Father Divine had been a charismatic, controversial, and formidable religious figure on the East Coast, and those looking for an approximation in Dallas could hear

Father J. Von Brown at his Lighted Church of Prayer. Father Brown also preached on the radio; he sponsored healing services for large audiences; and soon, like Divine, he would be in trouble with the law. But Bedford had no inclination for such religious shenanigans, and he happily returned to his family's New Hope Baptist Church.

The first thing for Bedford to do after moving in with his parents was to find a temporary job. He needed to earn money while he studied for the bar exam. Finding work, he learned, was not easy. It would have been virtually impossible to get a temporary job commensurate with his education, and he didn't try, but when prospective employers learned of his educational background, they became reluctant to hire him. Finally, he decided his prospects would improve if he did not reveal the extent of his education.

His former roommate Marvin Brotherton had been back in Dallas for a year now. He had not yet established the radio-TV repair shop that lay ahead for him, and he had found stopgap employment at Southwestern Medical School, a still-new institution consisting of a proliferation of Quonset huts in northwest Dallas. Two of Bedford's other good friends, Alfred Bowens and Herbert Chambers, had also been hired there. Chambers, who later became a physician, was employed in the library, and Bowens, who later became a high school teacher and assistant principal, worked for one of the doctors. They told Bedford that the medical school was a good place to work, and they encouraged him to apply. He did, acknowledging in his interview only that he had two years of college. He was hired.[11]

The job assigned to this law school graduate was as an animal caretaker, mainly dealing with mice, rats, and rabbits used in laboratory experiments. Sometimes there was also a monkey to care for. It was not an unpleasant experience. Each morning Bedford would feed the animals and replace old sawdust with new. Some of the white mice were kept in glass jars, away from any contamination, and Bedford lifted them out with long forceps, placed them in temporary jars, sterilized their regular jars, and then put them back in. Bedford held this job with pleasure until he passed the bar exam half a year later.[12]

A few months after he returned to Dallas, a letter arrived bearing unexpected news. It was from Gladys Webster, the young secretary at the Brooklyn YMCA with whom he had developed an intimate relationship shortly before leaving. She was pregnant. Bedford was the father.

He considered marriage, but at the time it did not seem realistic. "I had no money to bring her down to Texas, and I had no money to go there," Bedford said more than fifty years later. So, in New York Gladys bore the child, a girl whom she named Diane. Bedford over the years voluntarily "did what I could with what I had," sending monthly payments to help Gladys and Diane with their expenses. Bedford's parents accepted the news, but many years passed before Bedford saw his daughter. When he finally met her, Bedford's relationship with her grew close, and she would come to visit his family in Dallas. As an adult, Diane became a counselor in the public schools in New York City and a married mother of two daughters, the oldest of whom, Nicole Webster, became an attorney.[13]

Bedford, suddenly and unexpectedly faced with greater responsibilities than he had envisioned, studied for the bar exam. The questions would cover material distinctively different from much that he had learned at Brooklyn Law School. The community property laws of Texas were unique. And, of course, much else of what he must know—Texas oil and gas laws, for example—was essential.

For advice, Bedford visited the veteran attorney and family friend J. L. Turner and his son, J. L. Turner Jr., who had joined his father in his practice. The younger Turner, who had been an officer in World War II, was a storehouse of knowledge about the Dallas community, regaling Bedford and others with details about pioneer black families in the area. Bedford also came to know W. J. Durham and the attorney who shared office space with him, Crawford B. Bunkley Jr. These two men, the most prominent and visible black attorneys in town, had heard about Bedford's law degree and his pending bar exam, and they offered advice and encouragement. The dozen or so African American attorneys in town were close. They clung together for support, ineligible because of their color to join the Dallas Bar Association.

Durham, assisted by Bunkley and U. Simpson Tate, who had been hired as Southwest regional counsel of the NAACP Legal and Educational Fund, was involved as usual in several lawsuits aimed at breaking down racial segregation. One case making headlines this summer and fall of 1950 was the NAACP's effort to desegregate facilities of Texas's state parks, which by custom but not by law excluded African

Americans.[14] (In 1952, by court order, both city and state parks had to open their facilities to African Americans.)

Durham, Bunkley, and some of the other attorneys who were eager to assist the young law school graduate gave him some materials—old bar exam questions, primarily—to study. Because he was not aware of any preparatory courses for the exam (which would later be so common), Bedford was on his own in getting ready.

One requirement was that each applicant have a practicing attorney provide a character recommendation. Those authorized by the State Bar of Texas to give such references seemed to be members of big law firms in Dallas, all of them white. Bedford selected at random a lawyer on the list, a member of the leading firm of Strasburger and Price in the downtown Gulf States Building. Bedford put on his best clothes, called on the lawyer, and chatted with him for a few minutes, telling him about his experience at Brooklyn Law School, Prairie View, and his upbringing in Dallas. The lawyer, whose name Bedford later forgot, was pleasant, and he signed the requisite papers for the state bar association in Austin.[15]

Without actually knowing how difficult the questions would be, Bedford took the exam in fall 1950, a few weeks after his return to Dallas. The examination was held in the House of Representatives Chamber in the granite Texas State Capitol in Austin. Each applicant could sprawl out on the handsome, widely separated desks normally assigned to elected state representatives.

Glancing around that big room at the others taking the exam, Bedford could see only one other African American. As he soon learned, the man was L. Clayton Rivers, a World War II veteran who had attended the improvised Texas law school set up by the state legislature after Heman Sweatt's challenge. Rivers had not received his law degree, but as a World War II veteran, he was permitted to take the exam after two years at the school.

Following the exam, Bedford was curious to see the bar examiners call Rivers to them for a brief conversation. Afterward, Rivers and Bedford gravitated naturally to one another for their own introductions, and Bedford asked him about his exchange with the examiners. Rivers told Bedford they had asked about his legal education and whether he had enjoyed his experience. Were his professors good? Did he think it was a good school?

When the exam results later arrived in the mail, Bedford learned that he had made a grade of seventy-three, two points below the passing mark of seventy-five. Oddly, Rivers, who had studied at a makeshift and unproven school and had not actually finished his legal studies, had passed. What had been the difference? Bedford wondered whether the examiners, eager for the new Texas Southern to gain greater legitimacy, passed Rivers because of that.[16]

So, it was back to the books. The exam was offered again in Austin in spring 1951. This time Bedford passed. His letter from the State Board of Law Examiners advised that he had made the passing grade of seventy-five. He was now licensed to practice law in the state of Texas.[17]

His photograph appeared in the *Dallas Express* with an announcement: "Louis Bedford Jr., newly licensed attorney, has opened his office at his home, 3317 Thomas Ave. His telephone number is TE 3605." Except for basic announcements containing the barest of details, bar regulations forbade advertising. For his law office, Bedford took over a room on the house's first floor; he had no resources to rent space elsewhere. A sign went up in front of the house: "L. A. Bedford Jr., Attorney-at-Law." Bedford's parents purchased him a set of *Vernon's Annotated Statutes of Texas*, requisite for any lawyer, an expensive item they began paying off at ten dollars a month. Bedford furnished his office with a small desk, a couple of chairs, and the new set of *Vernon's Annotated Statutes.*[18]

It was disappointing but not unusual that hardly anyone called or stopped by his office in the first weeks. Eventually, a man who lived in West Dallas (then outside the Dallas city limits) needed representation for his divorce and asked Bedford to help him. The man's wife had filed a temporary restraining order against him, and he wanted Bedford to represent him in a hearing in District Judge Dallas Blankenship's court.

To Bedford's surprise, when he and his client appeared before the judge, the opposing attorney was none other than L. Clayton Rivers, who seemed in Bedford's eyes to exude confidence in telling the judge why the temporary restraining order should be granted. Judge Blankenship began posing questions directly to Bedford's client, who answered them without Bedford's assistance. Suddenly Judge Blankenship looked at Bedford and asked, "And who are you?" Bedford replied that he was the man's lawyer.

"I guess I was sort of awed," Bedford later said, chuckling about his wordless debut in the courtroom. He could not remember the judge's ruling.[19]

(Rivers soon moved to El Paso, where he was the only African American attorney in town. In 1965 he found himself in deep trouble, convicted in federal court for transporting a forged or falsely made security across state lines, a conviction upheld by the Fifth Circuit Court of Appeals.)[20]

As weeks passed without additional clients, Bedford began to wonder whether something was wrong beyond simply being a new attorney attempting to launch a career. He feared that he was being seen as a "homeboy" from the neighborhood, the same youth residents had always known—Louis and Callie's boy—instead of a promising attorney fresh from an East Coast law school at the beginning of his career. He wondered about his demeanor. Should he adopt a more aloof air of professionalism? Rivers and another young African American attorney just starting out seemed to have no such problems. To hear them, it sounded as if they were doing very well indeed.

To assume a more professional appearance, Bedford realized, he must establish a proper office away from home. Soon came the opportunity. A Lincoln High School teacher who also had a law degree, C. W. Asberry, owned a two-story office building in West Dallas. For the nominal sum of twenty-five dollars a month, Bedford rented one of the two upstairs offices at 1807½ Singleton Boulevard. A young African American dentist who was just beginning his practice, W. A. Hembry, rented the other one. A variety store owned by a friendly man named Ernest Dillard occupied the ground floor.

West Dallas was the poorest part of town, an area of small frame houses (many of them without plumbing), unpaved streets, auto and truck repair shops, and low-tech industry. Residents included impoverished whites and many African Americans and Hispanics. Although it was just across the Trinity River from downtown, it was not yet a part of the city of Dallas. (Bedford's new office was a few blocks down the street from where Clyde Barrow lived as a boy with his parents, behind the little filling station they had opened after coming to Dallas from adjacent Ellis County. Singleton Boulevard was where Clyde teamed up with Bonnie Parker in the early 1930s to begin their infamous crime spree.) Mean though it was, such a neighborhood, almost entirely lacking in professionals as well as in other amenities, might be a place where Bedford could do some good.

He could not even afford a telephone for his new office, but Dillard, the variety store owner, let Bedford list the store's telephone number on his new business cards as his own. When an occasional call came for Bedford, Dillard would shout up the stairway, "Telephone!" Bedford would hustle down the stairs and take the call.[21]

Bedford had no money for a car, either. Most days he took a bus to his office, but frequently, Dr. Hembry, whose residence was on Campbell Street only a few blocks away from Thomas Avenue, gave him a ride. They formed an enduring friendship. (Many years later, in 2002, Dr. Hembry's daughter Lisa was elected treasurer of Dallas County.)

In his first full discouraging year of practice, Bedford earned approximately fifteen hundred dollars. What made it worse was continuing to hear some of the other young lawyers, such as Rivers, talk about their growing practices. He wondered if their talk was true or if behind their bluster they were struggling as much as he was.[22]

Dr. Hembry, for certain, was doing well. He soon was able to purchase a house on Singleton Boulevard, which he converted into three offices, one for himself and the others to rent. Bedford moved to one of the offices, and another physician, Dr. Herbert Chambers, took the second.

Another new friend in West Dallas, also unmarried and with whom Bedford began to socialize in the evening hours, was J. B. Jackson Jr., a bright young man who had graduated from Booker T. Washington High School in Dallas and Morehouse College in Atlanta. At Morehouse, Jackson had been a member of the debate team with a fellow student named Martin Luther King Jr. Jackson, opinionated and outgoing, had gone to the University of Texas Law School for a while but had not graduated. Later Bedford speculated that Jackson had left law school because he alienated his professors with his constant challenges.[23] In the next decade, Jackson emerged as one of the leaders of the nascent civil rights movement in Dallas. Later a street was named for him.

Happy to be back in Dallas despite his struggles, Bedford missed certain aspects of his life in New York. He had enjoyed the abundance of public transportation, especially the subways, which meant a person didn't require an automobile to get around. If the tempo in Dallas were faster, he would have been pleased.[24]

Establishing a social life wasn't nearly as difficult as establishing a successful law practice. He merged easily back into his family's New Hope Baptist Church and the Moorland YMCA. He became a member of a group at Moorland called the Young Adults, composed of interesting young black people in the early stages of their careers. Many of the young women were schoolteachers. Bedford and some of them became part of Moorland's "junior board of directors," responsible for putting on a program once a year. Usually, they brought prominent speakers from around the country to discuss such things as the latest developments in desegregation efforts and civil rights. With the other Young Adults, Bedford centered his recreational activities at the Moorland YMCA, where they played volleyball and basketball and swam.[25]

The clients who eventually began to show up in Bedford's office were generally uncertain and often frightened about legal matters; they knew they were getting involved in a white man's system of justice, whose nuances they did not understand. They had turned to legal counsel only after difficult divorces, eviction from their homes, or unpleasant entanglements with the police or district attorney. By the time Bedford saw them, the "damage" might have already been done, and his options for them usually amounted to reducing further harm.

Potential clients often worried that Bedford, as a black lawyer, would be at a disadvantage. Some of them asked him plainly if he would be able to speak for them or if Bedford himself would need a white lawyer to appear in court. They knew that the legal system—judges, lawyers, clerks—was white and its members often friends with one another, and they clearly doubted the possibility of getting justice.[26]

A persistent problem Bedford soon encountered in West Dallas was the use of "contracts of sale" for low-income house buyers who could not qualify for typical mortgages with established lending agencies. In a contract of sale, a seller—too often an opportunistic one without a sense of moral obligation to his or her client—would offer unusually low monthly payments, with the understanding that the title to the house would be delivered to the prospective buyer after the house was completely paid for. Unsophisticated buyers did not realize that the low monthly payments represented little more than the interest on the loan. When a payment was missed, even after years of regular payments, the buyers frequently were evicted, understanding for the first time that no equity had been built up and that they did not even hold an encumbered title to the property. Even without missing any payments, buyers might realize after many years that they still owed as much as when they first entered into the contract of sale and that a payoff date was still far in the future. In such instances there generally was little that Bedford could do to assist his shocked clients.[27]

When the city of Dallas finally annexed West Dallas, not long after Bedford had set up his office there, its ramshackle houses and lack of utilities had to be brought up to code. Many of the houses had no sewer lines. An influx of con artists covered the neighborhood, accepting money for work that sometimes was never completed or for shoddy work that quickly fell apart.

Contractors would tell the homeowners that they would repair their houses. As Bedford later explained, they would say, "'Now you've got your deed; you don't need to give us your deed. You just keep your deed.'" Then they would have the homeowner sign a lien: "'We just want you to sign this. You don't have to worry about your deed, you keep your deed, because we're not going to mess with your deed.' People were signing away their rights without knowing a lien was being placed upon their home." A lawsuit was often useless if the work was done by a corporation, for the hastily improvised corporation would sell its notes to other holders. Hearing of more and more such instances reinforced the plight of the poor in Bedford's mind.[28]

On rare occasions some of these cases would go to trial with favorable results. One case involved new siding on a woman's house that began falling off. She had four to five thousand dollars' worth of liens on her house, and the jury found on her behalf, acknowledging that the contract had not been properly executed. But the judge, who happened to be a visiting judge, called Bedford to his side and gave him shocking news. He told him that he already had promised the other attorney that he would rule in his favor, so he was setting aside the jury's verdict and ruling for the defendant. He told Bedford that he could appeal the case and would surely win. "I appealed it, but because my client didn't have any money, the court reporter never would get my transcript ready," Bedford recalled.[29]

Bedford's first jury trial took place in County Court at Law No. 2 before Judge Grover Hartt Jr., the only Republican judge in the county—in fact, the first since Reconstruction—who had come to office in 1952 on the coattails of Dwight Eisenhower. It was an accident case, and Bedford, working alone as the defendant's lawyer, was uncertain how to handle himself in the courtroom. He confessed his uncertainties to a friendly bailiff, who gave him some simple advice, which he welcomed. The bailiff said that if Bedford could prove contributory negligence on the part of the plaintiff, a judge rarely if ever would hold for the plaintiff. "Whatever he [the opposing attorney] does, you just do the opposite," the bailiff said. "If he says one thing, you say the opposite." Bedford won the case after he was able to show contributory negligence on the part of the plaintiff.[30]

Inevitably, Bedford found himself handling both civil and criminal cases. Trips to the courthouse and county jail, or farther up the street to the police department's jail at city hall, were frequent. Most of his criminal cases involved misdemeanors. Discrimination toward him as an African American attorney was not overt—he never heard a judge use a derogatory name—but he sometimes heard people pass by and mutter epithets. On one occasion in a criminal case, an assistant district attorney used a derogatory term for Bedford's client, and the judge upheld Bedford's objection. Sometimes, in an effort to sway the jury, an assistant district attorney would try to tie Bedford and the case being heard to the NAACP. Bedford would object, and the judge always upheld these objections, too.

Collecting his fees, especially in criminal cases, was often a problem. Criminal lawyers typically require their payments at the time they are retained, but Bedford found himself susceptible to sad stories. Many times he was never paid for his work.[31]

On one occasion Bedford represented a man in Judge Shelby S. Cox's County Criminal Court. Bedford had heard that Cox, a former Dallas County district attorney, was racist, and he assumed that he would face special difficulties in his courtroom. Bedford's client was charged with gun possession, and when Bedford was summing up his case, he saw that Cox seemed to be recording his verdict in his docket already. "Judge, have you reached your conclusion?" Bedford asked. "Yeah, but you can go ahead with your argument," Cox replied. It seemed certain that the ruling would be adverse, but to Bedford's surprise the judge found in his favor. Only later did Bedford learn that Cox had been elected district attorney in 1923 as an avowed member of the Ku Klux Klan and that, fortunately for the client, the right to bear arms was important to him. In the ensuing years, Bedford and Cox had several amiable conversations.[32]

Sometimes an opposing attorney would tell Bedford that he didn't understand why he was even trying a case, since he surely knew he wouldn't win. Bedford would use a tactic he had learned from W. J. Durham and say, "I'm being paid, so I'm going to have to try it." Many of them had the idea that they would win their cases just because they were white and Bedford was black. Bedford saw this as an advantage, for sometimes these overconfident attorneys would be ill prepared or not prepared at all.[33]

As Bedford struggled to establish his practice, he was becoming acquainted with the handful of African American lawyers in town: the Turners, W. J. Durham, Crawford B. Bunkley Jr., Fred Finch, Romeo Williams, D. B. Mason, Robert Rice, U. Simpson Tate, and Rivers. None of these men were members of the Dallas Bar Association. That organization's attitude had not officially changed since 1943, when some senior members lobbied against the American Bar Association's decision to admit black members by arguing that to do so would lower the dignity of the organization. There were advantages for any lawyer to belong to the association. It was far more than a social club, although the ability to mix with other attorneys in a pleasant environment had its own advantages. It offered its members a substantive program of ongoing legal education so that they could stay abreast of the latest developments and discuss mutual problems. No similar organization existed for the city's handful of African American attorneys, who had no practical means of continuing their legal education and who also suffered from enforced isolation from the legal community in addition to the usual prejudices they encountered in the courtroom.

During Bedford's first year back in Dallas, John Lewis Turner Sr., the family friend and the one lawyer he had known earlier, died at the age of eighty-two. Turner had developed a good reputation for his expertise in probate and real estate law. Because of his race, though, he was not permitted to join the Dallas Bar Association, and in the courtrooms he endured the usual references to him as "boy."

Born on July 3, 1869, on a farm in what is now North Dallas, Turner studied under J. E. Wiley, then went to Chicago and enrolled at Kent College of Law. A story was often repeated about something his farmer father had told him on the eve of his departure for Chicago: "You can go on up there to study law, but when you get back the plow will be waiting for you."[34] Instead, he returned in 1898 to open his own law practice. His long and distinguished career in Dallas was never forgotten. Although he had not been the first African American to practice law in the city, he was the first to establish a lifelong practice. He died at his home at 1821 Allen Street on December 2, 1951. Even the *Dallas Morning News* recognized the significance of his passing, placing a photograph with his obituary and giving him a full story, at a time when newspapers rarely reported on African American deaths.[35]

Turner's life was memorialized the next spring, when several African American lawyers in town called a meeting to form their own legal association, one that eventually became the J. L. Turner Legal Association. The first meeting, attended by twelve attorneys, took place on the afternoon of May 4, 1952. As the first handwritten minutes of the organization, maintained by Bedford, reflected, their purpose was to form an organization through which common problems could be solved and experiences shared. It also would create a forum for fellowship.[36]

J. L. Turner Jr. agreed to serve as chairman until a president was elected, and a few minutes later, he found himself elected to that office, which he held until 1969. Bedford, still a fledgling lawyer but already recognized for his enthusiasm, was elected secretary. It would amount to a lifelong commitment, for Bedford held the records of the society for more than fifty years. Other officers included Romeo Williams, vice president; Durham, treasurer; Bunkley, parliamentarian; and D. B. Mason, chaplain.

Bedford later insisted his election as secretary reflected the fact that the more experienced members wanted to involve a young lawyer in the organization. They must have seen something in him, for there were other young lawyers who could have been named to the position but were not.

At that first meeting, the lawyers established three standing committees. Membership necessarily overlapped because there were so few individuals to choose from. Bunkley was named chairman of the constitution and bylaws committee. Members were L. Clayton Rivers and Jack Terry. Durham became chairman of the grievance committee, and he was joined by Rivers, Robert Rice, U. Simpson Tate, and Bedford. The chairman of the social committee was Kenneth F. Holbert, and serving with him were Williams, Bedford, and Durham. Bunkley was named chairman of the program committee, of which Tate and Rivers were members. Only one person who attended, C. W. Asberry, the teacher at Lincoln High, was not given an assignment.

Holbert, the chairman of the social committee, was an exact contemporary of Bedford's. He had graduated from Lincoln High School the same year that Bedford graduated from Booker T. Washington, and they were fellow church members at New Hope Baptist. Holbert earned his law degree from the University of Denver.

Tate worked for the NAACP as Southwest Region counsel, having been hired in 1948 by Thurgood Marshall. Tate was a graduate of Lincoln University in Pennsylvania and Howard University law school.[37]

Yet another matter was settled—temporarily, as it turned out—at this first meeting: the selection of a name for the organization. Two suggestions were made: the Dallas Lawyers Club and the Barristers Club. By a standing vote, the members selected Barristers Club, a name destined to be short-lived. The lawyers also agreed to have regular meetings from 6:00 to 8:00 PM on the third Tuesday of each month. Then, at 4:00 PM, the first meeting of the Barristers Club adjourned so the members could retreat to the Boll Street Church "in order to hear and enjoy the oratory ability of Mr. C. B. Bunkley," who had a speaking engagement there.[38]

At the second meeting of the Barristers Club, attended by ten members, U. Simpson Tate reported that the group had acknowledged three purposes for its existence. The first was "to effect cooperation between the members of the legal profession"; second, "to build and to promote fellowship between members"; and third, "to promote a program activity which shall be beneficial to all and have a public relations effect as well as for the benefit of the young and older lawyers."[39]

As to the last purpose, it was agreed that Durham would be the first speaker, and his topic would be pretrial proceedings. Topics covered in the future included summary judgments, special issues, and pleadings. In July, Tate discussed three-judge panels, in which federal judges heard challenges to State of Texas statutes.

Nowhere did the early minutes reflect members' discussion of the obvious fact that this association was organized for African American attorneys. Presumably, although unspoken, the Barristers Club would be open to white attorneys, as well. At the second meeting, the question was discussed as to whether the organization should affiliate with the Dallas Bar Association. Durham and Bunkley agreed to seek their own admission, perhaps as a means of testing the waters.[40]

Whether the two immediately followed up on their intentions is not recorded in the minutes, but the Dallas Bar Association's own records reflect that in 1956 an application for membership was received from "a colored lawyer." As Bedford remembered it, both Durham and Bunkley submitted their applications. A bar association committee was formed to study the matter, and at a meeting on January 12, 1956, the board of directors voted unanimously to defer the application. African American membership in the Dallas Bar Association thus was denied until the next decade.[41]

It soon dawned on the Barristers that they needed a new name. The term "Barristers" lacked meaning to most people. What better than to name their organization after the man who had been a role model for so many of them, J. L. Turner? Thus, several months after its 1952 founding, members of the Barristers Club voted without opposition to change the name to the J. L. Turner Legal Society (later J. L. Turner Legal Association).[42]

On many days, meanwhile, Bedford continued to sit in his office on Singleton Boulevard waiting for clients. To help earn extra money, he filed the necessary papers and posted the required bond to become a notary public. He was one of the few notaries public, if not the only one, in West Dallas.

Some days Bedford stayed only a short while at his office. He would drop by Durham's and Bunkley's offices and spend time there, soaking in the ambience of their routines, learning what he could by osmosis, asking occasional advice, and sometimes borrowing legal forms that he might need for routine procedures. Durham's office at 2600 Flora Street was only a few blocks from Thomas Avenue, where Bedford continued to live with his parents. Bunkley's office was nearby on Good-Latimer Expressway. One of the important lessons he learned from Durham—and Durham was always emphasizing this point—was the need to create an error-free record. "Durham's theory was you try a case like you're going to appeal it," Bedford later said. "Once you had a record, you could win on appeal." In the lower courts, all sorts of tomfoolery could reflect the institutionalized racism of judges and opposing lawyers, often through code words or easily understood subtleties, which made a courtroom triumph, especially before a jury, more difficult for an African American lawyer to obtain. Once the case was appealed, though, the appellate courts could make an objective judgment based on the record.[43]

Durham by no means limited his work to legal affairs. In 1953 he served as chairman of a committee to persuade department stores to end, among other things, their discriminatory practice of forbidding African American women from trying on clothes prior to purchase. Titled the Citizens' Committee to Abolish Discrimination against Negro Women in Dallas Department Stores, the group used Durham's Flora Street office as its headquarters. Durham reported to committee members that he had persuaded Morton Sanger, the manager of the E. M. Kahn store—which sold only men's clothing—to contact other store operators to see whether they would stop this discrimination. Stanley Marcus of Neiman Marcus reportedly responded that he was leaving on a trip, but upon his return he would study the matter to see what could be done about it. Marcus, identified then and in the future as a leading liberal figure in the city, did not change his own store's policies. Neiman Marcus would not permit black customers to sit next to white customers in its dining room or use the same bathroom until 1961, in conjunction with a citywide movement.

Representatives of other stores, Durham reported to committee members, refused to meet with them because "their business was their private business and they would operate it in such manner as they desired." Durham wrote that Morton Sanger of E. M. Kahn, bowing to the policies of the other stores, told him that "such action . . . left the management of the Kahn store to choose between two classes of business—white trade and trade from Negro citizens. Therefore, I can do nothing about the racial discrimination policy in force at the Kahn store."[44]

Bedford and his father were regular customers at E. M. Kahn, and later Bedford didn't recall experiencing any discrimination there. Yet, as Sanger acknowledged, there must have been a discriminatory philosophy in force at E. M. Kahn. Durham, in his letter to committee members, was harshly critical of the city's department stores. "The department stores' position is crystal clear; namely, that such stores will continue to insult Negro women . . . and if Negro men continue to trade in such stores, they will and must do so in the face of the fact that their women will continually be insulted and mistreated."[45]

Like Durham, Crawford B. Bunkley Jr. was also aggressively pursuing increased rights for African American citizens in Dallas, especially in his role as president of the Negro Chamber of Commerce. In 1955, shortly before Negro Achievement Day at the Fair—an attempt by officials to concentrate attendance by blacks on that particular day—he personally tested the 1953 decision of the board of directors of the State Fair of Texas to integrate its midway rides. Bunkley found that he was excluded from two rides in which physical contact between blacks and whites might occur.

As a result, through his prompting, the Negro Chamber of Commerce canceled its endorsement of Negro Achievement Day.

On the day before Negro Achievement Day, some of the more conservative Negro Chamber members, including Rev. E. C. Estell, called another meeting without Bunkley's knowledge or approval. In a night meeting that lasted until 1:00 AM, those attending voted to rescind the earlier action. Bunkley, disgusted at this capitulation, resigned his presidency in protest. The next morning, though, Juanita Craft, leader of the NAACP's Youth Council, had young picketers posted outside the fairground gates on Grand Avenue to protest Negro Achievement Day. In the usual opening parade of black organizations and schools, a number of the marching bands, including those of Booker T. Washington High and Wiley College, refused to cross the picket lines and declined to enter the grounds. As a result, state fair officials now reversed themselves—all rides would be open to blacks.

Bunkley and Bedford became close friends. Bedford considered Bunkley, four years older, to be like his big brother. Bunkley was a native of Denison, Texas, and he had practiced law in Sherman before coming to Dallas. Like Bedford, he held a bachelor's degree from Prairie View. Facing the same problem that all African Americans in Texas encountered if they hoped to become lawyers, he had gone north to the University of Michigan to earn his LLB degree.

Both men were ambitious, and it occurred to them in 1954 that an opportunity to expand their practices existed in Fort Worth, only thirty-five miles west. Despite its large population, the city had only two African American attorneys. Neither Bedford nor Bunkley wanted to move to Fort Worth, though, and they began looking for another attorney who would open the office.

One soon came to mind, Charlye Ola Farris of Wichita Falls, the first African American woman in Texas to pass the bar exam. The daughter of prominent, long-time public school educators in Wichita Falls, Farris had graduated from Prairie View at the age of eighteen. She taught elementary school for a year before entering Howard University to earn a law degree. Having completed her studies and passed the bar exam in 1953, she returned to Wichita Falls and was establishing her practice there when Bedford and Bunkley called.

The two men traveled to Wichita Falls to offer Farris the opportunity of opening their proposed office and becoming a pioneer black attorney in Fort Worth. Although it would mean leaving her hometown and her family's deep roots, Farris verbally agreed to their offer. Buoyed by this prospect, in June 1954 Bedford and Bunkley rented an office in Fort Worth, in the Masonic Building on the corner of Jones and 9th Streets, and hired a secretary. The primary tenant in the building was Fraternal Bank and Trust Co., one of the few black-owned banks in the state.

Farris decided to stay in Wichita Falls, though, where she would enjoy a long and honored career. Because neither Bedford nor Bunkley wanted to move, they began commuting to Fort Worth on alternate days to keep the office open.

Soon they identified another prospect, a young African American attorney in Waco named L. Clifford Davis, an Arkansas native and Howard University School of Law graduate. Bedford and Bunkley made him an offer, and Davis accepted and moved to Fort Worth to take over the office in a firm to be named Bunkley, Bedford, and Davis. No sooner had Davis arrived, though, than he was called into the military. Bedford and Bunkley continued to pay the monthly rent until Davis could return. When he completed his military obligation and returned to Fort Worth, they simply handed the whole practice over to him. Their dreams for a law firm named Bunkley, Bedford, and Davis thus ended.

For Davis the move to Fort Worth was fortuitous. With only two other African American attorneys in town in those early days, he affiliated with the J. L. Turner Legal Association in Dallas and drove regularly to its monthly meetings. Davis's practice in Fort Worth continued for more than five decades and brought him acclaim, notably for his role in the Mansfield public school desegregation case.[46]

In 1997 Davis was inducted into the National Bar Association's Hall of Fame, six years after Bedford received that honor, and in 2001 Charlye O. Farris was also inducted into the Hall of Fame. Bedford and Bunkley recognized talent when they saw it.

Heman Sweatt's successful lawsuit to be admitted to the all-white University of Texas Law School had made it apparent that the separate but equal doctrine, certainly as it related to public education, could not withstand continued legal challenge. Victorious in *Sweatt v. Painter* in 1950 and recognizing the advantage it now held, the NAACP moved quickly. In Topeka, Kansas, a black third-grade student named Linda Brown had to walk a mile through a railroad switchyard to get to her all-black elementary school even though a white school was closer. When her father attempted to enroll her in the white school, the principal refused to accept her.

At the father's request, the NAACP represented his daughter, and in 1951 this case was one of four other similar lawsuits filed in Southern states and argued before the U.S. Supreme Court by Thurgood Marshall. After lengthy and anguished anticipation, in 1954 the Supreme Court delivered its decision in *Brown v. Board of Education*, citing, among other cases, *Sweatt v. Painter*. For the first time the court held that separate schools for black children were inherently unequal, even if the facilities were precisely the same as for white children. *Brown v. Board of Education* was the most significant Supreme Court decision of the twentieth century, one with implications for almost every aspect of American life and that had a significant impact in Dallas.[47]

The rejection of the separate but equal doctrine changed everything for African Americans and for American society. It unleashed forces and feelings that had long lain dormant in black communities, giving them for the first time a legal standing to address the wrongs of segregation. For white communities it created uncertainty and fear about the widespread ramifications of the new doctrine.

In much of the white community, the fears focused on the NAACP, whose Thurgood Marshall had argued the *Brown* case before the Supreme Court and was now determined to see the decision enforced. In many quarters the very mention of the organization conjured up images of radical activists, inspired perhaps by Communists, intent on causing trouble and upsetting the social order.

Dallas was the center of NAACP activities in Texas and the Southwest. It had been the official site of the Southwest Regional Office since 1947, with U. Simpson Tate as regional counsel and Donald Jones as executive secretary. Dallas was also the site of the State Conference headquarters, of which A. Maceo Smith was executive secretary. The Southwest and State offices were in the building with Durham and Bunkley at 2600 Flora St. The local chapter was strong, second in size only to the Houston branch. Its members included Durham and Juanita Craft, the latter a prolific organizer and excellent youth leader. Bedford joined the chapter as a matter of course.

Just as Durham provided an invaluable role model for Bedford, so did Craft. Some historians have observed that in the civil rights movement "men led, but women organized," and perhaps no woman more so in Texas than Craft and Lulu White, the leader of the Houston branch. Craft, who joined the NAACP in 1935 and became the state organizer in 1946, was the first black woman in Texas to be deputized to sell poll taxes.[48]

The city's black ministers, always a powerful force, exerted an important role in the Dallas chapter of the NAACP. Some of the newer NAACP members felt that the president, Rev. Bezeleel R. Riley, should be replaced by a younger man. In 1954 a woman named Dickie Foster, active in civic circles, encouraged Bedford to seek election as president. With support from other friends, he agreed to stand for the office. Bunkley gave a nominating speech on his behalf at the election meeting at a church. But veteran minister E. C. Estell of St. John Baptist Church spoke against a change. Rev. Riley should be reelected, he said, because the times were too perilous to place an untested younger man in this important position. His argument held sway; Riley was reelected.[49]

As it happened, in the summer of 1954, two months after the *Brown v. Board of Education* decision was announced, the NAACP held its forty-fifth national convention in Dallas. A Texas setting seemed entirely appropriate. The NAACP's interest in the state had been intense since its first days, when the brutal lynching and burning to death of Jesse Washington in 1916 in Waco had given the organization the impetus to launch its prolonged nationwide antilynching crusade.

The Dallas convention was attended by the nation's foremost African Americans. Gaining the most attention was Dr. Ralph Bunche, a high-ranking United Nations official and the first black to win the Nobel Peace Prize (1950). Thurgood Marshall and his wife, who were staying at the residence of A. Maceo Smith, were present, and so were NAACP executives Walter White and Roy E. Wilkins.

More than seven hundred delegates were in Dallas from June 29 to July 4, 1954, and they were in a celebratory mood because of the *Brown* decision. They foresaw immediate results that would extend beyond school desegregation to include even housing. Dr. George S. Mitchell, executive director of the Southern Regional Council, said Negroes should be placed on local and state school boards as soon as possible, and he seemed to expect that they would be. Robert L. Carter, chief assistant to Thurgood Marshall, predicted a quick end to segregation on buses, on streetcars, and in train depots. "Folks are getting tired of buses being jammed and Negroes having to climb all over everyone to get to the rear," he said. Herbert Hill, labor secretary for the NAACP, said the trade unions would be targeted right away, for their activities doomed Negroes to "the dirtiest and hardest work for the least money." Marshall, in saluting the *Brown* decision, said, "I, for one, do not intend to waste my time . . . with some politicians of the South who are willing to 'wreck the law of the land' for their own political ambitions."[50]

Holding such an event in a Southern city, where only the small Powell Hotel in the State-Thomas-Hall area accommodated blacks, presented many obstacles. Attendees had to rely on the hospitality of private families. The convention program advised that "upon registering, persons from out of town will be assigned stopping places [room accommodations] which have been investigated by the housing committee." The fee for those staying in private homes was $2.50 per night.[51] By the same token, finding space for sessions was also difficult. The main site was Estell's St. John Baptist Church, located at the intersection of Allen and Guillot in the Thomas-Hall area.

Dallas Mayor Robert L. Thornton gave a welcoming address to the delegates. Thurgood Marshall addressed a general session at Good Street Baptist Church on Wednesday, which attracted about eleven hundred "sweating people" crammed into the sanctuary, with another three to four hundred listening outside to loudspeakers.[52] Earlier that evening a dinner for the national board of directors, of which A. Maceo Smith was a member, was held at a place familiar to Bedford, the Moorland branch of the YMCA.

The closing ceremony on July 4 was open to the public, and some seventy-five hundred people, including a sprinkling of whites, attended it at the Sportatorium, an unglamorous, drafty, tin-roofed structure used for professional wrestling. Walter White, executive director, spoke, but the major address came from Dr. Bunche, who declared that "Negroes will never accept anything less than their full rights."[53] He was hopeful, though, for he believed that the "prejudice of whites against Negroes is more veneer than deep grain and can be pulled off."[54]

Delegates must have been heartened during the convention by news from one of the city's major hospitals. Catholic-owned and -operated St. Paul announced that, for the first time, it would permit black physicians to practice there. The city's eighteen African American physicians were asked to form a committee and select five from among them, which they did.[55]

Brown v. Board of Education had given rise to a naïve but understandable hope among African Americans throughout the South that public school segregation would abruptly end. Only two months after the Supreme Court decision, the Dallas branch of the NAACP sent by special delivery a petition to Dallas school superintendent W. T. White, citing the *Brown* ruling, requesting an end to segregated schools, and offering to help with the transition. "As we understand these principles, children of public school age—attending and entitled to attend public schools—cannot be denied admission to any schools or be required to attend any school solely because of race or color." The petition, signed by Rev. R. C. McNeil of the Dallas chapter and thirty-two black parents, requested a hearing on the matter before the Dallas school trustees. They were disappointed in the school system's response. In rejecting the petition, White described the *Brown* decision as "mere philosophy" that would not pertain to the Dallas schools because they operated under state law.[56]

A year later the Dallas branch of the NAACP moved again, this time more deliberately. Attorney Kenneth Holbert, representing the organization as its secretary and accompanied by about a dozen African American supporters, appeared at a school board meeting in July 1955 and presented a petition to the school board asking for "immediate steps leading to the early elimination of segregation in public schools." School board president Edwin L. Rippy responded in the same fashion as White had a year earlier, saying that the Dallas Independent School District (DISD) was studying desegregation, but it would not put up with "undue pressure" from any group. Holbert, emboldened by the Supreme Court's May 31, 1955, elaboration on *Brown* (*Brown II*), in which it decreed that desegregation should proceed with "all deliberate speed," replied that the NAACP would be "impatient and disturbed by any prolonged delay."[57]

It was obvious that recalcitrant school districts throughout the South must be taken to court to gain their compliance. As had been true for the *Allwright* and *Sweatt* cases, the first step was to find suitable plaintiffs: students who had been barred from attending the white schools nearest to their homes. This process began at least by December 1954 in anticipation of the fall 1955 school term. U. Simpson Tate, as the Southwest NAACP regional counsel and adviser to individual branches, instructed activists first to locate children who could be potential plaintiffs, then to reveal the plans to their parents. "Great patience should be exercised in your efforts to get them to agree to let their children be used in this undertaking," he emphasized.[58] Tate later regretted this letter and other overt appeals to find clients, for it was presented as confirmation of what critics alleged about the NAACP's soliciting of plaintiffs.

In Dallas, Durham was more careful. He obtained signed contracts from parents, in which they designated him to be the attorney representing their children.[59] Knowing the importance of the case, wanting to present as united a front as possible, and recognizing that the other members of the tight-knit African American legal community in Dallas would want to join him in the suit, Durham circulated word that they were all welcome to be listed as attorneys. Bedford did not hesitate to add his name. Thus, on the petition that soon resulted, Bedford's name appeared third on the list, following Durham's and Bunkley's. After Bedford's name were those of Holbert, Tate, Turner, Robert L. Carter, and, finally, Thurgood Marshall.

On September 5, 1955, parents who had signed a contract with Durham took twenty-four black schoolchildren to six white schools and tried to register them. All were rejected. These minors, supported by their parents, became the plaintiffs in the petition Durham, Bedford, and the others filed in federal court that month, seeking an injunction against Edwin L. Rippy, president of the trustees of the DISD; eight school board members; W. T. White, superintendent of schools; six principals of the schools where the students had been rejected; and the Dallas Independent School District itself.[60]

The case was heard on September 16 on the second floor of the downtown U.S. Post Office and Court House in the courtroom of eighty-six-year-old U.S. District Judge William Hawley Atwell. If this aging jurist seemed to have come from another century, in fact he had. He had been admitted to the bar in 1890. In 1898 as a Republican, he was appointed U.S. Attorney for the Northern District of Texas by President William McKinley. President Warren G. Harding named him a district judge for the Northern District in 1923. In his many years of service, he became a familiar figure of authority in Dallas, a judge who meticulously insisted on decorum and proper attire in his court and one who, despite being a Republican, typified the typical old-school Southern gentleman.

Some 250 spectators gathered to hear the arguments. Somewhat unexpectedly, it was the attorney for the school board, Andrew J. Thuss, who visibly irritated the judge because of his long-winded introductory statements. Thuss need not have worried, for the judge had already made up his mind. What Bedford remembered most about that day in court was that Atwell began reading his decision even before hearing concluding arguments from Durham or the other plaintiffs' attorneys.

Surprised, one of them had the nerve to interrupt Atwell, pointing out to the judge that he had not even heard their closing. Atwell instantly recognized the truth of the statement and apologized. Now he would hear from the plaintiffs.

"The facts are undisputed," said Durham in his opening comments. "No effort has been made by the school board to start desegregation." Sitting alongside him were Bedford and the other attorneys of record, including Marshall, who had come down from New York City for the hearing. The school board's refusal to desegregate, Durham said, had been entirely arbitrary. "And you have your mandate, your honor, that desegregation shall be started forthwith," Durham added. Marshall, whose appearance in the courtroom was described in the newspapers as a surprise, asserted that the education now being offered white and black students was not equal. It was essential, he declared, to take immediate steps to desegregate the classrooms, so that black children could be given an education equal to that of whites.[61]

Having now heard from the plaintiffs, Judge Atwell promptly began reading the same decision he had started earlier. He denied the request for an injunction, but he acknowledged that eventually, the public schools in Dallas would be desegregated because the Texas laws requiring segregation were now unconstitutional. Meanwhile, he said, the trustees and school district officials were still studying a proper plan to eliminate segregation, and they should be given time to do so.[62]

The decision was appealed to the Fifth Circuit Court of Appeals. The arguments of the school board's pleadings—unrelated to the legal questions—indicated the depth of the emotions involved. For instance, it was asked, could a black teacher assert control over white children? "It is the opinion of the Board that under the present state of agitation, stimulated in some instances by their parents, white children will not submit to discipline, direction and teaching by negro teachers. This problem must be realistically solved, and, if not, the position of the negro teacher will suffer and also the scholastic standing of the white student."[63] Another point made was that black children would be "more at ease under negro teachers." A sudden and drastic introduction of white teachers would "result in tension and interfere with the ability of the negro students to retain instruction and make adequate progress."[64]

Atwell's rejection of the NAACP suit was overturned on appeal in a 2-1 decision by the Fifth Circuit Court of Appeals. He had been premature in dismissing the case, the court ruled. He should have conducted a full hearing. Instead of setting a date for such a hearing, Atwell tried to have the school board and NAACP meet and settle the issues. Rippy and White refused. A long legal battle to desegregate the Dallas public schools in accordance with *Brown v. Board of Education* ensued, shuttling back and forth from federal courts in Dallas to the Fifth Circuit Court of Appeals and not ending for several decades.[65]

Bedford was later modest about his role in the suit. "I wasn't on the front line," he told a reporter who in 1989 was writing about Bedford's pioneering role in civil rights legislation in Dallas. "I sat on the second row. But I enjoyed the fact that I was there . . . even if it was to carry books."[66]

The man whom Bedford came to know during these proceedings, the NAACP chief legal counsel—destined to become the nation's first African American Supreme Court justice—had already become a familiar figure in Dallas. Bedford, still an untried lawyer himself, became acquainted with Thurgood Marshall in personal settings away from the courtroom. He found him to be lighthearted and jovial, "a regular guy" who liked to give nicknames to everyone around him, but at the same time a man burning with a desire to end Jim Crow education and to give African Americans the full privileges they should have as American citizens.[67]

Born in Baltimore, son of a schoolteacher mother and a Pullman porter father, Marshall had been something of a hell-raiser during his high school and undergraduate years. The hometown University of Maryland School of Law, at the Baltimore campus, rejected his application to enroll because of his color, so he went to Howard University School of Law instead and finished first in his class. In his career Marshall was a tireless, brilliant attorney. He started working for the NAACP in 1934 and soon had the satisfaction of winning a courtroom battle to force the desegregation of Maryland's law school (*Murray v. Pearson*, 1936), and later seeing its law library named for him. He later forced the law schools at the Universities of Missouri, Oklahoma, and Texas to desegregate. Marshall became the NAACP's chief legal officer in 1938.

Then in 1954 came the great victory of *Brown v. Board of Education*. With that triumph, Marshall and the NAACP jumped to the front pages of the nation's newspapers in a way that was frightening to many public officials. But it was encouraging for blacks, bringing a boom in NAACP membership. The membership rolls of its Texas branches soared from 9,342 in 1953 to 16,672 by early 1956.[68]

In 1956 Bedford's friend L. Clifford Davis, who had taken over the NAACP office in Fort Worth at the organization's behest, became embroiled in an effort to desegregate the Mansfield, Texas, schools. Acting as the NAACP lawyer and representing three high school students, Davis brought suit in federal district court in late 1955 to force the small town—twenty miles southeast of Fort Worth, with a population of about 1,100 whites and 350 blacks—to open the high school to black students, who until then were bused to a Fort Worth high school. U.S. District Judge Joe Estes ruled against the plaintiffs, but in June 1956 the Fifth Circuit Court of Appeals reversed that judgment, declaring that the plaintiffs and all other Negro minors of the same class had the same rights as members of the white race to attend the school.[69]

When the three students attempted to enroll at the high school in fall 1956, an unruly, hostile mob of anti-integration protesters, some of them armed, stood in their way, and the students could not get inside. At this critical point the mayor and the police chief left town. When the students again tried to enroll the next day, the mob had grown to about five hundred, and scores of radio, television, and newspaper reporters were there. Demonstrators roughed up newsmen from Dallas and Fort Worth, an assistant district attorney, and an Episcopalian minister who was urging restraint. Bands of local whites created roadblocks to prevent "outside agitators" from entering town. Three effigies were hung, one downtown, one that stayed for days on the high school flagpole, and a third on an outdoor light above the school's front door.

Davis sent a desperate telegram to Governor Allan Shivers requesting assistance to uphold order. A reluctant Shivers, an ardent segregationist who called the violent situation an "orderly protest," sent two Texas Rangers and encouraged school officials to expel any student whose attendance could "reasonably be calculated to incite violence." When members of the press asked President Eisenhower, busy with his 1956 reelection campaign, about his reaction to these events, he warned only that "extremists on both sides" must moderate their behavior. Davis's telegram to the U.S. Justice Department seeking help from the federal government was stonewalled.[70]

Faced with violence if they attempted to enter the Mansfield school, the students declared that they would return to the Fort Worth school. The threatening, armed Mansfield mob, aided by intransigent local officials and unchallenged by state or federal authorities, had prevented enforcement of a federal court order. Mansfield was a test run for Little Rock, Arkansas, where, a year later, demonstrators also tried to turn away black students entering school under court order. Eisenhower, under growing pressure, sent U.S. Army troops to Little Rock to enforce the court-ordered desegregation. The Mansfield schools, though, were not desegregated until 1965.[71]

Knowing that further attempts to desegregate lay ahead, Governor Shivers actively tried to maintain the status quo. One of his approaches was to advise that integration meant all-black schools would be shut down. Many of the state's black citizens and educators, he contended, wanted to maintain their jobs and their separate schools. He was widely quoted as saying that Dr. W. R. Banks, by this time president emeritus of Prairie View, had begged him, "Don't let them take away our schools." Dr. Banks heatedly denied that he had ever made such a statement.[72]

Texas Attorney General John Ben Shepperd was furious over Thurgood Marshall's criticisms of Governor Shivers, which also implicated Shepperd as his legal adviser. He called Marshall's comments "just another concerted scheme by the NAACP to stir up hatred among the people of Texas."[73] Within days Shepperd announced a statewide investigation of all NAACP branches in Texas, with the Mansfield desegregation effort a central target. On September 21, 1956, he went to Tyler, in East Texas, and won a temporary restraining order from State District Judge Otis T. Dunagan that forced the NAACP to cease its operations in Texas. Shepperd charged the NAACP with barratry (instigating or soliciting lawsuits), operating in the state without a permit, illegally profiting from its Texas operations, and failing to pay taxes.[74]

The Dallas NAACP's upstairs office at 2600 Flora Street was shut down immediately. Bedford and other African American lawyers received letters accusing them of practicing barratry and threatening them with disbarment. Bedford vividly recalled being "very disturbed." He wondered what he could do if he lost his license and concluded that he would try to teach school.[75]

Marshall flew to Dallas that weekend, saying he had "dropped everything else" to work on the case and calling it "the most important battle on the integration front being waged today." He was in these early moments uncertain just how the NAACP would respond, but he told the *Dallas Morning News* that he was conferring with the other NAACP attorneys in Dallas to see what action to take. One of them was Louis A. Bedford Jr., and the others included Durham, U. Simpson Tate, J. L. Turner Jr., and Kenneth F. Holbert.[76] Bedford, Turner, and Holbert were not on the NAACP payroll, but they were a part of the informal think tank that customarily responded when called to consider such matters. The group's strategy session lasted until 3:00 AM Monday. Marshall, after little or no sleep, departed at 7:00 AM for New York City.[77]

The hearing over whether a temporary injunction against the NAACP should be granted lasted more than a month, opening in Tyler on September 28, 1956, amid a chaotic atmosphere. Outside a contingent of segregationist White Citizens Council demonstrators held Confederate flags and placards criticizing the NAACP. A smaller group of curious black spectators was also on hand. A large number of newsmen—reporters, photographers, and television cameramen—were there, too. Durham was the lead counsel for the NAACP, assisted by Bunkley and Tate. Ever present, though, was Marshall, directing the strategy and sometimes speaking to the court himself. Bedford, although not an official member of the NAACP team, occasionally made the trip from Dallas to lend support.[78] The nearest Bedford came to being an official member was when Durham and Bunkley considered sending Kenneth Holbert and him to Austin to file a document with the State Supreme Court, but the need disappeared.

Because there were practically no accommodations in Tyler for the four NAACP attorneys, they usually drove the 100 miles from Dallas for the day's hearing, then returned at night. Sometimes they found private accommodations, often through the efforts of Henry M. Morgan, who owned a barber college in Tyler. An African American attorney in Tyler, Charles Coleman, made his office available to the NAACP lawyers during the day. On the frequent occasions when the team drove back to Dallas late at night, they were acutely aware that their safety might be jeopardized in this deep East Texas area. Consequently, they armed themselves.

The challenge was formidable, for the state had made surprise raids on the homes and offices of NAACP officials and amassed considerable evidence showing that, indeed, the organization had actively sought out clients for the desegregation cases. State agents were keen on obtaining membership lists, and the NAACP chapters were just as determined not to release them, for fear of reprisals against individual members. More than four hundred exhibits obtained from NAACP files and testimony taken from courts of inquiry were admitted into evidence, despite objections from the NAACP attorneys. Testimony included such damaging statements as one by a seventeen-year-old African American student from Mansfield, who was quoted as saying to a reporter, "Mister, I don't want to go school in Mansfield. I'd rather go to school among my own people in Fort Worth. But I'll go to Mansfield if the NAACP makes me." And then there were the letters that U. Simpson Tate had sent out to branches throughout the state, in which he wrote of the need to find students to serve as plaintiffs. Two plaintiffs in the NAACP's suit against Texarkana College, a junior college on the Texas side of the border, testified that they had never met Tate, did not hire him, and did not know that he had filed a suit on their behalf until they read about it in the newspaper.[79]

The NAACP, Marshall pointed out in his closing argument, had done nothing more than try to get the people of Texas to obey the law of the land. Durham's closing comments were more emotional, bringing tears to some eyes in the courtroom as he described the heavy hand of the state's attorney general in gathering evidence.[80]

When the hearing was over, though, Judge Dunagan ruled against the NAACP, finding that it had violated the state's barratry statutes, had illegally engaged in political and lobbying activities, and was a profit-making organization that had failed to pay the state franchise taxes and other taxes. He enjoined the NAACP in Texas from soliciting funds for lawsuits, from requesting individuals to file lawsuits, from organizing chapters, or even from applying to the secretary of state for a permit to do business.[81]

For eight months the 102 local branches of the NAACP in Texas were shut down, unable to function, pending a hearing on a permanent injunction, which caused great consternation in the national office. The picture brightened, though, when a new state attorney general, Will Wilson, replaced John Ben Shepperd. Wilson had friends in the Dallas African American community. When he had successfully run for Dallas County district attorney just after the war, Bunkley had worked actively in his campaign. As district attorney, Wilson had worked with Durham as a special prosecutor on several cases. Now, as attorney general, he met with Marshall and Durham and worked out a compromise. Wilson allowed the organization to continue its operations, and he didn't challenge its nonprofit status. The NAACP agreed not to violate the state's barratry statutes, to pay the state franchise tax, and to comply with all state laws.[82]

The eight-month ban had an almost disastrous impact on the state's NAACP branches. The number of branches declined to forty-six, and membership dropped from 16,866 in 1956 to 7,785 in the following year. The momentum gained following the *Brown* decision was lost.[83]

For Bedford the experience at Tyler was especially meaningful. He had seen first-hand the behind-the-scenes maneuvering and courtroom strategies of the nation's most brilliant black attorney, Marshall. He had seen, as well, the wizardry of the man he was more and more considering a father figure, Durham, who, ironically, bestowed upon young Bedford a nickname he never understood: "Poppa."

In the 1950s Bedford's views about race relations had matured, as he realized—through his law practice and through his general experiences as an adult—the injustices suffered by African Americans. With the Korean War he had seen, for the second time in his life, men he had known at Prairie View risk their lives in war. Many of his friends, after completing the ROTC program there, became officers and NCOs and within a few years distinguished themselves in combat in Korea. They were "bleeding and dying in the [1950s] for a segregated society, same as World War II," Bedford said. Their war stories, when they returned, captivated him, and the injustice of their sacrifice for a society that did not recognize their full citizenship made a great impact on him.[84]

Later Bedford believed that for all the good it did, the immediate impact of the *Brown* decision and efforts to gain compliance with it only worsened relations between whites and blacks. Many whites, as well as local and state governments, believing that their backs now were to the wall, stiffened in their resistance to desegregation and grew more skeptical in their attitudes toward blacks.

"I never felt that the issue was integration," he said years later. "The issue was *desegregation*, and there was a difference between the two. The fact that the news media kept putting the word 'integration' into the headlines was unfortunate. Integration meant that black Americans wanted to be integrated into the white community. The idea of whites and blacks integrating was frightening to many whites. Desegregation says something different: it says that you can't tell me I can't go somewhere just because of my race or color. We were United States citizens, and we had a right to go where others went. Our lawsuits were to desegregate, not to integrate."[85]

1. Advertisements, *Dallas Express*, June 3, 1950, and June 2, 1951.
2. "Negro Serves on Petit Jury for the First Time in the History of Dallas County," *Dallas Express*, Apr. 16, 1949.
3. "Report on Negro Housing Market Data, 1950," Folder 4, Box 1, Dallas Negro Chamber of Commerce Papers, Dallas Public Library.
4. An extended analysis of these bombings is Jim Schutze's study *The Accommodation: The Politics of Race in an American City* (Secaucus: Citadel Press, 1986); see also Payne, *Big D*, 296–301.
5. Payne, *Big D*, 295.
6. *Dallas Express* advertisement, June 3, 1950.
7. William H. Wilson, *Hamilton Park: A Planned Black Community in Dallas* (Baltimore: Johns Hopkins University Press, 1998), 28–32.
8. Bunkley quotes are from Wilson, *Hamilton Park*, 55. Hamilton Park is discussed fully in that book.
9. Tushnet, *NAACP's Legal Strategy*, 107–109.
10. Advertisement, *Dallas Express*, Sept. 2, 1950.
11. Bedford, interview, Dec. 22, 2005.
12. Ibid.
13. Louis A. Bedford Jr., interview by Darwin Payne, Mar. 14, 2006.
14. "Negroes File Suit to Use State Parks," *Dallas Morning News*, Dec. 30, 1949; "Negroes Lose Decision on Parks Segregation," *Dallas Morning News*, Sept. 12, 1950.
15. Bedford, interview, Dec. 22, 2005.
16. Ibid.

17. State Board of Law Examiners to Bedford, May 24, 1951, "L. A. Bedford Jr. Personal" binder, Bedford Papers.
18. Announcement photograph and caption, *Dallas Express*, July 21, 1951.
19. Bedford, interview, Dec. 22, 2005.
20. "Friends for Rivers Fund Raising Committee" letter, signed by Rivers's son, L. Clayton Rivers Jr. It is undated but evidently was written in the late 1960s. "J. L. Turner Legal Society History of Black Lawyers" binder, Bedford Papers.
21. Bedford, interview, Dec. 22, 2005.
22. Ibid.
23. Louis A. Bedford Jr., interview by Darwin Payne, July 21, 2006.
24. Ibid., Dec. 22, 2005.
25. Ibid.
26. Ibid.
27. Ibid.
28. *Bedford Oral History Interview*, 23.
29. Ibid.
30. Bedford, interview, Dec. 22, 2005.
31. Ibid.
32. Ibid.
33. *Bedford Oral History Interview*, 25.
34. Louis A. Bedford Jr., interview by Darwin Payne, Mar. 24, 2006; undated letter to Ms. Frances Williams, "J. L. Turner Legal Society History of Black Lawyers" binder, Bedford Papers.
35. "John L. Turner Sr., Negro Attorney, Dies at Age of 82," *Dallas Morning News*, Dec. 3, 1951.
36. Minutes of J. L. Turner Legal Association, May 4, 1952, "J. L. Turner Legal Society History of Black Lawyers" binder, Bedford Papers.
37. Gillette, "NAACP in Texas," 137–38.
38. Minutes of J. L. Turner Legal Association, May 4, 1952.
39. Minutes of J. L. Turner Legal Association, May 20, 1952, "J. L. Turner Legal Society History of Black Lawyers" binder, Bedford Papers.
40. Ibid.
41. Minutes of Dallas Bar Association, Jan. 12, 1956, Bedford Papers.
42. Louis A. Bedford Jr., interview by Darwin Payne, Feb. 1, 2006.
43. Ibid.
44. W. J. Durham, "Citizens' Committee to Abolish Discrimination against Negro Women in Dallas Department Stores," circular letter, July 27, 1953, John O. and Ethelyn M. Chisum Collection, Box 1, Folder 2, Texas/Dallas History & Archives Division, J. Erik Jonsson Central Library, Dallas; quoted in Phillips, *White Metropolis*, 146.
45. Ibid.
46. Louis A. Bedford Jr., interview by Darwin Payne, Mar. 28, 2006.
47. *Brown v. Board of Education*, 347 U.S. 483 (1954).
48. Hine, *Black Victory*, 38.
49. Louis A. Bedford Jr., interview by Darwin Payne, Feb. 2, 2006.
50. "Interracial Meetings in South Urged to Speed Desegregation," *Dallas Daily Times Herald*, July 1,

1954; "Train Depot Segregation End Foreseen," *Dallas Daily Times Herald*, July 2, 1954; "Texas Unions Face Attack by NAACP," *Dallas Daily Times Herald*, July 3, 1954.

51. Official program for NAACP convention, Folder 2, Box 26, Juanita Craft Collection, Dallas Public Library.

52. "Interracial Meetings in South."

53. "Negroes Want Full Rights," *Dallas Express*, July 10, 1954.

54. "Bunche Sees End of Race Prejudice," *Dallas Morning News*, July 5, 1954.

55. "White Hospital to Admit Negro Doctors," *Dallas Express*, July 3, 1954. In 2005 St. Paul was consolidated into the University of Texas Southwestern Medical Center at Dallas as part of UT Southwestern University Hospital.

56. "Schools Petitioned to End Segregation," *Dallas Morning News*, Sept. 2, 1954.

57. "Rippy Vows Study of Desegregation," *Dallas Morning News*, July 14, 1955.

58. Tate letter quoted in Gillette, "NAACP in Texas," 306–307.

59. Ibid., 296.

60. *Albert Bell, et al., v. Edwin L. Rippy*, 133 F. Supp. 811 (N.D. Tex. 1955).

61. "Judge Atwell Upholds Delay in Integration," *Dallas Morning News*, Sept. 17, 1955.

62. *Bell v. Rippy*, 133 F. Supp. 811 (N.D. Tex. 1955).

63. Undated pleading, *Bell v. Rippy*, L. A. Bedford Jr. personal files.

64. Ibid., and *Bell v. Rippy*, 146 F. Supp. 486 (N.D. Tex. 1956).

65. Glenn M. Linden, *Desegregating Schools in Dallas: Four Decades in the Federal Courts* (Dallas: Three Forks Press, 1995), 22.

66. "Judicial Pioneer Recalls Milestones in Civil Rights," *Dallas Morning News*, Feb. 24, 1989.

67. *Bedford Oral History Interview*, 41.

68. Gillette, "NAACP in Texas," 255.

69. *Jackson v. Rawdon*, U.S. District Court, Texas, Civ. No. 3152, Nov. 21, 1955, 135 F. Supp. 936; *Jackson v. Rawdon*, U.S. Court of Appeals, Fifth Circuit, June 28, 1956, Civ. No. 15927. The Mansfield desegregation case is discussed fully by Robyn Duff Ladino in *Desegregating Texas Schools: Eisenhower, Shivers, and the Crisis at Mansfield High* (Austin: University of Texas Press, 1996).

70. Ricky F. Dobbs, *Yellow Dogs and Republicans: Allan Shivers and Texas Two-Party Politics* (College Station: Texas A&M University Press, 2005), 139; Ladino, *Desegregating Texas Schools*, 103, 107, 120.

71. Ladino, *Desegregating Texas Schools*, 116; s.v. "Mansfield School Desegregation Incident," in *New Handbook of Texas*, 4:489.

72. "Shivers Statement Denied," *Dallas Express*, July 24, 1954.

73. Ladino, *Desegregating Texas Schools*, 118.

74. "NAACP's Activity in Texas Blocked by Judge's Order," *Dallas Morning News*, Sept. 22, 1956; Ladino, *Desegregating Texas Schools*, 133; *State of Texas v. the National Association for the Advancement of Colored People, a Corporation, et al.*, 56 U.S. District Court 649 (1957) No. 56-649.

75. "Court Order Closes Dallas NAACP Office," *Dallas Morning News*, Sept. 23, 1956; *Bedford Oral History Interview*, 38.

76. "Court Order Closes Dallas NAACP Office."

77. "Group Maps Strategy for NAACP Side," *Dallas Morning News*, Sept. 24, 1956.

78. Gillette, "NAACP in Texas," 297.
79. Ibid., 268, 296, 306–307.
80. Ibid., 309–310, 314–15.
81. Ibid., 315–16.
82. Ibid., 320–21.
83. Ibid., 331.
84. Bedford, interview, Feb. 2, 2006.
85. Ibid.

5

TURNING THE CORNER

In the summer of 1954, a young entertainer in the early stages of a sensational career on stage and screen came to Dallas. Sammy Davis Jr. was performing for two weeks as an opening act for the legendary comedian Jack Benny at the cavernous State Fair Music Hall. Davis showcased his talents in an act known as the Will Mastin Trio Starring Sammy Davis Jr. Despite the inclusive billing, which included his "uncle" (Will Mastin, Sammy Sr.'s good friend) and his father (the "Trio" part), the show revolved almost entirely around the energetic Davis, a gifted singer, dancer, drummer, and impersonator—and later, of course, a movie star. African American patrons who wanted to see the show were relegated by custom to an upper corner of the hall's balcony. Because of the paucity of hotels and restaurants for blacks, lodging for members of the Will Mastin Trio was privately arranged. Davis stayed at the home of the executive secretary of the Negro Chamber of Commerce, John Rice.

As a thoughtful host, Mrs. Rice became concerned because of her guest's isolation in segregated Dallas. No matter how great his stage success before predominantly white patrons, the city's segregated restaurants and places of entertainment were off-limits to him. Mrs. Rice called Bedford and three or four of his friends to give Davis an evening of entertainment. Bedford was delighted at this opportunity. On the agreed-upon evening, he and his selected friends stopped by the Rice house and picked up the nimble performer for a night at the Empire Room on Hall Street. Davis, happy to be entertained for a change, proved to be personable and light-hearted while mixing easily with his new friends. At a lull in the Empire Room's scheduled show, Davis, unable to restrain himself, took the stage with no prompting and put on an energetic, free show for the patrons, singing and playing the drums with energy and joy. It was an evening Bedford and his friends never forgot.[1]

The night was unusual only because of the presence of the high-profile Davis, for as an eligible young black man in Dallas, Bedford enjoyed an active social life. He spent many evenings at a private club he and a number of other young business- and professional people had founded, the Nassau Club. They rented space for the club at what had formerly been a large private residence on Forest Avenue (later renamed Martin Luther King Jr. Boulevard) in South Dallas. (The Forest Avenue address was not far from the area where the 1950 South Dallas bombings had occurred, which in 1954 was rapidly completing its transition from white to black.)[2] Here Bedford was surrounded by friends. The Nassau Club's president was Bedford's close pal C. B. Bunkley Jr. Its treasurer was a man who had also become a warm friend, Haywood Sparks, an accountant whom Bedford had come to know after representing him in a legal matter.

The Nassau Club was a handy place for entertainment and fellowship. Music, dancing, food, and drink could be enjoyed in a comfortable setting. Bedford, an excellent dancer who enjoyed such social scenes, was a familiar figure at the club. When the Chicago Bears and New York Giants came to Dallas in August 1957 to play an exhibition football game at the nearby Cotton Bowl, five of the Bears' African American players stopped by. Bedford was among the several Nassau Club members who enjoyed their company that evening. His picture appeared with them in a group photograph in the *Dallas Express*.[3] The happy, event-filled nights he spent at the Nassau Club were so numerous that years later Bedford did not even remember the photograph with the football players.

One particular night at the Nassau Club at about the same time was unforgettable, for it was the evening he met the woman who would become his wife. At age thirty Bedford did not seem close to settling down. "I was trying to save up my marriage fund," he later said. He had vowed that he would not marry until he had a nest egg of a thousand dollars in the bank.[4]

He was still working on this fund when the young woman, Velma Bates, a teacher at Paul L. Dunbar Elementary School and a native Dallasite, stopped by the Nassau Club with a fellow teacher, Marguerite Williams, and her husband, Bernard. Velma, a beautiful and dignified young woman, caught the eye of Bedford, who lost no time in getting an introduction, and the two talked at some length that night. In the weeks that followed, Bedford ardently pursued the somewhat reluctant teacher. Although Velma had not known Bedford, she knew of his reputation as one of the city's few black attorneys.

Soon the spark became mutual, and one evening Bedford showed up with an engagement ring at her house near Dunbar School. Velma said yes. The wedding took place on June 7, 1958, at the Maria Morgan Branch of the YWCA, 3515 State Street. Bedford's pal Haywood Sparks was best man.[5] Velma's childhood minister, Reverend Bell, who moved from the city, returned to preside over the ceremony, and her friend Maxine Toles was maid of honor. After the wedding Velma joined her husband's church, New Hope Baptist, where he and his family were fixtures and would continue to be for many years. She became an enthusiastic member and a soprano in the church choir, an activity she was still engaged in half a century later.

Velma's parents, Hazel L. Bates and Carl Bates, both of whom lived in South Dallas, were divorced. Velma had been reared primarily by her grandparents in a neighborhood immediately north of Fair Park near Haskell Avenue. Although her mother lived next door, she worked "all the time," as Velma remembered it. As faithful churchgoers, Velma's grandparents took her with them to services three or four times a week. Velma's elementary school, then called Pacific Avenue School (later named Fanny C. Harris Elementary School), was near enough for her to walk. After that came two years at Julia C. Frazier School, and then in 1942 it was time for high school.

Bedford had been fortunate in living close to Booker T. Washington High School, but there was no high school for black students in Velma's neighborhood. She had to make a daily thirty- to forty-five-minute ride via bus and streetcar to the still-new Lincoln High School in South Dallas. Lincoln's opening in January 1939 had been postponed by several days because of bomb threats from disgruntled whites. With the beginning of school in September 1942, the threats continued. "They threatened it so often that I was afraid to go," Velma recalled later.[6]

Velma was a fine student, though, and upon graduation she enrolled in Bishop College in Marshall, Texas. She graduated *cum laude*, then returned to Dallas to accept a teaching position at Paul Dunbar Elementary School.

Velma fit in easily with her husband's family. The young couple spent much time at the house on Thomas Avenue. Before getting married, they often went to affairs catered by Bedford's father. One of Velma's fondest memories of her father-in-law was his excellence as a chef.[7]

The couple found an apartment on Meadow Street just off Hatcher Street in

South Dallas, a stone's throw from the cemetery where Bedford's maternal grandfather, M. M. Rodgers, was buried. They lived at the Southern Terrace Apartments for about a year, until they found a small, two-bedroom frame house with a large backyard, on Eugene Street at the corner of Diamond, a block from Central Expressway and near Charles Rice Elementary School. Bedford bought the house from the credit union of the Missouri-Kansas-Texas (Katy) Railroad employees, which not long before had foreclosed on it. The eighty-three-dollar monthly payments Bedford would have to make gave him some concern that the same thing might happen to him.[8]

Bedford found the house through a connection he had with the manager of the Katy Railroad credit union, a white man named Hubert Miller, who, as Bedford remembered him, was "a very, very kind fellow." Miller began to give Bedford some of the credit union's routine legal work, such as collecting debts and initiating foreclosures. Bedford was grateful for his support and business.[9] Miller also owned a furniture storeroom in the city's warehouse district (now the West End), and the Bedfords took advantage of his bargain prices to furnish their house, along with pieces they obtained from family members.[10]

The newlyweds enjoyed a wide circle of friends, including the Bunkleys, with whom they would share vacations, frequently in Colorado. Eventually, the two couples built houses three doors apart in the Cedar Crest area of Oak Cliff.

In Dallas and in other Southern cities, the criminal justice system, just like education, had separate if unofficial standards for blacks and whites. If a black man was accused of committing a crime against a white person, particularly a rape, police took an immediate active interest. Prosecutors routinely sought the maximum punishment. But for black-on-black crime, the situation was different. Police and prosecutors were almost indifferent. This lack of interest in prosecuting such crimes concerned black community leaders, who regularly urged more vigorous prosecution of black perpetrators, no matter what color the victim. Their pleas changed little or nothing. Sometimes, to ensure more effective prosecution, black families—with the district attorney's approval—would hire a lawyer, such as W. J. Durham, to act as a special prosecutor.

Bedford became more aware of this situation as he spent hours at the police station and courthouse. He also learned a new term that surprised him, "misdemeanor murder." This referred to a murder in which both the perpetrator and the victim were black, a crime so little regarded by the predominantly white legal system as to gain that nickname.

When a black man was accused of a crime against a white person, particularly a white woman and more particularly a *young* white woman, the pursuit of justice was swift and severe. One of the most sensational criminal trials of 1950s Dallas, one that rattled both the white and the black communities, involved just such a case. Its emotional impact, the manners in which it was publicized and prosecuted, and the outcome made Bedford's friend and mentor, Durham, who represented the defendant, swear afterward never again to involve himself in a criminal case.[11]

The crime occurred on Thursday evening, October 1, 1953, when a young mother, Venice Loraine Parker, waiting for a bus on Lemmon Avenue after leaving her job at a five-and-dime, was grabbed, taken beneath a bridge, raped, and left mortally wounded with a slashed throat. The twenty-nine-year-old woman was said to have gasped to a police officer with her dying breath that "a Negro took me under the bridge and slashed my throat."[12]

Much of the city had already been on edge before this brutal murder. Newspaper stories for the past two months had reported that Negro prowlers—sometimes said to be naked—were terrorizing Dallas women. Exacerbating the crime of Venice Parker's murder was the fact that she was the mother of a four-year-old son and the wife of an unemployed shipping clerk being treated for tuberculosis. In an apparent effort to save a nickel on her bus fare, she had walked to a more remote bus stop to take advantage of a zone change and lesser fare.

Shortly before the crime had been reported, police dispatchers broadcast an unrelated alert to officers to pick up a suspicious black male, wearing a white T-shirt and dark trousers, seen walking along Lemmon Avenue not far from the bridge. Such a person—only vaguely described, but already being sought in the vicinity of the killing—became the immediate suspect in the Parker homicide.

News of the crime immediately prompted a huge public response. On the night of the crime, some three to four hundred private citizens joined scores of police officers in searching for the assailant. Crowds at the crime scene were so large that four officers had to direct traffic. Searchlights probed a broad area. Police officers were kept overtime on the job.

Prowler complaints and tips swamped the police and sheriff's offices. In a broad sweep of possible suspects, including a dozen on the first day after the crime, police jailed and interrogated scores of black men. Many alarmed citizens armed themselves, and hardware and sporting goods stores reported a rush of gun and ammunition purchases. Friday afternoon the *Times Herald's* sensationalized news coverage, with huge banner headlines, inflamed the situation; on subsequent days the newspaper provided pictures of a married couple buying a pistol, of two elderly women aiming a pistol, and of two police officers bearing a shotgun.[13] For four consecutive days, Police Chief Carl Hansson urged citizens not to be trigger happy, but he did not discourage them from having firearms. "Be sure, if you do fire, that it is only at someone known to have murdered, raped, burglarized or robbed, and who is fleeing from the scene of his crime," he said.[14]

By Friday detectives were holding twenty-three African American suspects for questioning. Dozens of others had been questioned and released. "We still have about one hundred more Negroes to check on. We'll investigate each one as we have time to get to him," said Homicide Captain Will Fritz. (Ten years later Fritz gained national fame as the principal interrogator of Lee Harvey Oswald.) On Friday evening forty unmarked automobiles equipped with two-way ham radios patrolled the city streets along with the enhanced police patrols.[15]

The *Dallas Express* rivaled the *Times Herald* in the size of its banner headlines. In one of several articles with "Sex Slayer" headlines, the *Express* proclaimed, "The citizenry of Dallas is in a state of panic."[16] Two weeks later the newspaper recorded that although "hundreds of Negro men have been arrested and questioned," no evidence had been found. This led to a question asked in a page-one headline: "Is the Sex Slayer a Negro?" The newspaper observed that since no leads had been found, perhaps the police were following false leads. The murderer, according to the *Express*, might have been a white man posing as a Negro.[17]

But in late January 1954, nearly four months after the murder, a break came. While investigating the robbery of a service station, routine questioning of a nineteen-year-old former employee, Tommy Lee Walker, had led to the subject of Venice Parker's murder. After two hours of questioning by Fritz and without benefit of legal counsel, Walker, an African American, confessed to the murder but denied raping the victim, despite hospital reports that she had been raped. Walker said that after he forced the woman under the bridge and took her money, she had suffered her fatal injury because she started to run "and jumped into my knife." Fritz said there were elements in Walker's confession "that only the killer could have known—the way he threw away a comb and compact from her purse, for instance."[18]

The common belief in the black community that police routinely used high-pressure tactics to coerce African American suspects into confessions, even false ones, prompted widespread concern that this is what had happened to Walker, who was young and unsophisticated. Durham, sharing that alarm, stepped up, evidently at the request of Walker's family, to give him legal representation. Based on the personal investigation he had made in the previous few days, he said, he was "convinced that he is not the boy" guilty of the crime. "If I thought he were guilty I would not take the case," he said.[19]

Just before the grand jury was to consider the case, Walker, undoubtedly under Durham's advice, repudiated his confession, saying he made it because he "was afraid." He told newspaper reporters that at the time of the slaying, he had been at the home of his fourteen-year-old girlfriend, Mary Louise Smith, an evening he particularly remembered because she gave birth to their child the next day.[20]

Durham quickly moved to suppress other evidence that was to be presented to the grand jury. He argued that police took Walker from his home near Hall Street without an arrest warrant. Furthermore, the police's confiscation of two pairs of pants and a T-shirt from the home violated Walker's Fourth and Fifth Amendment rights and should be thrown out as evidence. Durham's motion before a district judge was ignored.[21]

With the first confession repudiated, Walker reportedly failed a lie detector test. A few hours later, he was said to have confessed to the crime once more, this time in a conversation with District Attorney Henry Wade. (Durham told Bedford that Walker was warned that only a confession would save him from the electric chair.)[22]

The grand jury, as expected, indicted Walker for murder. Durham tried in vain to dismiss the indictment on the grounds of racial discrimination, based on the fact that only one African American sat on the grand jury and that no African American served on the commission to select the grand jurors.[23]

At a bond hearing in March, the courtroom of Criminal District Judge Henry King overflowed with a crowd of 250 spectators, the majority of them black. Some of the spectators told a reporter for the *Dallas Express* that they had come to see for themselves "if the boy" had been "beaten."[24] When the trial began with jury selection later that month, the courtroom was similarly filled with predominantly African American spectators.

Bedford, following the case closely, was there, too. At one point an assistant district attorney reproached scores of African Americans waiting outside the courtroom door and urged them to leave. Sheriff Bill Decker, who was there, quickly countered the official. They had as much right to be there as anyone else, Decker told him. Besides, he pointed out, he, not the district attorney, was the official designated to maintain order.[25]

Crowds continued to fill the courtroom throughout the weeklong trial, even on the first day of jury selection. On Friday's first full day of testimony, after an all-white, twelve-man jury had been selected from a panel of 150 (women were still not eligible to serve on petit juries in Texas until November 1954), District Attorney Wade, heading the prosecution himself, introduced Walker's first repudiated confession as evidence. Durham made a strenuous protest, but Judge King accepted the confession for the jury's consideration. Two surprise witnesses appeared: the first said that from her passing car, shortly before the murder occurred, she had seen Mrs. Parker walking fifty to a hundred feet behind a black man she identified as Walker. The second witness, who had also passed by in a car, identified Walker as the man he had seen a block from the site of the crime. The repudiated confession and the two witnesses, whose identification of Walker was based on quick glances in the dark from their passing cars, constituted the main part of the prosecution's case against Walker.[26]

Durham, assisted throughout the trial by J. L. Turner Jr. and Ken Holbert, presented nineteen witnesses in two days, a number of whom gave alibis for Walker. One of them was Walker's young girlfriend, who testified that he had been with her on the night of the crime. The critical part of the defense came when Walker took the witness stand himself, denying any involvement in the murder and claiming that both of his confessions had been given out of fear.[27]

On Monday a huge crowd of African Americans, in a line that extended four deep for an entire city block, waited to get into the courtroom to hear the verdict.

Some had arrived as early as 7:00 AM, encouraged by the fact that many African American churches had formed prayer groups for Walker. When the jury foreman read the verdict and sentence—guilty, sentenced to death in the electric chair—Walker showed no emotion. But many of the spectators were emotional. Many of them left the courtroom prayerfully and in tears.[28]

U. Simpson Tate, the NAACP's Southwest Region counsel, watched the entire trial. As far as he was concerned, Judge King had made a consistent effort to see that Walker was given a fair trial. "I believe Judge Henry King did everything in his power to keep it on the highest judicial level," Tate said.[29]

Durham believed just the opposite. In his appeal Durham noted exceptions to the trial court action that filled 410 pages of the 12,000-page record. His appeals were unsuccessful, for the Court of Criminal Appeals held that there were no reversible errors. Durham's appeal to the U.S. Supreme Court was denied, as that court refused to review the case.[30]

On May 11, 1956, Walker died in the electric chair at the state penitentiary in Huntsville. When the warden asked him if he had any last words, Walker said, "I'm innocent."[31]

Durham was devastated, convinced that the white man's system of justice had failed to give Walker a fair trial. The admission of Walker's two confessions, made without benefit of counsel, was especially distressing to him. In his appeals he had emphasized the systematic exclusion of African Americans from the jury commission that chose the grand jury and from the grand jury itself. As was usual, there had not been any African Americans on Walker's jury. (The Court of Criminal Appeals noted that "one or two" Negroes had been on all but three Dallas County grand juries in the previous ten years.)[32]

So disgusted was Durham with the flimsy quality of the evidence and its acceptance by the trial judge that he vowed never again to accept a criminal case, and he didn't.[33]

Many in the African American community believed Walker innocent. Many others were convinced that the state had failed to prove its case and that Walker had been denied a fair trial. When his remains were returned to Dallas, some five thousand persons viewed the body at McGowen's Funeral Home. The *Dallas*

Express used eight columns of small type to print the names of individuals who signed the funeral home register. Every seat was filled at the funeral services at St. John Baptist Church. Many mourners were standing. Rev. E. C. Estell, officiating, said that if Walker was not guilty, he had been sacrificed as a young life on the altar of prejudice.[34]

Marion Butts wrote in the *Dallas Express,* "Yes, Dallas and Texas have killed young Tommie [*sic*] Lee Walker! But who is really satisfied? He was killed for a crime they thought he committed—a crime for which in this writer's opinion it was one of the most unjust uses of capital punishment that has occurred in recent years." Rev. Caesar Clark, pastor of the Good Street Baptist Church, declared that "Dallas has the blood of Tommie Lee Walker on her hands."[35]

Whether they accepted Walker's guilt or not, black Dallasites adopted him as a symbol of the overbearing, white-dominated justice system. Bedford, even after the passage of half a century, continued to see it that way.

As the 1959 Dallas City Council election approached, C. B. Bunkley Jr. and Bedford made a pair of important decisions: Bunkley would campaign for the Place 3 seat on the council, and Bedford would be his campaign manager. No black person had ever had the temerity to campaign for a council seat in all of Dallas's history.[36] There was no reason to think that 1959 was a good time, for the grip of the Citizens Charter Association (CCA) on city hall seemed ironclad. Mayor R. L. Thornton, a banker who through years of service had gained the nickname "Mr. Dallas," headed the CCA slate as he looked toward a fourth consecutive term in office.

Bunkley's campaign for the Place 3 seat was straightforward. He sought equal opportunity for minority workers at city hall, emphasized the need for greater basic services from the City of Dallas, and championed the rights of municipal workers to organize. His opponent, the highly favored pharmacist endorsed by the CCA, N. E. McKinney, acknowledged that he did not "know anything bad about Bunkley." The only real difference between them, he said, was that he was part of a team and Bunkley was an independent. Bunkley countered that he, as a lawyer, would be thinking for himself. He and other lawyers, he said, don't necessarily follow the thinking of a team.[37]

The campaign was marked by an especially heated challenge in the mayor's race by independent Earle Cabell, who forced Thornton into a runoff. The Interdenominational Ministerial Alliance, led by Rev. E. C. Estell, endorsed the establishment candidate, Mayor Thornton. Bunkley and Bedford took an opposite approach, endorsing Cabell and two other independents, Joe Geary and Elizabeth Blessing.[38] Only Geary, a lawyer, was able to prevail, becoming the only independent on the 1959–61 Dallas City Council. Bunkley's showing was respectable, 13,411 votes to McKinney's 34,360.[39]

The next year Bedford continued in his role as campaign manager. This time he managed the campaign of his own pastor, Rev. H. Rhett James, who sought election to Place 7 on the board of the Dallas Independent School District (DISD). James faced a formidable opponent, Tracy Rutherford, who was seeking her fifth consecutive term with the support of the Committee for Good Schools, the establishment group that controlled the school board just as effectively as the CCA controlled the city council.

James—thirty-two, married, and the father of four children—was a dynamic candidate. He sought votes based on an interest in "all of the children of Dallas and not in any particular segment."[40] James was well qualified, holding bachelor's degrees in sociology and divinity from Virginia Union University (in Richmond), and a master of education degree from Our Lady of the Lake College in San Antonio. He had taught for five years in the public schools in San Antonio, and he had taught at Virginia Union.

Two years earlier Rev. Caesar Clark had attempted to win a school board seat, and although he picked up more than 4,200 votes, he was defeated. James did better in the April 2, 1960, election, polling 7,478 votes, more than any of the other losing candidates and more than any black candidate in any DISD board election, but far behind Rutherford's 15,683 votes. James carried 22 of the 134 polling places in the city, and at the H. S. Thompson School polling place in South Dallas, he gained 617 votes, compared with 1 for Rutherford.[41]

After the election James, who had not campaigned as a black candidate, made harsh comments carried by both daily newspapers. He complained that there were many issues that directly affected his people and that the school board had been indifferent to the needs of black schoolchildren. Eight of the fourteen schools in the Dallas district without cafeterias were black schools, he pointed out.[42]

James was new to Dallas, but he would be heard from again.

The Bedfords began their married life at a time when American society was on the cusp of a revolution in race relations that rivaled the impact of Emancipation and Reconstruction. The segregated society in which Louis Bedford and Velma Bates had been reared was in the early stages of dismantlement.

The walls of segregation were already being slowly chipped away, but the goal still seemed far away until *Brown v. Board of Education*. Probably nothing brought home the reality of that ruling more forcefully than President Eisenhower's decision in 1957 to send U.S. Army soldiers to Central High School in Little Rock, Arkansas, to protect nine black students from threatening crowds.

Among African Americans, rising expectations regarding desegregation now transferred from schools to other institutions. If separation by race was wrong at school, how could it be right elsewhere? Why, for example, should African Americans be forced to sit in the back of public buses and streetcars? This was the question Rosa Parks asked in 1955 when she refused to move to the back of the bus in Montgomery, Alabama. Her arrest and the ensuing 381-day African American boycott of public buses in that city, led by an initially reluctant young minister, Martin Luther King Jr., achieved its goal.

When the U.S. Supreme Court refused in April 1956 to hear a federal appeals court decision that forbade separate sections on buses for blacks and whites in South Carolina, the end for segregated seating appeared certain. After studying that decision for three days, the Dallas Transit Company began removing the segregation signs from its 530 vehicles. (The city's streetcars were no longer in service.) The next day only two citizens called the company to complain.[43] Bedford recalled that most of the city's African American citizens were pleased that the separation of races on public transportation in Dallas ended so quietly.[44] In November 1956 the high court made an even more definitive decision banning segregated bus seating.[45]

If separation by race was unconstitutional in public schools and in public transportation, why then should restaurants deny African Americans the right to sit down for a meal? This was the question raised in February 1960 when a handful of black college youths, utilizing King's nonviolent tactics, staged a sit-in at lunch counters in Greensboro, North Carolina. Their actions spurred consternation, rioting, and arrests, but their courage inspired others to hold lunch counter sit-ins in such Southern cities as Atlanta, Birmingham, Chattanooga, Little Rock, Nashville, and Montgomery and in such Texas towns as Houston, Waco, Galveston, and—surprisingly—the little town of Marshall in East Texas, a few miles from the Louisiana border.

But earlier, while Bedford was still a law student in Brooklyn, Dallas had a lunchroom sit-in, which had been forgotten by the 1960s. It occurred on October 9, 1948, after a white Dallas woman, Lucy Krebs, who was active in the local Progressive Party, made arrangements for a Saturday morning breakfast at the downtown Dallas Central YMCA Grill and Dining Room to honor Lulu White, the NAACP leader from Houston, who was in town to help with the local membership drive. The YMCA accepted the reservation without realizing that White and three other African Americans would be among the guests. The mixed group initially sat down that Saturday morning for breakfast without challenge, but when it occurred to YMCA employees that the black guests could not be served in the segregated dining room, they asked them to leave. Krebs refused the request, insisting that her entire group remain in their seats until they were served. Thus, they sat. Morning turned to afternoon and then to night. The sit-in continued.

As darkness fell, some thirty to forty supporters bearing pickets appeared outside the building. Several signs bore this message: "The Negro YMCA Feeds White Guests—The White YMCA Refuses to Feed Negro Guests. Which One Is Christian?" The outside picketers began chanting, "Jim Crow Must Go, Jim Crow Must Go." Residents on the upper floors of the YMCA sprayed the demonstrators from above with a fire hose. At about 9:00 PM, a dozen hours after the sit-in had begun, as the protesters prepared to spend the night, friends and sympathizers brought pillows and blankets to send inside. Finally, at about midnight YMCA president Paul Carrington, a prominent white attorney, arrived to discuss the situation, finally acknowledging that he was ordering them to leave. Their point made, the demonstrators left peacefully.[46]

Bedford, and probably many African Americans who were in Dallas at the time, were not even aware of this incident, although it did receive minimal newspaper coverage. Only in retrospect did it seem to be a harbinger of future events.

The sit-in demonstrations beginning in 1960 were a different matter, occurring as the civil rights movement was gaining strength and receiving bold national headlines. In Marshall, Bedford, working with his fellow African American attorneys from Dallas, became involved in the experience that he later declared the most fulfilling activity of his life. Like so many of the other sit-ins across the South, those in Marshall took place with the now-familiar images of a large number of law enforcement officers, the use of fire hoses to disperse demonstrators, and accusations of Communist involvement.

A sleepy town of about thirty thousand residents located some 150 miles east of Dallas, Marshall, in Harrison County, seemed to be an unlikely place for such demonstrations. Its black population, outnumbering the whites, had accommodated itself for years to its secondary status, taking consolation in the two local black colleges, Wiley and Bishop, which stood as visible and important local institutions. Many of the state's outstanding black citizens were their graduates.

But Marshall, Harrison County, and East Texas remained culturally and emotionally linked to the Deep South in a way that Dallas had not been for many decades. On the eve of the Civil War, Harrison County had more slaves than any other county in the state, and it was a hotbed of anti-Union sentiment. Lynchings, all too common throughout the state, occurred most frequently in East Texas in the first decades of the twentieth century. In 1949 Marshall banned Elia Kazan's movie *Pinky* because of its portrayal of an interracial couple, a ban that the U.S. Supreme Court voided when it declared the city's movie code unconstitutional. With the outnumbered white population maintaining strict control in the city and county, racial tensions were just beneath the surface of daily life.

The inspiration for the Marshall sit-ins occurred on March 22, 1960, when an officer of the Southern Christian Leadership Conference (SCLC), a civil rights organization that had sprung from the Montgomery bus boycott, visited the town and spoke to a mass meeting of students at Wiley College. The SCLC officer, Dr. T. O. Simpkins, a Shreveport dentist, encouraged the students to be bold in seeking their civil rights. That same week students at both Wiley and Bishop Colleges launched a series of antidiscrimination demonstrations on their campuses.[47]

On Saturday morning, March 26, the student demonstrations spilled out from the two campuses into downtown Marshall, where nine students and a professor sat down at the segregated F. W. Woolworth lunch counter. The store manager refused to serve them. The group left quietly when the manager closed the store, but the sit-ins resumed at the Union Bus Terminal Café, where the counter was similarly closed. In the afternoon the demonstrators returned to the now reopened Woolworth lunch counter.[48]

The sit-ins resumed with greater force on Monday morning. This time police arrested some twenty-five students and gave them a "heart-to-heart talk" in hopes of averting further incidents, then released them without charges. In the early afternoon Marshall's city commissioners, concerned about what might yet happen, met and issued a statement:

> We must have law and order in Marshall.... Under this country's free enterprise system and under our laws a merchant has the legal right to select the patrons he serves. He is going to be protected in that right. Likewise, a customer has the right not to be forced to trade with a merchant with whom he does not want to deal.
>
> We recognize the right to demonstrate. But we call attention that the right to demonstrate in all cases is limited by the fact that, if there is any clear and present danger, that the demonstration will incite public disorder, it is unlawful and will be handled as a violation of the law.[49]

The student demonstrators, instead of heeding the commissioners and the police's earlier talk, now acted more forcefully and with greater organization. A much larger group of students sat in at the first two and now a third lunch counter on Wednesday, March 30. When police arrested them, others took their places. Police arrested the new demonstrators, too, and charged all of them with "unlawful assembly to interfere with the proper operation of a person's business." By afternoon fifty-seven students were in jail.[50]

Late in the day, as news of the arrests spread, a crowd of about four hundred sympathizers gathered on the courthouse lawn. When they began singing, the fifty-seven students in the jail could hear them, and from inside they lifted their voices in unison with the outside demonstrators, singing "God Bless America," "America the Beautiful," "The Battle Hymn of the Republic," "The Star-Spangled Banner," and the Negro "national anthem," "Lift Every Voice and Sing." As the numbers around the courthouse and jail grew, alarmed Marshall police and county lawmen summoned help from neighboring towns, the Texas Highway Patrol, and the Texas Rangers. Some two hundred lawmen soon surrounded the scene.[51] When the first protesters to appear were herded inside the Harrison County Courthouse, others began arriving, soon numbering about 150. Also showing up were white counterprotesters, a group of about fifty hostile young men who seemed ready to make trouble. Police persuaded them to leave, but the demonstrators remained. Unable to get them to depart, officers finally turned fire hoses on them. The cold, forceful spray accomplished the officers' goal, and the drenched demonstrators departed.[52]

Downtown business had suffered a sharp decline. District Attorney Charles Allen, eager to forestall further confrontations, advised the jailed students that he would not file charges against them if they would not repeat their actions. No promises were forthcoming, but the students were released.[53]

Many American whites, especially Southern whites, stiffened as they saw aggressive challenges to the social system under which they had lived their lives. Even moderate whites feared that such activism would stir up ugly responses from militant whites who could not be controlled. Black activists were seen as troublemakers at best and as inspired by Communists at worst. Many white citizens held even the NAACP in disdain, believing it to be a troublemaking organization, although it was increasingly viewed as too moderate by newer, more militant organizations.

Fearful of having his college tainted by allegations of Communist involvement, the president of Bishop College, Dr. Milton J. Curry Jr., announced on the day of the Wednesday demonstrations that he had requested the resignation of a professor, Dr. Doxey Alphonso Wilkerson, who had once belonged to the Communist Party. The *Dallas Morning News* reported his membership as part of its coverage of the sit-ins.[54] It mattered neither that Wilkerson had renounced his former membership nor that Curry declared that his service as a faculty member at Bishop had been exemplary and that he had nothing to do with the sit-ins. Wilkerson, who had earned his doctorate at New York University, was an active member of the Communist Party in the 1940s and 1950s, but he had made a public break in 1957, which Dr. Curry described as "abrupt, complete and final."

Dr. Curry further said that during the six months Dr. Wilkerson had been at Bishop, he had been "completely co-operative," had done "an effective job" as a professor, and was one of the most valuable men on the faculty. "We don't have any teacher who has been more Christian than he has. He is in regular chapel service attendance and attends churches in Marshall," Curry said. Nevertheless, Dr. Curry said, because of the demonstrations, he had requested the professor's resignation because he was "an unfortunate victim of circumstances." Wilkerson refused to resign. On the next day, Dr. Curry fired both him and his wife, also a Bishop faculty member.[55]

Dr. Curry's action may have been motivated by the fact that he was in the midst of a campaign to move Bishop College from Marshall to Dallas, where a committee of important civic leaders had been formed to raise $1 million to bring about the move. Or perhaps he had been intimidated by the action of Governor Price Daniel, who ordered Colonel Homer Garrison, head of the Texas Department of Public Safety, to investigate whether Wilkerson had had any part in demonstrations in Dallas and Houston.[56]

Tensions continued at the courthouse square in Marshall as law officers, with tear gas grenades at their sides, kept silent watch on the streets. Nonetheless, the students, perhaps inspired by the unexpected firing of Wilkerson, resumed their sit-ins. District Attorney Allen, having advised the fifty-seven students arrested on Wednesday that he would not file charges if they refrained from further sit-ins, now issued arrest warrants for them. Hearing this news, the students assembled peacefully that Friday on the campuses to await their arrests. Officers arrived and simply called out the students' names. Adhering to their commitment to nonviolence, the students followed the officers to their patrol cars to be taken to jail. By nightfall forty-seven of them were behind bars, charged with "failing to leave a store when requested by the management."[57] Before the arrests ended, more than seventy students were jailed for sit-ins and picketing.

One of the students—a junior named Mattie Mae Etta Johnson, from the small town of Mineola, halfway between Marshall and Dallas—wrote a letter immediately afterward to reassure her mother. She expressed concern that her involvement in the sit-ins might have had negative repercussions for her mother. Her letter vividly described the mood of the students and their experiences behind bars:

I guess you know by now we were arrested Friday evening. We were carried to jail about 8:00 p.m. Friday evening, and we stayed there about 26 hours. We got out Saturday night about 10 o'clock. There were 27 of us girls in my cell. Our lawyer is from Dallas [Romeo Williams]. We were bond[ed] out by Negro Citizens of Marshall. We are under $600 bonds. The night in jail was not to[o] pleasant but it was a comfort to know we were in there to serve a good purpose. We were in for a good cause and none of us minded it really. If it takes a few days in jail to get equality, I feel it's worth it. I feel that's least I can do. I know that God is with us because he has the whole wide world in his hands.

. . . I have lifted a burden from my heart because of my stand. In God's name we are going to get our freedom.[58]

With the jailing of the students, Bedford, who had been following the events in the newspapers, became directly involved. The jailed students needed legal assistance. Romeo Williams, who had been a charter member of the J. L. Turner Legal Association, was by now living in Marshall, his hometown, and, as Mattie Mae Etta Johnson indicated, was the first to help the students.

Williams, forty years old and a World War II veteran, had returned to Marshall in 1956. He had grown up there as the son of leading citizens. His parents owned the town's funeral home for black residents. Williams excelled in band, drama, athletics, and academics at Marshall's Pemberton High School before entering Bishop College. He took and passed the Air Corps examination, the first African American to do so; after he graduated from Bishop, he entered the Tuskegee (Alabama) Army Flying School and earned the Aviation Administration certificate. After the war Williams studied at the Lincoln University law school in St. Louis. Upon graduation he moved to Dallas to practice law as a junior partner to Durham.

The number of the students involved in the sit-ins was so great that Williams needed help. He turned to his attorney friends in Dallas—Bedford and other members of the J. L. Turner Legal Association.[59]

Bedford, Durham, Bunkley, Finch, and Holbert, all sympathetic to the students, agreed at once to join him. Over the next weeks and months, they drove back and forth between Dallas and Marshall, getting students out of jail, providing legal assistance, and representing them in the trials that soon occurred. The sit-ins, meanwhile, abruptly ended.[60]

Marshall's black citizens gained Bedford's admiration during this unusually stressful time. They guaranteed bonds as high as six hundred dollars for students they did not even know; many of the students had permanent residences elsewhere, often in other states. The students themselves were greater heroes to Bedford, though; they exhibited courage and maintained high spirits at a time when many questioned their motives and portrayed them as harming the city of Marshall. "In spite of the dangers they faced," Bedford later said, "[these young people] were willing to go to jail for equality. They handled this in a peaceful, but determined way. They knew they were subject to being mistreated in jail, but they were willing to risk their personal safety and put it on the line for what they thought was right."[61]

Dr. Curry was in a difficult position. Despite his seemingly misplaced punitive action against Wilkerson, he strongly defended the students several days later and declared that Wilkerson was an unfortunate "scapegoat," the victim of the *Dallas Morning News*, which had revealed Wilkerson's former ties to the Communist Party even though the professor had nothing to do with the demonstrations. The students, Curry said, were acting in full accord "with the aims of attaining human dignity and rights."[62] In a statement to the *Dallas Morning News*, remarkable in its tone because of the pending move of the campus and possible backlash, Curry described the newspaper's coverage as "character assassination by association," part of an evident plot to "destroy a small church-related college."[63]

As to the possibility of students damaging the fund-raising campaign to move Bishop to Dallas, he said he had urged them to "make their decisions on the basis of the highest ideals they know. . . . We could not in good conscience tell them in this crisis to stop thinking and accept blindly a solution which would guarantee us $1,500,000 for a new campus. Ideals are not thrown overhead so easily or so cheaply." It was impossible, he said, to "continually teach students the fundamentals of American democracy and seek to imbue them with its ideals generation after generation without running the risk that some of them will believe you mean what you say."[64]

The first student to face trial was Joel Rucker, a twenty-one-year-old Wiley College student from Bakersfield, California, who was charged in Marshall's municipal court with failure to leave private premises at the order of the lawful occupant. Rucker entered a plea of not guilty; Bedford, Bunkley, Williams, and Holbert represented him, with Bunkley taking the lead. Two witnesses testified for the city, the operator of the Union Bus Terminal Café and a sergeant for the Marshall Police Department. The defense offered no witnesses but presented six motions, three of them attacking the use of state powers to carry out the personal prejudice of a store owner, and three challenging the validity of the ordinance on which the cases were tried. At the end of the day, the jury found Rucker guilty and assessed a two-hundred-dollar fine.[65]

Other trials quickly followed that spring, some of them in a county court. All defendants were found guilty. Fines ranged from fifty to four hundred dollars. Durham and U. Simpson Tate joined the defense effort. Guilty verdicts may have been a foregone conclusion, but as Durham had always preached, what really counted in these cases was establishing a good basis for appeal.

Many of the trials were deliberately scheduled to be held in the summer, Bedford believed, because the Marshall officials knew most of the defendants did not live there and might not be able to return, thus forfeiting their bonds. To Bedford's knowledge, though, not a single student failed to show for trial.

Bedford and his lawyer friends based their work on their commitment to the ideals espoused by the students. They had no realistic expectation of payment, but the black citizens of Marshall formed a committee to help pay the legal expenses and guarantee the students' bonds. By June 1960 legal fees of $1,573.51 were submitted for approval. Bedford was to be paid $406 for three days in trial and eight days' briefing, an amount similar to that authorized for Williams and Holbert. Finch and Turner got lesser amounts. Durham and Bunkley were to be paid unspecified amounts by the NAACP Legal Defense and Educational Fund.[66]

Dallas residents also rallied to the cause of the students. A fund-raiser to help pay legal expenses was held at Bedford's New Hope Baptist Church, under the leadership of Rev. H. Rhett James. Students came to Dallas to give speeches and firsthand reports of their experiences.[67]

A tragic accident brought a sad ending to the drama of the sit-ins in August 1960. Mattie Mae Etta Johnson, the nineteen-year-old student who had written the poignant letter from jail to her mother, and a fellow demonstrator, Bernice Halley of Ogden, Utah, were in an automobile with Romeo Williams, who was representing them. Their trial was to be later that week. On August 16 a train struck their car not far from Bishop College. Williams and Johnson were both killed; Halley was critically injured. Williams's injuries were so severe that his casket was closed at his funeral.[68]

The tragedy cast a deep gloom over later events surrounding the sit-ins. On the day following the accident, though, Bedford and Bunkley dutifully went to the courthouse to represent another student in a county court trial. The judge said that in light of the accident, he was postponing the trial. But it was more than a postponement: the trial was never held, nor were any of the other pending trials.[69]

The fatal accident prompted Bishop president Curry to elaborate on his defense of the students and their sit-in demonstrations:

> They saw with clearer vision than their elders the crass moral corruption inherent in the practice and profession of segregation and discrimination based on race, and dramatized their protest in such a way as to give infinite and ultimate significance to a common, routine, unglamorous habit of Americans—namely eating when one gets hungry at lunch counters provided in stores that offer goods for sale to the public.[70]

He said that for years Negroes had bought shoe polish and trinkets at these stores and "looked on in their hunger" while other people sat and ate. "It never dawned on them that in their silence they condoned a practice whose immoral quality did violence to the whole Christian and democratic concept of essential equality, and which denied the indestructible dignity inherent in each human being." It was a practice, he said, that was a "cancer at the heart of the American body politic."[71]

In the sit-in cases, every student tried in municipal or county court was convicted. As Durham had preached to his law disciples, the appeal was especially important for African Americans. As Durham, Bunkley, Holbert, Finch, and Bedford studied the various possibilities for the most effective appeals, it was Bedford who saw a technicality that would cause all convictions to be reversed and the other trials to be simply dropped. Bedford's insight was based on the knowledge he had gained in the many concealed-weapon cases he had tried. He knew that the Texas Court of Criminal Appeals had ruled that the information—the means by which the students had been brought to court—had to be written as a conjunctive statement rather than disjunctive: it should include the phrase "on *and* about" rather than "on or about." The information documents by which the students had been brought to trial had failed to do this. Thus, on December 14, 1960, in two separate appeals, the Court of Criminal Appeals reversed the convictions of students S. J. Briscoe and Yvonne Tucker.[72] Bedford was pleased that he had been able to provide the insight that resulted in the reversal of these convictions. His involvement with the student demonstrators permitted him to see firsthand the dedication of this new generation of African Americans, the generation that immediately followed his own. There had been individual instances of courage in Bedford's generation of college students, but rarely if ever had such courage been demonstrated with such insight and passion by such large numbers.

Meanwhile, the suit filed in 1955 to desegregate the Dallas public schools, initiated by Durham and signed by Bedford and other J. L. Turner Legal Association members, had been bouncing back and forth between Judge Atwell and the Fifth Circuit Court of Appeals. The school district sought delays. Atwell was sympathetic to the district; the appeals court was not. While Thurgood Marshall was busy overseeing as many as one hundred desegregation cases across the nation, Durham was doing most of the appeals work for the Dallas case. Bedford—not intimately involved, even though his name was on the suit—participated occasionally in strategy sessions with the other attorneys.

Altering segregationist attitudes that had passed for generations from parent to child was a monumental task. When those attitudes had the official imprimatur of public school systems, legislative bodies, and private businesses, the task was almost insurmountable.

Yet, in Dallas, as in other Southern cities, there were hopeful signs that old attitudes, at least among more thoughtful citizens, were changing. When a civil rights meeting was held on January 8, 1956, at the Good Street Baptist Church, its key participants were both black and white. The sponsoring organization was a group called the Dallas Civil Rights Rally Planning Committee. Presiding over the meeting was Dr. Luther Holcomb of Lakewood Baptist Church. Two other white men, Rabbi Levi A. Olan of Temple Emanu-El and Fred Schmidt, secretary of the Texas State CIO Council, joined Holcomb as speakers on the topic "Civil Rights and Our American Democracy." The principal speaker was Roy E. Wilkins, executive secretary of the NAACP. Some twelve hundred persons attended the meeting.[73]

In April 1958 about three hundred white Protestant ministers, many of them leaders of their denominations, issued a joint statement declaring enforced segregation to be "morally and spiritually wrong." They urged churches, service clubs, community organizations, newspapers, and radio and television stations to "join together in seeking actively to promote the spirit of harmony and peace among all people." They presented their statement at a press conference presided over by Methodist Bishop William C. Martin, Episcopalian Bishop C. Avery Mason, Dr. John F. Anderson Jr. of First Presbyterian Church, and Dr. Foy Valentine, director of the Christian Life Commission of the Baptist General Convention. The names of all the signatories appeared in the *Dallas Morning News*, which gave prominent display to the news story.[74]

Two years later, though, the people of Dallas gave strong evidence that their sentiments had not changed. In a nonbinding election on whether they favored school integration, citizens voted against it by a margin of 30,324 to 7,416.

The ongoing school lawsuit still revolved around how soon and in what fashion desegregation should occur. By the time Thurgood Marshall came to town for an important 1959 hearing, Judge Atwell had retired.[75] Now presiding over the case was eighty-five-year-old T. Whitfield Davidson, who, like Atwell, was an avowed segregationist. Davidson overruled Marshall's motion to desegregate the schools that fall semester and instead ordered the school board to prepare a plan for the following year. When the school board next proposed a stair-step plan to integrate schools one grade at a time, beginning with the first, Davidson found this plan too sweeping and substituted his own "salt and pepper" plan, in which one white school and one black school would be integrated on a test basis. His attitude was summarized in a speech to a church men's club in which he alleged that "no country in history has ever amalgamated the two races without both races being the loser."[76]

Appeals to the Fifth Circuit Court by Durham, Bunkley, Bedford, and others were successful, and in 1960 the appeals court ordered the board to implement the original stair-step plan, beginning in fall 1961. Even with this tentative beginning, Mayor R. L. Thornton, "Mr. Dallas," was concerned about the community's possible negative response. He and other Dallas leaders were terrified that the kind of turmoil accompanying school integration in Little Rock and New Orleans might be repeated in Dallas, and they were desperate to avoid those experiences and the resulting negative publicity.

Thornton referred the matter to the powerful but unofficial body that ruled the city from behind the scenes, the Dallas Citizens Council. The group's president, C. A. Tatum Jr., a Dallas Power & Light Company executive, appointed a seven-member committee to address the school problem. Establishing himself as leader, he named civic leaders Karl Hoblitzelle, W. W. Overton, James Aston, Carr Collins, Julius Schepps, and John E. Mitchell to his committee, which decided to launch a massive public relations campaign to prepare Dallas citizens to accept peacefully what was inevitable—school desegregation. Realizing that the old ways of doing business might be futile as well as unwise, the committee decided to seek the black community's assistance, adding seven prominent African Americans to its member-ship. What became known as the "biracial committee" now also included Durham, A. Maceo Smith, Rev. E. C. Estell, undertaker C. J. Clarke, E. L. V. Reed, Rev. B. F. Joshua, and businessman George Allen. The all-male biracial committee began meet-ing privately every Friday afternoon, outside the gaze of newspaper or broadcast reporters. Its work was confidential; even Bedford had little idea of what the com-mittee was doing, other than working toward peaceful school integration.

Black members of the committee had a special task. They were expected to restrain the increasingly restive African American population while the committee worked quietly behind the scenes to prepare the community for peaceful desegregation. Demonstrations, most white members believed, might arouse hostility among short-tempered whites and create added difficulties.

Once it would have been enough to gain the cooperation of the Dallas chapter of the NAACP, the Negro Chamber of Commerce, and the Interdenominational Ministerial Alliance to represent the black community and send out the word to cooperate. The presence on the biracial committee of such influential leaders as Durham and Smith, whose aggressive past efforts toward African American equality were beyond question, would have guaranteed it.

But those times had changed. At Bedford's own establishment church, New Hope Baptist, Rev. H. Rhett James was not willing to sit back and wait for the goodwill of others. Beginning in October 1960 and continuing through the year, James organized regular picket lines outside the downtown H. L. Green Department Store, just across from Neiman Marcus, to force it to desegregate its lunch counters. A few white liberals joined the picket line. A few hecklers appeared.

Bedford, for the first and only time in his life, joined a picket line and carried a sign, outside the Green store. Velma approved but did not join her husband, although Bedford's good friend Haywood Sparks did. The two men bantered good-naturedly about how they might handle hostile whites who shouted epithets at them. Sparks, laughing, said he would be able to handle even the worst verbal insults without reacting, but if anyone spat on him, he didn't think he could refrain from violent retaliation. Fortunately, neither man's resolve was tested.[77]

In the white community, James was viewed as a maverick minister acting without the support of the city's African American churches and institutions. Bedford, as a faithful member of James's church, knew otherwise. The city's older ministers, he thought, encouraged James to see what he might accomplish. If James failed, they would escape blame because he would appear to have acted as an individual. As it turned out, James was an effective organizer, convincing churches, fraternities, sororities, and other organizations to take turns on the picket lines. During these tense times his church flourished, for in February 1961 it announced a $100,000 expansion program. Later that year James was elected president of the Dallas chapter of the NAACP.[78]

In early January 1961, the same month that John F. Kennedy spoke so idealisti-
cally to the nation in his inaugural address, two students at Southern Methodist
University's integrated Perkins School of Theology, one black and one white, challenged the segregation policies of a drugstore lunch counter across the street from
the campus. Denied service, they returned with about thirty other theology students
to begin a sit-in. The drugstore owner, furious, decided to fumigate his store, and he
sprayed the students as they sat peacefully with handkerchiefs over their faces. After
about an hour, the owner closed the store. Later that afternoon the students returned
with pickets. News of this event was reported by the Associated Press and appeared
in newspapers elsewhere, but not in the Dallas newspapers, which had decided to
put a moratorium on reporting this story for fear of stirring up further trouble.[79]

Clearly, the seven black members of the biracial committee could not contain
such activities. On the Sunday after the demonstrations at the drugstore near SMU,
Durham announced that the biracial committee's work, whose goals had been broadened to include desegregation at places other than schools, had "broken down"
because Mayor Thornton rejected a committee plan to desegregate Fair Park on a
year-round basis. Durham urged African Americans to boycott Dallas businesses that
practiced discrimination and to prepare themselves for sit-ins and demonstrations.[80]

This prompted James to declare that Durham and his fellow black biracial committee members "finally realized they were being used by whites to suppress peaceful demonstrations against segregation." Durham, alarmed at such an indictment,
pointed out that his own critical comments had been aimed at the operators of the
stores discriminating against African Americans. "We still have confidence in the
good faith and integrity of the white citizens with whom we worked," he said.[81]

James next targeted one of the city's major downtown department stores,
Titche-Goettinger, with the goal of halting the store's policy of refusing to let African
American women try on clothing. And at the drugstore across from SMU, some two
hundred students demonstrated against its segregationist policies. In February the
Dallas NAACP Youth Council staged demonstrations at two downtown theaters and
soon broadened the attack by asking African Americans to turn in their credit cards
to the downtown stores and refuse to buy any Easter clothes from them.[82]

No longer were black citizens of Dallas willing to accept a white timetable for their rights. This mood, already evident in other parts of the country, now had reached Dallas. Pressure, not patience, became the accepted wisdom. New leaders—such as H. Rhett James and Earl Allen, the black theology student at SMU who had organized the drugstore sit-in with a white student—emerged, beholden to no one and tired of delay. The possibility that their activism might spur retaliatory measures from white segregationists was a growing concern. It was a fear heightened by the approaching school desegregation.

The Dallas Citizens Council's goal of achieving peaceful school desegregation would not be enough. The pace of integration had to be picked up, and it would assume broader dimensions.

Quietly, the biracial committee began arranging for support from religious, service, fraternal, labor, and professional organizations to expand desegregation beyond the schools. Prominent citizens were recruited as speakers to emphasize to these organizations and clubs the city's need for peaceful school desegregation. Advertising executive Sam Bloom made a film, *Dallas at the Crossroads*; CBS broadcast newsman Walter Cronkite already famous before he began his long run as anchor of the *CBS Evening News*, was hired to narrate. In the film Cronkite and prominent Dallasites emphasized civic responsibility in the strongest terms. The film, shown always by an authorized speaker, was presented more than one thousand times to groups of all sorts across the city. More than one hundred thousand copies of the booklet *Dallas at the Crossroads* were distributed to churches. Inserts bearing the same basic message were distributed with employee paychecks in businesses across the city.[83]

Of special importance were quiet and successful negotiations to gain the cooperation of the city's restaurants in desegregating. The result was that in a carefully concerted but unannounced effort, on July 26, 1961, less than two months before school opened, 156 African American men and women spread about the city and sat down to eat at forty major restaurants and retail store dining rooms. The restaurants were thus desegregated without fanfare.[84]

Other steps were also taken. Desegregated seating began that summer at the State Fair musicals, where African Americans had previously been restricted to a balcony corner. Fair Park's midway area was desegregated. Progress was reported in persuading Dallas hotels to accommodate "mixed groups" at meetings. Visiting African American government leaders and other dignitaries were already being accepted at the hotels. One of the committee's studies had indicated that 139 types of jobs in the city were classified simply as "janitor" or "porter." These were properly reclassified so that a black man who had been doing the work of, for instance, a receiving clerk would now have that title instead of the general label of "porter." At the city's second largest bank, First National, a black man who had worked there for twenty-one years as a porter was promoted to teller.[85]

It was a small beginning, but official Dallas—largely the Dallas Citizens Council—was proud of these achievements. The announcement of this preliminary desegregation program came in August; in the following month, the real test would come: school integration.

More evidence of the Dallas Citizens Council effort followed. The Dallas City Council passed an "anti-mob ordinance," which prohibited persons from "standing, remaining or congregating on any public street or sidewalk . . . so as to obstruct, prevent, or interfere . . . with its use." Police officers received "mob control training." Dr. Luther Holcomb of the Greater Dallas Council of Churches urged Dallas pastors to talk about the need for peaceful integration in their sermons on the Sunday before the first day of school.[86]

On Wednesday, September 6, 1961, eighteen African American first-graders enrolled in eight previously all-white Dallas elementary schools. No more than four of them attended a single school. Two police officers guarded each integrated school, and a riot squad of one hundred officers was ready to move to any place of trouble. As it turned out, the day proceeded with hardly a word of protest.

President John F. Kennedy and his brother, Attorney General Robert F. Kennedy, praised Dallas for peacefully handling school desegregation, as did *Life* magazine and the *New York Times*. The latter publication said the city's peaceful integration "contrasted sharply" with the violence in Little Rock and the venom of New Orleans.[87]

Reverend James, writing in his column in the *Dallas Express*, was skeptical: "We have yet to see just how much integration will take place in Dallas."[88]

Indeed. Of the system's 128,563 students, 24,317 were African American. Only 18 attended formerly all-white schools. Not until a decade had passed would significant integration occur in the Dallas schools. Yet, a breakthrough had been made. Bedford was pleased to have his name on the lawsuit that had brought it about.

1. Louis A. Bedford Jr., interview by Darwin Payne, Jan. 31, 2006.
2. Ibid.
3. *Dallas Express*, Sept. 7, 1957.
4. Bedford, interview, Jan. 31, 2006.
5. *Dallas Star-Post*, May 10, 1958.
6. Velma Bedford, interview by Darwin Payne, Oct. 26, 2006.
7. Velma Bedford, interview by Darwin Payne, May 4, 2006.
8. Bedford, interview, Mar. 14, 2006.
9. Ibid.
10. V. Bedford, interview, May 4, 2006.
11. Joan Tarpley, interview by Darwin Payne, Mar. 24, 2006.
12. "Woman's Last Gasp Tells of Attacker," *Dallas Morning News*, Oct. 1, 1953.
13. "Grim Manhunt Intensified for Brutal Rapist-Killer," *Dallas Daily Times Herald*, Oct. 1, 1954; "Defense Unit Aids Hunt," Oct. 2, 1954; "Knife Expert Rape Suspect," Oct. 3, 1954; "Prowler Scare Keeps City Jittery," Oct. 4, 1954.
14. "Police Open All-Out Drive to Catch Woman's Slayer," *Dallas Morning News*, Oct. 2, 1953.
15. "Prowler Reports Swamp Officers," *Dallas Morning News*, Oct. 3, 1953.
16. "Sex Slayer Search Continues," *Dallas Express*, Oct. 10, 1953.
17. "Is the Sex Slayer a Negro?" *Dallas Express*, Oct. 24, 1953.
18. "Confession Made in Parker Murder," *Dallas Morning News*, Jan. 31, 1954.
19. "Parker Case Goes before Grand Jury," *Dallas Morning News*, Feb. 6, 1954.
20. Ibid.; "Parker Case Confession Repudiated," *Dallas Daily Times Herald*, Feb. 3, 1954; "Jury to Get Evidence in Parker Case," *Dallas Morning News*, Feb. 5, 1954.
21. "Attorney Advising Walker Not to Testify before Jury," *Dallas Morning News*, Feb. 11, 1954.
22. "Jury to Continue Parker Probe," *Dallas Daily Times Herald*, Feb. 8, 1954.
23. "Walker Trial Postponed; Jury Difficulty Foreseen," *Dallas Morning News*, Mar. 17, 1954.
24. "Accused Slayer Denied Bond," *Dallas Express*, Mar. 20, 1954.
25. Bedford, interview, Mar. 28, 2006.
26. "Witnesses Place Negro near Crime," *Dallas Morning News*, Mar. 27, 1954.
27. "Death Confessions Denied by Walker," *Dallas Morning News*, Mar. 28, 1954.
28. "Walker Sentenced to Death," *Dallas Morning News*, Mar. 30, 1954; "Walker Gets Electric Chair," *Dallas Express*, Apr. 3, 1954.
29. "Judge King Praised for Trial Work," *Dallas Morning News*, Mar. 31, 1954.
30. "Pleas Court Turns Down Convicted Rapist-Slayer," *Dallas Morning News*, Feb. 10, 1955.
31. "Walker Dies in Chair for Dallas Crime," *Dallas Morning News*, May 12, 1956.
32. "Pleas Court Turns Down Convicted Rapist-Slayer," *Dallas Morning News*, Feb. 10, 1955.
33. Tarpley, interview, Mar. 24, 2006. Tarpley recalled Durham's comments to this effect about five years later, when she was a new member of Durham's law firm.
34. "More Than 5000 View Tommie Lee Walker's Body," *Dallas Express*, May 19, 1956; "Thousands View Body of Walker," *Dallas Express*, May 19, 1956.
35. "Thousands View Body of Walker."
36. Donald Payton, "A Concise History: Black Dallas since 1842," *D Heritage* (June 1998): 29.
37. "Barbs Fly as Election Time Nears," *Dallas Morning News*, Apr. 3, 1959.

38. Postcard signed by Ernest C. Estell Sr. and R. E. Joshua, undated, Bedford Papers; postcard from Bunkley campaign committee, undated, Bedford Papers.
39. Payton, "Concise History," 29.
40. "Candidacy Announced by Pastor," *Dallas Morning News*, Mar. 2, 1960.
41. "3-Member Team Wins School Board Election," *Dallas Morning News*, Apr. 3, 1960.
42. "'My People' Need Voice, James Says," *Dallas Morning News*, Apr. 4, 1960.
43. "Segregation Notices Come Out of Buses," *Dallas Morning News*, Apr. 26, 1956.
44. Louis A. Bedford Jr., interview by Darwin Payne, Apr. 21, 2006.
45. "Segregated Bus Seating Ruled Down," *Dallas Morning News*, Nov. 14, 1956; *Browder v. Gayle*, 142 F. Supp. 707 (1956).
46. Articles about the sit-in appeared in the October 10, 1948, editions of the *Dallas Daily Times Herald* and *Dallas Morning News* and in the October 16, 1948, edition of the *Dallas Express*.
47. "Outside Influence in Sit-in Indicated," *Dallas Morning News*, Apr. 20, 1960.
48. "Sitdowns Staged at Marshall," *Dallas Morning News*, Mar. 27, 1960.
49. "Marshall 'Sit-ins' Lectured," *Dallas Morning News*, Mar. 29, 1960.
50. "Fire Hoses Used to Clear Crowd at Marshall Site," *Dallas Morning News*, Mar. 31, 1960.
51. Ibid.
52. Ibid.
53. "Deputies Arrest 47 Students after Marshall Sit-Ins," *Dallas Morning News*, Apr. 2, 1960.
54. "The Professor and the Reds," *Dallas Morning News*, Apr. 7, 1960.
55. "Professor 'Advised' to Resign," *Dallas Morning News*, Mar. 31, 1960; "Wilkerson Dismissed by College," *Dallas Morning News*, Apr. 1, 1960.
56. "Wilkerson Dismissed by College."
57. "Deputies Arrest 47 Students."
58. M. K. Curry Jr., "Last Will and Testament," *Bishop Herald*, Nov. 1960, 2.
59. Texas State Historical Association, s.v. "Romeo Marcus Williams," in The Handbook of Texas Online, http://www.tshaonline.org/handbook/online/articles/WW/fwibm.html.
60. Ibid.
61. "Lawyers with Commitment," *Dallas Bar Association Headnotes*, Sept. 1, 1998.
62. Ibid.
63. "Fired Professor Defended," *Dallas Morning News*, Apr. 8, 1960.
64. Ibid.
65. "Student Fined $200 in Marshall Trial," *Dallas Morning News*, Apr. 8, 1960.
66. C. B. Bunkley Jr. to Dr. Claude Williams, June 8, 1960, copy, Bedford Papers.
67. Louis A. Bedford Jr., interview by Darwin Payne, May 22, 2006.
68. "Two Marshall Case Figures Killed in Crossing Crash," *Dallas Morning News*, Aug. 17, 1960.
69. Bedford, interview, May 22, 2006.
70. M. K. Curry Jr., "Last Will and Testament," *Bishop Herald* (Nov. 1960): 2.
71. Ibid.
72. *S. J. Briscoe v. State of Texas*, No. 32347, Court of Criminal Appeals of Texas, Dec. 14, 1960; *Yvonne Tucker v. State of Texas*, No. 32612, Court of Criminal Appeals of Texas, Dec. 14, 1960; Bedford, interview, Apr. 21, 2006.
73. "NAACP Official Sees Bloc as Vote Factor," *Dallas Morning News*, Jan. 9, 1958; "Civil Rights Meeting" program, Jan. 8, 1956, Bedford Papers.

74. "Segregation Called Moral, Spiritual Ill," *Dallas Morning News*, Apr. 27, 1958.

75. A decade after his retirement a new public school was named for Judge Atwell. In 2006 that same school's media center was named for W. J. Durham.

76. Linden, *Desegregating Schools in Dallas*, 36.

77. Bedford, interview, Apr. 21, 2006.

78. Ibid.; "Baptist Church Begins Expansion," *Dallas Morning News,* Feb. 12, 1961.

79. Payne, *Big D*, 342.

80. Ibid., 342–43.

81. Ibid., 342; "Statement Challenged by Durham," *Dallas Morning News*, Jan. 10, 1961.

82. Payne, *Big D*, 343.

83. Linden, *Desegregating Schools in Dallas*, 42–43; "DCC Works for Peaceful Mixing," *Dallas Morning News*, Aug. 6, 1961.

84. "DCC Works for Peaceful Mixing."

85. Ibid.; "Bank Porter for 21 Years Promoted to Teller Post," *Dallas Express*, Sept. 21, 1963.

86. Payne, *Big D*, 344.

87. Ibid., 344–45.

88. Ibid., 345.

6

ENTERING THE RANKS

T ime seemed to be moving faster with John F. Kennedy in the White House. One momentous event followed another. A CIA-backed effort to invade Cuba and overthrow Fidel Castro failed at the Bay of Pigs, to the government's embarrassment. The East German Communists erected a wall as a barrier between East and West Berlin, and Kennedy activated some 150,000 National Guardsmen and Army Reservists as a show of strength. The U.S. Army sent more and more military advisers to South Vietnam, including members of the storied Green Berets. A tense confrontation over Soviet missiles ended when Nikita Khrushchev turned his ships around before their arrival in Cuba and agreed to dismantle missile sites already there. John Glenn became the first American to orbit the earth. A troubled Marilyn Monroe committed suicide by an overdose in her Los Angeles home; Eleanor Roosevelt died of natural causes at the age of seventy-eight.

In the American South, the civil rights struggle continued to make big news. Freedom Riders boarded interstate buses to demonstrate their new rights—and faced violent resistance. Amidst massive disorders, including fatalities and injuries, James Meredith became the first African American to enroll at the University of Mississippi. In August 1963 more than two hundred thousand demonstrators at the Lincoln Memorial heard Martin Luther King Jr. make his impassioned "I Have a Dream" speech. Medgar Evers, an NAACP field director, was shot and killed by a sniper on the driveway of his home, in Jackson, Mississippi.

The confrontations that made angry headlines in so many American cities bypassed Dallas. Public school desegregation was achieved without riots or other significant disturbances, although it wasn't until the early 1970s that significant desegregation would occur. Restaurants and hotels opened their doors to all races. The removal of signs on public buses separating blacks from whites was hardly noticed. These positive developments were not as unusual as some have conjectured. Recent scholarship has shown that civil rights gains were made in many Southern cities without violent confrontation, but that these gains were overshadowed by disturbances that did take place. It should be noted, however, that the fear of major disturbances in Dallas and other cities added a sense of urgency to making civil rights concessions.[1]

Good employment opportunities remained severely limited. Only a handful of black police officers wore the blue uniform and badge. Dallas's African American population accounted for about 30 percent of the city's total, but not a single black person represented them at city hall, at the county courthouse, or at the state capitol. Management positions in business were rare. Black professionals in law, medicine, and education rarely if ever served whites.

There were some signs that racist attitudes in law enforcement and at the courthouse might be eroding. An interesting example occurred when a diminutive, twenty-two-year-old white Freedom Rider from London, England, claimed that Tony Davis, a heavyset black former disk jockey and advertising salesman, raped her in her South Dallas hotel room. C. B. Bunkley Jr. and Charles Tessmer, one of the city's leading defense lawyers, co-represented the accused rapist, who claimed the woman had invited him to her room. An all-white jury found the accused rapist not guilty. No one could remember the last time a black man accused of raping a white woman had been found innocent.

Bedford by now was very well known in the black community. His civic activities had become widespread, for he enjoyed associating with others. His affiliations extended far beyond his work with the NAACP and the J. L. Turner Legal Association. He belonged to the Negro Chamber of Commerce; he was on the board of directors of the Moorland Branch of the YMCA; he was a member of Big Brothers; he served on the board of the Pioneer District of Circle Ten Boy Scouts; and he was a member of the Elks Lodge, Prince Hall Masonic Lodge, and the Omega Psi Phi Fraternity. (Social fraternities and sororities had not been permitted at Prairie View in his days there, but in 1956 Bedford affiliated with the Theta Alpha graduate chapter of Omega Psi Phi.) He was a leading member of the city's oldest black church, New Hope Baptist.

In 1962 Bedford moved his law office to the South Dallas area that was replacing the State-Thomas-Hall neighborhood as the main business district for the city's African Americans. It was a good move; he began making a decent income as a lawyer. His office was in a new two-story building at 2606 Forest Avenue (now Martin Luther King Jr. Boulevard), Suite 208, just six blocks from Fair Park, site of the annual State Fair of Texas. Sharing office space with him was Haywood Sparks, his accountant friend. Sparks hired a young secretary, Carmena Adams—a graduate of Lincoln High School and West Virginia State College—who soon began working for Bedford, too. Eventually, she would work exclusively for Bedford, remaining with him far into the twenty-first century.

Friends and businesses important to the black community were fellow tenants in the office building, and within a few years it would be an even more significant center for high-profile black organizations. Attorney D. B. Mason was already there. Foster Kidd, a dentist, was in the building, as was the Golden State Insurance Company. A new black-owned bank, Liberty National, occupied part of the first floor. Oddly, perhaps most important of all was a thriving barbershop, Graham's, which quickly became a primary gathering place for prominent black men not just for haircuts but for lively conversation about a multitude of topics, including politics. Four decades later the same barbershop remained a popular gathering place and a site television news reporters regularly visited to assess African American public opinion on current issues. (In 2008, however, Graham's moved to a new location.) Within a few years the Dallas branch of the Urban League, established at the request of the Dallas Citizens Council, took office space in the building, and so did the Southern Christian Leadership Conference.

Bedford, in his mid-thirties, was a model of respectability. He and Velma were the parents of two young children: Louis Arthur Bedford III had been born May 4, 1959, and Angela Renee Bedford was born April 25, 1962. Both births occurred at Parkland Hospital, a public facility that, unlike the city's private hospitals, welcomed all races. Bedford was an attentive father, sharing with Velma all aspects of their children's upbringing. Thanks to Bedford's parents and their willingness to babysit, Velma was able to maintain her career as a teacher.

The senior Bedfords no longer lived on Thomas Avenue. They had built a new house on Watts Street on the east side of Central Expressway not far from their longtime residence, which they had been forced to sell when the connection of the new

Woodall Rodgers Freeway to Central Expressway required their property for right-of-way. A bit farther to the west, the new freeway also caused the disappearance of much of the historic Little Mexico community.

In December 1962 a telegram arrived at Bedford's modest home on Eugene Street. It was from Hobart Taylor Jr., executive vice chairman of President Kennedy's Committee on Equal Employment Opportunity. Taylor advised Bedford that the vice president of the United States, Lyndon Baines Johnson, wanted him to come to the LBJ Ranch in central Texas to discuss community participation in, and support for, the program of Equal Employment Opportunity with LBJ "and some other friends." As exciting as the offer was, Bedford did not go.[2]

Bedford did not know what prompted this high-level invitation, but he had earlier become acquainted with Taylor through Bunkley, the two having been class-mates at both Prairie View and the University of Michigan Law School. (Taylor had graduated from Prairie View before Bedford enrolled there.)

In 1963 it had been seven years since Durham's application for membership in the Dallas Bar Association was rejected. By this time more and more DBA members believed that rejecting applicants because of their race was absurd. That summer the members of the J. L. Turner Legal Association decided that the time was ripe for another black attorney to try to gain membership in the DBA.

Furthermore, two years had passed since President Kennedy appointed the nation's first black man to be a U.S. District Court judge. James Benton Parsons—University of Chicago Law School graduate, former law school professor, and former assistant U.S. attorney—began his thirty-one-year career as a federal judge in 1961.

African American lawyers in Dallas wanted Bedford's close friend Bunkley to be the one to attempt DBA membership. Following the procedure required of any prospective member, Bunkley submitted his application. The admissions committee, charged with screening applications before presenting them to the overall member-ship, rejected his application without explanation, an act that normally would have prevented the question from reaching the rest of the membership. The committee seemed not to recognize that the times were changing.

The president of the bar did, though. H. Louis Nichols was a native Texan, SMU School of Law graduate, and attorney in Dallas since 1939. He and John

Louis Shook, an ex officio member of the board by virtue of his service as a director of the State Bar of Texas, were alarmed at the committee's rejection of Bunkley's application. The matter was not one that they could override as individuals, however. The association was governed by well-codified procedures, but those were subject to change.

Nichols and Shook discussed the situation with the DBA board of directors. At the insistence of Nichols and Shook, the directors agreed unanimously that in the future they would review any applications denied by the admissions committee. Further, Shook successfully moved that Nichols advise the admissions committee that the rules and bylaws of the Dallas Bar Association contained no provisions for rejecting a potential member on the grounds of race, color, or creed. In his appearance before the admissions committee, Nichols persuaded its members to suspend its action on Bunkley until the board of directors could hear their presentation.

On October 8, 1963, the admissions committee members attended the meeting of the directors to explain their reasoning in rejecting Bunkley. Nichols advised them that because of the sensitivity of the matter, their reasons should be good and sufficient. After a long discussion, however, the board approved the action of the admissions committee. Bunkley's application was denied.[3]

For a brief time the matter of membership for black attorneys in the Dallas Bar Association had ended again. And it had ended quietly. A change lay not far ahead, though. In June 1963 Durham, now being called "Mr. Civil Rights in Texas," had visited the White House at President Kennedy's invitation to discuss civil rights problems. How long could the Dallas Bar Association continue to ban black attorneys from its own doors?[4]

During the fall of 1963, when civil rights was one of the most widely discussed issues in the nation, Bedford decided that the time had come for him to step more directly into the fray. He had managed Bunkley's campaign for city council and James's campaign for the school board. Now he wanted to be a candidate himself.

The opportunity came when two Democratic representatives resigned from the Texas Legislature. A special election to replace them was called for November 9, 1963. A late September headline in the *Dallas Morning News* summed it up: "Negro Considering Race for Seat in Legislature."[5] That man of course was Bedford.

Only one black man had ever sought election as a state representative in Dallas. Thirty years earlier attorney Ammon S. Wells was one of sixty candidates who tried to replace Sarah T. Hughes when she vacated her at-large legislative seat to accept appointment as judge of the Fourteenth District Court. Wells did not win, but the campaign had revealed the lengths to which the Dallas establishment would go to maintain tranquility and white supremacy in the city.[6]

Nine years later, in 1944, Rev. Maynard Jackson had failed to be elected as a Dallas Independent School District trustee, despite his qualifications and well-run campaign. The campaign was marred by anonymous physical threats against him and his family. Not long afterward, despite longtime family ties to the city and to his New Hope Baptist Church, he accepted a pastorate in Atlanta, where the Jackson family began a new legacy.

Bedford's friend Bunkley had twice campaigned for Dallas City Council. Facing an overwhelming challenge because all council positions were at-large, he lost both times. More recently and more encouragingly, in April 1963 African American businessman George Allen had campaigned impressively for a seat on the council. Although he did not win, four white candidates had split the white vote, and black voters voted overwhelmingly in favor of Allen, who garnered 11,400 votes.[7]

The fact that voters throughout the city voted for all council and state legislative candidates rather than by single districts or neighborhoods always presented a handicap for minority or independent candidates. As for the city council, only those candidates endorsed by the business-dominated Citizens Charter Association could afford to mount a citywide campaign. As the Allen campaign had shown, even with white citizens splitting their votes among several candidates, the likelihood that a black candidate could win was slim. Although legislative races, unlike council campaigns, were partisan, the preponderance of white votes throughout the county made a black candidate's victory improbable.

The early article in the *News* about Bedford's candidacy reported that he was merely "considering" the race. In fact, he had already written the Texas secretary of state for an application. In early October his candidacy became official. He was a Democratic candidate for Place 7, a countywide position, as was the case for all legislative seats. Fourteen other individuals filed for the same seat. This, to Bedford, was good news, for he believed he could win almost all of the black votes and that white voters would split among the other candidates, as they had in Allen's city council race.

Actually, he could count on a number of liberal white votes, too, especially after the conservative Democratic County chairman, Lee Smith, infuriated many liberal and loyalist Democrats by personally endorsing individual conservative candidates in each of the two legislative elections rather than remaining impartial, as his position required.[8] Labor lawyer Oscar Mauzy and SMU professor Sydney Reagan were among those who quietly supported Bedford. As was typical, some white supporters who contributed to Bedford's campaign cloaked their donations for fear of backlash, masking their contributions as "fees" for unspecified services rendered.[9]

Mike Quinn, political writer for the *Dallas Morning News*, speculated that many loyalist Democrats, who were "bitterly opposed" to conservative chairman Smith, would vote for Bedford.[10] Keith Shelton, political writer for the *Dallas Times Herald*, observed that other than the Republicans, the African American vote was the only identifiable group supporting a single candidate.[11] "Chances of being elected . . . look good for Attorney Louis A. Bedford Jr., according to local political observers," reported a local African American newspaper, citing the expected support of black voters and the split among white voters. A picture of Bedford and Velma and their two children accompanied the article.[12]

Encouraged at his prospects, Bedford campaigned hard and tried to cover all bases. Early on he sent letters to the city's black ministers, always a potent force in guiding their congregations politically, asking for their advice and their support. He sent similar letters to others, including Durham, and he met with small groups throughout the city to seek their support. He was pleased with the interest and support the SMU community gave him.

His office at 2606 Forest Avenue served as his campaign headquarters. About one hundred supporters gathered there for its formal opening.

Bedford's platform, repeated many times in campaign literature, was broadly progressive. He supported congressional redistricting so that Dallas County could get a much-needed and justified additional seat in the U.S. House of Representatives. He also favored state senatorial and legislative redistricting to create nine separate districts of equal population, with candidates being elected by district rather than countywide. He favored increasing the minimum wage and maximizing payments allowable under workman's compensation laws. He wanted to abolish the poll tax, and he would seek broader educational opportunities for all citizens of Texas.[13]

Speaking before more than forty agents and district managers of Universal Life Insurance, he emphasized that the time had come for "all loyal Democrats to unite behind me" and stem the tide of Republicanism that had swept Dallas County. He was a loyal Democrat, and he had been so long before the Republicans had gotten a foothold in the county.[14]

That Republican foothold had begun in 1952, when city and county voters defected from the Democrats and favored Dwight Eisenhower over Adlai Stevenson, an election that saw upstart Republican candidate Bruce Alger defeat former Dallas mayor and conservative Democrat Wallace Savage for Dallas County's seat in Congress. Alger was reelected four times, defeating such popular Democratic Party stalwarts as District Attorney Henry Wade and State Representative Barefoot Sanders, before losing in 1964 to Democrat Earle Cabell, who had resigned as Dallas mayor earlier that year to campaign. Dallas had voted for Eisenhower in 1956; in 1960, in contrast to the rest of the state, the county gave an overwhelming majority of its votes to Richard M. Nixon over John F. Kennedy.[15]

Bedford was a liberal Democrat who intended to attract all voters, white and black. His hopes for victory depended on full support from the African American community, though, and at least partial support from white liberals. He was interested "in the educational, economic and industrial growth of Dallas for the benefit of all its citizens." Equal rights were important, and as "a member of a minority group," he said, "I believe that I could be of invaluable service to the Legislature of the State of Texas in its assumption of this responsibility."[16]

An editorial in the *Dallas Express* observed that in recent years too many black candidates, in contrast to Bedford, had thrown their hats into the ring and then done nothing except place a few placards here and there and send out a mailing piece or two. Too often these races had been undertaken, many believed, to siphon off Negro votes. The situation now was different, the newspaper stated. "Never before in history has the need been so great for Negroes to prove themselves a factor in the community," the editorial proclaimed. Some twenty thousand to twenty-five thousand black voters were now registered. Since it was generally agreed that the white vote would be split among the numerous white candidates, the race should be a "shoo-in for Mr. Bedford."[17] Bedford spent most of his time campaigning in the black community, although a meeting with some liberal white professors at SMU was encouraging to him.

Advertising executive Tony Davis recommended a campaign, which would cost eighteen hundred dollars, to include window cards, newspaper advertisements in both the *Dallas Times Herald* and the *Dallas Morning News*, and two paid television appearances. There was not enough money for all these, though.[18] Bedford raised enough money to pay for five thousand handbills and fifty placards, twenty-five thousand folders for a mass mailing, radio commercials, and a list of potential voters who had paid their poll taxes.[19]

In a letter to African American ministers, Bedford asked them to encourage their congregations to vote for him. "If every Negro who is registered to vote will exercise his or her right to vote, then victory is assured," he told them.[20]

That was a truthful statement, but it turned out to be unrealistic, for this contest was different from a nonpartisan city council race. Bedford's opponents were as varied as the faces of Dallas. Besides himself, there were four attorneys, an oil production–real estate man, two insurance men, a retiree, a student, a securities broker, and a rabid segregationist. The oil–real estate man, O. Hughes Brown, was a Republican who had the solid support of the GOP county executive committee. He based his platform on a national issue: the need to nominate Barry Goldwater for president in 1964.

There were no voter surveys or polls to indicate a likely outcome, and on the eve of the November 9, 1963, election, Bedford knew only that he had a good chance of winning if he got almost all the votes from the African American community.

But the strength of Dallas Republicans was too great for a Democrat of any stripe—liberal or conservative—much less a black Democrat. At home with his family and friends, Bedford listened to the results through radio reports. Voters gave Brown a solid victory with 27,638 votes. Bedford finished a respectable third, gaining 7,442 votes, trailing the second-place candidate, securities broker John Field, who had 12,244 votes. In the race for Place 6 (for the other legislative seat vacated by a Democrat), the Republican candidate, Jack Sampsell—who, like Brown, had tied himself to Goldwater and eschewed local or statewide issues— also won an easy victory.[21]

Voter turnout had been light in this special election, and light turnouts inevitably favored conservatives. GOP County Chairman John Leedom, echoing the themes the two Republican winners had emphasized, declared that their victories proved that Dallas County voters continued to "repudiate the socialistic New Frontier progress of the Kennedy administration."[22] This theme had resonance in Dallas.

Liberals in Dallas—moderates, too—were on the losing side in 1963. Right-wing sentiment had become increasingly virulent. By the time of the November 9 special election, Dallas citizens were obsessed with a far more important news story with lasting impact. Just two weeks earlier, United States Ambassador to the United Nations Adlai Stevenson had been roughly treated at a speech he gave in Dallas. With President Kennedy due to arrive in Dallas on November 22, great fears arose about what sort of reception he might receive. City officials and leaders were taking significant steps to insulate him from possible embarrassment or even harm.

At the Stevenson event, the audience was packed with right-wing extremists, who heckled and interrupted the ambassador as he spoke. Even before Stevenson could begin his speech, the leader of one right-wing group stood at the front of the auditorium with a bullhorn and shouted questions that implied a Kennedy alliance with communism. A huge banner spread across the top of the stage, planted the night before and bearing the words "Welcome Adlai," somehow was turned over in the midst of his speech to reveal an entirely different message: "U.N. Red Front." In the parking lot after his speech, Stevenson was struck on the head with a picket sign and spat on by a college student. Images of the tumultuous reception spread quickly over the nation via the evening newscasts and ugly headlines. Suddenly, the nation's attention was riveted on Dallas. What kind of treatment would the president receive on his arrival? The possibilities were frightening. Some prominent individuals urged the president to cancel his Dallas trip.

Bedford held Kennedy in high esteem. In the 1960 campaign Kennedy had emphasized eliminating racial and religious discrimination from American society, advocating greater voting rights, and increasing employment opportunities. His sympathetic telephone call to Mrs. Martin Luther King Jr. when her husband was jailed in Georgia won him an outpouring of goodwill in the black community. All of this gave him overwhelming black support in the election.

Once he was in the White House, Kennedy introduced the most comprehensive civil rights bill offered since Reconstruction, including, among other things, employment opportunities in private business, authority for the attorney general to initiate school desegregation suits, and equal accommodations in public facilities. It did not go as far as many civil rights leaders wanted, but Kennedy was fearful of the political consequences of going too far.

Bedford and most black leaders in Dallas understood the practical problems confronting Kennedy. They were willing to be patient. Overreaching would endanger other proposals, such as an increased minimum wage law and support for education, that would enhance life for African Americans.

Very few of Dallas's civic or political leaders supported the president, but they were concerned about the possibility of embarrassing demonstrations. They took well-publicized steps to ensure a reception for Kennedy that could restore the city's reputation for hospitality.

There was almost no chance for Bedford to be at the Trade Mart (part of the Dallas Market Center) to see the president he supported and admired give his scheduled address. The luncheon event, deemed "nonpolitical," was sponsored by the powerful conservative, business-minded Citizens Council. Only at the last minute, with protests erupting that Kennedy's loyal Dallas Democratic supporters were being frozen out of the event, were approximately one hundred tickets made available to them.

Bedford wanted at least to get a glimpse of the president, so he drove alone to the center of town, found a parking spot, and stood at curbside in the midst of the large, enthusiastic crowds on Main Street. Spectators cheered wildly as the president's black Lincoln convertible limousine, escorted by police cars and followed by other cars and press buses, passed by on its way to the Trade Mart—with JFK, his wife, Jacqueline, Texas Governor John B. Connally, and his wife, Nellie, all cordially waving and smiling at the happy onlookers.

When Bedford returned to his office some fifteen minutes later, he was told immediately that the president had been shot. "No," he replied, that couldn't be true, because "I just saw him."[23] But it was true, and the live radio and television broadcasts confirmed the shocking news right away.

Kennedy's death was a devastating blow. The assassination unleashed a torrent of emotions across the nation and world. Widespread hostility was immediately directed against Dallas.

If *Dallas Express* writer and photographer Marion Butts was any indication, many of the city's blacks felt that Dallas shared the blame for Kennedy's death. He wrote, "Dallas citizens must face up to the realization that because Dallas is a city where hate is bred, born, grows, and destroys the minds of its citizens, the President was murdered on our streets. . . . The sins of silent leadership, inactive complacency, and hypocritical lip service, have caught up with 'Big Friendly' Dallas."[24]

The city's leaders, who heretofore had tolerated the right-wing extremists in their midst, recognized that Dallas now faced the greatest crisis in its history. It might never recover from its extremist image. The damage could be economic as well. City leaders realized that a new tone of moderation must be adopted.

The postassassination comments of Mayor Earle Cabell, a conservative businessman who had become more moderate during his term in office, reflected the growing awareness that it was not enough merely to defend the city from its critics: significant changes must be made. Cabell's first instinct on the day of the assassination was to reject any notions of guilt for his city. "There are maniacs all over the world," he said, and reasonable people would realize that the assassination was the act of a maniac "with no relationship to the people of the community."[25] Later in the afternoon, he modified his stance. Although the assassination "could only be the act of a deranged mind," he said, "each of us, in prayerful reflection, must search our heart and determine if through intemperate word or deed we might have contributed in some fashion to the movement of this mind across the brink of insanity."[26] The following day the mayor declared a day of prayer, and he asked that the city's houses of worship remain open from midnight Friday until midnight Saturday. After Jack Ruby shot Lee Harvey Oswald on Sunday in the police station basement, Mayor Cabell issued yet another statement. "Now is the time for all of us to come to our senses," he said, "to resist hysteria and to quit casting around for someone else to blame." He called on his fellow citizens to dedicate themselves to "those principles of service and courage exemplified by the late John F. Kennedy."[27]

Perhaps it was because he realized that a dramatic change in attitude was occurring in the city that another African American attorney now decided to apply for membership in the Dallas Bar Association. He was Fred Finch, a Dallas native, a graduate of Booker T. Washington High, a *cum laude* graduate of Wiley College, and a Harvard Law School graduate. He had served as a second lieutenant in the U.S. Army Air Forces during World War II, and before entering Harvard, he had worked as a personnel officer at the Veterans Administration Hospital in Dallas from 1946 to 1951 (today part of the Dallas VA Medical Center). Bedford and his lawyer friends believed it would be difficult for the bar association to deny admission to a Harvard Law School graduate. How could it be said that he was not qualified?[28]

The admissions committee, however, still refused to budge. Finch's application was rejected, just as Bunkley's had been denied two months earlier. But Bunkley's rejection had prompted a change in DBA bylaws. As Nichols had insisted, all rejections now had to be reviewed by the board of directors, and he told his fellow board members on December 11, 1963, that he could see no reason to refuse to admit Finch. He persuaded the directors to approve Finch's application and submit his name to the full membership. The directors unanimously agreed, and at an open meeting on December 20, 1963, during which a full discussion was held, members of the Dallas Bar Association approved Finch as its first African American member.[29]

Without a doubt, the climate in Dallas after the Kennedy assassination became far more accepting, not just for African Americans and other minorities but also for average white citizens, who previously had not been able to participate in leadership roles. Early evidence of the change in attitude came in 1964 when Bruce Alger, an ultraconservative congressman whose strong states' rights philosophy and anti–federal government convictions had not been favorable to African Americans or minorities, was voted out after ten years in office, defeated by former mayor Earle Cabell, a moderate Democrat. Replacing Cabell as mayor was industrialist Erik Jonsson, founder of Texas Instruments who brought a worldwide perspective to office because of the company's worldwide operations. Jonsson's broad-based Goals for Dallas program was important in bringing new individuals into the decision-making processes of the city.

Kennedy's tragic death changed the national mood. The idealistic goals articulated so forcefully by this energetic young president seemed to have been abruptly ended by the act of a madman. It was as if America's bright future had been cut short.

The new president, Lyndon B. Johnson, immediately pledged himself to follow through on all of John F. Kennedy's goals, and the one goal he emphasized most strongly was civil rights. Five days after the assassination, Johnson declared, "No memorial or oration or eulogy could more eloquently honor President Kennedy's memory than the earliest possible passage of the civil rights bill for which he fought so long. We have talked long enough about equal rights in this country. We have talked for one hundred years or more. It is time now to write the next chapter and write it in the books of law."[30] In this speech, given before senators, congressmen, and Supreme Court justices, Johnson spoke eloquently: "Let us put an end to the teaching and the preaching of hate and evil and violence. Let us turn away from the fanatics of the far left and the far right, from the apostles of bitterness and bigotry, from those defiant of law and those who pour venom into our nation's bloodstream."[31]

Under Johnson's persistent prodding, Congress passed the Civil Rights Act of 1964, which was far broader than what Kennedy believed possible. Signed into law by Johnson on July 2, 1964, it tried to remedy the gross injustices that had relegated black Americans to second-class citizenship and made their interaction with the white community frequently intolerable for them. It prohibited racial discrimination in public places, such as theaters, parks, restaurants, and hotels; required employers to provide equal employment opportunities; and mandated uniform state standards for establishing the right to vote. It provided clear legal redress for basic human rights denied to African Americans and gave the attorney general the power to take legal action wherever he found a pattern of resistance. Especially important was its provision to guarantee equal employment opportunities for minorities through Title VII, which prohibited employment discrimination based on "race, color, religion, sex, or national origin." The next month the bodies of three missing young civil rights workers were found in an earthen dam in Mississippi. The nation's conscience shuddered. Pollsters detected a dramatic shift in public opinion from this moment.[32]

It was by far the most significant civil rights act yet passed in the twentieth century. Subsequent acts clarified and gave power to its provisions. In 1965 the federal Voting Rights Act outlawed the infamous literacy tests, which were used to deny the ballot to so many African Americans, and removed the onerous poll tax from voter registration.

The impact of the Voting Rights Act was dramatic, for the obstacles that Maceo Smith, Maynard Jackson, and W. J. Durham had been confronting for so many years in their efforts to register voters in Dallas disappeared. Throughout the South massive numbers of black voters were able to register to vote for the first time. As President Johnson observed in his autobiography, "Change, real change, was on the horizon."[33] Within four years of Johnson's Civil Rights Act of 1964, the enrollment of Southern black voters jumped from 58 percent to 83 percent.[34] The Civil Rights Act of 1968, often called the Fair Housing Act, prohibited racial discrimination in the sale or rental of houses. Introduced dramatically by people like Rosa Parks and Martin Luther King Jr., this was the beginning of a revolution in American life that guaranteed new rights not just for African Americans and other minorities, such as women and Mexican Americans, but for the aged, the infirm, the poor, and other forgotten citizens.

The civil rights movement and the turmoil surrounding it were far from over. Beyond the Civil Rights Act of 1964 were freedom walks; urban rioting; the rise of the black power movement as more aggressive civil rights leaders who disdained civil disobedience stepped onto the national scene; and the assassination of Martin Luther King Jr.

Real progress—over and above the Civil Rights and Voting Rights Acts—took place throughout the rest of the decade. Racist attitudes did not magically disappear in an instant, but long-ingrained biases began to change. Later generations of both white and black youths would be surprised to learn that their parents and grandparents had lived in a society where separate drinking fountains for whites and blacks were common.

One restaurant in Dallas that had not willingly desegregated in 1961 was the Piccadilly Cafeteria downtown on Commerce Street, part of a small statewide chain. Beginning on May 30, 1964, a group of protesters led by Rev. Earl Allen, pastor of Hamilton Park United Methodist Church, and Ted Armstrong, a senior at Bishop College (which had moved from Marshall to Dallas in 1961), began picketing the restaurant. Police forcibly removed eleven of the demonstrators from the alcove of the cafeteria. This did not discourage the demonstrators, who began daily picketing of the cafeteria. Their presence was evidence of the growing power of the new civil rights groups, which were beginning to display their strength. Allen had been one of the SMU theology students involved in the sit-ins at the drugstore across from the campus. He now headed the Dallas Coordinating Committee for Full Civil Rights. Armstrong was chairman of the Dallas chapter of the Congress of Racial Equality (CORE). After twenty-eight days of demonstrations, the cafeteria agreed to open its doors to blacks when President Johnson signed the Civil Rights Act.[35]

Less than three hours after the president signed the act, the associate pastor of the Boll Street CME Church, Rev. John Bethel, a member of CORE, tested the cafeteria by showing up alone to eat. He was admitted without incident. "Everyone was polite and the food was good," he said afterward.[36]

A year later Dallas experienced its first massive civil rights demonstration. Bedford was among three thousand or so who marched from Good Street Baptist Church to Ferris Plaza in downtown Dallas. It was the largest such rally he had ever attended. The demonstration, part of a nationwide movement encouraged by the NAACP, was prompted by the beating death in Selma, Alabama, of a white Unitarian minister, James Reeb, who had been in the city in support of the voting rights movement. The Reverend B. L. McCormick, president of the Dallas chapter of the NAACP, addressed the crowd, as did Clarence Laws, regional director of the NAACP; W. J. Durham; and Rabbi Levi Olan of Temple Emanu-El.

Dallas city officials were determined to have a peaceful demonstration, and that is what took place. Some three hundred regular police and reserve policemen were on hand. A fifty-member police riot squad was out of sight, poised to respond if trouble occurred. Police Chief Jesse Curry personally helped escort the demonstration. Police arrested five young white men, one of them carrying a Confederate flag and others bearing anti–civil rights placards.[37]

The event received huge headlines in the Dallas newspapers. In the nation's capital, Congressman Earle Cabell extolled the march's peaceful nature as proof of Dallas's harmonious racial relations.

Bedford clipped a newspaper article and added it to the scrapbooks he had begun concerning racial issues, particularly those in Dallas. Clipping such articles about individual achievements by African Americans—published in the two dailies, as well as in the black weeklies—had become a habit for him.

Before the decade of the 1960s was over, a black man, Edward W. Brooke, was elected to the U.S. Senate, the first African American to serve in that august body in eighty-five years. In 1964 Martin Luther King Jr. was awarded the Nobel Peace Prize. In 1967 a Texan, President Lyndon B. Johnson, nominated Thurgood Marshall to be an associate justice of the U.S. Supreme Court; the Senate confirmed the nomination, and Marshall was sworn in, the first African American ever to sit on that bench. Tennis player Arthur Ashe became the first black man to win a major tennis tournament when he captured the 1968 U.S. Open. Charles Evers, Medgar's older brother, was elected as the first black mayor of a biracial town in Mississippi since Reconstruction.

In retrospect, Bedford believed he had been premature in his effort to break the color barrier in his 1964 race for the state legislature. Had he waited a couple of years, the outcome almost certainly would have been different, and he might have become Dallas County's first black legislator. Bedford intended to campaign once more in 1966 and believed he would enjoy the backing of most of the black attorneys. Bunkley offered once again to be his campaign manager. Velma was worried, though. How could they take care of their two young children if he won and spent so many months in Austin?

Young black attorneys—such as E. Brice Cunningham, Berlaind Brashear, James Hopkins, Sam Hudson, Walter Irvin, LaWanda Lacy, Cleo Steele, and Joseph Edwin Lockridge—were beginning to establish practices in town. Lockridge and Cunningham created a partnership with Fred Finch, establishing the law office of Finch, Lockridge, and Cunningham on Oakland Avenue not far from Bedford.

Just as Durham, Bunkley, J. L. Turner Jr., and a handful of others had been available to encourage Bedford, he now found himself in the position of mentoring these new attorneys. One of them he grew particularly close to was Lockridge, who was also interested in the 1966 legislative race. Lockridge had good connections within Dallas's politically powerful African American ministry. His father had been pastor at Golden Gate Baptist Church, and his brother was also a local minister. He could count on the support of Rev. S. M. Wright and the Interdenominational Ministerial Alliance, a formidable black organization. In 1964 Lockridge had been unanimously elected the first black president of the Dallas Pastors' Association.

This time it was understood that the African American candidate who was anointed by the majority of the black community would have an excellent chance at winning, for the Democratic power brokers in town had decided to give open and full support to that individual. They had seen in the 1964 election that the division of votes among the Democrats had resulted in a Republican victory. They didn't want that to happen again.

Finally, Bedford chose not to run. He would have been willing to battle his friend Lockridge, but he listened carefully to his wife's concerns about how his absence would affect their children, and he followed her wishes.[38]

Joseph Lockridge won the endorsements of the black community and of the two daily newspapers, Democratic Party groups, and groups representing both business and labor in Dallas County. In the Democratic primary for Place 5, he swept past the incumbent, conservative Ben Lewis, who had fallen into disfavor. In the November 1966 general election, he defeated Republican Hank Gilliam, 79,188 to 70,809. Lockridge thus had the honor of being the first black person from Dallas County elected to the Texas Legislature.[39]

Lockridge, in his mid-thirties and an Army veteran of the Korean War, was a native of Waco who had moved to Dallas with his parents when he was four years old. The tenth of eleven children, Lockridge graduated from Lincoln High School in South Dallas and earned an undergraduate degree from Southern University in Baton Rouge, Louisiana. His law degree came from Howard University School of Law in Washington, D.C., where he had been president of his class. His classmates there included E. Brice Cunningham and future Democratic powerhouse Vernon Jordan. Lockridge and his wife, Eva, a teacher at H. S. Thompson Elementary School in South Dallas, were the parents of one son.

Lockridge entered the state legislature the same year as two other new black legislators, both from Houston: Barbara Jordan, the first black person elected to the Texas Senate since 1895, and Curtis Graves, elected to the Texas House of Representatives. Lockridge's success was immediate. Fellow legislators elected him Rookie of the Year. In November 1967 Lockridge applied for membership in the Dallas Bar Association and just over two weeks later was admitted. He became the organization's second black attorney, following his law partner Fred Finch.[40]

H. Louis Nichols, now the Dallas Bar Association's immediate past president and still a member of the board of directors, moved that Bunkley's application be reconsidered. Leonard E. Hoffman Jr., the DBA secretary, personally visited both Bunkley and Durham to solicit their membership. Durham declined, saying he no longer needed it. Bunkley once more submitted his application, and less than two weeks later—on April 19, at the recommendation of Hoffman and DBA president Philip Wilson—he was voted into membership. (Although documentation on his election is clear, Bunkley's membership card in the DBA files does not indicate that he ever paid his dues to activate his membership. Bedford later was under the impression that Bunkley never became a member.)[41]

Four days after Bunkley's admission, Bedford submitted his own application. Lockridge and Hoffman signed as his sponsors, and on May 24, 1968, Bedford was voted in, the fourth African American member of the Dallas Bar Association.[42] He was one of seven new members, all the others being white, elected at the time. Three months later, on July 19, 1968, E. Brice Cunningham became the fifth black member of the Dallas Bar Association. Samuel W. Hudson followed in 1969. On September 18, 1970, Joan Tarpley Winn was voted into membership as the first black woman lawyer in the DBA.[43]

About three weeks before Bedford's admission to the bar association, Lockridge asked him to accompany him to Prairie View A&M, where he was to give a speech. If Bedford would go with him, he told him, Lockridge would drive his car so the two could have a leisurely visit on the trip. If not, Lockridge would make commercial flight arrangements and go alone. Bedford decided not to go, and Lockridge made reservations on Braniff Airways. On the return flight from Houston, the propjet airplane encountered a fierce thunderstorm and crashed near Buffalo. Lockridge and all the passengers and crew, eighty-four of them, died. It was the worst air crash in Texas history. Bedford forever after lamented his decision not to accompany Lockridge by car.[44]

Lockridge's successor to the legislature was another black man, Rev. Zan W. Holmes, pastor at Hamilton Park United Methodist Church. Holmes won the special election from a field of eighteen candidates. As did Lockridge, Holmes had the endorsement and support of the Dallas establishment, and at the time he was a member of the Dallas County grand jury.[45]

For some years the Dallas Bar Association headquarters had been on the top floor of the high-rise Adolphus Tower in the heart of downtown Dallas. It was a well-appointed gathering place for the city's most prestigious attorneys and a convenient location for lunch, social events, seminars, committee meetings, and informal gatherings. Here one found judges and attorneys mixing easily. Lawyers who had argued vehemently against one another in the courtroom might be seen sharing a drink after hours.

Becoming involved in the association's activities was not a simple or automatic matter for Bedford and the handful of other African American attorneys who had become members. Bedford felt isolated on his first visits there, and he did not go there for lunch. "It wasn't the most pleasant experience," he said of his early days. However, there were no displays of hostility, and he had no sense that whispered comments were being made behind his back. On the contrary, he heard many sincere expressions of welcome from members who were painfully aware that black attorneys should have been admitted many years before.[46]

As he was invited to committee appointments, Bedford began to feel more comfortable. Far more than any of the other new black attorneys, he became involved in the association's activities. Before his first year as a member ended, he was appointed vice chairman of the traffic committee for 1969, responsible for making reports and recommendations concerning traffic laws and regulations to the City of Dallas.[47] More significant was his service in 1996 as vice chairman of the Law Day Committee, with Doug Lang as chairman. The next year Bedford chaired the committee. He was interacting with a large number of DBA members and public officials in a pleasant way.[48]

Attorneys from the city's largest firms dominated the Dallas Bar Association membership rolls and leadership positions. A large number of white lawyers—generally, by personal choice—still did not belong. By 1965 Dallas County had 2,443 lawyers, and membership in the DBA totaled only 1,426.[49] Those who chose not to belong tended to be sole practitioners. Almost all of the members were men; women were eligible and had been accepted into the organization since 1920, but Dallas County had very few female practitioners. By the end of the 1960s, they numbered only about 150, although in the next decade barriers would fall, and the legal profession would become a popular option for women as well as for African Americans.[50]

Bedford's participation in the Dallas Bar Association was lengthy, honorable, and satisfying. He became one of its most familiar and appreciated members, a trustee of both the foundation and the association, recipient of the Justinian Award in 1991, first recipient of the Martin Luther King Jr. Award in 1993, and Trial Lawyer of the Year in 1998.[51]

In 1966, the same year that Lockridge was elected to the legislature, the coordinator of the Dallas municipal courts, Hugh Jones, called Bedford and invited him to city hall to visit him and James B. Gamble, the chief judge. Bedford accepted the invitation. At the meeting Jones and Gamble told Bedford that an associate judgeship was open, a position that required someone who could work on weekends, some evenings, and weekdays. They were wondering whether this would be something Bedford might like to try (not that he was being offered a judgeship just yet). Bedford told the two men he would be interested in such a position. After the meeting both Bunkley and Durham encouraged him to accept an offer, if it came.

Not long afterward the city attorney, Alex Bickley, called and asked Bedford to come to his office to discuss Bedford's possible appointment as an associate municipal judge. The interview was perfunctory, with questions directed to Bedford about his civic activities and general qualifications. Bickley seemed pleased. He said he'd get in touch with Bedford.

On June 29, 1966, Bedford wrote a letter itemizing his qualifications and formally declaring his interest in the position. Less than three weeks later, on July 19, Bedford took the oath of office to become a municipal or corporation court judge for the City of Dallas. On that Saturday, July 23, he found himself presiding in a courtroom in city hall.[52]

Louis A. Bedford Jr. had become the first African American judge in Dallas County history. It was a position he held until 1980, when he resigned to run for Dallas City Council. Because he normally heard cases only on weekends and evenings, Bedford was able to maintain his private law practice.

Those who appeared before him in the municipal courts were charged with violating city ordinances, especially traffic offenses, zoning violations, and Class C misdemeanors. Jury trials were possible but rarely if ever used in Bedford's court. His duties also involved issuing search warrants and giving Miranda warnings to persons under investigation for felony crimes.

The uniqueness of Bedford's position of authority in what had previously been a white man's system of justice meant that he was being carefully watched. This scrutiny came from city prosecutors, police officers who appeared in court, lawyers, defendants, and the general public. There were no protests from accused white persons who appeared before him, but he sometimes observed the surprise of those who passed by his courtroom and saw him on the bench. Sometimes they even stopped and did a double take.

Bedford's appointment could have been perceived to be a token gesture in those changing times, but the black community did not see it that way. As Albert Lipscomb, future mayor pro tem for the city, later recalled, "That was no Uncle Tom appointment. That was a real appointment. Boy, we sure felt good about that."[53]

There was no training for his judgeship. Bedford simply took a seat at the bench and began hearing cases. He was grateful to Bill Boyd, the white police officer assigned to his court as bailiff. Boyd told Bedford he would do everything he could to help him, and he did so without fail, pointing out all the intricacies that only his long experience could bring. The fact that such significant help came from a white police officer was a welcome surprise to Bedford. "He was like a mother hen," Bedford later said in appreciation. Boyd became a close friend and remained with Bedford until resigning a few years later to become a bailiff in a Dallas County courtroom.[54]

Within days of Bedford's appointment, Dallas radio station WFAA invited him to be a guest on its Sunday show, *Newsmakers*. Expecting to be asked about his role as a corporation court judge, Bedford was surprised when the show's three veteran reporters immediately turned to Martin Luther King Jr.'s decision to move his protest marches from the South to the North to address poverty and segregated housing. Disgruntled whites in Cicero, Illinois, adjacent to Chicago, heckled and assaulted the demonstrators there, leading many people to question the appropriateness of King's new campaign in the North.[55]

Bedford responded quickly. King had the absolute right, he said, to demonstrate wherever he pleased. The fact that some people reacted by rioting did not negate that right. The problem lay in the people who chose to riot, not in the demonstrators. He thought of an analogy: "It's like me going to a football game where everybody is rooting for the Dallas Cowboys and I'm the only one rooting for the Redskins. Do the Cowboy supporters have a right to stone me?"[56]

Two months later, in September 1966, Dr. King visited Dallas to speak at an international assembly of Christian Churches (Disciples of Christ). When he stopped by the Nassau Club (on the street that in a few years would be named for King), Bedford challenged him to a game of pool. Bedford, a more than competent player, felt that he might have the honor of beating King in a friendly game. They played eight ball, and King played poorly at first. Then he warmed up and started putting balls in the pockets with ease. Finally, King sank the eight ball in a corner pocket, winning the game handily. Pleased with himself, King put up his cue stick. This was the first time he had played since his school days, he told the somewhat deflated Bedford.[57]

One of the early surprises for Bedford as a municipal judge came on a Friday evening in early October 1966. It was the annual Texas-Oklahoma football weekend. The Longhorns and Sooners' traditional rivalry game, then played at the Cotton Bowl, is held during the Texas State Fair. On the eve of the 1966 game, fans of both teams, as always, partied downtown, drinking heavily, making loud noises, and generally behaving in an outrageous manner. Such pregame shenanigans were often shocking in their intensity, and every year police arrested scores of fans for drunkenness and disorderly conduct. So many store windows were broken during this annual bacchanalia that hotels and retail establishments had taken to boarding up their windows.

On this night in 1966, the partying went on until at least 2:00 AM Saturday. Bedford found himself reading the rights to some 150 to 200 rowdy fans as they had been arrested throughout the evening for various offenses. Some had thrown mattresses and chairs out of hotel windows. Some had even broken the huge iron doors at city hall. Bedford had never witnessed this kind of rowdyism. He could not avoid an overriding realization: If these had been black revelers committing such outrageous deeds, an immediate crackdown would have been demanded to end the problem then and forever. The National Guard might even have been called in.[58]

In general, Bedford tried to be a fair judge to everyone who appeared before him. One time, though, a city prosecutor went to Judge Gamble and corporation court administrator Jones and stated that Bedford seemed to be especially harsh on black defendants. After investigating the docket sheets, Gamble, Jones, and other city prosecutors found nothing to warrant the allegation, and the prosecutor withdrew his complaint.[59]

At one point in his judgeship, Bedford offended some Special Services police officers by dismissing a number of cases they had brought for alleged drinking after hours. Bedford soon began receiving odd telephone calls from anonymous white women, asking him to take them out on a "date." Bedford feared that the calls, which soon ended, were part of a trap set by officers to result in his arrest and cause him to lose his position.[60]

More than once a lawyer said to Bedford, "Judge, you're so great, I'd vote for you for a public office. If everybody were like you we wouldn't have any problems." Such comments, he believed, reflected deep-seated prejudices, the assumption that the masses of blacks were not good citizens.[61]

Bedford's work as an associate corporation court judge was satisfying, though, and it brought extra income, $51.44 for each day he spent on the bench. In 1971 City Councilman George Allen, who headed the municipal court committee, asked Bedford to become a full-time judge. Bedford declined.[62] He did not want to be a full-time corporation court judge mainly because of the lack of job security. He would be serving at the pleasure of the Dallas City Council. He also knew of one corporation court judge who had fined the secretary of one of the city's leading citizens, then found himself called to that citizen's office to explain his decision. While it was not mandatory for a corporation court judge to respond to a private individual in such a demeaning manner, Bedford believed there were pressures to do so.[63]

For a while, though, Bedford was intrigued with the possibility of becoming a full-time judge on the state level. With Dolph Briscoe as governor and with liberal Dallas Democrat Mike McKool, Bedford's friend, as a state senator, he thought an appointment might be possible. His first thought was to be a juvenile court judge. "I felt that some of the youth, especially the young black males, were not fully understood, and that there needed to be somebody who could decipher what was really the problem." A white judge from an affluent background, he believed, might be less able to grasp the complicated situations of black youths. Bedford wrote a letter expressing his interest to both Briscoe and McKool.

When the juvenile court possibility faded, Bedford turned his attention to a vacancy for a domestic relations judgeship and wrote a letter of application.[64] A conversation with Fred Finch changed his mind. As Bedford recalled later, Finch asked him whether he really wanted to be a domestic relations judge, who would be faced regularly with difficult decisions. "Do you want to start every day by hearing someone say that he didn't pay child support because he had lost his job or his mother got sick? Your practice is building up. Do you really want to give it up? And if you do give it up and don't get reelected, you'll have to start all over again." Full-time judgeship would also mean losing flexibility to be involved in community affairs. Finch talked and Bedford listened. Then Bedford wrote the governor a letter asking to withdraw his name from consideration.[65]

Bedford was indeed doing much better in his law practice. In the same year that he became an associate corporation court judge, 1966, he and Velma purchased a lot in an undeveloped part of the Cedar Crest section of Oak Cliff and began building a brick, four-bedroom home. The couple spent many late afternoons at the site with Angela and Louis III, noting with growing anticipation the progress made each day. The location was a bit farther away from his office than the modest house on Eugene Street, but it was a straight shot southwest down Forest Avenue (modern Martin Luther King Jr. Boulevard), which changed its name to Cedar Crest Boulevard as it crossed the long bridge over the Trinity River.[66]

The neighborhood, a pleasant one with wooded, rolling hills, had an interesting past, and its transition not long before from white to black provided an intriguing case study on the dynamics involved. Just one block away from the Bedfords' new homesite was the public Cedar Crest Golf Course.[67]

A large-scale neighborhood transition had occurred in the early 1950s in South Dallas, where a large stock of inexpensive frame houses existed. The transition there was accompanied by considerable strife, including the dynamiting of houses. After South Dallas's transition and even with the opening of Hamilton Park in 1954, there continued to be a shortage of good housing for black families, especially those who could afford larger and better homes.

By the 1950s the Cedar Crest community was populated by middle-class whites, who lived in comfortable, moderate-sized brick houses, many of them valued from fifteen thousand to twenty thousand dollars. In 1959 the first African American family bought a house in the neighborhood. That fact, coupled with information that an area apartment development was to be designated for blacks, prompted the Cedar Crest Home Owners' Association to meet in September 1959 and begin raising money to fund a legal battle against the integration of the neighborhood.[68] In April

1960 a district judge issued an injunction prohibiting the sale of two houses there to blacks, but in 1961 the Texas Supreme Court reversed that decision.[69]

After the resulting first panicky rush of white families out of the neighborhood, the situation became relatively stable. But in January 1962 a blast shattered a vacant duplex whose next occupant was to be a black family. A few months later, the Dallas Independent School District designated the neighborhood elementary schools, Roger Q. Mills and Albert Sydney Johnston, for African Americans. Mills had been integrated the previous year with a single black child; now white students would be sent to other schools.[70]

Insofar as achieving an integrated neighborhood was concerned, the effect was devastating. The white pastor of an area Baptist church saw the situation this way: "Those people who objected to living next door to Negroes left early. When I came here 17 months ago, I moved into a block which was pretty well mixed—Negro, Mexican and white. We were living side by side. There was little animosity." When the Dallas Independent School District designated the two schools for blacks, however, white parents who had initially been willing to remain in the neighborhood began moving out, he explained. Many of the families had only a single car, and it was difficult for them to send their children to another school.[71]

The Cedar Crest community's white churches showed some promising signs of coexistence. In 1963 the all-white South Loop Baptist Church, part of the Southern Baptist Convention, voted to admit a thirty-two-year-old African American woman and her two children into membership. It was believed to be the first time any Southern Baptist Convention church had ever admitted blacks.[72]

Generally, though, the white churches sold their properties to black churches and relocated. By the time the Bedfords moved to the neighborhood, it was almost entirely African American. It was attracting many of the city's leading African Americans, including Bunkley, who lived down the street from the Bedfords; future congresswoman Eddie Bernice Johnson; and future Dallas school board member Dr. Emmett Conrad.

By the late 1960s, Bedford had become well known and respected by the white legal profession as well as the black, largely because of his patience, his good work, and his expertise as an attorney. However, there had been skilled and personable African American lawyers before him in Dallas, and the gates had not opened for them. What was primarily different, of course, was the change in American society. The realization that the separation of the races and the subjugation of minorities was inherently evil had taken wider hold, extending gradually from blacks and white liberals into a growing segment of moderate middle-class whites.

In 1967 the Citizens Charter Association (CCA), the political group that for so long had controlled municipal politics, made its first gesture toward black representation on the Dallas City Council. When Joe Moody, the independent councilman from Pleasant Grove, resigned his seat in April 1967, the CCA appointed black realtor C. A. Galloway to succeed him. It was the first time in Dallas's history that a black man sat on the council. The remainder of the unexpired term was brief, just two weeks, but a precedent had been set. When it was time to endorse candidates for the next election, however, the CCA nominated a white man for Galloway's post.

Just as the CCA had dominated city hall for so many years, so had the establishment-supported Committee for Good Schools (CGS) controlled the Dallas Independent School District. For seventeen years the organization had swept school board elections, but in 1967 the progressive, multiracial League for Educational Advancement (LEAD) arose to challenge its dominance. LEAD counted among its membership some of Dallas's leading citizens who had become dissatisfied with the board's conservatism. Two of LEAD's candidates upset their CGS opponents in the spring elections. One of the victors was Dr. Emmett Conrad, a black physician, who became the first African American to serve as a Dallas school board trustee. (In 1964 another black physician, Dudley V. Powell, had gained a number of white votes in the school board election in a losing campaign.) The other LEAD winner was Dr. Marvin Berkeley, an executive with Texas Instruments, Inc.

Conrad's election was another manifestation of the rapidly changing times. Educated at Southern University (in Louisiana), Stanford University, and Washington University School of Medicine (in St. Louis), Conrad had been in Dallas eleven years. He commented at some length on the new black leadership emerging in Dallas. "The new breed is somewhat younger," he said. "The older leaders were faced with bargaining with those in control, and the only thing they could bargain for, was that people in control would maintain goodwill and a sense of fair play. They were at a disadvantage." The older leadership had to fight apathy, for in the past black citizens had a tendency to shrug their shoulders and say there was no use in voting: "'We never win anything and never will, so why vote?'" This attitude, Conrad said, was changing.[73]

In 1968 a legal challenge by losing city council candidate Max Goldblatt resulted in a change in residency requirements to greatly favor minorities seeking elected office at city hall. For the first time, eight of the eleven council members had to live in designated districts rather than being elected citywide. One of the new districts was in South Dallas and was predominantly black. For that place the CCA nominated moderate businessman George L. Allen, who had been in Dallas since 1938 and whose early attempt to integrate the University of Texas had been largely forgotten. Allen was elected, beginning a long career in public office, which eventually extended to his election as mayor pro tem and then as justice of the peace. One of the Dallas County courthouses was later named after him.

In the following year, 1969, Bedford received a letter from Judge Jerome Chamberlain of the Criminal District Court. Chamberlain, a former municipal court judge whom Bedford had known at city hall, named him to serve as a grand jury commissioner, responsible for selecting four grand jury members who, along with other members, would have the important responsibility of weighing evidence and either indicting or no-billing individuals charged with crimes. If Bedford was not the first black man to be a grand jury commissioner in Dallas County, he was *one* of the first. Bedford ensured black participation in the grand jury when all four of the members he selected were African Americans.[74]

In this era of the late 1960s, a prominent African American such as Bedford found himself with opportunities never before offered. When U.S. Senator Ralph Yarborough was honored at an appreciation dinner at Dallas's Memorial Auditorium in September 1969, Bedford was one of a group of national, state, and local officials who gathered to pay tribute to the longtime liberal politician.[75] Bedford also accepted an invitation to be on the board of the Friends of the Dallas Public Library, serving with some of the city's most prominent citizens.

Bedford received an even more intriguing possibility during this time. A new member of the GOP state executive committee, future county GOP chairman and future U.S. district judge Robert W. Porter, called Bedford to see whether he could meet him to discuss an important matter. The Republicans, more and more powerful in the county and state and destined to control the Dallas County courthouse, were looking to diversify their slate of candidates in upcoming elections. How would Bedford like to run for an office as a Republican at some future date?

Bedford was surprised, of course. Certainly, he responded, he had nothing against the Republican Party, describing the role that his grandfather, M. M. Rodgers, had played as a prominent Republican in Texas. Bedford said he could see himself as a "Rockefeller Republican," that is, a liberal Republican with civil rights as a priority. But he could never be a "Goldwater Republican." The conversation ended amiably, but no further overtures were made.[76]

Bedford's thriving church, New Hope Baptist, decided in the mid-1960s to construct a new facility on South Central Expressway in South Dallas, leaving its longtime home at San Jacinto and Bogel. Bedford played a leading role as chairman of the building committee. The church, the oldest congregation in Dallas founded by blacks, held its dedication service in the new sanctuary in June 1968. A year and a half later, in that same sanctuary, funeral services were held for Bedford's father, who died on December 28, 1969, from colon cancer. He was seventy-seven years old. He had provided for his son a stern but loving model of rectitude and responsibility.

1. For a recent discussion of the civil rights movement in Dallas, see Brian D. Behnken, "The 'Dallas Way': Protest, Response, and the Civil Rights Experience in Dallas and Beyond," *Southwestern Historical Quarterly* 111, no. 1 (July 2007): 1–29. Others have speculated that Dallas's civil rights gains did not go far enough because of the absence of more-violent demonstrations. See Phillips, *White Metropolis*; Dulaney, "Whatever Happened?"; and Schutze, *The Accommodation*.
2. Hobart Taylor Jr., executive vice chairman of the President's Committee on Equal Employment Opportunity, telegram to Bedford, Dec. 14, 1962, "L. A. Bedford Political Races" binder, Bedford Papers.
3. Payne, *As Old as Dallas Itself*, 232–33.

4. Durham photograph and caption, *Dallas Express*, June 22, 1963; the caption describes the visit to the White House.
5. *Dallas Morning News*, Sept. 27, 1963.
6. The incident is described in Chapter 1.
7. "Mayor Cabell Wins by Large Margin; CCA Men Take Seven Council Seats," *Dallas Morning News*, Apr. 3, 1963.
8. "Young Democratic Club Hits Smith Endorsement," *Dallas Morning News*, Oct. 16, 1963.
9. Will Wilson to Bedford, May 15, 1961, "L. A. Bedford Political Races" binder, Bedford Papers; Louis A. Bedford Jr., interview by Darwin Payne, June 29, 2006.
10. Mike Quinn, "Unique Battle to Unfold in Special Ballot," *Dallas Morning News*, Nov. 3, 1963.
11. Keith Shelton, "GOP Still Holds Edge in Legislature Race," *Dallas Times Herald*, Oct. 6, 1963.
12. "Attorney Bedford Hopeful in Bid for State Legislature," newspaper unknown, 1963, "L. A. Bedford Political Races" binder, Bedford Papers.
13. Ibid.
14. Typewritten news release, Oct. 1963, "L. A. Bedford Political Races" binder, Bedford Papers.
15. "Dallas County Vote Canvass Gives 60,000 Edge to Nixon," *Dallas Morning News*, Nov. 13, 1960.
16. Political mailer, 1963, "L. A. Bedford Political Races" binder, Bedford papers.
17. "Editorials," *Dallas Express*, 1963, "L. A. Bedford Political Races" binder, Bedford Papers.
18. Tony Davis of Davis & Associates to Bedford, 1963, "L. A. Bedford Political Races" binder, Bedford Papers.
19. Invoices and statements from various printing firms, 1963, "L. A. Bedford Political Races" binder, Bedford papers.
20. Form letter to "Dear Reverend," 1963, "L. A. Bedford Political Races" binder, Bedford Papers.
21. "GOP Lassoes All but One," *Dallas Morning News*, Nov. 10, 1963.
22. "GOP Wins Said JFK Loss; Democrats Lament Turnout," *Dallas Morning News*, Nov. 10, 1963.
23. Louis A. Bedford Jr., interview by Darwin Payne, June 15, 2006.
24. "A City That Breeds Hate: The President Is Murdered," *Dallas Express*, Nov. 30, 1963.
25. "Cabell Says Shocked by Slaying," *Dallas Morning News*, Nov. 23, 1963.
26. "Mayor Cabell Declares Day of Prayer for J.F.K.," *Dallas Morning News*, Nov. 23, 1963.
27. "Cabell Asks People to Use Sense," *Dallas Morning News*, Nov. 25, 1962.
28. Bedford, interview, June 15, 2006.
29. Payne, *As Old as Dallas Itself*, 234.
30. Quoted by Doris Kearns (Goodwin), *Lyndon Johnson and the American Dream* (New York: Harper & Row, 1976), 174.
31. Ibid.
32. Joshua Zeitz, "1964: The Year the Sixties Began," *American Heritage* 57, no. 5 (Oct. 2006): 43.
33. Lyndon Baines Johnson, *The Vantage Point: Perspectives of the Presidency, 1963–1969* (New York: Holt, Rinehart and Winston, 1971), 167.
34. Hine, *Black Victory*, 6.
35. "Piccadilly Serves Lone Negro Pastor," *Dallas Morning News*, July 3, 1964.
36. Ibid.
37. "Dallas March," *Dallas Times Herald*, Mar. 15, 1965; "'Smooth as Silk,'" *Dallas Morning News*, Mar. 15, 1965.

38. Louis A. Bedford Jr., interview by Darwin Payne, June 28, 2006.

39. "Two Negroes Win Contests," *Dallas Morning News*, May 9, 1966; "Democrats Win; One Race Close," *Dallas Morning News*, Nov. 9, 1966.

40. Dallas Bar Association, Application for Membership, Nov. 10, 1967.

41. Ibid., Apr. 8, 1968.

42. Bedford, interview, June 15, 2006; Leonard Hoffman, interview by Darwin Payne, June 17, 2006.

43. *Dallas Bar Association Weekly Bulletin*, Apr. 15, May 20, and July 19, 1968; May 5, 1969; and Sept. 14, 1970.

44. Bedford, interview, June 28, 2006; "84 Killed in Crash near Corsicana," *Dallas Morning News*, May 4, 1968.

45. "Holmes Wins Special Race for Place 5," *Dallas Morning News*, June 19, 1968.

46. Bedford, interview, June 15, 2006.

47. Hugh L. Steger to Bedford, Mar. 18, 1969, "L. A. Bedford Jr. Personal" binder, Bedford Papers.

48. Bedford, interview, June 15, 2006.

49. Payne, *As Old as Dallas Itself*, 236.

50. Ibid., 275.

51. Ibid., 234.

52. Bedford, interview, June 15, 2006; Bedford's personal calendar, reproduced in "L. A. Bedford Jr. Personal" binder, Bedford Papers.

53. "'He Had Vision,'" *Dallas Morning News*, Feb. 24, 1989.

54. Bedford, interview, June 29, 2006.

55. "Dallas' First Negro Judge on 'Newsmakers,'" *Dallas Morning News*, July 23, 1966.

56. Bedford, interview, June 15, 2006.

57. Louis A. Bedford Jr., interview by Darwin Payne, Feb. 26, 2008.

58. Ibid., June 29, 2006.

59. Ibid., June 15, 2006.

60. Ibid., June 29, 2006.

61. *Bedford Oral History Interview*, 45.

62. "Ranger to Air Decision Friday on Judgeship," *Dallas Morning News*, July 4, 1973.

63. "Action by City Judge Poses Legal Question," *Dallas Morning News*, Mar. 1, 1967; Bedford, interview, June 15, 2006.

64. *Bedford Oral History Interview*, 32.

65. Bedford, interview, June 15, 2006.

66. Ibid.

67. Cedar Crest had been a private club that opened amid gala festivities on January 1, 1918. In 1927 Walter Hagen, playing at Cedar Crest with the rest of the world's best golfers, won the PGA Championship for the fourth consecutive year, becoming the first golfer to achieve such a streak. The club ran into financial difficulties in the 1930s, and in 1946 it was sold to the City of Dallas, and the course became open to the public.

68. "Area Seeks Negro Ban for Homes," *Dallas Morning News*, Sept. 15, 1959.

69. "Judge Bars House Sale to Negroes," *Dallas Morning News*, Apr. 2, 1960; "Right to Sell Home to Negro Affirmed," *Dallas Morning News*, May 11, 1961.

70. "Blast Shatters Vacant Duplex," *Dallas Morning News*, Jan. 13, 1962; "Church in Changing Sector," *Dallas Morning News*, Aug. 5, 1962.

71. "Church in Changing Sector."

72. "3 Negroes Accepted by Church," *Dallas Morning News*, July 18, 1963.

73. "Dr. Conrad: Dallas Negro Leadership," *Dallas Morning News*, May 13, 1967.

74. Judge Jerome Chamberlain, Criminal District Court, to Bedford, Mar. 10, 1969, "L. A. Bedford Jr. Personal" binder, Bedford Papers; Louis A. Bedford Jr., interview by Darwin Payne, Sept. 20, 2006.

75. "Officials Invited to Dinner for Ralph," *Dallas Morning News*, Sept. 21, 1969.

76. Bedford, interview, June 29, 2006.

Mack Matthew Rodgers, Bedford's grandfather, was a politician, educator, and businessman.
Here he is pictured in front of his LaGrange, Texas, home surrounded by his son, six daughters, and two
grandchildren. Bedford's mother, Callie, is at the far left. (Courtesy of L. A. Bedford Jr.)

In his later years, M. M. Rodgers maintained an office for his church and fraternal work in the
Knights of Pythias building in Dallas, where his daughter Callie worked with him. (Courtesy of L. A. Bedford Jr.)

The Bedford house at 3317 Thomas Avenue in Dallas provided a comfortable home for Louis A. Bedford Jr. and his sister Deborah. (Courtesy of L. A. Bedford Jr.)

Along with her husband, Callie Bedford, whose mother died shortly after she was born, was a thoughtful, loving presence for her two children. (Courtesy of L. A. Bedford Jr.)

Siblings Deborah and
Louis Bedford Jr. were
well-behaved youngsters.
(Courtesy of L. A. Bedford Jr.)

In 1947 Lee G. Brotherton
(at left) and Ben Thomas became
the first two African American
police officers in Dallas. Despite
the police car in this photo,
they patrolled the State-Thomas
neighborhood on foot. (Marion
Butts Collection, Texas/Dallas
History & Archives Division,
Dallas Public Library)

Bedford regularly passed through these front doors to the Brooklyn Law School between 1947 and 1950, competing for the first time with white students. (Courtesy of Brooklyn Law School.)

Bedford, at right, often studied for his law school classes with good friends Nathan Mitchell, at left, and Hugo Madison. They were among a handful of black students there. (Courtesy of L. A. Bedford Jr.)

J. L. Turner Sr. was an early Dallas lawyer and Bedford family friend who provided a role model for others. Dallas's first organization of African American lawyers was named for him. (Marion Butts Collection, Texas/Dallas History & Archives Division, Dallas Public Library)

W. J. Durham was a brilliant civil rights attorney involved in many significant cases such as *Sweatt v. Painter*, which in 1950 was a prelude to the epochal *Brown v. Board of Education* decision. (Marion Butts Collection, Texas/Dallas History & Archives Division, Dallas Public Library)

Crawford B. Bunkley Jr. was a close friend and attorney colleague of Bedford. (Marion Butts Collection, Texas/Dallas History & Archives Division, Dallas Public Library)

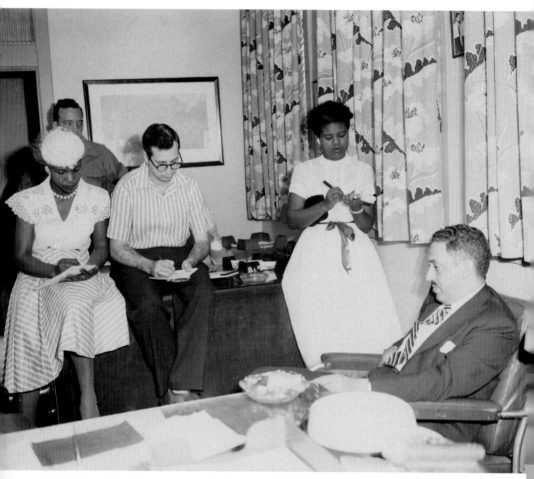

Thurgood Marshall is interviewed by reporters while visiting Dallas for the 1954 NAACP national convention. At left is Julia Scott Reed, who later became the first full-time black reporter hired by the *Dallas Morning News*. (Marion Butts Collection, Texas/Dallas History & Archives Division, Dallas Public Library)

In late 1960 and early 1961 organized pickets marched in front of the H. L. Green department store to force the desegregation of its lunch counters. Bedford was among the demonstrators.
(Marion Butts Collection, Texas/Dallas History & Archives Division, Dallas Public Library)

The H. L. Green store had a separate lunch counter in the basement for its black customers.
(Marion Butts Collection, Texas/Dallas History & Archives Division, Dallas Public Library)

A panel discussion at New Hope Baptist Church in the 1960s brought together white and black leaders. Bedford is standing in the rear. At the far left is the church's pastor, H. Rhett James. A. Maceo Smith is seated, second from the right. Standing at right is C. B. Bunkley Jr. (Marion Butts Collection, Texas/Dallas History & Archives Division, Dallas Public Library)

In 1979 Bedford campaigned for a seat on the Dallas City Council. Here he addresses a group at the Moorland YMCA, a place familiar to him since his childhood. (Courtesy of L. A. Bedford Jr.)

In the mid-1960s, Bedford headed the building committee for a new facility for the New Hope Baptist Church. Here (second from right) he hands a key to the new facility to the pastor, Rev. H. Rhett James. (Marion Butts Collection, Texas/Dallas History & Archives Division, Dallas Public Library)

An estimated 3,000 demonstrators gathered at Ferris Plaza in downtown Dallas in March 1965 to show their support of civil rights activists in Alabama. It was said to be the largest such gathering in Dallas up to that time. (Marion Butts Collection, Texas/Dallas History & Archives Division, Dallas Public Library)

A memorial service at Bishop College for Martin Luther King Jr., slain in 1968, attracted a large crowd that participated in a processional from the library of the college to the chapel. (Marion Butts Collection, Texas/Dallas History & Archives Division, Dallas Public Library)

Bedford (at right), nattily attired in the hat, joined E. Brice Cunningham, (in the center with the briefcase), when Cunningham argued a Dallas school desegregation case before the U.S. Supreme Court in 1979. (Marion Butts Collection, Texas/Dallas History & Archives Division, Dallas Public Library)

In 1966 Bedford (at left) joined other municipal court judges in taking the oath of office. He became the first African American judge in Dallas's history. (Marion Butts Collection, Texas/Dallas History & Archives Division, Dallas Public Library)

Ron Kirk (center) was one of the successful African American attorneys who represented a new generation in Dallas. He was elected mayor by a wide margin in 1995 and served into 2001. With him is Al Ellis, former Dallas Bar Association president. (Courtesy of Dallas Bar Association)

Royce West (at left), who began a long tenure as state senator in 1992, and Sam Lindsay (at right), who was the first African American to be appointed as a federal judge for the Northern District of Texas, both credited Bedford (center) with giving them political advice. (Courtesy of Dallas Bar Association)

Rhonda Hunter became the Dallas Bar Association's first African American president in 2004. Here she's pictured with Bedford at a lawyers' social function. (Courtesy of Dallas Bar Association)

In 2006 Craig Watkins was elected the first black district attorney in Dallas County and the state of Texas, making national headlines with the exoneration of prisoners falsely convicted. He chose Bedford, right, to swear him into office on January 1, 2007. (Courtesy of Rex Curry)

7

A BURST OF ENERGY

The social upheaval of the 1960s seemed to gain momentum as the decade transitioned into the 1970s. The entire era was rife with change—expanded boundaries for personal freedoms, distrust of government authority and established institutions, glorification of the young and distrust of the old, and an emphasis on the benefits of a return to nature. Whites and blacks as well as a growing number of Hispanics shared in this new outlook that was big enough to contain the civil rights movement. Demonstrations for civil rights evolved into massive protests against the war in Vietnam. The popular 1968 Broadway musical *Hair* glorified the long hair and beards that typified this new mood. Young black men wore bushy Afro hairstyles and beards as a badge of their black activism.

In this freewheeling period of bell-bottom trousers, wide ties, and generally flamboyant attire, Bedford was known to sport clothing with flair. At a National Bar Association meeting, he splurged and bought a handsome leather briefcase with a shoulder strap. This was before the addition of shoulder straps to men's briefcases had become common. He took lighthearted teasing from other attorneys, and even from a district judge, who referred to it as his "purse."[1]

Bedford went a step further in 1970 when he stopped shaving while spending two weeks at home with the flu. The idea of a beard appealed to him. He decided to keep it as a personal statement to contradict the stereotype that black men with beards were a threat to society. As a judge, lawyer, husband, father, and civic worker, he wanted to contrast that fierce image. He believed that whites and police officers who saw a black judge with a beard might question their own prejudices. His beard also reflected his identification with the new generation's mood and his approval of their goals, which in his view were long overdue. He maintained a short beard for the next three decades, into his eighties.[2]

The activist groups that had made national headlines in the turbulent 1960s now made inroads in Dallas. Their aggressive, attention-getting tactics overshadowed the work of the local chapter of the NAACP. Bedford came to know well the leaders of these new organizations, and he did not disapprove of them. The Congress of Racial Equality (CORE), the Southern Christian Leadership Conference (SCLC), the Student Nonviolent Coordinating Committee (SNCC), the National Urban League, and the Black Panthers had small presences in the city. There also were local groups with such names as Black Citizens for Justice, Law and Order.

Age-old racial barriers that had plagued Bedford and his parents and all black people continued to tumble, one after the other. These new activists, experiencing the familiar rising tide of expectations associated with revolutionary movements, wanted more. And they wanted it faster. If to many whites they seemed overly aggressive, most of their goals were reasonable, for there was so much more to be achieved, especially in jobs, housing, and education.

Their strategy sessions and activities emanated from South Dallas and Forest Avenue, now the heart of Dallas's African American population. The old Forest Avenue High School for white students had been converted to a black high school in the late 1950s and given a new name, James Madison High. The broad thoroughfare of Forest Avenue was lined now with the same sort of small businesses that had marked Thomas Avenue and Hall Street. Soon its name would be changed to Martin Luther King Jr. Boulevard.

The central location for the new activist groups turned out to be the building where Bedford and Sparks shared their office, the Negro Business and Professional Building, generally referred to as simply the Professional Building. There on the second floor with Bedford were the Dallas Urban League, the new black weekly *Post Tribune*, and attorney D. B. Mason. By 1971 the second floor was also home to a third attorney involved in the civil rights movement, Brice Cunningham of the NAACP, as well as the Block Partnership Program, the Equal Employment Opportunity Commission, and the SCLC. Foster Kidd, a dentist, was still there. Graham's Barber Shop on the ground floor remained a popular social center as well as a place for haircuts, as it did for decades to come.

Often members of this newer generation of African Americans sat in front of 2606 Forest Avenue in folding chairs, bantering, brainstorming, and discussing current affairs, especially the state of civil rights in Dallas. Bedford did not spend much time on the street corner with them, but he inevitably became friendly with them, and he identified with their commitment to eliminate the racial barriers that had oppressed them and their forebears for so long. In these informal meetings along Forest Avenue, they developed ideas and strategies for pushing ahead to achieve racial equality and redress past wrongs.

Sometimes they simply gathered in Graham's Barber Shop, and often Bedford would be there, more than just an onlooker. Al Lipscomb, one of the younger activists, recalled that Bedford "would hold court in that barber shop, and we would all assemble around him." Lipscomb described the skill with which Bedford was able to mingle with the different segments of the black community. "He had vision. He knew it took all of us. As Jesse Jackson put it, 'A little agitation to get things clean.'"[3]

Perhaps the most militant of the new groups was the Student Nonviolent Coordinating Committee, founded in North Carolina in 1961 by college students as a follow-up to their lunch counter sit-ins. In the mid-1960s, under the leadership of Stokely Carmichael, SNCC began to be influenced by Marxism and black nationalism. Separatism rather than integration began to be emphasized. Carmichael's term "black power," repeated time after time, startled the nation. In 1967 Carmichael's successor as chairman was H. Rap Brown, who declared that violence was "as American as cherry pie." Nonviolence was dismissed as a strategy of weakness. In 1968 the word "Nonviolent" in the organization's name was replaced by "National," the name becoming the Student National Coordinating Committee. This organization, then, had come to represent a distinctly different approach from those of the NAACP, the SCLC, and the Urban League.

The leaders of the new Dallas SNCC chapter were among those who were spending much of their time on Forest Avenue, often sitting in front of Graham's Barber Shop. In casual fashion Bedford came to know them: Ernest McMillan, the field secretary; Matthew Johnson, the director of political activity; Fred Bell; Charles Beasley; Ed Harris; and others. Bedford was becoming involved with this emerging generation, which would rely not so much on legal challenges as on social pressure.

Much of the older leadership in the African American community disapproved of the aggressive tactics and posture of these activists. And this younger generation, in turn, disapproved of the old leadership—especially the Interdenominational Min-isterial Alliance, the Negro Chamber of Commerce, and even the NAACP. These older leaders were, in their eyes, too gradualist in their approach, too willing to com-promise, and too willing to postpone their goals. Bedford found much to appreciate in this new breed.

"Certainly I didn't feel that they were out of step," Bedford later said. He had seen the conciliatory approach, had grown up in it, so he knew a hard and constant push would be necessary for continued progress.

Bedford's friend Bunkley felt the same way. He became so dissatisfied with the accommodationist stance of his minister at St. John Baptist Church, Rev. E. C. Estell, that he transferred his membership to Bedford's New Hope, whose Rev. H. Rhett James was a social justice activist. U. Simpson Tate of the NAACP transferred from St. John to New Hope, too.[4]

Bedford's behind-the-scenes involvement with the new SNCC chapter began in 1968, when SNCC first made its presence known by picketing OK Supermarkets, a small grocery chain with outlets in South Dallas and black neighborhoods in Oak Cliff. Owned by three white men, these stores, SNCC field secretary Ernest McMil-lan charged, exploited black patrons with higher-priced, inferior products, compared to OK stores in white neighborhoods. The underlying complaint was the conviction that African Americans, not whites, should own the stores in black communities. Certainly, SNCC contended, white owners needed to hire more African American employees in managerial positions.

Working out of Mount Olive Lutheran Church, five blocks down Forest Avenue from Bedford's office, SNCC pickets took their places at the stores on July 19, 1968. Their impact was immediate. Business sharply declined.

Bedford did not himself demonstrate, but with Brice Cunningham, Marcus Ranger, and a few others, he served as legal counsel for SNCC. Years later one of the picketers, Edward Harris, said that he and the others were pleased to have Bedford's support when so many conservative leaders in the African American community chastised them, claiming that their activities should have been cleared with the established leaders.[5]

At first the stores tried to ease the tension by giving free cigarettes and ice water to the demonstrators, who were walking in temperatures approaching one hundred degrees.[6] But the goodwill evaporated as picketing became more aggressive. A number of arrests occurred when picketers were said to have threatened employees and customers who crossed their lines. Tactics escalated: demonstrators moved inside the store on Oakland Avenue, loaded up shopping carts, and abandoned them in the aisles. In a climax to the hostilities, some two dozen protesters broke juice bottles, smashed two watermelons, spilled a container of milk, and dumped sugar on the floor.

Bedford realized the SNCC had at that point crossed a line. "Picketing was okay, but I was worried when they began taking things off the shelves. I never favored blatant violation of the law when it involved destroying another person's personal property."[7]

SNCC's McMillan was paraphrased by the black-owned *Post Tribune* as saying that "the stores had done nothing wrong other than being 'white' and operating in a Negro community, and that his group was going to boycott all white-owned stores operating in the Negro community until they were out of business."[8]

Only a week after the picketing had begun, the pressured owners agreed to sell their chain of stores to any African American or group of African Americans who could pay them approximately six hundred thousand dollars. A truce was declared. Felton Alexander of the Dallas Urban League, whose office was adjacent to Bedford's, arranged the meeting between the picketers and store owners.[9] (Eventually the stores were sold, and OK Supermarkets disappeared.)

In the aftermath two leaders of the picketing episode, McMillan and Matthew Johnson, were charged with felonies for destroying private property. Represented by a white attorney, Vincent Perini, and a Mexican-American attorney, Frank Hernandez, both defendants were found guilty in a criminal district court and sentenced to ten years.[10] Before the year was over, two other demonstrators, Fred Bell and Charles Beasley, were charged with a more serious felony, robbing a bank in Ladonia (seventy miles northeast of Dallas). Soon afterward Beasley was arrested when he attempted to hijack an Air Canada passenger airplane with an intention of forcing it to fly to Cuba. The Dallas chapter of SNCC faded away.[11]

A number of other individuals were arrested during the OK Supermarkets pickets and charged with lesser crimes. The young black attorney Marcus Ranger, then working with Fred Finch, called a meeting of some of the J. L. Turner Legal Association members and urged them to represent the demonstrators pro bono. Bedford and the others agreed to do so. One of those arrested during the demonstrations was Edward Harris, who had come to know Bedford casually in those frequent gatherings on Forest Avenue. In jail and needing someone to bail him out, Harris called Bedford, who responded promptly and arranged for Harris's release on what was called an attorney's bond. Bedford represented Harris in a county criminal court and won a not-guilty verdict for him. "He saved my ass on many occasions," Harris said years later, recalling his days as an activist with SNCC.[12]

The two developed a relationship. "He became a mentor for me," Harris said. With Bedford's encouragement, he enrolled in the University of Texas at Arlington and got a bachelor's degree in criminal justice and a master's degree in urban affairs. "It was all brought about by Bedford," he said. Harris went to work for the federal government's Department of Housing and Urban Development (HUD), later becoming a consultant on housing developments in Dallas.[13]

Fears that a disturbance with racial overtones might break out in Dallas reached a peak with the OK Supermarkets boycott. This fear continued for several years. How far would such aggressive tactics go? What if massive numbers of demonstrators began destroying private property in other establishments? In August 1968 the city council passed an ordinance giving the mayor broad powers in the event of a civil disturbance. Dallas police quietly made plans for such an eventuality. The *Dallas Times Herald* handed out contingency assignments to reporters to follow if outbreaks occurred. The Dallas Bar Association worked out a plan for the efficient processing of large numbers of persons apprehended in such an outbreak, with volunteer attorneys serving as defense lawyers, prosecutors, and magistrates. Bedford, although an associate municipal judge, was designated to represent defendants in case of civil disorder.[14]

In December 1969, over a year after the OK Supermarkets boycott, SCLC national headquarters in Atlanta sent Peter Johnson to Dallas. Johnson was a twenty-four-year-old Louisiana native who had been involved in the civil rights movement since he was fifteen. The organization he represented had begun in 1957 out of Rosa Parks's refusal to move to the back of the bus in Montgomery, Alabama. Under Martin Luther King Jr.'s direction, the group captured the nation's attention through a successful series of nonviolent mass demonstrations. By the time King was assassinated in Memphis in April 1968, the movement had begun to address broader problems: the Vietnam War and the elimination of poverty and hunger.

Johnson's arrival as regional director of SCLC represented one of the city's greatest fears, an outside agitator from an organization with a confrontational strategy. Even Dallas's traditional black leaders were hesitant to accept Johnson, for they saw SCLC as a threat to their control over the community. Newer leaders—Albert Lipscomb, J. B. Jackson, and others—welcomed him.

Johnson's first assignment in Dallas was to promote the film *Martin Luther King: A Filmed Record . . . Montgomery to Memphis*, especially in the black community. His assignment was not as easy as it seemed. When the Reverend S. M. Wright, president of the Interdenominational Ministerial Alliance, declined to speak on behalf of the film, the feud between the older black leadership and the new radicals began in earnest.

When Johnson attempted to find office space, he encountered many obstacles. No one seemed willing to rent space to SCLC. One day Johnson was approached by a well-dressed man named J. H. Glenn, the owner of the Forest Avenue building in which Bedford had his office. Glenn had heard of Johnson's problems, and he offered to rent him space in his Professional Building. Johnson took Room 209. Immediately adjacent in Room 208 was Louis A. Bedford Jr. Johnson had not met Bedford, but he had heard about him even before his arrival in Dallas. He was eager to meet him. Bedford did not share the fears of the Interdenominational Ministerial Alliance about Johnson. He welcomed him, and the two became friends. Soon Bedford was acting unofficially as the unpaid legal adviser to SCLC in Dallas, just as he had done for SNCC.[15]

Johnson, Jackson, Lipscomb, and other emerging leaders became involved in a simmering controversy over a planned expansion of Fair Park that would require condemning low-cost houses for blacks in South Dallas. Some critics said the proposal was racist because its unspoken intent was to eliminate the black housing at Fair Park's eastern border. The homeowners complained that the city was offering too little compensation for their houses, making it impossible for them to find comparable housing elsewhere. Out of concern for the homeowners, the Greater Dallas Council of Churches initiated the Block Partnership program, in which white churches developed partnerships with residents and worked with them to solve their housing problems. Block Partnership, which soon moved its offices to the Professional Building, provided a structure for the homeowners to organize and register their grievances.

As activists such as Johnson emerged and gained influence, however, the white churches in Block Partnership faded into the background. Johnson assumed leadership of the Fair Park homeowners and threatened to lead massive demonstrations to force better compensation for them. The issue was so intense that the CBS television show *Sixty Minutes* sent journalist Mike Wallace to Dallas to report on it.

Although Johnson and Block Partnership had offices in his building, Bedford managed to avoid involvement in this controversy. The Fair Park housing situation dragged on for a couple of years, into the early 1970s. The remaining homeowners gradually accepted the prices offered to them and relocated. But the black community and the new leaders that had emerged realized more than ever the impact they could make. In the process, the split between the more conservative Interdenominational Ministerial Alliance and the new leaders was highlighted. At one point a visiting official of SCLC said Rev. S. M. Wright, president of the alliance, was doing everything possible "to keep us black folks quiet for his white friends."[16]

Johnson's next targets, in keeping with the goals of the SCLC's Operation Breadbasket, were three Safeway grocery stores. The huge national chain Safeway, Inc., had forty-four stores operating in Dallas, including two in South Dallas and one in the Cedar Crest area of Oak Cliff. In this campaign Bedford assumed a role as unofficial, unpaid adviser to Johnson and SCLC. Johnson drew up a list of complaints, which included poor food quality, lack of cleanliness of stores, insufficient advertising in the black media, inadequate use of black construction contractors, and too few black employees. In July 1970 two Safeway officials met with Johnson, but Johnson complained that they lacked "policymaking power." He had no alternative, he said, but to "call on the people of Dallas to boycott beginning immediately."[17]

Thus ensued an on-again, off-again boycott of the three Safeway stores. Bedford regularly advised Johnson about the legal requirements in picketing a store. Every night, in planning the next day's demonstrations, the picketers would try to create provocative signs, even identifying specific individuals. As the days went on, the signs grew more and more pointed. Bedford, seeing this, called Johnson into his office, advising him that the demonstrators were opening themselves to possible slander and libel suits. The messages were toned down.[18]

Even so, to many in the black community, the Safeway demonstrators went too far. The *Post Tribune* described them as a "typical example of leadership not consulting the community about problems." The black community had neither ordered nor directed SCLC to lobby on its behalf, the newspaper wrote in an editorial titled "Wanted—New Leadership."[19] The title acknowledged, though, what seemed to be a fact: Johnson and others had emerged as the presumed leaders.

Rev. A. L. Bowman, a spokesman for the Interdenominational Ministerial Alliance, said his organization considered the boycott to be "ill-advised, misdirected and wrong." Even the local NAACP criticized the picketing. Boycotts should be used as a last resort, said Rev. B. L. McCormick, president of the local NAACP, and "singling" out Safeway for boycott was "wrong." His own dealings with Safeway in the past, he said, had been satisfactory, for the company always had "proven amenable to the grievances of the black community."[20]

The differences in opinion reflected a growing diversity. The *Post Tribune*, founded in 1962 as a successor to the *Dallas Star-Post*, was not an organ of conservative blacks, even though serving on its board were some of the city's more conservative black ministers, such as the Reverends E. C. Estell and Caesar Clark. The board included, as well, such activists as W. J. Durham, U. Simpson Tate, and A. Maceo Smith.[21] Although this diversified board had concluded that Johnson was acting improperly, Bedford did not share the newspaper's criticism of Johnson. He openly supported SCLC.

Finally, Dallas City Councilman George Allen, viewed as a moderate, intervened by calling a meeting between Safeway officials and SCLC to try to bring a resolution to this issue that had split the black community. Bedford was there at Allen's office on Ross Avenue, advising Johnson and other SCLC officials. After a five-hour meeting, the parties came to an agreement. Safeway made numerous concessions that placated both the conservatives and the demonstrators. The company would hire eighty additional minority employees by the end of the year, including four store managers and three assistant store managers; it would invite qualified African American contractors to bid on construction projects; and it would continue to advertise in minority-owned media.[22]

At the height of the Safeway boycott, Johnson recalled more than three decades later, a friendly white police officer had tipped him off that unknown persons would come to Johnson's office that night. If they found Johnson there, they would kill him. Johnson called Ralph Abernathy, King's successor as president of SCLC, to advise him of the threat. Abernathy told him to go straight to the airport and fly to Atlanta. Johnson followed his advice, and that very night, he said, "hooded white men" with automatic weapons went to his apartment on South Boulevard and put a gun to his roommate's head to ask where he was. After some days passed and the immediate threat was over, Johnson returned safely to Dallas and resumed his activities.[23]

Years later Peter Johnson interpreted the boycott as consisting of two separate fights: "One was with the white Dallas oligarchy, and the other was with the conservative black leadership."[24]

Each Saturday during those tumultuous years, SCLC and people sympathetic to its causes met at the Warren United Methodist Church to rally for Operation Breadbasket. Sometimes as many as three to four hundred people would attend. One Saturday Bedford was invited to be the speaker. Those attending typically came in casual dress, but Bedford, as a dignified lawyer and judge, showed up in coat and tie. Bedford's talk, inspired by a familiar gospel hymn, was titled "This Little Light of Mine, I'm Going to Let It Shine." Peter Johnson was "flabbergasted" to see the way that Bedford—this "always thoughtful, easygoing" man, speaking, as usual, without notes—energized the audience with his dynamic message. "To this day I can remember his speech," he recalled. "He blew the roof off."[25]

On such public occasions Bedford, his presence often unpublicized, was there to advise Johnson. "I talked to him every day during that period," Johnson later said. "He was a very astute counselor and a shoulder to cry on. We took more of his time than those who were paying him."[26]

There was plenty to talk about. In October 1970 Minyard's supermarkets signed an agreement similar to Safeway's. That same month the Reverend Jesse Jackson, national director of Operation Breadbasket, came to town to speak at one of the meetings at the Warren United Methodist Church. And when the vocal group the Jackson Five was booked by a white promoter to come to Dallas for a concert, Johnson worked behind the scenes and managed to have it cancelled. Black promoters, not white ones, should be the ones to bring in black entertainers, Johnson said.[27]

In March 1971 Johnson, promoting his Operation Breadbasket movement, urged the Dallas City Council to establish a department of human resources, with five hundred thousand dollars in emergency city funds, to attack the problem of hunger in the city. The council sidestepped the issue by referring it to the city attorney for study. Disgusted with the inaction, Johnson that night began a hunger strike on the Harwood Street steps of city hall, vowing to subsist only on orange juice until the council undertook "positive action" to alleviate hunger. He was accompanied throughout that first day by sympathizers bearing signs with such messages as "Jesus Fed Hungry People" and "In God We Trust, In Dallas We Starve."[28]

A week later, with Johnson's fast continuing, Romie Lily of SCLC appeared at a city council meeting and handed Mayor Erik Jonsson two loaves of bread and some fish, advising him to "go out and feed the multitudes." Taking the offering in his hands, Jonsson responded, "It seems to me if you know where the hungry people are, you could use these to better advantage."[29]

Dallas's leaders and many others were deeply skeptical that any of its citizens could be suffering from hunger. Starvation didn't seem possible for a city so mindful of its image. As the days wore on and Johnson continued his often-lonely vigil on the city hall steps, a number of churches came to his support, tacitly acknowledging the possibility of hunger as a problem. Even the presiding bishop of the United Methodist Church in Dallas and Fort Worth, Rev. W. Kenneth Pope, announced his support of Johnson and Operation Breadbasket. After Johnson had been fasting for a week, some fifteen to twenty churches committed a ton of food a month for Operation Breadbasket to distribute to the poor. Whether indigent people were actually hungry was still uncertain, but the food was welcome.[30]

Bedford visited Johnson several times during his hunger strike to encourage him, although the fast was Johnson's idea alone. As newspaper headlines continued to describe Johnson's protest and television newscasts showed him resting under a blanket on the city hall steps, the city was embarrassed. Two weeks after the fast began, a way out of the dilemma arrived when the president of the Interdenominational Ministerial Alliance, at this time the Reverend O. H. Lakey, appeared before the city council and asked its members to sanction a community antihunger movement called Operation Assist. Council members voted to support the program, which sought emergency survival service and the coordination of the resources of some 121 welfare agencies. Johnson's original goal to create a human resources department with five hundred thousand in emergency city funds was disregarded, but Lakey's action was enough to prompt Johnson to end his two-week hunger strike.[31]

An allegation arose afterward that the Interdenominational Ministerial Alliance had interceded at city council simply to defuse Johnson's hunger strike and to prevent further embarrassment to the city. Lakey appeared before an SCLC meeting to deny that he was "playing politics."[32]

Another interesting episode in these racially charged days involved Johnson's attempted boycott of KKDA, a white-owned radio station that catered to black audiences. In November 1971, to emphasize the point that businesses catering to blacks should be owned by blacks, Johnson organized pickets to march in front of the station. He sent letters to black businesses across the nation that were advertising their products on the station, urging them to cease. The station, he alleged, did not take the economic development of the black community seriously, and its employment practices were not in line with the best interests of the black community.

The radio station challenged these tactics, contending that Johnson's letters amounted to an illegal secondary boycott, and KKDA's management questioned the legality of the pickets. When the case was heard in District Judge Leonard Hoffman's court, Bedford, joined by Brice Cunningham, represented Johnson and SCLC. A few years before, Hoffman had signed Bedford's application for membership in the Dallas Bar Association. Now, after the hearing Hoffman issued a temporary restraining order to prohibit SCLC efforts against the advertisers. The conflict soon ended without resolution.[33]

Although Bedford was not paid for his work as an unofficial adviser, SCLC later recognized his services with a certificate of appreciation for "morally and financially supporting our national civil rights and humanitarian endeavors."[34]

Johnson, having created a stir in Dallas as SCLC's regional director, returned to Atlanta. He came back to live in Dallas in the 1980s, not as an official of the SCLC but as a construction contractor attracted by the city's economic promise.[35]

It might have appeared to some in the early 1970s that Bedford was walking a tightrope. He did not think so, though. On weekends and some evenings, he was presiding as an associate judge in the city's municipal courts. This part-time position permitted him to maintain his regular daytime law practice. During the daytime and some evenings, he was conferring with the new generation of leaders, who were aggressively seeking to expand rights for the city's African American citizens. Bedford did not participate in any of the demonstrations, nor did the organizers want him to. As Johnson told him, they wanted him to stay out of trouble so he could help get them out of jail. In case of a potential conflict between his roles as judge and as adviser to SCLC and others, Bedford was ready to recuse himself.

During these tense years in Dallas, Bedford may have been an unofficial adviser and confidant to leaders of SCLC and SNCC and a sympathetic friend to many of the other activists who so alarmed official Dallas, but he was also an associate municipal judge at city hall, a respected member of the Dallas Bar Association, a leading church member at New Hope Baptist, and a civic worker with a commendable record with the YMCA, Big Brothers, the Boy Scouts of America, and other such organizations.

Was this incongruous? Not at all. Bedford understood that the advances the activists sought were long overdue and more than fair. They would not be granted by the white power structure without pressure. The cry of "Black power!" and the emergence of black nationalism, frightening though these may have been to white America, were prompting among young blacks a sense of self-esteem and pride that had been missing during Bedford's younger days when newspaper advertisements encouraged hair straightening and skin whitening.

A turning point for the nation's attitudes had been signaled in 1968 when the Kerner Report, the findings of the National Advisory Commission on Civil Disorders, confirmed the deep-seated convictions existing in black communities about the nation's ingrained racism. This committee, appointed by President Lyndon B. Johnson after the widespread urban disorders in 1967, concluded that the nation was split into two sections—one black and one white, separate and unequal. The system had been created and maintained by white institutions and white society. There was pervasive discrimination in employment, education, and housing, all of which must be addressed by drastic actions. "White racism," the Kerner Report charged, was "essentially responsible for the explosive mixture which has been accumulating in our cities since the end of World War II."[36]

The Kerner Report lamented another sad fact: national and local media rarely showed black faces. African Americans deserved to be portrayed in television commercials, in television shows, in newspaper and magazine articles. The report urged broadcasters and journalists to include minorities among their ranks in visible roles.

Some 740,000 copies of the paperback edition of the report sold within two weeks. There was much yet to be done, but with the turmoil of the 1960s and 1970s, the nation and attitudes were changing.

The old order in Dallas was under siege in both the white community and the black community. The organization that had dominated city hall for so long, the Citizens Charter Association, began to lose its power under the liberalizing influences of the 1970s. An independent, Wes Wise, was elected mayor in 1971. In 1976 the CCA, having already become more diversified in its endorsements, ceased operations. A lawsuit filed by Al Lipscomb, Peter Johnson, J. B. Jackson, Elsie Faye Heggins, and others challenged the citywide method for electing councilmen as unconstitutional. Election of council members by districts surely would permit minority neighborhoods to elect their own officials.

In 1970, the same year he grew his beard, Bedford testified before the state's House Criminal Law Study Committee as an expert witness. The subject was the marijuana possession laws, which Bedford believed were too severe. His recommendations to the committee were characterized by the committee's vice chairman, Phil Burleson, as "very interesting" and "helpful."[37] State legislators soon agreed to soften the penalties.

In December of that year, there occurred the death of a man who had been an important role model for Bedford and other African American attorneys, the man acclaimed as the foremost civil rights attorney in Texas. That man, of course, was W. J. Durham, whose death was attributed to heart problems.[38] Durham's death, though duly noted in the press, did not receive the attention that his exemplary life merited. His primary methods of achieving social justice through the ballot box, through legislation, and through court challenges (integrating the University of Texas law school, banning the all-white Democratic primary, gaining equal pay for black teachers, and more) were being overshadowed by activists who were achieving results through dramatic actions and threats. Durham already seemed to be part of a different time.

If Bedford had viewed Durham as a father figure, he had seen Crawford B. Bunkley Jr. as his big brother. The two men were close, having been united in so many cases, having been members of the same civic organizations, having discussed so many times the unfair social conditions they knew so well, having taken vacations together with their families, and having lived just around the corner from one another in the Cedar Crest area. Bunkley was just five years older than Bedford. In June 1974, at the age of fifty-two and at the peak of his legal career, he died of a brain tumor. Services were held at the church he had favored because of its civil rights activism, New Hope Baptist Church. The Reverend H. Rhett James presided.[39]

The Dallas City Council passed a resolution of "Special Recognition" for Bunkley, describing him as a man of "great sensitivity and fairness" and "one of the city's ablest leaders, [who] believed profoundly in the ideal of equal opportunity for all of the citizens of these United States."[40]

The J. L. Turner Legal Association remembered Bunkley as one of its founders by establishing an award in his name, the C. B. Bunkley Jr. Community Service Award. Bedford was an obvious choice as the recipient of the award, and it was presented to him in 1982.

Lyndon B. Johnson's War on Poverty had included the creation of legal services agencies to provide assistance to the poor. These agencies required the participation of local legal communities, especially their bar associations. All that was needed to obtain federal funding were agreements from local bar associations to sponsor such a project. The Dallas Bar Association as well as the Junior Bar Association and Dallas County Criminal Bar Association agreed to be sponsors. Thus, the Dallas Legal Services Project (DLSP) was established with the understanding that the "core" of its activities would be its "educational aspect."[41]

This somewhat innocuous goal was quickly superseded. The DLSP was staffed with young, aggressive, and idealistic attorneys, who, rather than merely responding to requests for legal assistance from the indigent, soon turned their actions toward righting many of the wrongs they believed society had inflicted on the lower classes, including the African American community. The DLSP's aggressive tactics in the late 1960s and early 1970s infuriated many and had a significant impact on Dallas, especially on the black population.

The DLSP's attacks on the problems of poverty included a series of class action suits. The agency's attorneys did not try to hide their political sentiments. Ed Polk, a staff attorney who became director in 1970, said plainly that his goal was to "improve life for poor people," and if that constituted revolution, then he was a revolutionary. On his office wall were two posters, one bearing the image of Malcolm X, and the other of Che Guevara. Polk resigned under intense pressure because of the controversies he stirred up. Marcus Ranger, an African American attorney who succeeded Polk as DLSP director, explained that if problems of poverty were class problems, then the best tool to eliminate such problems was the class action suit. Within one three-month period in 1971, the DLSP filed more than thirty class actions or law reform cases.[42]

In such a mood of reform, it was difficult for the DLSP to ignore the delaying tactics of the Dallas school board in meaningful desegregation of its public schools. Many other Southern cities had made far more progress than Dallas. Fifteen years after the monumental *Brown v. Board of Education* decision (1954), the majority of black students in Dallas continued to attend all-black schools.

Sam Tasby was the father of two sons who had to ride the bus each day past the almost all-white Thomas J. Rusk Junior High to reach their own school for African Americans. It seemed to him and to other critics that the DISD was continuing to operate basically a dual system, one for whites and another one with inferior facilities for blacks. He requested and received legal assistance from the DLSP. The ensuing *Tasby v. Estes* case was heard in the federal district court of William Mac Taylor, who agreed that desegregation in the Dallas public schools was proceeding at too slow a pace.[43]

In 1971 Judge Taylor ordered that one-race schools in the district be ended. In his many-faceted decision, the judge ordered the institution of a number of changes and programs—including busing—that soon would effectively end the dual system in Dallas. Thus began "white flight" by parents who moved their children to suburban districts. The result brought about a school district whose students were almost entirely minority—African American and Hispanic—children.[44] Federal court supervision of the Dallas school district as a result of this case continued for close to forty years, before it was held that a "unitary status" had been achieved and federal supervision was lifted.

Neither Bedford nor any of the other attorneys who had been a part of the original desegregation case played a direct role in *Tasby v. Estes.* In summer 1970, however, Bedford was appointed to the DLSP's board of directors. His appointment came after anguished outcries arose in the Dallas community as well as within a large portion of the Dallas Bar Association over the aggressive manner in which the DLSP was acting as a lightning rod for social upheaval. These critics, and there were many of them, believed that the DLSP was overstepping its original purpose. In response, and under intense pressure, the Dallas Bar Association made several changes, including the appointment of ten additional attorneys to what had been its predominantly grassroots board of directors. Bedford was one of the additional attorneys named to the board.[45]

Loud and harsh debates among community leaders and the more conservative lawyers often marked board meetings. Many of the white lawyers resented being challenged in these give-and-take sessions by black community leaders. They were unaccustomed to being addressed in such fashion by persons whom they considered to be of little standing. The issues revolved repeatedly around the proper role of the Dallas Legal Services Project. Should it concentrate on serving the immediate and basic legal needs of the poor—disputes with landlords, employment problems, divorces, and the like—or should it be attacking broader social problems through class action suits? Bedford thought it should attempt both.[46]

Perhaps the most divisive of the DLSP's suits occurred in October 1971, when the DLSP filed on behalf of four Dallas County prison inmates a class action suit alleging that the county jail's conditions violated minimal standards. The case was heard by U.S. District Judge Sarah T. Hughes, who ruled in favor of the plaintiffs and oversaw the implementation of her recommendations for the next several years. Ultimately, she ordered the county commissioners to build a new jail, the Lew Sterrett Justice Center.[47]

Racial breakthroughs, both social and political, had occurred in Dallas, but as the decade of the 1970s moved forward, Bedford continued to be the only African American judge in the city. Change was just ahead, though. In 1972 he was joined on the municipal bench by one of the new generation of promising young black lawyers who were beginning to be attracted to the legal profession and who no longer had to leave the state to study law. He was Berlaind Leander Brashear, a graduate of Lincoln High School in Dallas, Prairie View A&M University, and Texas Southern University School of Law (in Houston); and a former U.S. Marine. Brashear, twenty-eight years old, was appointed by the Dallas City Council to be the first full-time black municipal judge in Dallas.[48]

There still were no African American judges at the Dallas County Courthouse. Although county and state judges were elected by the voters, when vacancies occurred, as was often the case, the governor appointed replacements for state courts, and the commissioners court appointed county judges. At election time the appointees had to campaign but could do so as incumbents. Appointment was the quickest avenue to the bench for African Americans.

An opportunity for Bedford arose in 1973 when a newly created county criminal court of law required the appointment of a judge. The Pylon Salesmanship Club submitted L. A. Bedford's name to the commissioners court. Appearing before the commissioners, Clyde Clark III, representing the Pylon Club, pointed out that there were still no black judges at the Dallas County Courthouse and that appointing Bedford would correct that situation. The commissioners stalled. Commissioner John Whittington asked Clark to submit one or two additional black candidates. "I know [Bedford] is capable, but I like a choice," Whittington said.

Tony Davis, chairman of the Pylon Club's public affairs committee, made it clear that Bedford was the club's choice. However, he agreed to submit other names.[49]

But this time the commissioners were not ready to name an African American to the judgeship. Two years later, though, they broke the barrier by appointing two black men, George L. Allen and Cleophas Steele Jr., to be justices of the peace. Others would follow.

In 1977 Berlaind Brashear left his municipal court post to accept appointment as judge of the newly created County Criminal Court No. 6, a position he held until 1990. Aside from having been the city's first full-time municipal court judge, Brashear now became the first African American to preside in a criminal court in the county.

With Allen's departure from city hall to become justice of peace, the longtime NAACP crusader, youth leader, and organizer Juanita Craft, was elected to succeed him on the city council. She joined another black woman on the council, Lucy Patterson, who had been elected in 1973 under the endorsement of the increasingly moderate establishment political organization, the Citizens Charter Association. Recognizing the changing times and smarting from accusations of elitism, the CCA was attempting to broaden its appeal with such endorsements.

The unelected leaders of the African American community were more aggressive than their predecessors. One was Albert Lipscomb, a Lincoln High School graduate and World War II Army veteran, who began showing up regularly at city council meetings and speaking bluntly at the podium about a myriad of issues. After losing a race for mayor in 1970 as the first African American to run for that office in Dallas (and having been fired from his job with Block Partnership when he announced his candidacy), Lipscomb became one of the city's best-known African Americans, serving on the Dallas City Council from 1983 to 1991 and 1993 to 2000.

Another who had emerged as an unelected leader in the Fair Park housing controversy was J. B. Jackson Jr., Bedford's old friend from his bachelor days. Jackson, less visible than Lipscomb, was no less dedicated to personally monitoring community affairs as they pertained to the black community. In the 1980s he began holding his own "Tuesday Night Town Hall" meetings, at which like-minded African American citizens were tutored in the political ways of city hall. He counted among his protégés Elsie Faye Heggins, who succeeded Juanita Craft at city hall but who was much more aggressive in championing the cause of African Americans, and another future city council firebrand, Diane Ragsdale. A future leader who came under Jackson's early influence was John Wiley Price.[50] Jackson eventually became a public official himself, serving on the original board for the Dallas Area Rapid Transit (DART). A South Dallas DART station and street were named for him.

During these years in the 1970s, when Bedford appeared with some frequency at the courthouse, he came to know the legendary Dallas County district attorney Henry Wade, who held that office from 1951 to 1987. Wade and his assistant district attorneys gained nationwide attention for their aggressive prosecution of criminals and their insistence on unusually lengthy prison sentences, sometimes as long as a thousand years.

In 1961 it had appeared that President Kennedy would appoint Wade as a federal district judge. When news of the impending appointment was revealed in the Dallas newspapers, liberal lawyer Oscar Mauzy (later associate justice of the Texas Supreme Court) met with W. J. Durham and C. B. Bunkley Jr. to plan a strategy to derail the appointment. They favored the loyal Democrat Sarah T. Hughes, who had made an energetic but seemingly failed effort to gain the judgeship. They recalled the 1956 congressional campaign Wade had conducted against Republican incumbent Bruce Alger, in which Wade had made strong segregationist statements. How could President Kennedy appoint someone who had expressed such sentiments? The three decided to fly to Washington, taking with them news stories and advertisements documenting Wade's segregationist stands, to present to Attorney General Robert Kennedy. A meeting was arranged, and Wade's appointment was circumvented. Soon the announcement came that President Kennedy would appoint the liberal activist judge Sarah T. Hughes to the bench.[51]

In these years Bedford, without personally knowing Wade, viewed him with disfavor. As time went on and he came to know him, especially during the last years of Wade's time in office, they began to communicate. Bedford discovered that Wade—despite his reputation and despite the 1956 campaign—was more enlightened and affable than popular opinion held. Bedford was pleased to learn that Wade had even joined the NAACP, even though he believed it was for political purposes.[52]

At Wade's retirement a roast was held in his honor, and Bedford was asked to participate. Knowing that Wade and some of his attorneys had frequently stated in death penalty cases that they would gladly walk the last mile and pull the switch on the electric chair for the convicted, Bedford had an electrician friend mount a portable switch. When it came Bedford's turn at the podium, he said that throughout his career Wade had said he wanted to pull the switch, and "so here's the switch;" Wade could pull it as often as he wanted.[53]

Bedford also said that Wade owed his record-breaking longevity as district attorney to the black community, for when Wade had campaigned in 1956 to replace Alger in Congress, African Americans had voted against Wade almost to a person, keeping Wade in his district attorney position. "At the end I thought Henry was a pretty good fellow," Bedford allowed many years later.[54]

1. Louis A. Bedford Jr., interview by Darwin Payne, Nov. 29, 2006.
2. "Facial Hair: Not a Four-Letter Word," *Dallas Times Herald*, n.d., "L. A. Bedford Jr. Personal" binder, Bedford Papers.
3. "'He Had Vision.'"
4. Louis A. Bedford Jr., interview by Darwin Payne, Aug. 15, 2006.
5. Edward Harris, interview by Darwin Payne, July 27, 2006.
6. "Boycott of White Owned Business in South Dallas," *Dallas Post Tribune*, July 31, 1968.
7. Bedford, interview, Aug. 15, 2006.
8. "Boycott of White Owned Business."
9. "Store Chain to Sell," *Dallas Morning News*, July 26, 1968; "Store Threats under Study," July 27, 1968.
10. "SNCC Leaders Given 10 Years," *Dallas Morning News*, Aug. 24, 1968. Before sentencing, McMillan jumped bond and fled the state, only to be arrested three months later in Cincinnati.
11. "Prints Awaited," *Dallas Morning News*, Sept. 12, 1968; Dulaney, "Whatever Happened?" 87.
12. Louis A. Bedford Jr., interview by Darwin Payne, July 12, 2006; Harris, interview, July 27, 2006.
13. Harris, interview, July 27, 2006.
14. Dallas Bar Association, "The City of Dallas, Texas: The Administration of Justice during a Civil Disorder" and "Court Personnel," July 1, 1968, L. A. Bedford Jr. personal files.
15. Peter Johnson, interview by Darwin Payne, Aug. 7, 2006.
16. "SCLC Aide Blasts Dallas Minister," *Dallas Morning News*, Apr. 27, 1970.
17. "Safeway Target of SCLC Boycott," *Dallas Morning News*, July 25, 1970.
18. Johnson, interview, Aug. 7, 2006.
19. "Wanted—New Leadership," *Dallas Post Tribune*, Aug. 15, 1970.
20. "2 Groups Criticize Boycott," *Dallas Morning News*, Aug. 11, 1970.
21. Rev. I. B. Loud, "Loud Talk," *Post Tribune*, Mar. 17, 1962.
22. "Safeway Boycott Over," *Dallas Morning News*, Aug. 15, 1970.
23. Johnson, interview, Aug. 7, 2006.
24. Ibid.
25. Ibid.
26. Ibid.
27. "Church to Host Director of Operation Breadbasket," *Dallas Morning News*, Oct. 5, 1970.
28. "Fast on City Hall Steps Receives Added Support," *Dallas Morning News*, Mar. 10, 1971; "Johnson Continues Hunger Fast," *Dallas Morning News*, Mar. 11, 1971.
29. "Mayor Accepts Food, but Rejects Challenge," *Dallas Morning News*, Mar. 16, 1971.
30. "Pastors Join Fasting Group in Worship," *Dallas Morning News*, Mar. 18, 1971.
31. "Hunger Aid Plan Ends Fast," *Dallas Times Herald*, Mar. 23, 1971; "Council Backs 'Assist'; Johnson Ends Hunger Fast," *Dallas Morning News*, Mar. 23, 1971.
32. "Lakey Denies Move Was to Defuse Fast," *Dallas Morning News*, Mar. 27, 1971.
33. "KKDA Obtains Court Injunction," *Dallas Morning News*, Nov. 11, 1971.
34. Certificate signed by Dr. Joseph Lowery, president, Southern Christian Leadership Conference, n.d., Certificates binder, Bedford Papers.
35. Schutze, *The Accommodation*, 178.

36. National Advisory Commission on Civil Disorders, *Report of the National Advisory Commission on Civil Disorders* (The Kerner Report) (New York: Bantam Books, 1968), 203.
37. Phil Burleson to Bedford, Oct. 14, 1970, "L. A. Bedford Jr. Personal" binder, Bedford Papers.
38. Bureau of Vital Statistics, "Texas Death Records" (Austin: Texas Department of Health, 1970), no. 93178.
39. "Rites Set Monday for C. B. Bunkley," *Dallas Morning News,* June 9, 1974.
40. "Prominent Civil Rights Attorney Succumbs," *Dallas Post Tribune,* June 1974, "Memorials for Attorneys" binder, Bedford Papers.
41. Payne, *As Old s Dallas Itself,* 241.
42. Ibid.
43. *Tasby v. Estes,* 517 F. 2d 92 (5th Cir. 1975).
44. Linden, *Desegregating Schools in Dallas,* 66–81.
45. Payne, *As Old As Dallas Itself,* 242.
46. Louis A. Bedford Jr., interview by Darwin Payne, July 21, 2006.
47. *Taylor v. Sterrett,* 344 F. Supp. 411 (1972), 499 F. 2d 367 (1974), 532 F. 2d 462 (5th Cir. 1976), and 600 F. 2d 1135 (5th Cir. 1979).
48. "The Life and Legacy of Judge Berlaind L. Brashear," a summary of his life distributed at his funeral, June 2000, "Memorials for Attorneys" binder, Bedford Papers.
49. "Blacks Press for Judgeship," *Dallas Morning News,* June 26, 1973.
50. "Longtime S. Dallas Advocate J. B. Jackson Jr. Dies of Stroke," *Dallas Morning News,* July 1, 1998.
51. Darwin Payne, *Indomitable Sarah: The Life of Judge Sarah T. Hughes* (Dallas: SMU Press, 2004), 214–15.
52. Louis A. Bedford Jr., interview by Darwin Payne, Nov. 7, 2006.
53. Ibid.
54. Ibid.

8

A TIME FOR REFLECTION

olitical campaigns continued to intrigue Bedford. In 1977 he headed the steering committee for Crawford B. Bunkley III, the son of his late friend and associate, in his campaign for the Texas Legislature. This race—a sign of times to come, in which the African American community no longer would speak with a single voice—split the black leadership. Bedford and Dr. Emmett Conrad worked for Bunkley; Juanita Craft and Lucy Patterson campaigned for his female opponent, Lanell Cofer, a realtor. Bedford saw the contest as based on gender; many African American women supported Cofer because they believed a woman's time had come to hold political office. Cofer commanded the larger campaign chest and won the race.

Bedford next turned once more to his own campaign for the Dallas City Council. The possibility of an African American winning those days had become far more realistic. By now four African Americans already had held seats on the council: Galloway (however briefly), Allen, Patterson, and Craft. The latter two were serving simultaneously, and they didn't seek reelection in 1979 when their terms expired.

In previous days city council candidates could live anywhere in the city and campaign for the seat of their choice. This changed in 1975 when the federal courts decreed that eight of the eleven seats must represent specific geographical districts. That change, combined with the fact that the once-dominant Citizens Charter Association had disbanded, opened the door to independents, who only had to worry about garnering votes from their own neighborhoods. Bedford lived in Patterson's Place 8 Oak Cliff district. With his family affairs in order, he believed he could dedicate himself to a campaign to succeed her and also be able to devote the many hours of service that would follow.

Velma was at this time a fifth-grade teacher at A. S. Johnston Elementary School in the Bedford neighborhood, where she had been since 1958, when she transferred from Paul L. Dunbar Elementary. She had achieved an enviable record in her profession. State Senator Royce West had recommended her for, and Governor Preston Smith appointed her to, the Teachers' Professional Practices Commission, a body on which she served for five years. She was on the textbook committee for the Dallas Independent School District. She had been chosen 1977–78 East Oak Cliff Teacher of the Year for the East Oak Cliff Sub-District. She was as busy as her husband, for she had a long list of civic activities, including a term as president of the Dallas Barristers' Wives. She had successfully woven herself into the fabric of the Dallas Bar Association. In the early years of Bedford's membership, she had been the only black member of the Dallas Lawyers Auxiliary, where she made good friends and was pleased to find that she was "always treated royally."[1]

As a teacher at a school in her own neighborhood, she was able to know many of her students and their parents on a familiar basis. When the Dallas Independent School District finally experienced widespread desegregation in the early 1970s, she was offered a transfer to a white school that would have a modest influx of African American students. "I refused," she later said. "If I had anything I wanted to give, I wanted to give it to black students. I could be of better service to them."[2]

Living in the same neighborhood as her students was important to her. "I meet and greet my students each time I step out of the house," she said. "When you live in the neighborhood, you must be a friend and an example of what you teach."[3]

In 1979 Louis Arthur Bedford III, who had graduated from Skyline High School, was a sophomore at the University of Houston. Angela had followed her brother to Skyline, a huge new facility that had opened in 1971 as a fully integrated school in southeast Dallas. In New York the other daughter of Louis Bedford Jr., Diane Paige Webster, had graduated from St. John's University, then earned a master's degree, and was now married and a counselor in the New York public schools. When she had married, Bedford responded to her request that he give her away by traveling to New York for that honor.[4]

In January 1979 Bedford announced his candidacy for the city council election scheduled for the first week of April. To concentrate on his campaign, he resigned as associate municipal court judge, having served with much satisfaction in that office for thirteen years. As a resident of the predominantly black Cedar Crest section of Oak Cliff and a high-profile leader in the African American community with long ties to the city, Bedford was the favorite to succeed Lucy Patterson in District 8. His principal opponent, Fred Blair, was less well known. Blair was a thirty-nine-year-old real estate broker and a former member of the City Plan Commission who had been removed from that body in the middle of his term because of excessive absenteeism. A third candidate was attorney B. D. Howard, a thirty-year-old graduate of Texas Southern University Law School who had unsuccessfully sought the Democratic nomination for Congress in 1976 and had worked in campaigns for U.S. Representative Barbara Jordan.[5]

To Bedford's dismay, before he could even launch his campaign, the April election was indefinitely postponed because of U.S. Justice Department requirements that the city realign district boundaries in an effort to ensure greater minority representation on the council. The reason normally would have pleased him. In a city where blacks represented some 40 percent of the total population but held only two of the eleven city council seats, the goal was to change district lines so that at least three city council districts would have a voting population of at least 68 percent African Americans.[6]

But when the Justice Department finally approved the new boundaries in November 1979, Bedford found that his home was not in District 8 anymore. Although most of District 8 was still composed of Oak Cliff, it now excluded Bedford's neighborhood, which was within the new District 6 boundaries. District 6 was still mostly composed of South Dallas, where Bedford's law office was. He had not been campaigning in District 6, though—he'd been campaigning where he resided, in the old District 8.

The January 19, 1980, election was only a couple months away, and if Bedford wanted to remain in the race for District 8, he had until December 30 to move into the district. Its border was less than a block away from his home.[7] "The earth moved and I got caught," he told a reporter from the *Dallas Morning News*.[8] A quick solution would have been to move into an apartment in South Dallas, which is what B. D. Howard, caught by the same residency restriction, did. Bedford declared that he would do no such thing. Fred Blair was left as the only candidate for District 8.[9]

A major problem for Bedford concerning switching his candidacy to District 6 was the fact that several strong candidates had already been campaigning there for more than a year. Three of them were women. Elsie Faye Heggins, a real estate broker who had extensive involvement in South Dallas and who had unsuccessfully opposed Juanita Craft in the previous council election, was one of these. She had good grassroots support and name recognition. Heggins, along with Al Lipscomb, Peter Johnson, J. B. Jackson, Pancho Medrano, and others, had been an original intervenor in the case that had overturned the old at-large method of citywide elections. Mabel White, also a real estate agent, had an even stronger record of civic service in South Dallas and had won the endorsement of many organizations. Sherry Ferguson was a twenty-seven-year-old political science graduate of Southern Methodist University. She had been an administrative assistant to former State Representative Eddie Bernice Johnson. And now there was also Howard, who, like Bedford, faced an uphill battle.

Weighing his chances, Bedford was not pleased. He had only two months to campaign in the new district. Finally, though, he did decide to join the District 6 race.

There was not much difference in the candidates, but it was refreshing that African Americans had a choice. All the candidates emphasized the need for neighborhood improvement, more municipal services, greater help for low-income and elderly citizens, and effective leadership. The differences lay in personalities, in organization, and in funds available for campaigning. Heggins was more confrontational, White more moderate, and Ferguson youthful and promising. Bedford was a seasoned attorney, and Howard a youthful attorney.

The required December 10 financial report showed Bedford trailing White in funds raised. White had $5,005, Bedford $3,305. Then came Howard with $2,973 and finally Heggins, who had lent herself $1,176 for the campaign.[10]

With so many candidates, a runoff between the top two seemed inevitable since gaining more than 50 percent of the votes would be sufficient. Bedford finished third, with 590 votes or 11.3 percent. White led with 2,061 votes, or 39.6 percent of all votes cast, followed by Heggins with 1,529 votes (29.4 percent). These two would be in the runoff.[11] Conservative developer Robert S. Folsom was returned to the office of mayor with a 75 percent majority.

Left on the sidelines for the February 2 runoff, Bedford was importuned by both candidates for his endorsement. Even though he knew Mabel White better and liked her, Bedford chose the more confrontational Heggins, believing that White would be too trusting of the white establishment to promote black interests. Although White was considered the frontrunner in the hotly contested runoff election, Heggins was an upset victor by a margin of just 18 out of 4,322 votes cast.[12] Blair sailed easily to victory in Place 8.

Afterward, Bedford asked Councilwoman Lucy Patterson whether she believed the new district lines had been drawn deliberately to exclude him from District 8. While she could not say they had been, her response strongly suggested that possibility. And indeed, the next year the lines were redrawn again, and Bedford found himself once more in District 8.

Both Blair and Heggins went on to be elected to three terms on the council, providing distinct contrasts in their attitudes. Blair operated comfortably with his fellow white councilmen and proved to be moderate in his approach. Before leaving the council, he was elected mayor pro tem. Heggins preferred working independently, tying her allegiances directly to her constituents rather than seeking a working relationship with her fellow council members. To a far greater degree than George Allen, Lucy Patterson, or Juanita Craft, she examined each issue before the council for its impact on the black community. Heggins gained a reputation for creating controversy because of this insistence.

After Dallas police officers were involved in several questionable shooting incidents with minorities—incidents that stirred resentment and threatened to lead to the kind of urban disorders that had struck so many other cities in similar circumstances—Heggins was quick to criticize the police department for its alleged racism, heightening tensions rather than calming the situation. Police Chief Billy Prince even claimed that she was "gonna end up creating a Watts in South Dallas."[13]

Blair and Heggins both resigned from the city council in 1984 to campaign as political partisans for the same position on the Dallas County Commissioners Court. Although service on the city council was without party affiliation, both now campaigned as Democrats.

But a surprise awaited these two well-known city hall veterans. While press reports focused on the duel between them, a third African American candidate, the youthful and aggressive John Wiley Price, won the race. Price was an administrative assistant for Justice of the Peace Cleophas R. Steele Jr. and a former supporter of Heggins. He was less well-known than his two opponents, but he, unlike them, enjoyed the advantage of having worked diligently in party politics and enjoying the support of an established apparatus. A native of Forney (in Kaufman County, just southeast of Dallas), Price continued to be reelected for term after term, holding office into 2008, becoming probably the most-recognized African American official in Dallas.

Following Heggins at city hall and even more outspoken in her support of black issues was Diane Ragsdale. Fred Blair's successor was Albert Lipscomb, the former perennial political gadfly, who now began a long, controversial career as an elected councilman at city hall. Heggins, Ragsdale, and Lipscomb demonstrated that this new generation, owing no debt to the once-powerful Ministerial Interdenominational Alliance, now led the black community.

Up and down Forest Avenue amid the commercial establishments were two-story houses, reminders of the day when the street was primarily residential and an integral part of the Jewish community in South Dallas. Two doors from Bedford's office in the Professional Building stood a once-handsome but now vacant and partially burned two-story frame house. A black physician named Eugene Dorsey owned 2626 Forest, which he intended to restore in order to move his office there. When Dr. Dorsey changed his mind, Bedford purchased the structure, renovated it with the help of a client named James Epp, moved his office there, and put up his attorney-at-law sign in the front yard.[14]

Moving with him to his new office was his faithful secretary, Carmena Adams, who had served him and his friend Haywood Sparks for so many years. She has remained with Bedford to the present time. Soon after Bedford's move, the Dallas City Council authorized a name change for Forest Avenue: it would henceforth be known as Martin Luther King Jr. Boulevard.

There was more than enough space in the new building, and in the following years Bedford rented space to a series of African American attorneys, including Gene Gaines, Carl Gaines, Roy Jeffers, Ricardo Jordan, Robert Beckels, Fred Landers, Larry W. Baraka, and Josephine Dye.

Baraka achieved unique distinction. He had grown up in a twelve-story housing project in St. Louis, Missouri, won a scholarship to Cornell College in Mount Vernon, Iowa (near Cedar Rapids), and then earned his juris doctorate at the University of Houston. Upon graduation in 1976, he moved to Dallas and joined District Attorney Henry Wade's staff as a prosecutor. He was in private practice between 1978 and 1985, during which time he and Bedford developed a close relationship. In 1984, at the age of thirty-four, Baraka campaigned for election as judge of Criminal District Court No. 2. In a sign of the changing times, he became the first black man in Dallas to be elected to a district judgeship, holding that position through 1990.[15]

Baraka's election as a district judge at the courthouse occurred the same year that John Wiley Price was elected a county commissioner. The white, good old boy culture of the courthouse that Bedford had encountered in 1951 was changing—in fact, it had disappeared.

In 1984, also, Bedford was interviewed for a *Dallas Life Magazine* feature story on various residents and their relationships with Dallas. An appealing photograph of him gesticulating in front of his law office accompanied the piece. Bedford's views on his hometown revealed a trace of disappointment, clearly related to his loss in two political races and to his sense that as a native Dallasite, he would like to have had an even larger, more public voice in its affairs.

"Dallas isn't bad for me," he said. "I haven't gotten by any means rich, and maybe I haven't been able to do all the things I'd like to do for the city. At one time, I thought I had something to offer Dallas, and I would have liked to exercise my interest.

"I'm not unhappy with this being my home. I'll put it this way. There was a song called 'It Had To Be You,' but I think the part I liked is 'with all your faults, I love you still.' So with all its faults, I still love Dallas."[16]

The city had grown over the years, he thought, primarily because of the dedication and perseverance of its white leaders, even though they had operated it as "sort of a closed town." Bedford's perception was that the "old guard" of white leaders preferred dealing with blacks who were newly arrived from New York, California, or Chicago rather than those born and reared in Dallas.[17]

As the years passed, Bedford's law practice underwent a gradual change. No longer was he accepting criminal cases or divorce cases. He found it difficult to collect his fees in advance in criminal cases, as was the custom, and divorce cases were simply too emotional. What he began to appreciate and specialize in was less confrontational: probate law. To hone his skills in this field, he completed the advanced estate planning and probate course offered by the State Bar of Texas as part of its Professional Development Program.[18]

With a new generation of black attorneys graduating from law schools and establishing practices without the hardships facing earlier African American lawyers, Bedford had assumed a new and exalted position. An article in the *Dallas Morning News* in 1985 reflected his new status. He was only fifty-nine, but he was being described as a "pioneer" who had made a racial "breakthrough" as a judge.[19] Many of the new black law school graduates made an effort to meet him. Bedford welcomed their overtures; he was keenly interested in them, as well. He wanted to give them the same courtesies that Durham, Turner, and others had extended to him when he was young and "wet behind the ears."[20]

As he exchanged visits with these new attorneys, camaraderie inevitably blossomed. As news and feature articles about Bedford's circle of new young attorneys and other African Americans appeared with more frequency in Dallas's two daily newspapers, Bedford's habit of clipping the articles for his three-ring binders intensified. He had a compelling need to document the achievements of fellow African Americans.

One of these lawyers who would consider herself to be a Bedford protégé and who exemplified the energy of this group was Joan Tarpley. In earning her degree in 1968, she became one of the first African American women to graduate from SMU's law school, and she was the first black woman to practice law in Dallas. Tarpley (later elected district judge under her married name of Winn) was a Dallas native who grew up on her aunt and uncle's farm in the area north of White Rock Lake (northeast of downtown), commuted to Booker T. Washington High School for her studies, and then graduated from Dillard University (in New Orleans) with a degree in psychology. Before entering law school, Tarpley joined the Peace Corps and taught for two years in Nigeria.[21]

After law school she encountered a remnant of prejudice against her as a woman of color and prejudice against all women attorneys. Major law firms in Dallas were reluctant to hire them. Tarpley joined W. J. Durham in his law practice. She later remembered the practical legal advice Durham gave her, the same sort of advice he had given Bedford nearly two decades earlier: "The answers always lie in the library," he told her. Rather than ask someone, he said, he always looked it up himself.[22]

Upon leaving Durham's practice, Tarpley took a position as trial attorney for the U.S. Labor Department in Dallas and then later served as assistant regional appeals examiner for the U.S. Civil Service Commission. In 1975 the Dallas County Commissioners Court appointed her a judge of a county court at law. When a vacancy opened on the 191st District Court, Governor Dolph Briscoe appointed her to that bench, making her the first black woman in the state of Texas to preside over a district court.[23]

The J. L. Turner Legal Association was undergoing its own transition during these days of change. From its inception as a small organization of men who had banded together for mutual support, it had remained a male-dominated organization. Its first president, J. L. Turner Jr., had held that office for seventeen years, until he was succeeded by C. B. Bunkley Jr. and then by Cleophas Steele Jr. But in the 1970s many new African American attorneys, including women such as Tarpley, were arriving in Dallas. The organization entered a new era in 1978 when one of the new female African American attorneys, Joan Sessoms Ford, was nominated for the presidency. She remembered that there was considerable resistance to her because of her gender, but after a "tug of war" at the meeting, she was elected as the first woman president.[24]

In Ford's opinion, the Turner Association in previous years had been a good old boys club. Members got together for lunch, and the guys sometimes went out "for drinks and to smoke." Under her presidency the organization began to have annual banquets and become more professional in its activities.[25]

In the years that followed, women presidents of the organization would become common. Elected to the presidency were DeMetris Sampson, 1989–1990; Rhonda Hunter, 1991–1992; Josephine Dye, 1993–1994; Sonya D. Hoskins, 1999; Monica McCoy Purdy, 2000; and Buena Vista Lyons, 2005.

An earlier change for the Turner Association had occurred in 1977, when the attorneys in Tarrant County, now numerous enough to have their own association, decided to establish their own Tarrant County Black Bar Association. Its first meeting was held in L. Clifford Davis's office in Fort Worth.

Recognition of Bedford's contributions to Dallas's civic, legal, and church affairs began to come regularly from both white and black organizations. His church, New Hope Baptist, presented him with its Gold Centennial Award for his many years of leadership. The Big Brothers organization, with whom he had been affiliated since practicing law in West Dallas, honored him in 1973 for his fifteen years of service. In 1976 he was named Honorary Mr. Homecoming at his alma mater, Prairie View A&M. His new status as a revered senior lawyer was signified by the roast given him in March 1977 by his friends at Amvets Post 99.[26]

When the Dallas Bar Association held a three-day conference at Lake Texoma (on the Red River north of Dallas) in 1974 to set goals, Bedford was among the distinguished conferees, joining such individuals as U.S. District Judge Sarah T. Hughes, future U.S. Supreme Court nominee Harriet Miers, SMU President Paul Hardin, and a host of other community leaders and attorneys.[27]

In 1978, upon the recommendation of future congresswoman Eddie Bernice Johnson, President Jimmy Carter appointed Bedford to the Commission for Nominating Federal Circuit Court Judges for the Fifth Circuit.[28] That was also the year Bedford received a signal honor from Texas Governor Dolph Briscoe, who commissioned him as an admiral in the Texas Navy. Of course, the state of Texas had no navy, but such honorific "commissions" were occasionally given to friends or persons of influence.[29]

When in 1984 a vacancy occurred on the Dallas Bar Association Board of Directors, Bedford's name was placed in nomination. At the May 22 board meeting, he was unanimously elected.[30] In the following year he was named a fellow of the Texas Bar Foundation, and soon afterward a fellow of the Dallas Bar Foundation.

A tragic incident shocked the Dallas legal community in 1986. Harvard-educated Fred J. Finch, the first black member of the Dallas Bar Association, and his wife, Mildred, a community college math teacher, were stabbed to death in their sleep in their South Dallas home by an intruder. The attack appeared to be random. Not long afterward a twenty-five-year-old parolee who had fled a minimum-security halfway house was arrested and charged for the murders. Kenneth Wayne Thomas had in his possession a number of items from the Finch household, including a Rolex watch, a suit of clothes, and shoes. Thomas seemed to have no knowledge of his victims' identities.[31]

Bedford had lost a fine friend in Fred Finch, and the legal community lost one of its outstanding attorneys. In addition to working with the NAACP in desegregating the Dallas public schools, Finch, sixty-six at the time of his death, had represented the first black students to attend the University of Texas at Arlington (then Arlington State College). Before his death he had founded the second weekly newspaper for the black community, the *Dallas Examiner.*

South Dallas, where Finch lived and where Bedford maintained his law office, had become a predominantly depressed area, noted for a high degree of poverty and crime and sometimes referred to as "the ghetto." Not long before Finch's death, a black physician had been killed in his office on nearby Grand Avenue. Many people began to ask Bedford whether he shouldn't move his office to a safer neighborhood. He preferred to stay, but he safeguarded his office by placing burglar bars on the windows and by locking the doors even during daylight hours.

Another incident caused safety concerns and reinforced the need for burglar bars. On her way to an afternoon PTA meeting at her Johnston School, Velma was assaulted by a robber who grabbed her purse. In the melee she broke her hip.

In November 1987 William L. Johnson Jr., another of the black legal pioneers in Texas, died. He was Bedford's classmate at Prairie View, and Johnson's wife and Velma were undergraduates together at Bishop College in Marshall. In 1966 Johnson became the first black lawyer in the U.S. Attorney's Office for the Northern District of Texas.

Another death in 1987 was even more personal for Bedford. His mother, Callie, died of natural causes at the age of ninety-five. Services were held at the family's New Hope Baptist Church. She was buried in southeast Dallas at Lincoln Cemetery next to her husband.

Dallas in the 1980s was a far different place from the town Bedford had returned to from Brooklyn in the 1950s to begin his legal practice. Attitudes had been transformed in both the white and the black communities. With only a few unenlightened exceptions, those in the white community had realized and acknowledged the massive injustices perpetrated against black Americans for so many generations. Those in the black community, in large part, had discarded the prevailing pessimism of earlier days for a far more confident and aggressive attitude.

Of course, there was still a great distance to go, especially in the upper reaches of the legal community. As a 1987 news story in the *Dallas Times Herald* summarized the situation, "Decades after the civil-rights movement helped minorities move into society's mainstream, most of the country's lawyers are still white males, and few blacks and Hispanics have moved into the uppermost levels of the profession."[32]

The president-elect of the J. L. Turner Legal Association, Andrew Dunlap, described the legal profession as "the last bastion of elitism and the ante-bellum tradition of excluding minorities from society. The law profession, which has brought all kinds of changes through the civil-rights movement, doesn't live what it preaches."[33] The Dallas Bar Association was mindful of the problem. The DBA had an active Minority Participation Committee, summer programs to persuade minority students to practice law in Dallas after graduation, and a scholarship program at the SMU School of Law for minority students.

In the early 1950s Bedford had occasionally begun to attend annual meetings of the National Bar Association, the organization formed for African American attorneys when they were not eligible for American Bar Association membership. Getting to those early meetings and finding places to stay was often a problem. To get to his first meeting in 1952 or 1953 in New Orleans, he and Kenneth Holbert rode with one of Durham's friends. Bedford and Holbert stayed in dormitory rooms at Dillard University. Most of the lawyers in attendance were from cities like New York, Chicago, and Detroit, and to Bedford they appeared unusually well dressed and mentally sharp. "It was very, very encouraging to see black lawyers who seemed so obviously successful," he said years later. For his return to Dallas, Bedford took a Greyhound bus; Holbert rode with someone else as far as Texarkana, then made his way back to Dallas from there.[34]

Beginning in the 1960s, Bedford attended every annual meeting of the National Bar Association. As the years progressed, he enjoyed seeing old friends, rejoicing in their accomplishments, and meeting new friends from various parts of the nation. When the organization met in Dallas in 1988, it honored Bedford with the Gertrude E. Rush Award, named for the female cofounder of the NBA. Three years later the organization placed Bedford in its Hall of Fame.

He reminisced at these annual conferences with old friends, such as Aloysius M. Wickliff Sr., a Houston attorney who had been Bedford's ROTC company commander when he was a freshman at Prairie View. Wickliff had enjoyed an exemplary career, and in 1997 he joined Bedford in the National Bar Association Hall of Fame.

Another longtime friend he saw regularly at NBA meetings was Theodore R. Johns of Beaumont, who had been a year behind Bedford at Prairie View. Johns represented the NAACP in court in 1956, when he argued successfully to desegregate Lamar State College of Technology in Beaumont. When black students tried to enter the college that fall, though, they were met with burning crosses and a persistent outbreak of violence from one hundred or so belligerent picketers. Police, reluctant at first to enforce order, finally gave in to pressure from the local newspaper and the mayor to clear the picketers from the campus so that the students could enter. Twenty-six blacks enrolled during the second week of classes. Plenty of stories like this one were shared at these annual NBA meetings.[35]

Craig A. Washington, a fellow Prairie View graduate who began practicing law in 1969 after graduating from Texas Southern University Law School, offered proof in Bedford's mind that just because someone had not attended a more prestigious law school did not mean he or she couldn't be a superior lawyer. Washington won what Bedford considered to be the hardest criminal case he had ever heard of. Washington defended a state penitentiary inmate who had killed an assistant warden and a prison guard to stop them from beating him—and won a not-guilty verdict from the jury. Washington was later a state representative in Austin for nine years and a congressman in Washington, D.C., for six years.[36]

A distinctive honor came when Bedford was profiled and his portrait painted for the 1989 Miller High Life calendar titled "Gallery of Greats: Counsels for the Cause." His brief biography included this comment by Bedford: "I've always believed that my actions could make a real difference. And I could never stand by and witness an injustice without putting up a good fight." His original portrait and those of eleven other black legal honorees—one for each month—were displayed in galleries throughout the United States.[37]

The time seemed to have arrived for such reflections. A 1989 article in the

Dallas Morning News titled "'He Had Vision'," with the subtitle "Judicial Pioneer Recalls Milestones in Civil Rights," gave a flattering profile of Bedford, accompanied by a large, close-up photograph of him in a reflective mood. In the article some of the city's leading African Americans paid tribute to Bedford and the role he had played in inspiring them.

One of them was attorney Royce West, who had been elected the first African American president of the Student Congress at the University of Texas at Arlington before earning a law degree at the University of Houston. In 1993 West was elected to the Texas Senate, beginning a long and distinguished career there. West had been in the fifth grade when he met Bedford, the first lawyer he had ever met, and West said Bedford was indirectly responsible for his decision to go to law school.[38]

"Whether he's in South Dallas on Second Avenue or whether he's at the top of San Jacinto Tower, he's the same L. A. Bedford," West said. "He's not the type of person who will change to fit the environment. He's real steady and he's real constant."[39]

In 1990, when Bedford was sixty-four years old, he wrote an imaginative, thoughtful article for the Dallas Bar Association's *Headnotes*, describing what he would say about his life when he no longer was able to "stand before the bar."[40] (Perhaps he was too young to write his reminiscences, but during his lifetime so many dramatic changes had taken place that it must have seemed to him that he was already very old.) There had been joys but also tribulations in his own practice, he wrote, and the tribulations left the deepest and most lasting impressions. In his early practice he had felt like a pioneer surrounded by a "sea of whiteness" that—except for the janitors, who were "invisible"—covered the courthouse.

His central theme was the debt he felt he owed to the African American lawyers who had inspired him through their courageous work and made it possible for him and others to have a legal career. He wanted these "intent and brilliant" men to be remembered:

> I will recall J. L. Turner, Sr., a very small man of stature, but [who] stood as tall as a giant when he walked into the Dallas County courthouse in 1896, and proclaimed to all that he would practice law and protect the

property rights of his people. I will ask those who will listen to imagine the pain, humiliation, bias, and injustice he must have endured. Also imagine the courage, boldness, and Mr. Turner's ability to overcome fear and apprehension in the hostile environment existing in the halls of justice of Dallas County, in the year of 1896, almost a hundred years ago.

W. J. Durham was his "leader, idol and mentor," an emancipator who removed "so many legal shackles from our arms and legs." Durham, he said, had the ability to transform the hostile environment he found in most courtrooms into an impartial and equitable setting, winning favorable verdicts for African Americans when the juries, judges, opposing attorneys, and opposing parties were white. That so few young African American lawyers now even knew his name was shocking and saddening.

He remembered his "big brothers," C. B. Bunkley Jr. and J. L. Turner Jr., and how they "walked with me and guided me along the way." Bunkley he treasured as one of his dearest and closest friends. "I will speak of his ability to make impromptu speeches which would stir the souls of those who heard him. A gentleman, he was, yet bold, aggressive, and unyielding in and out of the courtroom when fighting against inequities and [for] the right to be treated with respect." Turner, known as "Brother Turner," was a "scholar, philosopher, quiet, dignified, reliable, a true friend, and a son who held his father, J. L. Turner, Sr., in high esteem."

He recalled in particular the decades of the 1950s and 1960s. The 1950s he remembered as a time when African American lawyers were subjected to retaliation for representing and participating in civil rights cases. Disbarment for barratry was an ever-present threat for those who attacked unjust laws. Yet, although the times were hostile, those were the most rewarding days. The caring and trust among those few compatriots could never be appreciated by those who had not experienced those times firsthand, he wrote.

I will tell of the 60s and the fire that swept over the college campuses. Young men and women burning with the desire to become first class citizens in their own lifetime. I will tell all who will listen about the students who attended Wiley and Bishop colleges, both then located in Marshall, a small East Texas town. I will speak in reverence, with tears in my eyes, of Romeo Williams, my friend and fellow lawyer, and Mattie Mae Ella Johnson, a student at Bishop, both of whom lost their lives in a tragic accident shortly after leaving the Harrison County Courthouse. I will always remember with pride and respect those students who faced the criminal justice system, physical abuse, and possible death for the cause of justice and equality.

. . . I will tell all who will listen that no accumulation of wealth can bring the joy and satisfaction that one receives by knowing that his efforts helped to loosen the legal shackles which we as a people have borne for more than 300 years. . . . I will tell them that I earned less than $2,000.00 my first year of practice. During my early years, African American lawyers received no Court appointments from the Civil or Criminal benches, therefore, we were deprived of fees generated from such appointments. Only white lawyers, some with considerably less experience and ability, were appointed as Ad Litems and to represent indigent defendants. Needless to say, neither the public or private sector, regardless of one's qualification, engaged the services of African American lawyers. If my listeners may ask how I survived during my early years, I will tell them that I was sustained by faith, family and friends.

He urged his readers not to forget the lessons of history, to be mindful that racial oppression could arise again. In Germany there had been many wealthy Jews who were unable to save themselves from the political pogroms of Adolph Hitler. In the United States native-born citizens of Japanese ancestry, without due process of law, were placed in internment camps for the duration of World War II. "I will also remind my listeners that no person of German or Italian ancestry, native born, naturalized or unnaturalized, suffered the denial of their basic constitutional rights. I will ask if racism triumphed over the Constitution."

Finally, he wrote about his contemporary colleagues: Fred Finch, Joseph J. Lockridge, and E. Brice Cunningham. Of Finch, a Harvard Law School graduate who spoke with pride of his alma mater Wiley College but never mentioned Harvard. Of the memory of Lockridge, who had the most promising future of all, but who had taken an airplane that crashed and ended his life. And of Cunningham, the last of a breed who could try any type of case and had "stepped into Durham's shoes and traveled over the State trying cases which resulted in single member districts, deseg-regation of public schools and equal employment opportunities."

When Bedford's career at last was over, he wrote, he would "walk slowly away, my sun setting, but in my heart, I will be watching the sun rise as I see young African American lawyers taking my place before the Bar."[41]

The J. L. Turner Legal Association was thriving. From the original dozen or so black attorneys who had organized it in 1952, membership was approaching one hundred by 1990. Many, if not most, of the members also belonged to the Dallas Bar Associa-tion. A separate bar organization had arisen in Dallas for another minority group, also. Mexican American lawyers banded together and formed their own associa-tion, the Mexican-American Bar Association of Dallas (today known as the Dallas Hispanic Bar Association).

Not so many years before, in 1943, members of the Dallas Bar Association had sought to chastise the American Bar Association for removing racial barriers to membership. Indeed, all of enlightened society had changed. With the awakening of America's racial consciousness, the Dallas Bar Association became a model of progressivism.

Its Sarah T. Hughes Diversity Fellowships, started in 1981 and funded by the Dallas Bar Foundation, provided full scholarships to minority law students at SMU. In its first twenty-five years the program awarded more than $1.2 million to students. Recipients of the Hughes Fellowships began making an impact in the city after they earned their law degrees. John Loza became a Dallas city councilman and mayor pro tem. Irma Ramirez became a U.S. magistrate. T. J. Johnson became an assistant U.S. attorney. Diane Jones became a Dallas County criminal courts judge.

Through its Collins Summer Clerkships, the DBA paid the salaries of minority law students who worked for six weeks in the district attorney's office, the public defender's office, the city attorney's office, a district court, the Fifth District Court of Appeals, and the Texas Supreme Court. In the mid-1980s the DBA began sponsoring receptions to introduce minority law clerks to city officials and to encourage them to return to Dallas when they began their practice.

The presidents of the J. L. Turner Legal Association and the Mexican-American Bar Association were ex officio members of the DBA Board of Directors. A reduced dues policy was instituted for minority lawyers who belonged to those organizations. Minority bar members were now playing important leadership roles in the DBA's various committees.[42]

In 1990 DBA president Al Ellis took another step by appointing a task force on opportunities in the profession for minorities. Bedford was an automatic choice to be a member of the committee.

Ellis remembered well a discussion that was a turning point in whether to make the presidents of the J. L. Turner Legal Association and the Mexican-American Bar Association voting members of the DBA board, rather than ex officio members. He met with key attorneys, including Bedford, Hispanic lawyer Adelfa Calleja, incoming DBA president Douglas S. Lang (later a justice on the Fifth Court of Appeals), and board member Orin L. Harrison III. "L. A. and Adelfa told their stories and swayed them right away," Ellis recalled later, "and Orin made a convincing speech."[43]

The DBA board accepted their recommendation and voted unanimously to ask the membership to ratify this historic bylaw change. On January 21, 1991, a day chosen because it was within a week of Martin Luther King Jr.'s birthday, the membership approved the change.[44]

"I can't help but believe," wrote Royce West, "that the faithful few that organized J. L. Turner Legal Association envisioned a day when every lawyer, regardless of ethnic background, would be an integral part of the Dallas Bar Association.

"I know they will be watching from that great courtroom in the heavens. . . . They will witness this historical vote and say, 'Our work is done. We can now rest. The future is in good hands.'"[45]

Bedford was sixty-five years of age and in fine health. "To retire at 65 is not something to be considered," he said.[46]

One of the signal honors for a Dallas civic leader was the Justinian Award for Community Service, given to an "unsung hero" for conspicuous public service each year by the Dallas Lawyers Wives' Club (in 1992 renamed the Dallas Lawyers Auxiliary). Bedford's civic service had been conspicuous indeed, and in 1991 he was named the ninth recipient of this prestigious award. His list of service was long: he was a member of the boards of directors of the Black Chamber of Commerce, Dallas Metropolitan YMCA, Friends of the Dallas Public Library, Dallas Legal Services, North Texas Legal Services, Dallas Community Health Center, Southern Christian Leadership Conference, Interracial Council for Business Opportunity, Dallas Human Relations Committee, Martin Luther King Recreation Center, Moorland Branch YMCA, and West Dallas Social Center. He was a member of the steering committees of Big Brothers and the Pioneer District Circle Ten Council of Boy Scouts. He was a past president of the Prairie View A&M University National Alumni Association and the Washington-Lincoln High School National Alumni Association, a board member of the Dallas Urban League, and a former commissioner on the Dallas County Grand Jury. He was a director of the Dallas Bar Association and a fellow of the Dallas Bar Foundation. He was a fellow of the State Bar of Texas and a member of the National Bar Association and the American Judicature Society.[47]

In accepting the award at a luncheon at the Anatole Hotel, Bedford credited individuals in the past who had influenced and encouraged him: his parents, his teachers at Booker T. Washington High School, his professors at Prairie View, the attorneys in the African American community who had befriended and helped him when he began his career, and his wife and family. "I would not be standing here today without all of them," he said. "They taught me civic pride, gave me a sense of dignity, encouraged me, lifted me up."[48]

That day the luncheon speaker was Edith H. Jones, circuit judge of the U.S. Court of Appeals, Fifth Judicial Circuit. "What is it," she asked, "that impels a man like Louis Bedford to strive not just for the well-being of himself and his family, but also for his profession, his community, and the nation?" She answered the question herself, saying it was an effort to address the "unfinished business" of society, a business of attacking the ills of the community, nation, and world, which would never be completed.[49]

The American Bar Association, so late in embracing minorities among its membership, now was pursuing them. A 1986 ABA task force reported that the legal profession "must aggressively promote ethnic diversity." Despite good intentions, the profession continued to be largely segregated. It was estimated that of the nation's 677,000 lawyers, about 10 percent were minorities and 15 percent were women. In Dallas County minorities made up less than 6 percent of the 8,000 lawyers. Most were employed in small firms or worked as individuals. An important goal now was for them to land more lucrative positions as partners in the dominant large firms. By 2007 progress had been made in this regard—out of 867 equity partners in the major firms, 38 were persons of color.[50]

Another significant breakthrough had been made at city hall, and it had come through legal action. Two African American activists, Roy Williams and Marvin Crenshaw, filed suit in federal court to challenge the manner in which city council members were elected. Both men had failed to be elected to the council—Crenshaw four times and Williams once. Their suit in federal court contended that the number of African Americans elected to the council did not begin to reflect a representative proportion of the city's African American population.

In March 1990 U.S. District Judge Jerry Buchmeyer responded to the suit and agreed that the 8-3 system (eight members elected from geographical districts, and three at-large) was insufficient to satisfy constitutional requirements. A tense, drawn-out debate, much of it conducted in public, ensued as to how to satisfy the judge's ruling. Judge Buchmeyer finally ordered a 14-1 plan for the city, in which only the mayor was elected at-large. Boundaries for new council districts were drawn to result, in theory, in seven whites, five African Americans, and two Mexican Americans being elected to the council. To achieve this proportion, the boundaries largely disregarded the preservation of communities.

A new era had arrived. In 1999 minorities were a majority on the city council. The same was true for trustees at the Dallas Independent School District. In the late 1990s Dallas had an African American mayor, police chief, school superintendent, county commissioner, congresswoman, and state legislators. Such a situation would have been beyond the imagination of the little boy nicknamed Brother living on Thomas Avenue in the 1930s and 1940s.

By now Bedford was a senior attorney who had seen much and who approved of what he had seen. The blatant discrimination he had suffered as a child and as a young man had disappeared. Now his attention turned to preserving the story of that transition and becoming a historian of the movement.

He had not forgotten how far he and other minorities had come. He was the archivist of the J. L. Turner Legal Association. His interest in the history of African

American lawyers and the civil rights struggle in Dallas was keener than ever. His thick three-ring notebooks, bulging with information, grew almost every day. In them he was continuing to document the progress of black lawyers and the continuing struggle for civil rights by collecting photocopies of old city directories, his handwritten minutes of the J. L. Turner Legal Society, newspaper and magazine articles, letters, photographs, programs, and various ephemera. He had been a history major at Prairie View. History, especially of black progress, was an interest he never abandoned.

As his fellow attorneys were regularly acknowledging now, Bedford was himself an important part of that history. Honors continued to come, not just for him but for other African American attorneys, as well. In 2004 Rhonda Hunter was elected president of the Dallas Bar Association, the first African American to hold that office. (When a young attorney, Paul Stafford, was visiting Bedford and discussing Hunter's ascendancy to the presidency, Bedford looked calmly at Stafford and said, "You're next." His prediction was accurate: a few years later Stafford held a Dallas Bar Association office that would lead to the DBA presidency.)

Hunter had previously been president of the J. L. Turner Legal Association. Born in Philadelphia, she moved to Dallas as a child and attended Dallas public schools before earning a bachelor of arts degree from the University of Texas and a juris doctorate from Southern Methodist University School of Law.

Another female African American attorney, Josephine Dye, settled comfortably into Bedford's building to establish her private practice just around the corner from Bedford's own office. Dye, a native of Milwaukee and one of seven children, was the daughter of a carpenter and a teacher's aide. After graduating from the University of Wisconsin Law School, she took a position with the Greater Boston Legal Services, providing aid to the poor. In 1987 she came to Dallas as a staff member with Legal Services of North Texas, eventually becoming managing partner. In 1997 Dye left that position to begin private practice in Bedford's space at 2626 Martin Luther King Jr. Boulevard. In her private practice she emphasized family law and probate and served a term as president of the J. L. Turner Legal Association. Among Dye's honors was the Chrys Dougherty Award for legal services to the poor, awarded by the State Bar of Texas in 1995.[51]

Yet another of the new generation to distinguish himself was Sam Lindsay, who in 1998 became the first African American federal district judge for the Northern District of Texas. Lindsay, nominated by President Bill Clinton, won unanimous approval from the U.S. Senate. Lindsay was a native of San Antonio and a graduate of the University of Texas School of Law.

Lindsay came to Dallas after graduation and immediately contacted Bedford, who gave him names and places to look for work. His efforts to find a position with a corporation or in a big law firm failed, but following Bedford's suggestion, he approached the City of Dallas and was given a position as an assistant city attorney. Intending at first to stay only temporarily, he was appointed city attorney in 1992 by the city council after a dozen years on the job. He was the first African American city attorney for Dallas, and he served in that position until his presidential appointment to the federal bench.

When Lindsay took the oath of office of federal district judge, Bedford was asked to comment. He was mindful of the significance of the occasion. His opening words, "It's about time," drew a rousing cheer from the crowd. Bedford recalled that not so long before, blacks were not even accepted as members of the Dallas Bar Association. "Today, this date, Sept. 11 [1998], is the first time we've had African Americans who've served in every aspect of the judicial system," he said.[52]

Lindsay was one of a trio of African American classmates at the University of Texas School of Law who came to Dallas following graduation. The best known of the three is Ron Kirk, who was elected Dallas's first black mayor in 1995, serving into 2001 when he resigned to campaign unsuccessfully for the U.S. Senate as a Democrat. Kirk, the son of a postal worker, was a 1979 law school graduate. He won his initial mayoral race with 62 percent of the vote, having gained support in both the black and the white communities, and was reelected in 1999 with 74 percent of the vote. He already had achieved partnership in one of the state's major law firms, and prior to his election as mayor, he was the secretary of state of Texas. Returning to private practice after his Senate campaign, Kirk began serving on the boards of major national corporations and remained active in Democratic politics. He was a major adviser to presidential candidate Barack Obama on his Texas strategy, and he campaigned widely for him. As had Lindsay, Kirk made Bedford's acquaintance when he first came to Dallas. Later Kirk called him an "inspiration."[53]

The third member of the UT Law trio was DeMetris Sampson, who was the first African American woman to become a partner in a major firm in Dallas, rising to the position of managing partner of Linebarger, Goggan, Blair & Sampson. She earned her law degree in 1980 from the University of Texas and her master of laws in taxation in 1986 from Southern Methodist University. Three years later Sampson was elected president of the J. L. Turner Legal Association. By the year 2000 she had become a powerful figure in Dallas, active in local, state, and national civic affairs as well as in politics. Sampson too counted Bedford as one of her early inspirations.

As this second millennium began, Bedford and other African Americans could look around the federal, state, county, and municipal courtrooms and be proud. There were twenty-five black judges, from Lindsay on the federal bench to Elizabeth Davis Frizell, presiding municipal judge of the tiny suburb of Balch Springs in southeast Dallas County.

A year later the president of the Dallas Bar Association, Elizabeth Lang-Miers, selected Bedford as one of two Trial Lawyers of the Year, an honor presented to him at the seventh annual Bench/Bar Conference at the Del Lago Golf Resort and Conference Center near Houston. Honored alongside him was veteran attorney John Estes, a former Dallas Bar Association president and a member of the Locke, Purnell, Rain, and Harrell law firm. Both men were honored for having given a lifetime of commitment to trial practice; to the legal profession; and to local, state, and national bar associations.[54]

In 2002 Legal Services of North Texas presented Bedford with the Equal Justice Award for serving the legal needs of the poor with distinction. That same year the Texas Bar Foundation honored Bedford with an Outstanding Fifty Year Lawyer Award, and he was interviewed at length for an oral history that was transcribed and printed as a fifty-two-page booklet. A lifelike pencil portrait by artist J. Longacre, appearing on the cover, depicted the calm gaze of a veteran lawyer whose experiences transcended the careers of almost any of his peers.

One of the finest honors accorded him was the Dallas Bar Foundation's creation of the L. A. Bedford Jr. Scholarships for minority law students. The need had long been apparent to Bedford, but it became acutely apparent in 1997 when a young woman won the Sarah T. Hughes Scholarship to attend SMU law school but could not afford a preparatory course for the admissions exam. The next year the foundation established the Bedford Scholarships to pay for Law School Admission Test (LSAT) preparation courses for needy minority students in the Dallas area. The Princeton Review Foundation soon joined with the Dallas Bar Foundation in expanding this scholarship program.

In 2006 grants were awarded to twelve students, all of whom were required to write essays explaining their needs. Two of the winners for 2006 were refugees from Hurricane Katrina who had settled in the Dallas area. As was true for all the winners, they wanted to contribute to society.

In the eighty-second year of his life, Louis Arthur Bedford Jr., in excellent health and nearly as vigorous as ever, drove his late-model Lexus down Cedar Crest Boulevard every weekday morning, over the long bridge crossing the Trinity River, onto Martin Luther King Jr. Boulevard, and then pulled to the rear of the two-story frame building that had been his office for more than twenty-five years. He would be the first one there; his longtime secretary, Carmena Adams, would arrive around noon. Shortly after he got to the office, Bedford would walk a couple of doors down the street to Graham's Barber Shop, where old friends greeted him as "Judge." There the coffee was always ready, and he would pour himself a small Styrofoam cupful, exchange lighthearted repartee with the barbers and patrons, and leisurely stroll back to his office. The daily newspaper's crossword puzzle awaited him in a room whose walls were filled with plaques and photographs attesting to his long, successful career. There would be occasional phone calls, generally concerning a probate matter, and sometimes he would have to go to the courthouse on routine business. Old friends and new ones often dropped by unannounced, and there was usually time for a chat.

Velma Bedford, retired from teaching since 1979, stayed busy with volunteer work, spending many hours at a retirement center and continuing her church work, which included the presidency of the New Hope Baptist choir. The Bedfords' children had long since been gone from home. Angela Renee Bedford-Walker earned an undergraduate degree at Spelman College in Atlanta and a master of arts degree at Washington University in St. Louis, Missouri. She was back in town, though, a counselor at the Family Place, a Dallas agency for women subjected to violence.

Louis Arthur Bedford III, who earned his degree at the University of Houston, was working as an environmental agent at a hospital in Houston. And he had given his parents two grandchildren: Louis Arthur IV, born March 12, 1993, and Darcy Marie, born February 23, 1997.

To the younger generations of African American lawyers, now so numerous that he long ago had lost the ability to know all of them personally, Bedford was an icon, a figure who had experienced firsthand the days of enforced segregation they had only read about. The newer ones would not have feelings of isolation Bedford experienced when as a young lawyer he saw only white faces at the courthouse. Neither would they have tucked into their memory banks the fear Bedford and others of his generation had felt as youths whenever a white police officer approached.

When this new generation of lawyers went to the courthouse, they saw in all the offices African American officials or employees; they might appear in court before an African American judge; they might encounter County Commissioner John Wiley Price in the hallways. They knew that beginning in 2007, the district attorney of Dallas County was a black man, Craig Watkins, elected to that office over a white veteran prosecutor who held a vastly superior campaign chest. They also knew that Watkins had chosen Bedford to give him the oath of office.

Watkins, who had grown up in Dallas seeing Bedford as a role model, graduated from Prairie View A&M and earned his law degree from Texas Wesleyan University School of Law. He gained national attention when he intensified a program to give DNA tests to prisoners whose convictions seemed questionable. The number of convictions that were overturned as a result of this scientific evidence was astonishing. As a *New York Times* editorial observed in 2008, Dallas County was "turning into a model for the rest of the nation."[55]

The Democratic sweep of the Dallas County courthouse in November 2006, which included Watkins's election, gave proof of a strong change in demographics that would bring even more minority judges to the courthouse in the future. The new African American lawyers knew that one of the area's most influential members of Congress was Eddie Bernice Johnson, who had held office there since 1993, and that in 2001 she was named by *Ebony* magazine as one of the ten most powerful black women in the nation. They knew that one of the most important state senators in Texas was Royce West, who had held the 23rd Senatorial District seat since 1992. They remembered that from 1999 to 2003 the police chief in Dallas was a black man, Terrell Bolton, and they knew that a significant number of patrol officers and detectives (26.4 percent as early as 1992) were members of minority groups.

The world had changed. Viewed over the perspective of a single lifetime, it had been altered with astonishing rapidity, faster and deeper than anyone could have anticipated. Micro improvements were won through painstaking courtroom battles, until progress gained sudden impetus following Rosa Parks's courage in refusing to go to the back of the bus. Awakened by the success of this movement, others quickly joined the surge to expand civil rights—women, Hispanics, gays, and Native Americans. These groups gradually realized that the discrimination they had suffered for years need no longer be tolerated; following in the steps of African Americans, they joined in the effort to make American society a more just society.

Bedford knew well that Durham, Bunkley, and all the others who had sacrificed and worked for decades for the slightest gains could not have imagined how far and how quickly the tide would change. But economic disparities between blacks and whites, though diminished, persisted. Too many young African Americans failed to take advantage of the opportunities for higher education that had been won after so much effort and sacrifice. The black family, once so strong, had by now given way to predominantly single-parent households. The number of children born out of wedlock skyrocketed. Such developments were disturbing and profound in their consequences.

In the beginning years of the twenty-first century, economic and corporate power still resided almost exclusively in white hands. Bedford was reminded of this as he regularly scanned a weekly column in the *Dallas Morning News* that carried photographs of promoted business executives, hoping to see black faces but rarely having that pleasure. Yet, continued progress in the private sector seemed inevitable.

These economic and social challenges would be fought by a new generation, but from the advantage of a far stronger base than that of pioneers, such as Bedford, who had won civil and educational rights in previous decades. If the playing field had not been leveled entirely, nothing could have symbolized these advances more than the dramatic election of an African American, Barack Obama, to the presidency, the highest office in the land. Louis Arthur Bedford Jr., looking happily back over a life that had begun eight decades earlier and measuring the progress made, could only regret that previous generations upon whose shoulders he and others stood had not lived to see the rewards of their good work.

1. V. Bedford, interview, Oct. 26, 2006.
2. Ibid.
3. "The Open Line: Miss Bedford Wins Teaching Award," *Dallas Morning News*, Apr. 12, 1978.
4. Bedford, interview, Mar. 14, 2006.
5. "36 Panel Members Removed Despite Opposition," *Dallas Morning News*, July 28, 1977.
6. "Judge OKs City Election," *Dallas Morning News*, Nov. 20, 1979.
7. Robert S. Sloan, Dallas city secretary, to Bedford, Nov. 23, 1979, "L. A. Bedford Political Races" binder, Bedford Papers.
8. "Judge OKs City Election."
9. Ibid.; "District 6 Maintains Minority Rule," *Dallas Times Herald*, Dec. 27, 1979.
10. "Haggar, Stahl Head List on Campaign Donations," *Dallas Times Herald*, c. Dec. 1979, "L. A. Bedford Political Races" binder, Bedford Papers.
11. "Council Assured of Three Minority Seats," *Dallas Times Herald*, Jan. 20, 1980.
12. "Heggins Scores Upset; Medrano, Tucker Win in Council Contests," *Dallas Times Herald*, Feb. 3, 1980.
13. "Firing of Policeman," *Dallas Morning News*, Nov. 16, 1983.
14. Bedford, interview, July 21, 2006.
15. "Judge Runs Bench in His Own Way," *Dallas Times Herald*, n.d., Bedford Papers.
16. "Dallas on Dallas," *Dallas Morning News*, Aug. 12, 1984, *Dallas Life Magazine*, 14.
17. Ibid.
18. State Bar of Texas, certificate from the Professional Development Program, June 1986, Bedford Papers.
19. "Pioneering Blacks Reflect on Breakthrough as Judges," *Dallas Morning News*, Feb. 6, 1985.
20. Bedford, interview, Sept. 20, 2006.
21. "New Judge Is an Individual, Not a Crusader," *Dallas Times Herald*, July 13, 1975.
22. Ibid.
23. "She's Taken the Law into Her Own Hands," *Dallas Morning News*, May 9, 1980.
24. Joan Sessoms Ford, interview in *J. L. Turner Legal Association*, DVD.
25. Ibid.
26. Amvets Post 99, Bedford roast program, Mar. 11, 1977, Bedford Papers.
27. Dallas Bar Association, "Goals for the Dallas Bar Association," Tanglewood Country Club, Pottsboro, Texas, Oct. 4, 5, 6, 1974, Bedford Papers.
28. "'He Had Vision.'"
29. The commission was dated Dec. 22, 1978. Bedford Papers.
30. "New Directors Named: DBA and SBT," *Dallas Bar Association Headnotes*, June 18, 1984, 1.

31. "Noted Lawyer, Wife Slain," *Dallas Morning News*, Mar. 17, 1986; "Finch's Watch Linked to Murder Suspect," *Dallas Morning News*, Feb. 20, 1987.
32. "ABA Conference to Study Dearth of Minority Lawyers," *Dallas Times Herald*, 1987, Bedford Papers.
33. Ibid.
34. Bedford, interview, Mar. 28, 2006.
35. Shabazz, *Advancing Democracy*, 168–180.
36. Louis A. Bedford Jr., interview by Darwin Payne, Nov. 7, 2006.
37. "Dallas' Bedford in Calendar of Legal Greats," *Dallas Black Chamber of Commerce Update* (Jan.–Feb. 1989): 1, 3.
38. "'He Had Vision.'"
39. Ibid.
40. "When I Become an Old Lawyer and Can No Longer Stand before the Bar," *Dallas Bar Association Headnotes*, Nov. 19, 1990, 1, 10.
41. Ibid.
42. Al Ellis, "President's Report: Can We Talk?" *Dallas Bar Association Headnotes*, Sept. 17, 1990, 4.
43. Al Ellis, interview by Darwin Payne, June 6, 2006.
44. "By-Law Amendment: An Historic Step . . . ," *Dallas Bar Association Headnotes*, Jan. 21, 1991, 1.
45. Ibid., 4.
46. "Three of Dallas's Most Active Seniors View Age as Opportunity to Serve," *Dallas Weekly*, Nov. 28–Dec. 4, 1991.
47. "Justinian Award to Louis Arthur Bedford, Jr.," *Dallas Bar Association Headnotes*, Feb. 18, 1991.
48. "L. A. Bedford Receives DLWC Justinian award," *Dallas Bar Association Headnotes*, May 15, 1991.
49. Ibid.
50. "ABA Conference to Study Dearth"; Cheryl Hall, "Law Firms Remain White Bastions," *Dallas Morning News*, Nov. 11, 2007.
51. Al Ellis, "Unsung Hero: Josephine Dye," *Dallas Bar Association Headnotes*, n.d., L. A. Bedford Papers.
52. "Lindsay Sworn In as Judge," *Dallas Morning News*, Sept. 12, 1998.
53. Ron Kirk, interview in *J. L. Turner Legal Association*, DVD.
54. "Lawyers with Commitment," *Dallas Bar Association Headnotes*, Sept. 1, 1998.
55. "More Than a Steak Dinner," *New York Times*, Jan. 10, 2008.

AFTERWORD

The Shoulders We Stand On
Black Professionals and the Transformation of U.S. Society

I
n her presidential address delivered to the convention of the Organization of American Historians in Washington, D.C., on April 12, 2002, Darlene Clark Hine invited the future generation of historians to delve deeply into "the layers of our country's past in order to bring into the bright light of history all those whose struggles and resistance made freedom more than a dream. We have work to do." She observed that "World War II was a watershed in the history of the black professional class. It brought to the forefront ideological tensions that reverberated throughout the black community. The struggles of black professionals to carve for themselves a niche within 'separate but equal' gave way to a determination to end Jim Crow." In the half century before the war, a professional class of African Americans emerged and helped establish a set of parallel institutions under the theoretically "separate but equal" framework to which the 1896 *Plessy v. Ferguson* decision of the U.S. Supreme Court had granted constitutional sanction. Professor Hine, in an address that brilliantly culminated her many years of careful research and numerous books and articles on the black professional class, pointed out that "the development of the black professional class and of the educational and practice facilities in which its members were trained and worked seemed to imply acquiescence in segregation. But such institutions never silenced internal dissent. Ideological tensions between parallelism and integrationism haunted black discourse throughout the twentieth century." It is in this liminal context, fraught perhaps with a measure of DuBoisian double consciousness, that Louis Bedford Jr. entered law school and then the legal profession in 1950s Dallas.[1]

Black professionals were central to the long movement for African American freedom in the United States, but their role was seldom played out as part of a conscious strategy for some comprehensive overturning of the system of Jim Crow racism. Instead, as we see in Bedford and the organizing of the J. L. Turner Legal

Association as a parallel association to the State Bar, black professionals challenged the day-to-day discrimination and restrictions on their professional work in numerous ways, sometimes direct and overt, but more often, in a manner that did not threaten the fundamental premises of a white supremacist society. As a class, they were amply equipped to make these challenges and to make them in a way that more modern sectors of the white professional class found increasingly difficult to ignore, especially in the context of a Cold War where the United States had assumed the position of leader of the Free World.

Until recently, however, the place of men and women like Bedford in the critical years of the civil rights movement, 1954–65, has not been well appreciated or understood. In this vein, Hine points out that "many diverse contributories flow into the ocean of social change. Historians must revise the time line and bring into history those less prominent and less visible contributors whose struggles forged foundational moments in the long movement for black liberation. There are many more events and individuals worthy of historical investigation. The study of the civil rights odyssey of diverse segments in communities of African Americans is far from exhausted." From the study of the history of Dallas and of the influential figures on Bedford and his generation, from the prominent men like Richard T. Hamilton to Bedford's mother, this kind of revised history is beginning to emerge. "The maneuvers of black professionals to end segregation," states Hine, "expanded and enriched the arsenal of protest strategies that equipped activists in the classic civil rights movement, the one so well studied by historians, sociologists, and popular writers: the strategic use of the media, appeals to diverse publics, dramatic confrontations with white authority, cultivation of relations with high-ranking white leaders, behind-the-scenes negotiations with white adversaries, avowal of the principles of democracy, demonstration of intellectual and professional competence, and the invocation of the rhetoric of moral outrage against white supremacy." We historians still have work to do.[2]

One important area of study is to critically discern how black professionals helped engineer "less prominent and less visible" changes in society by developing alliances and support for change in the white community. In *Standing Against Dragons: Three Southern Lawyers in an Era of Fear*, Sarah Hart Brown studies the careers of three lawyers who advocated racial equality and fought for civil liberties in the two decades that followed World War II. The left-liberal white Southern attorneys "served their region and the nation well," she writes, "if only as critics, examples, and facilitators." She highlights the uncommonness of the subjects of her study who, in an anticommunist and white supremacist Cold War era that was plainly dangerous for those who dissented from the norm, "joined a minority of their professional contemporaries who championed liberal constitutional remedies for the compelling inequities of the American Century." What makes them interesting, however, is not how uncommon it was for Southern white attorneys during the Cold War era to cast their lot with African Americans and others who were outside of the racist, anticommunist orthodoxy of the times, but that any did so at all.[3]

Before the deep suffering of the working masses of black folks pushed its way onto the front pages, the prime-time news programs, and ultimately, the political agendas of U.S. power brokers from the Oval Office to city councils and corporate boardrooms, it was the microstruggles of African American lawyers and other black professionals that facilitated the emergence of white allies and the adjustment of the firmly closed apartheid society of the South. The 1948 episode at the Dallas Central YMCA Grill and Dining Room is a clear example of a small challenge that caused some questioning among whites. Likewise, when Bedford and his friends C. B. Bunkley Jr. and W. J. Durham began to challenge the notion and legal policy of "misdemeanor murder" in Dallas courthouses, their actions called into question the mind-set of white judges, prosecutors, law enforcement officials, and politicians. When Bedford managed Bunkley's 1959 campaign for a seat on the Dallas City Council, the very act pushed whites to new modes of thinking about black capacity and competency. Their actions evoked not mere sympathy from whites, but the beginning of a sense of blacks as equals who had something to offer (or threaten) in material and political terms. Ultimately, in 1963, when the Dallas Bar Association approved Fred Finch's application for membership, followed by that of Bedford and others, a process of change was solidly set in place that had already placed many progressive and forward-thinking whites on the side of dismantling the Jim Crow regime. The Civil Rights Act of 1964 would embolden more African Americans, especially those of the younger generation, to speed the pace of change and to widen and deepen it. Black professionals had, however, done much of the critical preparatory work of identifying the problems, removing the legality of racial discrimination, and fostering among white allies a healthy debate and critical engagement with anti-racist ideas and action. When Bedford became Dallas County's first African American judge in 1966, his appointment was tangible evidence of more than two decades of work by black professionals to *make a way out of no way.* The election of black physician Dr. Emmett Conrad and Texas Instruments, Inc. executive Dr. Marvin Berkeley in 1967 to the Dallas school board was further evidence that this process of change was gaining momentum. Permanently, *a way* to a new, antiracist Dallas had been made out of the *no way* of a white supremacist society that had reigned from the days of chattel slavery to the mid-1960s with only a brief interruption during Reconstruction.

Another critical research area is to examine how the internal tensions among members of the black professional class became part of a wider class conflict between an increasingly upwardly mobile African American petit bourgeoisie and working-class African Americans. The parallel social structures and the segregated spaces of African American life, as limited and unequal as they were under America's Jim Crow regime, were the means by which most African Americans, especially workers, married and sustained families, educated their children, buried their dead, made sense of their material lives vis-à-vis their spiritual strivings, and formed their hopes and brought their dreams to fruition. Many African Americans were not interested in symbolic victories or token gains that might benefit a small black professional class while leaving the majority to endure inequality, structural racism, residential segregation, low wages, and restrictions on their working roles and private lives. Moreover, many were less interested in racial assimilation than in tangible improvements in their economic opportunities and a broadening of the life chances and choices available to them. In other words, the black community was never monolithic. African Americans were and remain a complex and diverse ethnic group. In 1960, when the student movement exploded in Marshall, Texas, with antidiscrimination demonstrations and then a nonviolent sit-in action at F. W. Woolworth's segregated lunch counter and later at the Union Bus Terminal Café, the black community did not respond with uniform support for the brave Wiley and Bishop College students and professors who were involved. The firing of Bishop College professor Doxey Wilkerson, one casualty of the student insurgency, likewise revealed fissures in the community. Bedford occupied an interesting position amid the various tensions and differences in black Dallas. He was not a typical representative of the black professional class, but one of its more visionary leaders. He embraced the impatient militancy of the young activists of the 1960s like Ernest McMillan of SNCC, even while sharing memberships and history with older members of the NAACP, the Negro Chamber of Commerce, and the Interdenominational Ministerial Alliance. When the Dallas Legal Services Project moved from addressing basic legal needs of the city's poor to class-action lawsuits that fomented what to some seemed like a class war against established wealth and power, Bedford did not see an either-or situation but supported both kinds of legal approaches.

Albert Lipscomb accurately expressed the kind of leader Bedford represented: he was a visionary. Not all African American professionals have as well thought out a vision of society as Bedford did. It takes a special kind of person to see the future in the past and to use that vision to guide action in the present. The lawyer Abraham Lincoln was that kind of leader. The lawyer Barack Obama has emerged as that kind of leader. The lawyer Louis Bedford Jr. was such a leader, too. In history such leaders are often referred to as transformational figures. They help enable society to go through times of monumental change without turning completely upside down or falling apart. In African American history there is still a great deal of work to do to properly record and interpret such transformational figures in U.S. society. This telling of the story of Louis Bedford Jr. constitutes a great contribution toward this end.

---

1. Darlene Clark Hine, "Black Professionals and Race Consciousness: Origins of the Civil Rights Movement, 1890-1950," *Journal of American History* 89, no. 4 (2003): 1279. The black professional managerial class as a force in history and contemporary society has interested me since my undergraduate studies as a student of William "Sandy" Darity. See his "The Class Character of the Black Community: Polarization between the Black Managerial Elite and the Black Underclass," in *Black Law Review* 7 (1980): 21–31; "The Managerial Class and Surplus Population," *Society* 22 (November–December 1983): 54–62; and "Underclass and Overclass: Race, Class, and Economic Inequality in the Managerial Age," in *Essays on Economic Discrimination*, ed. Emily P. Hoffman (Kalamazoo: W. E. Upjohn Institute for Employment Research, 1991), 67–84. Some other writings that piqued my curiosity for their analytic framework include Barbara Ehrenreich and John Ehrenreich, "The Professional-Managerial Class," in *Between Labor and Capital: The Professional Managerial Class*, ed. Pat Walker (Boston: South End Press, 1979); Nicos Poulantzas, *Classes in Contemporary Capitalism* (London: Verso, 1978); and Erik Olin Wright, *Class, Crisis, and the State* (London: Verso, 1979).

2. Quotation from Hine, "Black Professionals and Race Consciousness," 1294. Alabama-born Dr. Richard T. Hamilton of Dallas, Texas, is an example of a member of the black professional class who tried to work within the system of segregation to enlarge African American access to higher educational opportunities as well as other tangible, material improvements for African Americans. In my book *Advancing Democracy: African Americans and the Struggle for Access and Equity in Higher Education in Texas* (Chapel Hill: University of North Carolina Press, 2004), 25–28, he gets some historical treatment, but more work can and should be done on him.
3. Sarah Hart Brown, *Standing Against Dragons: Three Southern Lawyers in an Era of Fear* (Baton Rouge: Louisiana State University Press, 1998), 263, 268.

Amilcar Shabazz is chair of the Department of Afro-American Studies at the University of Massachusetts, Amherst. He is the author of *Advancing Democracy: African Americans and the Struggle for Access and Equity in Higher Education in Texas.*

SELECTED BIBLIOGRAPHY

Archival Sources

Louis A. Bedford Jr. Papers, in his possession, Dallas.

Juanita Craft Collection, Texas/Dallas History and Archives Division, Dallas Public Library.

Dallas Negro Chamber of Commerce Papers, Texas/Dallas History & Archives Division, Dallas Public Library.

Books and Articles

Alexander, Charles C. *The Ku Klux Klan in the Southwest.* Lexington: University of Kentucky Press, 1965.

Bedford, L. A., Jr. *L. A. Bedford Jr.: Oral History Interview.* Austin: Texas Bar Foundation, 2002.

———. "M. M. Rodgers: A Study of a Negro in the Age of Transition." Paper submitted for bachelor of arts degree, Prairie View University, Division of Arts and Science, 1946. Louis A. Bedford Jr. Papers.

———. "When I Become an Old Lawyer and Can No Longer Stand before the Bar." *Dallas Bar Association Headnotes*, November 19, 1990.

Behnken, Brian D. "The 'Dallas Way': Protest, Response, and the Civil Rights Experience in Dallas and Beyond." *Southwestern Historical Quarterly* 111, no. 1 (July 2007).

Branch, Taylor. *At Canaan's Edge: America in the King Years, 1965–68.* New York: Simon and Schuster, 2006.

Brown, Charles S. "The Genesis of the Negro Lawyer in New England," pt. 1. *Negro History Bulletin* 22, no. 7 (April 1959): 147–52.

Campbell, Randolph B. *An Empire for Slavery: The Peculiar Institution in Texas, 1821–1865.* Baton Rouge: Louisiana State University Press, 1989.

Cheek, William, and Aimee Lee Cheek. *John Mercer Langston and the Fight for Black Freedom, 1829–1865.* Urbana: University of Illinois Press, 1989.

Contee, Clarence G. "Macon B. Allen: 'First' Black in the Legal Profession," *Crisis* 83, no. 2 (February 1976): 67–69.

Dobbs, Ricky F. *Yellow Dogs and Republicans: Allan Shivers and Texas Two-Party Politics.* College Station: Texas A&M University Press, 2005.

Dulaney, W. Marvin. *Black Police in America.* Bloomington: Indiana University Press, 1996.

———. "Whatever Happened to the Civil Rights Movement in Dallas, Texas?" In *Essays on the American Civil Rights Movement*, edited by John Dittmer, George C. Wright, and W. Marvin Dulaney. College Station: Texas A&M University Press, 1993.

Friedman, Lawrence M. *A History of American Law.* New York: Simon and Schuster, 1973.

Gillette, Michael L. "The NAACP in Texas, 1937–1957." PhD diss., University of Texas at Austin, 1984.

Goodwin, Doris Kearns. *No Ordinary Time: Franklin and Eleanor Roosevelt: The Home Front in World War II.* New York: Simon and Schuster, 1994.

Hales, Douglas. *A Southern Family in Black and White: The Cuneys of Texas.* College Station: Texas A&M University Press, 2003.

Hauer, John L. ("Jack"). *Finest Kind! A Memorable Half Century of Dallas Lawyers (plus a few from out-of-town).* Dallas: Dallas Bar Foundation, 1992.

Hine, Darlene Clark. *Black Victory: The Rise and Fall of the White Primary in Texas.* Columbia: University of Missouri Press, 2003.

Jackson, Kenneth T. *The Ku Klux Klan in the City, 1915–1930.* New York: Oxford University Press, 1967.

Johnson, Lyndon Baines. *The Vantage Point: Perspectives of the Presidency, 1963–1969.* New York: Holt, Rinehart and Winston, 1971.

Kearns (Goodwin), Doris. *Lyndon Johnson and the American Dream.* New York: Harper & Row, 1976.

Ladino, Robyn Duff. *Desegregating Texas Schools: Eisenhower, Shivers, and the Crisis at Mansfield High.* Austin: University of Texas Press, 1996.

Langston, John Mercer. *From the Virginia Plantation to the National Capitol, or The First and Only Negro Representative in Congress from the Old Dominion.* Hartford: American Publishing, 1894.

Linden, Glenn M. *Desegregating Schools in Dallas: Four Decades in the Federal Courts.* Dallas: Three Forks Press, 1995.

Malcolm X. *The Autobiography of Malcolm X.* As told to Alex Haley. New York: Grove Press, 1968.

McDonald, Bobby. *Out of Darkness: The Black Face of Hopkins County.* Vol. 3. N.p.: Bobby McDonald, c. 2002.

Meier, August. *Negro Thought in America, 1880–1915.* Ann Arbor: University of Michigan Press, 1968.

Payne, Darwin. *As Old as Dallas Itself: A History of the Lawyers of Dallas, the Dallas Bar Associations, and the City They Helped Build.* Dallas: Three Forks Press, 1999.

———. *Big D: Triumphs and Troubles of an American Supercity in the 20th Century.* Dallas: Three Forks Press, 2000.

———. *Indomitable Sarah: The Life of Judge Sarah T. Hughes.* Dallas: Southern Methodist University Press, 2004.

Payton, Donald. "A Concise History: Black Dallas since 1842," *D Heritage*, June 1998.

Phillips, Michael. *White Metropolis: Race, Ethnicity, and Religion in Dallas, 1841–2001.* Austin: University of Texas Press, 2006.

Pitre, Merline. *In Struggle against Jim Crow: Lulu B. White and the NAACP, 1900–1957.* College Station: Texas A&M University Press, 1999.

Prince, Robert. *A History of Dallas from a Different Perspective.* Dallas: Nortex Press, 1993.

Rowan, Carl T. *Dream Makers, Dream Breakers: The World of Justice Thurgood Marshall.* Boston: Little, Brown, 1993.

Schutze, Jim. *The Accommodation: The Politics of Race in an American City.* Secaucus, NJ: Citadel Press, 1986.

Segal, Geraldine R. *Blacks in the Law: Philadelphia and the Nation.* Philadelphia: University of Pennsylvania Press, 1983.

Shabazz, Amilcar. *Advancing Democracy: African Americans and the Struggle for Access and Equity in Higher Education in Texas.* Chapel Hill: University of North Carolina Press, 2004.

Smith, J. Clay, Jr. *Emancipation: The Making of the Black Lawyer, 1844–1944.* Philadelphia: University of Pennsylvania Press, 1993.

Tushnet, Mark V. *The NAACP's Legal Strategy against Segregated Education, 1925–1950.* Chapel Hill: University of North Carolina Press, 1987.

Williams, Juan. *Thurgood Marshall: American Revolutionary.* New York: Times Books, 1998.

Wilson, William H. *Hamilton Park: A Planned Black Community in Dallas.* Baltimore: Johns Hopkins University Press, 1998.

Woolfolk, George Ruble. *Prairie View: A Study in Public Conscience, 1878–1946.* New York: Pageant Press, 1962.

———. "W. R. Banks: Public College Educator." In *Black Leaders: Texans for Their Times,* edited by Alwyn Barr and Robert A. Calvert. Austin: Texas State Historical Association, 1981.

Newspapers

Bishop Herald
Dallas Bar Association Headnotes
Dallas Bar Association Weekly Bulletin
Dallas Times Herald (*Daily Times Herald* prior to Sept. 13, 1954)
Dallas Morning News
Dallas Express
Dallas Examiner
Dallas Post Tribune
Dallas Star-Post
Dallas Weekly Herald

DVD

J. L. Turner Legal Association: Over Fifty Years of Service in Dallas, DVD. Dallas: J. L. Turner Legal Association, 2005.

Court Cases

Bell v. Rippy. 133 F. Supp. 811 (N.D. Texas, 1955).
Bell v. Rippy. 146 F. Supp. 485 (N.D. Texas, 1956).
S. J. Briscoe v. State of Texas and *Yvonne Tucker v. State of Texas.* No. 32347 and No. 32612 [respectively], Court of Criminal Appeals of Texas, Dec. 14, 1960.
Browder v. Gayle. 142 F. Supp. 707 (1956).
Brown v. Board of Education. 347 U.S. 483 (1954).
Hill v. State of Texas. 316 U.S. 400 (1942).

Jackson v. Rawdon. U.S. District Court, Texas, Civ. No. 3152, November 21, 1955, 135 F. Supp. 936; U.S. Court of Appeals, Fifth Circuit, June 28, 1956, Civ. No. 15927.

Nixon v. Herndon. 273 U.S. 538 (1927).

Smith v. Allwright. 321 U.S. 649 (1944).

State of Texas v. the National Association for the Advancement of Colored People, a Corporation, et al. 56 U.S. District Court 649 (1957) No. 56-649.

Sweatt v. Painter, et al. 339 U.S. 629 (1950).

Tasby v. Estes. 517 F. 2d 92 (5th Cir. 1975).

Taylor v. Sterrett. 344 F. Supp. 411 (1972), 499 F. 2d 367 (1974), 532 F. 2d 462 (5th Cir. 1976), and 600 F. 2d 1135 (5th Cir. 1979).

INDEX

D A R W I N   P A Y N E is professor emeritus of communications at Southern Methodist University. He's the author of biographies of U.S. District Judge Sarah T. Hughes (*Indomitable Sarah*, SMU, 2004), and the writers Owen Wister and Frederick Lewis Allen. He's written extensively on Dallas history, including *Big D: Triumphs and Troubles of an American Supercity.*

Hannah K. Payne

Dedication

I dedicate this book to my children, husband, parents, grandparents, and others who have taught me caregiving lessons.

Contents

Introduction

As I wrote this book, I couldn't help but think about you, the many caregivers I've met along my journey. I've heard your stories. I've heard your hurt and frustration. Some of your stories resonate with me, because some of your stories are also my experiences. Some of you are feeling guilty for what you have or have not done for the loved one you are caring for. Some of you have a longing just to do what you want to do. Some of you want to give up. Some of you are in the middle of the caregiving journey. Some of you have just ended a caregiving experience.

So, what do I have to offer you in this book? I know there are many books about caregiving in the bookstores and libraries. Caregiving has an emotional impact that changes us, breaks us, molds us, and sometimes even makes us better. As caregivers, we want and need to tell our stories. It is a therapeutic process.

In this book, I offer you the wisdom that has grown out of my experience. And my experiences are woven together with scripture to offer you a message of hope and show you that you have enough and are enough for this caregiving journey.

Use what you have. When I think about using what you have, I am reminded of the scripture about the widow who had only a little oil. She went to the prophet Elisha, because her husband had been a servant of the Lord.

Elisha knew her husband and knew that her husband had died. The woman owed a debt that she couldn't pay. Her sons were in danger of being taken away as slaves in order to settle her debt. Elisha told her to get some empty jars from her neighbors. He told the widow not to ask for just a few. Afterward, she was to go inside her house with her sons and close the door. The sons handed her the jars and she poured the oil she had into the available jars. They used all the jars and she still had some oil left over. The oil had continued flowing until they ran out of jars.

2 Kings 4:7 reads, "She went and told the man of God, and he said, 'Go, sell the oil and pay your debts. You and your sons can live on what is left.'"

Things are never quite as they seem to be when God is involved. Whatever we have, God can multiply it. Whatever we have, God can change it to make it work for us. Whatever we have, God can do far more with it than we can ask or imagine.

Perhaps these words are just what you need. Perhaps these words will even inspire you to share your unique story. Or perhaps these words are just what you would like to share with someone you know who is a caregiver.

All experiences have a purpose and place, even if we don't understand what the experience, situation, or circumstance means at the time. I can see in hindsight how my life experiences helped me navigate my journey. God's timing is perfect. I pray that even more insight will be revealed to you and to me as we continue the journey.

I needed to write this book. I needed to tell my story for me. It is a bonus if it is helpful to someone along the way. I pray that you will find some comfort, humor, and insight to support you on your own caregiving journey.

CHAPTER 1
Karen's Story

I was born in Washington, DC, to Paul L. Walker and the late Irene M. Pattillo Walker. I was raised in a home with both parents and am the oldest of two children. From my perspective, my brother, Paul K. Walker, and I were raised as though each of us was an only child. We called my brother Kevin. I would describe our family as middle class and we lived in a house in the town of Glenarden, which is located in Maryland. My parents were great providers. However, I felt that we had very little emotional support. I thought this was probably due to the way both of my parents were raised.

I was expected to be responsible at a very young age. My godmother told me that I was born old, which I thought was an odd thing to say until I reflected on my life. Not only was I the oldest child, but both of my parents were the youngest children in their families.

Think about that for a moment. I lived with three family members who were used to being taken care of and accommodated. I can't really describe what that was like. Two of my cousins told me that I was always held responsible for Kevin. They remember me being told that it was my job to watch him. I do remember being responsible for getting him to his activities and picking up and dropping off his friends and him after I got a driver's license. I think my caregiving duties started before I realized what I was doing.

As I grew into adulthood, my parents asked me to take the lead on vacations and making travel arrangements for funerals or other family occasions. Even after I was married with a family, my parents depended on me to facilitate things in their lives. I never thought about it much until after my mother passed. With her death, I was officially a matriarch, which put a whole new level of responsibility and pressure on me. At this point, it was clear that if I didn't take action, holiday meals and other family traditions would never happen again. I now feel responsible for making life (activities and events) happen not only for my husband and children, but also for my father. Both my father and Kevin have depended on me to keep them connected to our extended family.

REFLECTION: How would you describe your childhood in a snapshot? Reflect, and then write your thoughts in a journal or on a "My Reflections" page in this book.

PRAYER: Gracious God, you have created me for your purpose. Show me how the plans for my life work together to achieve your perfect will. Give me the patience to be comfortable with not knowing everything I want to know about this caregiving journey. In the name of Jesus, amen.

CHAPTER 2
The Calling

Most Christians are familiar with the word *calling*. I believe that sometimes we are called to do things for a lifetime and sometimes we are called to do things for a season. Or maybe the things we do in a season support the overall calling. I have provided caregiving support for my husband, mother, and father with aging and health issues. Over the years, I have also supported others placed in my path. I've supported people in the hospital. I've had the opportunity to support friends of friends. I've supported people in support groups. I've supported other patients in a dialysis center. I've prayed for others. I've provided resources to others. And I've encouraged others who found themselves as caregivers and those who have found themselves with health issues.

John 15:16 reads, "You did not choose me, but I chose you and appointed you to go and bear fruit—fruit that will last. Then the Father will give you whatever you ask in my name."

I can attest to the fact that I have seen fruit. As I reflect on the scripture from John, I can see how I have served as a caregiver and encourager. I have also seen the fruit. Even when I served as a Local Pastor, I believe that one of my strengths was my way of being while visiting the sick and shut in. (In the United Methodist Church, my denomination, the term *Local Pastor* refers to someone who answers God's call to serve the mission of Jesus Christ, usually by serving a local UMC congregation. Although Local Pastors aren't ordained, they are licensed to perform the usual duties of a pastor within that setting.) There is nothing as humbling as people allowing you to minister to them during their most vulnerable times. Yes, that was a caregiving experience in itself.

I think when the opportunity presented itself to serve as a caregiver, I sensed and naturally gravitated to what needed to be done. Of course, I believe that this was through the power of the Holy Spirit.

Most of us know other eligible folks who could have taken on the caregiving needs of our loved one. However, you are the only one who has made yourself available for the task. It doesn't mean that everything is nice and easy, but God has given you what you need to free yourself up to do what is needed for this time. Before becoming a caregiver, I had a very successful career. Over the years, I have served in the private, public, and nonprofit sectors. In the private and public sectors, I spent most of my career working in the area of procurement and human capital management for organizations ranging from a university to businesses to an aerospace agency. As I mentioned earlier, my experience in the nonprofit world consists of approximately five years as a Local Pastor in the United Methodist Church.

Do I believe that non-Christians can have a calling? Absolutely, but it is still in the context of God calling the person. I believe in the prevenient grace (attributed to

John Wesley) that existed before we even knew that God was in our lives.

In the book of Acts, Saul, who persecuted the Christians and was converted while on the road to Damascus, and whose name thereafter was Paul, had a calling on his life to preach the Gospel to the Gentiles. In my journey, I did not hear a voice directing me to be a caregiver, but I did feel that the Holy Spirit moved me in that direction. I certainly believe that it is a huge part of who I am and how I am called to serve other people.

REFLECTION: What is your sense of calling? How has your sense of calling connected to your role as a caregiver? Reflect, and then write your thoughts in a journal or on a "My Reflections" page in this book.

PRAYER: Gracious God, I thank you for choosing me for the important work of caregiving. Continue to give me insight into how I was already being prepared for the task. May my efforts be pleasing and demonstrate the fruits of the spirit (love, joy, peace, patience, kindness, goodness, faithfulness, gentleness, and self-control) in all that I say and do. In the name of Jesus, amen.

My Reflections

_____

_____

_____

_____

_____

_____

_____

_____

_____

_____

_____

_____

_____

_____

_____

_____

_____

_____

_____

_____

_____

CHAPTER 3
Kendrick's Story

Kendrick O. Weaver, my husband, was born in High Point, North Carolina. He is the oldest of six children. He moved from North Carolina to Maryland when he was about 12 years old, and entered the seventh grade. I met him at Thomas Pullen Junior High School in Landover, Maryland, in the eighth grade. He was very active in sports and was a gifted athlete. He has always had a lot of friends. Neighborhood kids and classmates somehow found their way to his home. His house was always filled with people. It was common for his friends to be fed at his house. There were even times when others spent the night there.

While Kendrick was in college, his father passed at 38 as the result of a heart attack. This experience changed Kendrick's life forever. His father died over the Thanksgiving holiday in 1976. I remember it, because I was in Pennsylvania with my family. We were visiting my grandparents, which was a common tradition for my family. Kendrick was supposed to drive up to be with me and my family, but his father passed on his travel day.

His father had been home recovering from a health event. Kendrick remembers that before he passed, his father asked for his Bible and that the bedroom door be closed.

Death is always a major life event, especially when it

is unexpected. It was particularly difficult for Kendrick and his family because his father was the primary bread-winner. Kendrick's mother had been working as a home-maker and doing some babysitting for a few neighbors. It was a major adjustment for the family to lose the only parent who was working outside the home. It was also amazing how well his mother was able to do many things that she had never done in the past. She went into the workforce and started to take over administrative activities that she hadn't had to worry about in the past. As the oldest child, Kendrick felt the weight of the loss of his father in addition to his own grieving. I soon felt the weight as well, since we were married a few months later, in spring 1977.

REFLECTION: How has your relationship with your loved one impacted your feelings as a caregiver? In what ways has your relationship made your role easier or more difficult? Reflect, and then write your thoughts in a journal or on a "My Reflections" page in this book.

PRAYER: Father God, I thank you for your perfect timing even though it is difficult to understand at times. Continue to focus me on your will for my life at the moment. Let me not be distracted by what has happened in the past, what is happening in the present, or what may come in the future. In the name of Jesus, amen.

CHAPTER 4
The Setup

Every caregiver can remember the beginning of his or her journey. My caregiver story started in 1995. It was at the end of February. Kendrick, my husband, hadn't been in bed long when around 2:00 a.m., I heard a thump and realized he was on the floor. When I first looked down on him from the bed, I thought that he was playing. He often played tricks. But then I quickly understood that something was wrong. I called 911.

Kendrick couldn't speak or get up. The paramedics came and asked me questions about his use of drugs and alcohol. It was so sad that those were their first thoughts. My husband had just gotten off work. He was an assistant manager at a Safeway store in Washington, DC. He had a stressful job and was probably planning to go back to work early the next day, after getting a little rest.

I couldn't help but think that our being African American wasn't helping us in this situation. I wish the medics had thought about the impact of hypertension on the African American community instead of spending so much time on questions about drugs and alcohol. Kendrick was never one to engage in destructive behaviors. Yes, we had an occasional social drink, but we were focused on raising a family and working.

Finally, Kendrick was taken to the hospital by ambulance.

I called his mom and my parents. I woke up Kendrick D., and Jason, our two sons, and we went to the hospital. It was still in the early hours of the morning. Strange that I can remember that night so clearly.

Kendrick was 39 years old, or maybe I should say 39 years young. He would never drive or work again. Well, that's not totally true. He spent the first few years after his stroke driving the car around the neighborhood. He even ventured out of the neighborhood at one point and went to his mother's house. But I'm getting ahead of myself. That's another story.

In the hospital, we were told that Kendrick had about twenty minutes to live. A blood vessel had broken in the middle of his head, and there was no way to stop the bleeding. They would have needed to drill a hole into his head to relieve the pressure of the blood that was flowing. The doctors thought about flying him to Baltimore to another hospital. It was thought that a bigger hospital could better accommodate the complexity of the stroke. In the end, the doctors decided not to send him, because they didn't think Kendrick would survive the journey.

As a result, I was told to inform the family and to call everyone who needed to know that Kendrick's brain would probably shut down in about twenty minutes. I made those calls, and those people called other people. We got Kendrick's other son, Corey, to the hospital. That's another story that you will read more about later. I still have that image of Corey sitting beside his father with one of the mothers of Ebenezer United Methodist

Church. Her name was Sister Agnes. She was reassuring Corey that everything was going to be all right. Sister Agnes has since that time gone to be with the Lord. I should have been reassured that everything was going to be all right just by her words. I always felt that she had a special connection with the Lord.

Within the next twenty-four hours, we had close to a hundred people come to the hospital, praying and supporting my family and me. I sensed that the staff was wondering, *Who is this guy?* Yes, Kendrick is an amazingly friendly and charming man, but it was God's work that night.

Then it happened. The bleeding stopped, and I was told that my husband was being moved to a critical care unit. The doctor in charge sounded almost disappointed, because he had been so sure that Kendrick was going to die that night. He obviously didn't understand the power of prayer. My husband is not famous, but we have the right connections. We were told that Kendrick would go to critical care and we would have to wait and see what happened.

The bleeding stopped. And we did see God at work. Kendrick survived the night and started his stay in intensive care. Now, I realize that not everyone reading this book may be a Christian, but that is my frame of reference. I think my faith played a key role in my surviving Kendrick's health episode. I prayed very short "Help me, Jesus" prayers. I watched family and friends pray for us. Then there was our church family. Some came to the hospital and prayed. Some stayed at home and prayed. A phone tree was created. Each one called another one to pray. It was powerful.

Of course, while all of this was happening, I had no idea that I was being set up and prepared for my future caregiving roles, which would go beyond the care of my husband.

> **Exodus 3:10–12 reads, "'So now, go. I am sending you to Pharaoh to bring my people the Israelites out of Egypt.' But Moses said to God, 'Who am I, that I should go to Pharaoh and bring the Israelites out of Egypt?' And God said, 'I will be with you. And this will be the sign to you that it is I who have sent you: When you have brought the people out of Egypt, you will worship God on this mountain.'"**

The setup is that moment when we are face-to-face with the opportunity for which God has been preparing us. Moses was prepared for his leadership role from the time he was a baby. He was nurtured by Pharaoh's daughter, and he learned the customs and traditions of the Egyptian people. Moses was prepared for his leadership in the wilderness when he fled to the wilderness and served under Jethro, who was his father-in-law. There Moses was taught how to live in the wilderness, even though he didn't know those lessons would support him later in his life.

The setup is placed in front of us. We are in the lineup to serve. You may not feel it's fair. Maybe you don't feel equipped or qualified, but the task is definitely assigned to you. Yes, you may have five other siblings, but the task to take care of your momma or daddy is your task. You may have a full-time job, but the task still belongs to you. You may have dreams that you want to fulfill, but the assignment still belongs to you.

I am often reminded by God that some things are not options. I see the road ahead. I may not want to go down that road, but God has spoken and told me that I will go down that road. And yes, you will be required to sacrifice your time, your money, and your energy. I'm sure some of you can think of other things that you've sacrificed as well.

REFLECTION: What happened to make you realize that you would be taking on a caregiving role? What did you have to sacrifice? Reflect, and then write your thoughts in a journal or on a "My Reflections" page in this book.

PRAYER: Awesome God, I know you are the master planner of my life. Thank you for using me. I put my trust in you and know that by your grace I will be able to complete my task. Continue to guide me on this journey of faith. In the name of Jesus, amen.

My Reflections

_____

_____

_____

_____

_____

_____

_____

_____

_____

_____

_____

_____

_____

_____

_____

_____

_____

_____

_____

_____

_____

CHAPTER 5
Kendrick and Karen Meet

Kendrick and I met in junior high school. When Kendrick came to Maryland, he started school in the seventh grade. We met in the eighth grade. He was very polite, which made him stand out from other boys his age. I could tell that he wasn't from the Washington, DC, area. He had a different way of talking, and he had a different way of being. I think of junior-high-age children as being at that age where you really don't know what you don't know. Plus, you are not trying to find out what you don't know. It is also the time of adolescence, which adds a whole other dynamic to the school experience.

I remember Kendrick being in my math and Spanish classes. In our Spanish class, he was Carlos and I was Carlota. I also remember him making me a plaque in his shop class. The plaque had the initials *KW* on it. We both had the initials *KW*, since my maiden name was Walker and his last name is Weaver. I made him a stuffed monkey out of socks. I still tease him about the fact that he doesn't have the monkey. Where did it go? Truth be told, he let his niece play with it and that's the end of that mystery.

Kendrick and I went to different high schools, but still remained friends. Our relationship was rekindled when we were in college. He played football for McDaniel College in Westminster, Maryland. It was called Western Maryland College at the time. His football team was playing my college football team. At the time, I was attending Georgetown University in Washington, DC. And somehow things just started back again, just like we had never been separated.

One of my friends, Rev. Rose (who is a minister), refers to Kendrick as my Boaz. In the book of Ruth, Boaz served as the redeemer for Ruth. Boaz was Ruth's protector and saved her from a life of insecurity. They married and later had a child who would be in the generational lineage of Jesus, the Son of God.

Kendrick has always been my protector. Even with his own health issues, he has continued to do whatever he can for me. Sometimes it is to his own detriment. It may cause him to lift things he shouldn't lift or even climb ladders he shouldn't climb.

I'm sure you are wondering why I am telling you all of this. I want you to have an appreciation for the fact that Kendrick is not just my husband; we have been friends for a very long time. He knows the good, the bad, and the ugly. This friendship has played a key role in our lives and in the caregiving journey. We were married, divorced, and remarried. Remember when I talked about getting his other son to the hospital? Corey was only eight when Kendrick had his stroke. When he suffered a stroke, my care and concern went beyond him being my spouse. Kendrick and I have been longtime friends. I take my role in his life very seriously.

Kendrick has always been a very extroverted person. He

loves people and loves to help them. He wants to tell his story, and he wants to know other people's stories.

Kendrick and I married young by today's standards. He was twenty-one and I was twenty-two when we married. I had just graduated from college in December 1976. We married in 1977. We had our first child, Kendrick D., in 1978. Four years later, we had our second child, Jason. We separated and were divorced for about three years. We had been remarried for eight years when Kendrick suffered the massive stroke I described earlier.

REFLECTION: What do you know about your loved one's story that has helped you be a better caregiver? Reflect, and then write your thoughts in a journal or on a "My Reflections" page in this book.

PRAYER: God, thank you for my faith journey. And thank you for allowing me to be a believer in God the Father, Son, and Holy Spirit. Lord, continue to sustain me. Holy Spirit, continue to guide me. Focus me on the gift of the overall journey. In the name of Jesus, amen.

My Reflections

_____

_____

_____

_____

_____

_____

_____

_____

_____

_____

_____

_____

_____

_____

_____

_____

_____

_____

_____

_____

_____

CHAPTER 6
The Healing Journey Continues

W hen it was time for Kendrick to go to a rehabilitation center, I was very picky. Trust me,
this was no easy task. It was an experience
just trying to find a rehabilitation center where Kendrick
wouldn't feel isolated because of his age. Many of the rehabilitation centers were filled with elderly people. I wanted
Kendrick to be in a place where he could see and interact
with younger people. He was only 39 at the time. I was
fortunate to have a family friend, John, who helped me
in my search. John and his wife, Robin, were a tremendous support to my family. Their son, Adrian, was one of
Jason's best friends. John and Robin provided hands-on
support for Kendrick, me, Kendrick D., and Jason.

I remember visiting rehabilitation centers in Laurel, the
District of Columbia, Largo, and Forestville. I ended up
requesting that Kendrick be sent to Mount Vernon in
Virginia. And all of this was done in a very short amount
of time. As some of you know, once a person is ready to
go to a rehabilitation center, the hospital doesn't give the
family much time to decide where you want your loved
one to go. (This process would prove to be helpful in my
next caregiving experience.)

Mount Vernon Rehabilitation Center was definitely the

right place. Kendrick's roommate was a teenager who had fallen off a bike, which resulted in a head injury. In addition to the fact that it had younger people on-site, I liked the location of the center. It was far enough from Prince George's County (our neighborhood) to give us some space from the curiosity seekers. I felt that Kendrick needed the space. I knew *I* needed the space.

Isaiah 53:5 reads, "But he was pierced for our transgressions, he was crushed for our iniquities; the punishment that brought us peace was upon him, and by his wounds we are healed."

Kendrick was learning how to speak, walk, and process information. He was literally starting over, learning some very basic skills. A therapist explained to me that having a stroke was like all the books falling on the floor from your library shelves (which would be your brain). The difficulty is getting the books not only back on the shelves, but in the proper order. Kendrick was taking speech therapy, occupational therapy, and physical therapy. He had good and bad days. There were times when he could barely get his wheelchair back to his room. I am sure it was exhausting for him, because it was exhausting for me to watch him.

The doctors and nurses were trying to get him to do everything by himself, so that he could move toward being as independent as possible. Then he had to adjust to being helped with everything, even the very basic skills of life that we often take for granted. Progress seemed slow, but it was still progress. Within a month, the insurance company decided that Kendrick was ready for outpatient therapy. The fun continued.

REFLECTION: What have you observed or learned from the healing journey? What healing has taken place inside of you? What healing are you still in need of? Reflect, and then write your thoughts in a journal or on a "My Reflections" page in this book.

PRAYER: Holy God, thank you for the gift of healing. I acknowledge that I am also being healed in the process of watching my loved one be healed. I understand that healing comes in many forms. And sometimes I know that healing comes through our transition from life to eternal life. Whatever is your will, help me to walk faithfully with you. In the name of Jesus, amen.

My Reflections

_____

_____

_____

_____

_____

_____

_____

_____

_____

_____

_____

_____

_____

_____

_____

_____

_____

_____

_____

_____

CHAPTER 7
The Wilderness Experience

Then Kendrick came home. I can't describe the fear that came over me when Kendrick came home from the rehabilitation center. I know the scripture tells us that God did not give us a spirit of fear. Second Timothy 1:7 reads, "For God did not give us a spirit of timidity, but a spirit of power, of love and of self-discipline." Well, I can at least say I was very concerned.

Kendrick was thrilled. He was still in a wheelchair, and I wasn't sure how we were going to manage. Now that I think back, I really don't remember how we managed. My dad installed bars in the bathrooms on the top level and the main level. Ronald, Kendrick's brother, made a ramp for the wheelchair. Kendrick D. and Jason, my children, were probably in shock, because I had been a try-to-do-everything kind of mom. I had learned from my mom, so I didn't know there were other ways of doing things. I couldn't keep up with my normal activities. I'm sure this was about the time that Kendrick D. and Jason learned how to do laundry. I think they just got tired of waiting for me to wash their clothes.

I was really busy. On most days, I was exhausted and couldn't wait to get in the bed.

So, the new routine started. I was taking Kendrick to speech therapy. I was still working. At the time, I was a procurement analyst in the public sector for an aerospace agency. I was primarily responsible for reviewing and updating procurement policy. I can't remember how, but my supervisors during those early years (especially) were very accommodating. This was way before the days of telework. I had to go to the office in order to get paid. Work life was not as flexible as it is today, but my supervisors did everything possible to support me.

My dad was taking Kendrick to physical therapy. Our schedule was busy. I can't remember how we managed. My parents and others were helping us along the way. When Kendrick came home from the hospital, it took two to three years to get used to a new normal. Of course, as Kendrick got better, there were new challenges. He was driving the car while I was at work. We would argue, because I would take the keys to work to keep him from driving. He didn't want to be treated like a kid. What was I to do? He had no peripheral vision on either side and was paralyzed on his right side, which is the side for your driving foot. Plus, he now had no driver's license or insurance.

All of this had the word *unsafe* attached. He will say that that is not true, but just quietly move up beside him and stand next to him. That's all I will say.

> **Exodus 13:21 reads, "By day the Lord went ahead of them in a pillar of cloud to guide them on their way and by night in a pillar of fire to give them light, so that they could travel by day or night."**

This was a wilderness experience for both Kendrick and me. I can't imagine what my sons were experiencing. I would like to think we were all following God's lead. In hindsight, I remember open doors and closed doors. We were given support from places we were not familiar with. Places we had once been invited to go were no longer an option. When people see a situation such as ours, they make a lot of assumptions about where and what you will be invited to do. Some people were sent to be in our path, and some stopped associating with us. I believe we were following God's lead, but we didn't know it was God's lead. Neither of us had ever experienced anything like what we were experiencing. We didn't know what to expect.

One vivid memory I have is the impact on our finances. I just could not make ends meet with our reduced income. I told Kendrick that we needed to give more money to the church. He was still not totally well, but he was well enough to ask me if I was crazy. I told him, "I've tried everything else. Let's trust the scripture and see what happens." Malachi 3:10 reads, "'Bring the whole tithe into the storehouse, that there may be food in my house. Test me in this,' says the Lord Almighty, 'and see if I will not throw open the floodgates of heaven and pour out so much blessing that you will not have room enough for it.'" I did it. And we were blessed beyond what either of us could ever have imagined. People we knew and people we didn't know very well gave us financial gifts. There was a major fundraiser, which I talk about in the next chapter, that blessed us spiritually, emotionally, and financially. Some people from our church also brought us meals. It was an amazing time of watching the movement of God. Now, you have to know that this was not my Local Pastor faith. This was before it was revealed to me what God was going to do in my life regarding ministry.

When I think of the wilderness, I think about the unknown and being without the basic necessities of life. Or maybe the necessities of life are there, but we don't know where. It is usually a place where we are not comfortable and where we encounter a lot of unknowns and uncertainty.

Then there was the adjustment for Kendrick's former coworkers. At first, they wanted to visit him and ask him questions about what they should do at work. They were actually trying to get him to solve their work problems. He had always been the "go-to" person. His employees adored him. Eventually, people realized that Kendrick was not the same. He had some processing issues. He certainly was not able to navigate his former work life. The reality of "who are Kendrick's real friends" came into play.

Fortunately, Kendrick does have a few faithful friends. Some are more faithful than others, but he does have real friends. And to this day, I know I can call at least one or two and they will respond. It is hard, though, when you experience a health event such as a stroke. People will stick with you for a while, but eventually everyone goes back to their routine called life.

When Kendrick came home from the rehabilitation center, neither one of us really understood that things were never going to be the same. The old way of life was gone forever. The longer we kept trying to make things exactly like they had been, the harder it was for us to determine what a new normal looked like. It has been my experience (in hindsight) that once you have a wilderness experience, things will never be the same. *You* will never be the same.

REFLECTION: What does your own wilderness experience as a caregiver look like? How has God protected you throughout your caregiver journey? Reflect, and then write your thoughts in a journal or on a "My Reflections" page in this book.

Prayer: Father God, you led the Israelites through the wilderness, and you are leading me through the wilderness. I am grateful. In the name of Jesus, amen.

REACHING UP FOR COMFORT
My Reflections

_____

_____

_____

_____

_____

_____

_____

_____

_____

_____

_____

_____

_____

_____

_____

_____

_____

CHAPTER 8
Things Come Together

Our family eventually found the new normal after Kendrick's stroke. It sounds so easy when I say it now, but it was hard and sometimes painful getting to a new normal. I think when something this devastating occurs, it is difficult to look for the new normal, because you are still holding on to the way things were.

What do I mean by new normal? We grew to have a better understanding of Kendrick's disabilities and of the limitations regarding my time. The stroke had also impacted us financially, emotionally, and spiritually.

Getting to the new normal was not something I did on my own. We had cheerleaders along the way. Our friend John took the lead in helping to keep Jason active in the Glenarden Boys Club track team. Jason was flown to his track events around the country at no cost to my family. Kendrick and I had been very active parents. Now we were depending on other people to do things that we had just done without any thought. I know it was still hard for Jason, because we did miss some of his best track events.

Kendrick D., our older son, was in the process of searching for colleges. I just couldn't make the number of trips that I wanted to, to help him in his search. He was an amazing student in high school. I wanted him to be happy in college.

Of course, God got him to American University not by chance. We had a cousin, Marion, who worked at American University. She really looked out for him during his stay.

Change is difficult, but it happens with or without our consent. My faith sustained me along the way as I was encouraged to go with the flow and make a new life for my family.

Romans 8:28 reads, "And we know that in all things God works for the good of those who love him, who have been called according to his purpose."

I am appreciative to this day for all the support we received. Whenever there is a major change, it is helpful to have support. And as I mentioned before, my parents, and Uncle Johnny and Aunt Dorothy (both of whom have since passed) were with us every step of the way. Kendrick's mom and younger brother, Ronald, also helped. Ronald would come and take Kendrick on rides to look at houses. It may sound like a small thing, but it was a big deal for Kendrick. And of course, there were others, such as my church family and my supervisors, who made our life much easier as well. Kendrick got better, and family life got easier. Oh, and I can't forget to mention the fundraiser and how we were supported by financial donations from Kendrick's co-workers for two years. The fundraiser was a celebration of Kendrick's life, with music, and kind words, and lots of food. The program focused on telling the story of who he is. At the time, Kendrick was still using a wheelchair. The theme of the fundraiser centered on how in the end, he would continue to run the race of life. And he has in many ways. Even today with all of his health challenges, he encourages others at the dialysis center, where he goes three times a week.

REFLECTION: During the caregiving journey, when have you witnessed all things coming together for your good? What does that look like for you? What emotion or emotions can you attach to this experience? Reflect, and then write your thoughts in a journal or on a "My Reflections" page in this book.

PRAYER: God, I thank you for continuing to remind me that you are in the midst of all that is happening. You can bring all things together. Let me not take my eyes off you. In the name of Jesus, amen.

My Reflections

_____

_____

_____

_____

_____

_____

_____

_____

_____

_____

_____

_____

_____

_____

_____

_____

_____

_____

_____

_____

CHAPTER 9
Another Storm

By 1998, Kendrick was in kidney failure. The journey became more complicated. It was one of those times that just when you think things are getting better, something else happens.

The impact of hypertension had taken a toll on Kendrick's kidneys. He had to have an emergency procedure to obtain an access, or entrance, that would allow his blood to travel to a dialysis machine.

It was a scary time. My parents were right there with us. I took Kendrick to dialysis at 6:00 a.m., on my way to work. My dad would pick Kendrick up around 10:00 a.m. I don't know exactly what this experience was like for Kendrick, but I know it had to have been difficult. He seemed to go with the flow in spite of the difficulty. I remember his doctor telling the dialysis center to give us whatever schedule we requested. He wanted it to be as easy and accommodating as possible. With Kendrick's personality, he quickly formed relationships with the other patients and the staff.

> **Matthew 8:23–27 reads, "Then he got into the boat and his disciples followed him. Without warning, a furious storm came up on the lake, so that the waves swept over the boat. But Jesus was sleeping. The disciples went and woke him, saying, 'Lord, save us! We're**

going to drown!' He replied, 'You of little faith, why are you so afraid?' Then he got up and rebuked the winds and the waves, and it was completely calm. The men were amazed and asked, 'What kind of man is this? Even the winds and the waves obey him!'"

As I reflect on this time, I realize there was just too much going on. It was like a storm, because this health event caught us totally by surprise. Trying to do it all—work, school, caring for Kendrick, and supporting our sons--was tough. Kendrick D., our older son, was now in college. Several years later, I learned that my cousin Marion had helped him with buying books. I felt sad that I was so out of touch that I didn't know he was in need of something. I know my cousin did it without any thought of us being bad parents, but it made me realize just how out of touch I was with all that was going on.

Where was my faith? I had faith. I didn't really know what was going to happen to Kendrick's health. I did realize that everything was going to be all right. I knew that I just had to hang in there. I just needed to keep Kendrick and myself encouraged.

We often take our normal bodily functions for granted. This was a huge awakening for me that anything could shift at any time. I thought I had realized that when Kendrick had his stroke, but his losing his kidney impacted me even more than the stroke. I think the stroke experience left me thinking that we'd had all the surprises one could have for a lifetime. Like the disciples, though, I wondered how long the storm was going to last. When would the end be in sight? I've often heard it said that we are either in a storm, coming out of a storm, or entering a storm. Scary!

REFLECTION: When is the last time you felt like you were in a storm? How did you navigate the storm? Reflect, and then write your thoughts in a journal or on a "My Reflections" page in this book.

PRAYER: Lord, remind me that you can calm any storm with your presence. Provide me with the peace I seek. In the name of Jesus, amen.

My Reflections

_____

_____

_____

_____

_____

_____

_____

_____

_____

_____

_____

_____

_____

_____

_____

_____

_____

_____

CHAPTER 10
God's Compassion

We waited for Kendrick to get a kidney. We prayed for a miracle. We kept doing what we needed to do. There was some talk of perhaps one of Kendrick's five siblings giving a kidney, but I don't think any of them ever went to get tested. I have only one kidney, so I didn't get tested. We didn't think about the children. Kendrick D. was in college. Jason and Corey were even younger.

In the meantime, Kendrick had several medical appointments. Many of the therapy sessions had stopped. We were doing some things on our own, like swimming. Unfortunately, Kendrick got a bad cold as a result of swimming, so we stopped that venture. I don't remember us complaining about being tired. I'm thinking that was because we were focused on trying to improve Kendrick's quality of life. But I'm sure we got tired. It makes me tired just thinking about it now.

Lamentations 3:22–24 reads. "Because of the Lord's great love we are not consumed, for his compassions never fail. They are new every morning; great is your faithfulness. I say to myself, 'The Lord is my portion; therefore, I will wait for him.'"

Then the miracle happened. Kendrick was on dialysis for only a few months. Our oldest son, Kendrick D., went to the Transplant Clinic at Washington Hospital Center to be tested. I don't even remember if he told us before he made the trip. We eventually found out that he was a five-out-of-six match. However, Kendrick D. had to have all of the conversations with the transplant manager. It was their policy that the potential donor had to work directly with the Transplant Clinic staff, so he or she would not feel pressured. The staff wanted to make sure the potential donor had all the information needed to determine whether he or she wanted to move forward. As a result of the testing and the conversation, Kendrick D. offered to serve as a living kidney donor. Yes, this was a huge blessing, but it was also scary. Kendrick D. ended up giving a kidney to his father over his college summer break. I remember our other son, Jason, saying that is a lot to do. I think he was pretty impressed, and so were my husband and I.

What was the challenge? Kendrick D. had never been in the hospital before. We took his favorite pillow and a quilt made by his grandmother to the hospital. We did everything possible to make him comfortable. Kendrick D. did great, but there was more to come before he got out of the hospital.

When I think about caregiving for my husband and my son, I am reminded of God's compassion. What we need doesn't come from the Lord like a package from the United Parcel Service. It comes cup by cup and sometimes a spoonful at a time. It comes bit by bit. Morning by morning new mercies or compassion I see.

If you are a caregiver, then you know what I'm talking about. There is no big dose to sustain us for the complete journey. We are literally going back to God on a continuous basis, trying to navigate one day at a time. If you are not going back to God on a continuous basis, then you are missing out on the doses of grace that can sustain you on this journey.

REFLECTION: How has God revealed his compassion on your journey? What does it look like? Reflect, and then write your thoughts in a journal or on a "My Reflections" page in this book.

PRAYER: God, every time I experience and see the manifestation of your compassion, I am reminded of how much you love me and my family. In the name of Jesus, amen.

My Reflections

_____

_____

_____

_____

_____

_____

_____

_____

_____

_____

_____

_____

_____

_____

_____

_____

_____

_____

_____

_____

CHAPTER 11
Unexpected Surgery

After the transplant, the doctors realized, based on the number of arteries on the kidney placed in my husband, Kendrick, that they hadn't closed off one of Kendrick D.'s arteries. As a result, the doctor had to go back and open up Kendrick D.'s body for another surgery. I was not happy, but my mother was extremely stressed just thinking about Kendrick D. having another surgery. This was her first grandson. This was her baby. I just kept praying that our son who had come to the hospital healthy would leave healthy.

That night after all the surgeries, I stayed at the hospital all night long. I remember sleeping in a chair. I was alone. This was one of those times when everything has gone quiet and you are left with yourself and your thoughts. A cleaning woman came and told me to sleep on top of my pocketbook or it might not be there when I woke up. I thought that was very helpful of her.

Deuteronomy 31:7–8 reads, "Then Moses summoned Joshua and said to him in the presence of all Israel, 'Be strong and courageous, for you must go with this people into the land that the Lord swore to their forefathers to give them, and you must divide it among them as their inheritance. The Lord himself goes before you and will be with you; he will never leave you nor forsake you. Do not be afraid; do not be discouraged.'"

Kendrick D. was in the recovery room overnight, since he had had two surgeries. It is amazing how God has designed our bodies to heal. At about five o'clock the next morning, I was allowed to go into Kendrick D.'s recovery room to talk with him. I asked him why he had given his father a kidney. He said he had given his dad a kidney because his dad needed a kidney. He felt that he had something that someone else needed. I still get chills just thinking about the gift. This has been a powerful testimony of God's faithfulness regarding the healing brought to our family. And my husband gets teary anytime he thinks or talks about it.

I was encouraged, because God was with us. God had been with us through everything. I wasn't as clear about it that day, but I am clear about it today. And when I think about the heaviness that Joshua must have felt while listening to the words of Moses, I'm sure his knowing that the Lord would be with him as he led the Israelites had to be of some comfort.

Kendrick D. was a great patient, but this was still quite an experience. He was not used to being in the hospital. Once during his stay, he called me at work and told me he was dying. I knew then that he was done with the hospital. He was tired of being in pain and tired of everything that went with the hospital. Grandma's homemade quilt and his pillow from home were not helping his state of mind anymore. Plus, he was probably feeling better. I told him that if he was dying, he would not be calling me. I assured him that if he was dying, someone else would be calling me. I assured him that I would be there soon.

My husband, Kendrick, started getting better right after receiving the new kidney. He was eating and chatting with everyone in sight, including hospital staff. I needed to get my son home quickly. It was a joy being his caregiver. So, we made it through the kidney transfer, which led to many years of Kendrick being able to enjoy life without dialysis.

Whenever there is a life-threatening event, I think there is the potential for us to shift our paradigms. I looked at my son in a different way after the experience of him giving my husband a kidney. How had he come to think this way? It was really way beyond what I knew my husband or I had given him. This was God at work in his life and in our lives. Healing would not take place overnight, but it just made sense to focus on what was going right. God was at work. Healing was happening. And sometimes when things are overwhelming, it helps to focus on the positive in the midst of everything that is going on. God is with us all the time.

REFLECTION: When is the last time you acknowledged the presence of God? How often do you acknowledge the presence of God? Reflect, and then write your thoughts in a journal or on a "My Reflections" page in this book.

PRAYER: Awesome God, I am so grateful that you are always with me even when I don't acknowledge your presence. Teach me to be more mindful of your constant presence in my life situations and circumstances. In the name of Jesus, amen.

My Reflections

_____

_____

_____

_____

_____

_____

_____

_____

_____

_____

_____

_____

_____

_____

_____

_____

_____

_____

_____

CHAPTER 12
Mom's Story

My mom, Irene Mae Pattillo Walker, was born in Altoona, Pennsylvania. She was the youngest of three children and the only girl. Her mother died when my mother was about four. I don't think my mother ever recovered from the emotional loss of her mother. She seemed to grieve silently her entire life. Her father was able to keep her and her brothers together, but my understanding is that several people lived in their house at various times to help care for my mother and her brothers. It appears that my grandfather may have even remarried at one point. My mother didn't always have the benefit of a loving home. Her father suffered from alcoholism. And her first cousin even shared that my mother was sometimes abused in the form of punishment from other adults living in the house.

Fortunately, my mother had a strong support system with her mother's sisters. I fondly remember three of them who kept a close eye on her: Aunt Barbara, Aunt Sarah, and Aunt Alice. She was also very close to her mother's brother—Uncle John—and his wife, Aunt Pauline. Her cousins Mahulda, Gladys, and Donald also played significant roles in her life. They were Aunt Barbara's children. Her cousin Willie was also a key figure in her younger years. It is my understanding that Cousin Willie was on her father's side and came to care for my mother and her brothers at some point. Even though her father's family was in Arkansas, it appears that she had a strong connection with them as well. I've had the opportunity to connect with her cousins Sally Sue and Jimmie Frances, both of whom are in their eighties.

My mother was a very extroverted person who definitely got her energy from being around people. She worked as a nurse. She was also a faithful Christian, church member, and Bible class student. She even got a certificate in Biblical Studies from Washington Bible College. After she retired, she made quilts, having a great eye for color and pattern. She was known for remembering birthdays and for having family gatherings for every occasion. Before one holiday ended, she was talking about plans for the next one. She loved family. She was faithful to her sick and shut-in friends. Even after Kendrick had recovered from his stroke, he was paralyzed and unable to work. My mother would take him with her to visit the sick and homebound. She was a very caring and supportive mother and mother-in-law to my husband and to me.

CHAPTER 13
Embrace the New Season

Mom needed a pacemaker in 2007. I started my journey as a caregiver to my parents after my mother had heart trouble and later, a loss of kidney function. My mom was talking on the phone in her kitchen with one of her best friends, Mel (who would eventually become one of my best friends as well), when she dropped the phone and passed out. My father was in the kitchen with her at the time.

Of course, my father rushed to her to see what was going on. After he was able to get her alert enough to go to the hospital, he called me. I met them at the hospital. She was in the waiting room for a short period before she was able to see a doctor. While in the waiting room, she vomited. That key piece was missed while she was in the hospital. Once she was seen by a doctor, the doctor focused on her heart and determined that she needed a pacemaker. A pacemaker made sense, but no one realized that the pacemaker was not the end of the medical attention she needed. She was scheduled for surgery to put in a pacemaker, and the surgery went well.

We thought that things would go back to somewhat normal in the near future. That was our mistake. When people have a major health event, it is usually a sign that life is getting ready to shift. Little did we know that this was the beginning of a journey that would go on for months and years. When she had vomited in the waiting room, some of that fluid had gone down into her lungs. There was so much focus on her heart and the pacemaker that the doctors didn't realize that there was fluid in her lungs. As a result, her lungs were compromised. It wasn't until she was in crisis mode that the doctors realized what had happened. She started having problems breathing and was flown from the local community hospital in Lanham, Maryland, to a larger hospital in Baltimore. Her body actually filled with fluid. She ballooned. The doctors in Baltimore struggled to get fluid off her, which led to her getting too much medication. As a result, her kidneys shut down. With her age being a factor, the kidneys never restarted. She then had to go on dialysis. She stayed in the hospital for several weeks.

Then the hospital told us she was being released. My dad and I had only a few days to decide which rehabilitation center to use. Boy, did that sound familiar! I couldn't help but think how my experience with my husband had already prepared me for this scenario. I was trying to do some quick research before we actually made visits. It really helps to make some phone calls before you start visiting rehabilitation centers. Of course, I was trying to take location and accommodations for her needs into consideration. The most difficult piece was that she still had a tube in her trachea for breathing. As some of you may know, not every rehabilitation center can accommodate the care required for a tracheostomy tube. Dad and I visited several places that could accommodate her needs.

Where did we go? We settled on a rehabilitation center

in Ellicott City. It could accommodate a patient with a tracheostomy tube. I also wanted a place that had a dialysis center in-house. This was one of the few centers (from my research) that provided that medical service. Mom spent several weeks in Ellicott City. She was an amazing patient. Even though she wanted to go home, she didn't really complain about the place or the food. It has been my observation in making hospital visits over the years that most of the time people will complain about the place and the food. I felt that the rehabilitation center in Ellicott City was a good selection. My mother also had a good relationship with her roommate. When my mom was ready to be released, she was saddened to hear that her roommate refused to go home and opted to stay in the assisted living part of the facility permanently. My mom couldn't imagine someone not wanting to be with his or her family.

I had been the driver throughout this part of the journey. I had taken my dad back and forth to the hospital in Baltimore. Now I was taking him back and forth to the rehabilitation center. Neither of these facilities was close to where we lived, but I managed to make the trip after getting off work and attending to my family's needs. Again, I was probably doing an okay job, but not doing a good job anywhere.

After a few weeks, the doctor gave my mom clearance to go home. By this time, she was off the tracheostomy tube. The transition home was a real turning point for my mother even though she didn't realize it. Even after she no longer needed the tube, she had to be on oxygen all the time. This would prove to be an issue once she got home. She didn't want anyone to see her with oxygen. I can't begin to tell you how hard it was to get her to comply with the oxygen requirement.

My mother went home with the thought that she'd be able to pick up right where she had left off. I am sure her efforts to do everything she had done in the past led to her further declining health and death. I could see that she wasn't going to be able to just resume her usual routine. My mother was used to taking care of everything for everybody. My dad had been waited on hand and foot. I remember when she first went into the hospital and my dad asked her how to make the coffee. It was so sad. He was very pampered and really didn't know how to take care of himself. He went from my grandmother taking care of everything to my mom taking care of everything. Little did I know that I was next in line.

Ecclesiastes 3:1 reads, "There is a time for everything, and a season for every activity under heaven."

As I think back on this experience, I know neither my parents nor I were prepared for the changes coming. They didn't really like to talk about preparing for the future in terms of declining health and death. They preferred to think that life would continue the same way forever. It was a very naïve approach to life. I think it made me angry at times to hear them talk this way. I have always tried to prepare for what is yet to come. And I know a plan is only a plan. We really have no control over what God will allow to come into our lives, or how. Maybe because I had been living with Kendrick and his health issues for such a long time, I was more sensitive to the fact that life can change in a moment. I have also learned that most people don't think the things you are experiencing will ever happen to them. Why? I don't know.

Now the pressure was really on me. I had probably thought the weeks of travel back and forth were rough, but my mom being home added another level of stress. My parents really needed a reality check. I was doing a very poor job of making them aware of the difference between what they wanted life to be like and what was actually happening.

I worked full-time, took care of my house, and at one point cooked for my parents seven days a week. It was overly ambitious of me, to say the least. I eventually reached out to a caregiving agency for some outside support. That certainly helped the situation, but it was still over-whelming.

My mother came home with oxygen and was on dialysis. My dad had never taken care of himself. Now he was the primary person driving her back and forth to dialysis. I constantly worried about my mother being with my dad. I felt that she wasn't getting the care she needed. I was doing what I could, but I never felt comfortable leaving her. When she came home from rehabilitation, she couldn't accept that she could no longer take care of my father. She finally got to the point where she couldn't physically do anything for him. She was totally dependent on my dad and me. When she came to my house, she would sit and watch me wash dishes or cook, and say, "I wish I could help you." I knew that she really meant those words. I'm sure it was very frustrating for her not to be able to support people like she had in the past. I remember my husband struggling with similar feelings when he became disabled.

As I focused my concern on my mother, I didn't realize the toll that all of this was taking on my dad. She kept saying that my father was having problems keeping up with things, but I never thought much about the comments. I assumed that he was experiencing normal aging issues. It was later that I discovered that my dad was bagging trash and then putting the trash in boxes. Then he was putting the boxes in the garage and the shed. Fortunately, none of it was garbage, but it was trash. The season of life had definitely changed at my parents' house, but they were not budging. It was like the weather had changed to summer but they were refusing to take off their winter coats.

REFLECTION: How have you embraced the new seasons in your caregiving journey? How has your loved one embraced the new season? What has been the greatest challenge for both of you? Reflect, and then write your thoughts in a journal or on a "My Reflections" page in this book.

PRAYER: God, thank you for the seasons of life. I know that things constantly change. Keep me focused on you so that I can adjust to what's happening at this moment. Encourage me along the way. Holy Spirit, be my advocate for the things I need but don't know I need. In the name of Jesus, amen.

My Reflections

_____

_____

_____

_____

_____

_____

_____

_____

_____

_____

_____

_____

_____

_____

_____

_____

_____

_____

_____

_____

_____

CHAPTER 14
Do the Best You Can

Even though my mother was very sick, she was still particular about her appearance. She never considered going out of the house without makeup. She still wanted to perm her hair and wear curlers at night. Help me! Getting her to the hair salon was a big challenge, especially as her health declined even more. I tried to persuade her to cut her hair and wear it natural to make things easier. She already had short hair, so it wouldn't have been a big transition. And even short, natural hair requires some maintenance.

My mother still insisted on getting a perm and putting curlers in her hair at night. I tried to accommodate her request to keep doing what she was used to doing. As one might imagine, it was not sustainable. I continued to do my best to fit her hair and nail appointments into my calendar. I took her to those appointments. It was a struggle even getting her in and out of the car, but we did it until the very end. I tried washing her hair at home with dry shampoo when we really couldn't make the journey. That came with its own challenges.

At one hair appointment, my mother actually passed out because of the heat from the dryer. That caused quite a commotion with the stylists and the other clients. Plus, she was using a walker. Then our hairstylist moved from that shop into her home. I was trying to keep the same stylist, so we followed her. Our stylist was now doing hair in her parents' basement. This required me to navigate down a hill (which was part of her driveway) to the basement level and then get my mother into the salon. It was a challenge getting her from the chair to the room with the washbowl and back. What was I thinking? It sounds funny and crazy just thinking about it now. We ended up wheeling her in a chair so that we wouldn't have to keep moving her from chair to chair.

Colossians 3:23–24 reads, "Whatever you do, work at it with all your heart, as working for the Lord, not for men, since you know that you will receive an inheritance from the Lord as a reward. It is the Lord Christ you are serving."

Matthew 11:28–30 reads, "'Come to me, all you who are weary and burdened, and I will give you rest. Take my yoke upon you and learn from me, for I am gentle and humble in heart, and you will find rest for your souls. For my yoke is easy and my burden is light.'"

When I think about my experiences and the scripture above, I must admit that I was weary. I don't think that is the right thing to say, but it is the truth. It was very difficult trying to help someone understand that things were not the same. My mother struggled to maintain what she had always known even though it often didn't make sense. Not only was the way she wanted to maintain her hair unsustainable, but my good intentions were taking a toll on my health with all the other things going on. I didn't know the answer to this dilemma then, and I still don't know the answer. I did the best I could, but it was at a cost.

REFLECTION: How have you served your loved one in the best way you know how? What was the cost? Reflect, and then write your thoughts in a journal or on a "My Reflections" page in this book.

PRAYER: God, thank you for continuing to remind me that all that we do is for you and not to bring glory to ourselves. Give me the wisdom to establish boundaries so that I can maintain my own health for the journey. In the name of Jesus, amen.

REACHING UP FOR COMFORT
My Reflections

_____

_____

_____

_____

_____

_____

_____

_____

_____

_____

_____

_____

_____

_____

_____

_____

_____

_____

_____

_____

CHAPTER 15
A Moment of Gratitude

My mother was in the rehabilitation facility over the Christmas holiday. Fortunately, the weather was good. It wasn't a short ride, but it was one that I wanted to take alone. After getting breakfast for my husband, I made my way to Ellicott City. Usually, I was the one driving my dad and my brother to see my mother. I noticed that every time I went to visit with my dad and brother, they wanted to do just that—visit. They just wanted to sit and look at her. They wanted to have some conversation and then go. I could see that things needed to be done. My dad would always say, "Leave that for the nurse." I realize now that I already had the caregiver spirit that I needed for the tasks that were ahead.

So, on that Christmas morning, I needed to go and visit my mother alone, because I wanted to be of support, not just a visitor. I was her daughter. My mother was surprised to see me. I don't remember her exact words, but I knew that she really appreciated the extra effort and was not expecting it. I would be back later in the day with my dad.

First Thessalonians 5:16–18 reads, "Be joyful always; pray continually; give thanks in all circumstances, for this is God's will for you in Christ Jesus."

On that day, I gave her a large-print Bible, something she

had asked for in the past. Now that I'm older, I certainly understand why it was such an appreciated gift. As you get older, it is difficult to read small-print Bibles. I actually have the Bible (that I gave her) at my house now. In fact, I use it as my primary Bible.

Caregiving is not just something for when your loved one gets home. When a person is aging or disabled, caregiving starts wherever he or she is. And you can do a lot of caregiving in the hospital as well. I've learned over the years that nurses and nursing assistants have only so much capacity. They are trying to care for several people, which means that they are focused on medications and doing what absolutely must be done. It is important for loved ones to have advocates to support them on their journey. Those in need of care still need their pillows adjusted and their feet repositioned or rubbed. There are cups of water to be poured. And messes to be cleaned up. I was very grateful for that one-on-one time. I give thanks for that time with her.

REFLECTION: What are you grateful for? Reflect, and then write your thoughts in a journal or on a "My Reflections" page in this book.

PRAYER: Lord, thank you for allowing me to make the choice to be grateful. Open my eyes that I may be able to see more of the blessings in the moment. In the name of Jesus, amen.

CHAPTER 16
Know that God Is Able

K endrick had another major surgery in 2008. Kendrick was doing fairly well, although he still struggled with his blood pressure. One of his doctors decided that perhaps his native kidneys were causing his blood pressure to stay high. Of course, he still had his transplant kidney as well. The surgery happened about two weeks before Kendrick D., our oldest son, got married. I didn't think that was a good idea. Did you read what I just wrote? I didn't think that was a good idea. And now I can say without hesitation that it was not a good idea.

Kendrick had surgery to remove his two native kidneys right before Kendrick D.'s wedding day. As a result of the surgery, one of his adrenal glands was damaged. I just recently found out that that is a common problem with this type of surgery. I don't remember anyone telling us about it being a possibility at the time. As a result of the adrenal gland being damaged, he had to start taking an additional medication that he'll be on for the remainder of his life. Kendrick was drained of energy on the day of the wedding, but his spirits were high. My mother was struggling physically to keep up a good front on that day as well. Like Kendrick, she was determined to experience the full day.

We made it through the wedding. Did I mention that I

also officiated at the wedding? Yes, I was also performing the wedding ceremony. So, it was a long day. And I haven't even mentioned that there were family members from out of town and I was scheduled to preach the next day, after the wedding. We went to the reception, which was also very nice. Everything was at Wesley Seminary in Washington, DC, if any of you are familiar with the grounds. It was a beautiful day! There was a little difference of opinion about the reception bill, but other than that, everything went smoothly.

After the wedding reception, Kendrick and I came home only to find a voice message from his doctor. The doctor knew that this was the day of Kendrick D.'s wedding. He apologized, and then went on to say that Kendrick's blood work wasn't what the doctor thought it should be. There was a concern about the functioning of the transplant kidney. The doctor said something along the lines of, "Mrs. Weaver, I know you are just getting home from the wedding. I'm sorry to tell you this, but Kendrick needs to go to Washington Hospital Center immediately." In other words, his working kidney did not appear to be working as well as the doctor thought that it should. We had to go to the emergency room at Washington Hospital Center right away.

Did you read what I just said? We had to go to the emergency room across town at that very moment. We were exhausted from the day. Since I was preaching the next morning, this scenario made for an interesting evening.

Let me stop and just laugh out loud at myself. Even though

most of this situation was out of my control, I still kept thinking that I could have committed to do less overall for that weekend, which would have helped some. I didn't call Kendrick D., Jason, or Corey. I didn't even call my parents at that moment. I didn't want my oldest son to find out and worry while he was off on his honeymoon. We made it through the evening, but Kendrick had to stay in the hospital. I preached the next morning. I don't remember what I preached about that day. It certainly wasn't one of my best preaching moments, but I did have real points. Then there was something going on with the caterer after the wedding reception, so in the midst of everything else, I was also dealing with that by phone. All the relatives left on Sunday after church as best as I can remember. Kendrick was released from the hospital within a few days. What an experience that was!

Genesis 18:14 reads, "Is anything too hard for the Lord? I will return to you at the appointed time next year and Sarah will have a son."

I can truly say that nothing is too hard for the Lord. Those words were said to Abraham when the Lord revealed that Sarah, Abraham's wife, would have a child. She laughed. I probably did a lot of laughing on that wedding day myself, if only about the fact that we made it through the wedding without incident. In fact, probably no one outside the family even knew what we were going through in order to get through the day. When I think about all the fanfare that goes along with a wedding, I still can't believe I was able to preach the next day. I remember going over my sermon in the emergency room of Washington Hospital

Center. It sounds so crazy when I think about it. And yes, I really believe I was far from feeling prepared, but God gave me a word. Kendrick and I still chuckle about my final sermon preparations in the emergency room.

REFLECTION: How has God shown you that nothing is too hard for him? Reflect, and then write your thoughts in a journal or on a "My Reflections" page in this book.

PRAYER: Almighty God, I know that you are able. Thank you for showing up just in time. I'm leaning on you and you only. In the name of Jesus, amen.

CHAPTER 17
Grieving Is a Process

om died in 2012. My mom died on a day when she had dialysis. I was actually feeling ahead of the game that day, because I had prepared several meals for my parents and it was still early in the day. My mom's access got clogged, so she had to go to the access center to get it cleared, then go back to the dialysis center. I told my dad I would meet him at the house, since I was bringing down food. *It is always amazing how the things we think are important are not important. I had no idea that it was my mother's last day on earth.*

I went to the house and waited for my parents. When they got there, my dad told me that my mother had been vomiting at the center. She was complaining of indigestion. We helped her upstairs to the bathroom. Then she started to have diarrhea. I was trying to clean her up and get her into the bed. I got her to the bed, but I was concerned about her pain. Of course, she didn't want to go to the hospital. She kept saying that she needed some medicine for the indigestion.

I called the doctor, but her doctor was not in the office that day. I told the doctor on call what was happening. He told me to get some pills for indigestion and give that a try. Randy, a family friend, was there, and he went to pick up the over-the-counter medicine for me. Afterward, I worked to get Mom up to give her the medicine. Then her eyes glazed over and she fell onto her side. I thought she had choked on the tablet.

Psalm 31:9 reads, "Be merciful to me, O Lord, for I am in distress; my eyes grow weak with sorrow, my soul and my body with grief."

I called my dad. Randy left. He said we had a lot going on and he didn't want to be in the way. I told my dad to call 911, but he just couldn't do it. He was trying to see if my mom was okay. Finally, I took the phone and made the call to 911. I talked to the 911 dispatcher and explained what was going on. She told me how to position my mother on her side. The paramedics came and asked a lot of questions. Now that I'm thinking about this experience, I realize it was very similar to my experience with the medics when Kendrick had his stroke.

Then they started stressing over which one of them was going to do CPR. The medics were white, and I believe they were stressing over who was going to perform CPR on an African American woman. I couldn't help but think once again that our being African American was not helping our situation. There were three medics. They asked my dad and me to leave the room. It took them only a few minutes to prepare to take her to Doctors Hospital, a local hospital that was close to their Bowie neighborhood. Dad and I followed. When we got to the hospital, they told us that my mom had passed in the ambulance. They were trying to bring her back and asked how long they should keep trying. We were in shock and told them they did not have to keep trying if they could see it was not working.

We went into the room. My mom was gone. I started to call folks, including my husband and children. Two conversations I clearly remember were with Randy, our family friend, and my brother. Randy had just been there with my parents and me at the house. He was in shock as I expected, since he had just been with us.

I also called my brother. I told him I didn't care where he was or what he was doing, that he had to come to the hospital now. I know that I scared my brother with my words. However, I believe that my approach was appropriate for what was going on.

If it wasn't difficult enough to lose a parent, I had to be interviewed by a police officer. I was told that there was an investigation to make sure there was no foul play. I agreed to be interviewed, because I didn't want my dad dealing with questions.

Then there were the funeral preparations. I had officiated at my grandmother's funeral, so I knew it was going to be a lot of work. Then of course there are all the people you have to deal with. There are people who mean well. There are people who are nosy. Then there are people who are just curious.

My father was dependent on me to make it happen. He was also naïve regarding how much planning it took and how much it cost. Even so, my mother's death was a loss. At that point I was almost numb to loss. My husband's stroke years earlier had put me in a state of experiencing loss each and every day. Even now, each time Kendrick loses more mobility or language processing, I go through a grieving process. I'm sure there were times that I didn't even realize that I was grieving those little losses day by day, month by month, and year by year.

Elisabeth Kübler-Ross talks about the stages of grief: shock, denial, anger, bargaining, and acceptance. As a caregiver, I think the grieving process is constant. We lose so many things, including the health of a loved one, our own way of life, the relationship with the person we are caregiving for, and on and on.

I don't think people often realize that when you are caring for a loved one, you are also grieving. If nothing else, you are grieving the way things were in the past.

REFLECTION: What are some of the things you have grieved throughout your journey? What does that grief look like (shock, anger, denial, bargaining, acceptance)? Reflect, and then write your thoughts in a journal or on a "My Reflections" page in this book.

PRAYER: God, comfort me day by day in the many losses that I am experiencing. In the name of Jesus, amen.

CHAPTER 18
Dad's Story

My dad, Paul L. Walker, was born in Hollidaysburg, Pennsylvania. He is the youngest of three children. He had one brother and one sister. My grandparents were not rich, but they were well off. They were very active in my life and the lives of their other grandchildren. I had a very close relationship with my grandmother, so I had the benefit of hearing stories about my dad.

My father was pampered. My grandmother told me he would come home from school at lunchtime to change his clothes. To this day, he is very particular about what he wears and what he eats. He dresses like someone going to a business meeting every day. And getting him to eat is no easy task. Breakfast consists of two eggs over easy, two pieces of bacon, a waffle or toast, coffee, water, and orange juice. Lunch and dinner can be a little challenging at times. I operate like a restaurant and try to give my dad choices, so that he will eat. And now, he usually refuses to eat anything that is green. When my mother was alive, she would iron his underwear and T-shirts.

My dad was a very good student, and even skipped a grade. He was an athlete in high school. He served in the Korean War and retired from a successful career in the public sector. My cousins always laughed, because no one really knew what he did. He was working for the National

Security Agency at the time. I think some of those earlier restrictions are no longer in place, so employees can share some information about what they do for a living. He was a good provider, father, and husband. I always remember him being in school or taking some kind of class. He didn't show emotions, so it was always difficult to read him except when someone hurt his feelings. He was very dependent on my mom for coordinating family and social activities. I don't know what we would have done without her pushing to make social and family things happen.

CHAPTER 19
Honor Your Parents

Dad was living alone. After my mother's funeral, he immediately fired Lily, the lady who was cooking for him and my mother. I shouldn't say fired. He is such a polite person. He basically told her that he didn't need any more support, because in his mind, Lily was there to help only because my mother was sick. I am not sure what he was thinking. No, let me be truthful: I'm sure he was thinking he didn't need support.

At the funeral, Kevin, my brother, told me that although I could probably get through the weekend, I needed to get Lily back. I immediately told Lily to continue showing up the following week. Kevin and I knew that things were not going to get easier. My father had never taken care of himself.

Now I really felt like I had another full-time job. I was going back and forth to Dad's house. I was worn out with worrying. I was worn out with preparing. And then he stopped eating the food that Lily prepared. I was throwing away food before she came back, because I didn't want her feelings to be hurt. That sounds crazy, I know. I thought maybe she was making too much food or that his eating alone was affecting his appetite. I wasn't sure what was going on. All I knew was that more food was being wasted and I was tired of thinking of things he would eat.

It wasn't only the food. It was the clothes, changing the bed, and so on. Even with someone else cooking, there was a lot to do in trying to keep two houses. My husband needed a lot of attention as well. And I was still working full-time and as a Local Pastor part-time. And anyone who has served in ministry knows there is no such thing as part-time ministry.

> **Ephesians 6:2–3 reads, "'Honor your father and mother'—which is the first commandment with a promise—'that it may go well with you and that you may enjoy long life on earth.'"**

Even though my mother has passed, I think the memory of her has helped me tremendously in caregiving for my father. She would have wanted me to take care of him. My mother even told my husband at some point that if she died before my dad, I would have to take care of him. She believed there were no other options.

At first, it was difficult for me because my father does not think very highly of women. He is very partial to men, especially Kevin and my sons, Kendrick D. and Jason. Somehow, I think just hanging in there with my dad has been a way of honoring not only him, but my mother.

REFLECTION: What kept you going when things became difficult? Or what is keeping you going now through your difficult moments? Reflect, and then write your thoughts in a journal or on a "My Reflections" page in this book.

PRAYER: Holy God, thank you for your commandments and your grace as a result of the sacrifice that your Son Jesus made on the cross. May I continue to walk humbly and yet boldly in knowing that the word can sustain me on this journey. In the name of Jesus, amen.

My Reflections

_____

_____

_____

_____

_____

_____

_____

_____

_____

_____

_____

_____

_____

_____

_____

_____

_____

_____

CHAPTER 20
Let Go

Caregiving is not easy. If you are a caregiver, then I know I am preaching to the choir. There are many times in the journey when I have to just let go. The work never stops. There is always something to do. There are medicines to manage and administer. There are clothes to be washed. There are meals to be prepared. There are loved ones who need to be cleaned and dressed. There are medical appointments. At some point, you have to just stop and leave the remainder of the tasks for another day.

Caregiving can also be a lonely job. Most of the time the work falls on one person unless you are blessed to have someone to share the responsibility with you. Unfortunately, it is usually a single effort.

It is almost as if people hear the word *caregiving,* think about what it really means—then run. Remember that wonderful line in *Forrest Gump* where his friend tells him, "Run, Forrest, run! Run, Forrest!" That's the image I have in my mind when some people hear the word *caregiving*.

Although we assume that people, especially family members, will understand that we need help, it doesn't work that way. There comes a point in time where you have to let go of the resentment against family members who don't have a clue about what you are going through. Some people just don't know what they don't know. Some people are too self-centered to think about other people. That is not a judgment, but an observation. You have to let go and get the help you need in the best way you can. Sometimes folks really think they are doing their part, but you just can't figure out what it is they are doing. And it is easy to say let it go, but it is not so easy to do.

> **Philippians 4:6–7 reads, "Do not be anxious about anything, but in everything, by prayer and petition, with thanksgiving, present your requests to God. And the peace of God, which transcends all understanding, will guard your hearts and your minds in Christ Jesus."**

Especially in caregiving for my parents, I talked about my hurt and frustration with anyone who would listen. You know how people say in general conversation "How are you?" Most of the time, they really don't want to know. They want you to say "Fine" and ask them how they are so they can say "Fine" and life can move on. I took this general conversation opener literally and really let people know how I felt. And as one might expect, people got tired and are tired of hearing my story. People really don't want to hear complaining.

And don't talk to a Christian. You will hear scriptures and all the good sayings that go along with being a Christian: Honor your mother and father. Live the true meaning of your wedding vows. Well, those are the right things to do, but hearing those lines isn't always helpful to the person who is a caregiver. It's like people telling you that your loved one who died has gone to a better place. Maybe they have, but hearing that isn't helpful in the moment.

So how did I let go? And how do you let go? Well, it takes prayer if you are a person of faith. It may also take therapy. The practice of Christian meditation and yoga also helped me. I have also been able to embrace a regular exercise routine.

And we must forgive. I found that the hurt inside of me was hurting only me. The hurt inside of you is hurting only you. I had to say my piece to those people in my life who caused pain, but then I had to let them go and let go of the hurt.

REFLECTION: What do you need to let go of? What have you learned to let go of? Reflect, and then write your thoughts in a journal or on a "My Reflections" page in this book.

PRAYER: God, thank you for allowing us to let go of the weight of our sin. Teach us to let go of the hurt that we experience because of others. In the name of Jesus, amen.

My Reflections

_____

_____

_____

_____

_____

_____

_____

_____

_____

_____

_____

_____

_____

_____

_____

_____

_____

_____

_____

_____

CHAPTER 21
Acknowledge the Lord in All You Do

How did I stop Dad from driving? At the end of 2014, Kevin took our dad to a car dealer, where they decided to lease a new car for Dad. I already knew something was wrong with Dad, but his Alzheimer's disease had not been diagnosed yet. Kevin knew this was going to be an issue for me. He called and said, "You're going to kill me." I knew that was his way of saying, "You are not going to be happy with what I am about to tell you." He told me Dad had gotten a new car because Dad wanted a new car.

Well, really, who doesn't want a brand-new car? So now my dad had two cars at his house. I had already been thinking about how to get him to stop driving. First, I worked on getting him to give the older car away. Dad decided to give his car to Kevin's brother-in-law. I thought that was a good idea. Unfortunately, my dad knew how to drive the old car, but the new car was a challenge. Now in his late eighties, he had trouble learning to navigate the fancy bells and whistles.

With the old car gone, he was left with the new car. He was basically driving it back and forth to McDonald's or other local places if he thought he needed or wanted to buy something. I tried to stay on top of what he was thinking about getting so I could get it for him. It helped a little, but of course Dad wanted to drive his new car. So, I hid the keys. I told only my husband. Kevin didn't think it was a problem for Dad to drive. I had heard horror stories about people with memory issues going a short distance and making a wrong turn and getting very lost. After hiding the keys, I finally took them to my house. Did that help? Well, my dad found another set of keys for the car.

Proverbs 3:5–6 reads, "Trust in the Lord with all your heart and lean not on your own understanding; in all your ways acknowledge him, and he will make your paths straight."

Then I wrote a letter to the Motor Vehicle Administration. Buddy, a longtime family friend, had already shared with my husband and me that Dad had made a left turn from the middle lane of a major road. I had my girlfriend Lisa sign the letter, and I mailed it. Oh, I thought I was doing something. Well, that did no good. We didn't hear anything for months. I called the MVA to follow up on the letter. The MVA told me that elderly people have rights. They would eventually investigate, but probably my dad would have to take a test at most. I was told in so many words that unless his doctor put it in writing that Dad should not be driving, I was fighting a battle I was not going to win.

After my dad's Alzheimer's disease was diagnosed, an MVA representative did come out to the house and visit with him. Dad told the MVA representative that although he had received a diagnosis of Alzheimer's disease, the paperwork did not say he couldn't drive. He even showed the representative the paperwork from the doctor. Lily, the lady who cooked for my dad, was at the house that day. She filled me in on the details of the visit, since she witnessed the conversation.

Eventually, the MVA sent Dad the paperwork asking him to retake the driver's test, since his doctor had not given any indication that driving was a problem. I took all the keys to my house and told him I didn't know where they were.

By this time, Dad was moving to my house. Once he had moved in, I had to make up a story about how I had found the keys. Lying always gets people in trouble. Then I asked Kevin to take the car to his house. Eventually I was able to get the leased car transferred to someone else. That was about five years ago, and my dad still has his license. So much for being proactive! He once told a caregiver that someone came to his house when he was sixty-five or sixty-eight and took his license from him. Oh my!

REFLECTION: What are some of the challenges you have faced during your journey as a caregiver? Reflect, and then write your thoughts in a journal or on a "My Reflections" page in this book.

PRAYER: Lord, thank you for getting me through difficult times. Holy Spirit, continue to guide me on this journey. In the name of Jesus, amen.

REACHING UP FOR COMFORT
My Reflections

_____

_____

_____

_____

_____

_____

_____

_____

_____

_____

_____

_____

_____

_____

_____

_____

_____

_____

_____

_____

CHAPTER 22
Troubled and Afraid

D ad's Alzheimer's disease was diagnosed in **2015.** Only a few years had passed after my mom's death before I noticed that something was going on with him. In 2014, he called me up and said he was getting a lot of money back on his tax return. He asked me to come down and take a look at his return. I discovered that he had made an error when entering the information. This was not usual for my dad. He has always been good with numbers or any activity that involved numbers. But I didn't think much about the tax return. Anyone could make that type of mistake.

Then my dad started to ask me the same questions over and over. Around the same time, Lily, who was cooking and providing some light housekeeping duties, told me that he was wearing the same clothes several days in a row. Dad has always been very particular about what he wears. He has always been obsessed with being neat, and still is, even with Alzheimer's disease.

It was October. My husband and I were preparing to go out of town. I was actually concerned about leaving my dad. When I got to Williamsburg, Virginia, I called him. He asked me about some information that we had just talked about before I left town. I called his doctor, but the doctor didn't think too much of what I was saying. I had suggested to my dad that we go see his doctor, but

Dad told me that was not necessary. The doctor did offer to talk with him. After I got back home, the doctor and I somehow persuaded him to go in for a visit. His primary doctor did some blood tests to see if he could find an explanation for the memory issue. The following February 2015 my dad got a diagnosis of Alzheimer's disease. Kevin didn't believe the doctor's diagnosis, so I took my dad to a neurologist. The result was still the same.

John 14:27 reads, "Peace I leave with you; my peace I give you. I do not give to you as the world gives. Do not let your hearts be troubled and do not be afraid."

Wow! I wasn't sure what to do with this information. My dad's response was that the doctor never gives good information. I was trying to wrap my mind around what this might mean for my dad's future and my future. I automatically wanted him to come and live with Kendrick and me. I'm not sure why. I think it was because I thought it was the best and responsible thing to do. Of course, Dad didn't want to even entertain the idea. I really had no idea what I was saying, because I was underestimating how this would work with my current home situation. Kendrick had a lot of health issues and was starting to lose kidney function again. We were going back and forth to the hospital a lot. I was still working full-time and serving as Local Pastor as well.

My dad didn't want to come. I tried once again to take on the challenge and continued to take care of both houses with this new reality. When I think about the scripture above, I realize I was definitely troubled and afraid. I was searching for a sense of peace.

What was I going to do? My mother was the only one I knew who could help and make a difference, and she was not here. Now that I look back on this situation, I wonder if I could have done something different. We can always do something different. However, I believe that in most situations, we are doing the best we can with the information and emotional capacity we have at hand.

REFLECTION: What caregiving challenge caught you by surprise? How did you navigate the challenge? Reflect, and then write your thoughts in a journal or on a "My Reflections" page in this book.

PRAYER: God, I know you are bigger than my problems. Help me to focus on you and not on my problem. In the name of Jesus, amen.

My Reflections

_____

_____

_____

_____

_____

_____

_____

_____

_____

_____

_____

_____

_____

_____

_____

_____

_____

_____

_____

_____

_____

CHAPTER 23
Jesus Is Always the Same

Dad moved in with Kendrick and me. I tried to support my dad in his home with some outside caregiver support, but Kendrick's health continued to decline. I could no longer manage both houses, even with the caregiver's support. She was basically doing meal prep (lunch and dinner), changing sheets, and doing laundry. I was trying to fix Dad's breakfast in advance to keep him from using the stove. One day I came over, only to find the frying pan in the backyard. It looked like it had caught on fire. My dad told me he didn't know what had happened to the pan or how it had gotten in the backyard. Really?

Finally, I had to trick my father into coming to stay with me. Kevin told my dad that he was going to take him golfing, but that Dad had to meet him at my house. I picked my dad up and brought him to my house, where he met Kevin. They went golfing, and then we didn't take him home. When he came back from golfing, he said he needed to shower and get his clothes. I had everything ready upstairs in his new bedroom. Lisa, my girlfriend, had helped me get the remainder of my dad's things before he returned from golfing.

Dad ended up with two rooms in our house. He has a bedroom and a room for his stationary bike and computer. He is no longer using a computer or cell phone. He put something on Facebook one time, and I knew it was time to bring that to closure as well. Later, I was even able to get his piano moved to my house. It took some adjusting for all of us.

Now my dad has his routine, which appears to be a nice way of life. One day he, Kendrick, and I were having a conversation about parents living with children. I have no idea how we got on that topic. My dad said he thought it was best if parents did not live with their children, but that he was very comfortable. We all laughed.

Hebrews 13:8 reads, "Jesus Christ is the same yesterday and today and forever."

As a part of this transition, I tried to have Lily, the lady who had supported both of my parents, come to my home to support us. She had provided care for both my parents and then for my father after my mother died. It worked for a few months, but after some time I realized that we needed a change. By then, I was attending support groups for caregivers. Even though everyone's story is different, I was encouraged to start looking for support that could help as my dad's condition changed.

My dad's condition has changed slowly, but it has changed. We are now at the point where he needs assistance taking a shower. He had been taking baths, but then one time he slipped in the bathtub. I ended up taking the tub out and putting in a walk-in shower.

I needed a caregiver who was comfortable enough to give my dad a shower. By working on that change before the need came, my dad had an easier transition with having someone help him. Reana, his current caregiver, helps him with his shower, or I do. I was concerned about this transition, especially since my dad is such a private person.

As a caregiver, you know that finding caregiving services is a very stressful process. We've had many caregivers. I've used four different companies. My biggest issue has been that you can't get the same person unless you commit to a schedule. I'm glad I figured that out sooner rather than later. I was going crazy meeting a new person every other day. I had to explain our routine over and over again. It was painful.

Overall, I've met some amazing caregivers along the way. However, I've also met people I don't want to see in my house ever again. Fortunately, it is almost five years later (working with my dad) and we finally have a regular caregiver whom I am very grateful to have. The other challenge for me was that my husband had to be comfortable with the caregiver on duty as well. It was a journey, and it still isn't over, but it is working. The caregiver definitely had to pass my husband's screening level of comfort. It was painful, but now Dad appears to be comfortable with his life here with my husband and me. Kendrick is also pleased with our current caregiver. And I couldn't have made it to this point without Natalie, the case manager with the company I use. She has listened to my stories and always tried to support my changes in schedule. I am grateful.

REFLECTION: What physical moves have taken place to support your loved one? What was your biggest challenge? How did you manage the move physically and emotionally? Reflect, and then write your thoughts in a journal or on a "My Reflections" page in this book.

PRAYER: God, I thank you for being the same yesterday, today, and tomorrow. Even when we are in the middle of moves or change, you are our one constant. In the name of Jesus, amen.

CHAPTER 24
Don't Worry About Tomorrow

Dad needed prostate surgery. He was losing kidney function. His primary doctor had a theory that his prostate might be enlarged and causing problems for the kidney. I took him to a urologist, who suggested a simple procedure to check my dad's prostate.

The day of the procedure the doctor found much more than he expected. My dad had tumors growing on his prostate. So, the doctor asked Kevin and me for permission to remove the tumors. This made the surgery a little more invasive than anticipated. My dad ended up staying in the hospital for a day or two. He was totally confused. He kept asking when he was going to have his procedure, but the procedure had already been completed. Plus, he was wearing a catheter, and that was uncomfortable and confusing.

I realized that Dad couldn't be left at the hospital by himself, because he was so confused. Fortunately, he is a very passive person, so we made it through the two days. If that ever happens again, I will hire a caregiver to stay with him. With the changing of shifts, it is difficult for the nurses to keep up with the background of the patients. When a loved one has Alzheimer's disease, the information does not always get passed on from nurse to nurse with shift changes.

Matthew 6:34 reads, "Therefore do not worry about tomorrow, for tomorrow will worry about itself. Each day has enough trouble of its own."

As a result of the surgery, we had to follow up with the urologist. My dad had a PSA level of over 600, which is very high and not normal, resulting in a diagnosis of Stage 4 prostate cancer. The doctor started him on hormone therapy. The cancer would not go away, but the goal was to keep the tumors from growing.

My dad is still losing kidney function and has a low blood count, but the primary care doctor attributes this to the aging process. Fortunately, his numbers have been stable for almost two years.

My dad is amazing. He is still up and around. He is still able to dress and use the toilet. I was concerned about traveling. His primary care doctor told me to take him on trips and enjoy the moment. I was able to take him to his sister's granddaughter's wedding in Pennsylvania in 2018. In addition, I've taken him back to his hometown in Pennsylvania for the past two years for our traditional Sunday School Picnic.

REFLECTION: When have you had to tell yourself, let tomorrow take care of itself? What did that look like for you and your loved one? Reflect, and then write your thoughts in a journal or on a "My Reflections" page in this book.

PRAYER: Lord, teach me to take one day at a time. In the name of Jesus, amen.

My Reflections

_____

_____

_____

_____

_____

_____

_____

_____

_____

_____

_____

_____

_____

_____

_____

_____

_____

_____

CHAPTER 25
Do Not Grow Weary

D **ad has also had skin cancer.** My dad's doctor told me that Dad's Alzheimer's disease appeared to be moving slowly, which might make it difficult to assess when a shift has taken place. I found this to be true. Dad had a fall in the bathtub, and then about a week later, he fell in the hallway. Both were a result of tripping, but I knew I had to step up the safety measures. As previously mentioned, I had his bathtub removed and a shower installed. Now either a caregiver helps him with his shower or I do. As a result, we started to notice things about his body. He had a strange black, crusty-looking spot on his back near his waistline. I thought it was a bruise, so I asked his primary care physician about it during a regular visit. The doctor suspected it was skin cancer and encouraged us to go to a dermatologist.

When the dermatologist looked at it, she too thought it was skin cancer, but she wasn't sure what kind. She did a biopsy at that visit. After numbing the area, she took off a piece of skin about the size of a dime. Then we had to wait about a week to get the results. My challenge was caring for the wound. It wasn't a big area, but it still required care so that it would not get infected. I eventually got the routine down, and the caregivers provided great advice as well.

I didn't realize it at the time, but this wound care was

preparing me for my dad's next procedure. The results from the biopsy indicated that my dad had skin cancer, but fortunately it wasn't the kind of skin cancer that spreads all over your body. The dermatologist said it was from the sun and there may be more spots to come. I scheduled a time for the skin cancer spot to be removed.

> **Galatians 6:9–10 reads, "Let us not become weary in doing good, for at the proper time we will reap a harvest if we do not give up. Therefore, as we have opportunity, let us do good to all people, especially to those who belong to the family of believers."**

After the surgical procedure, I had to take care of the wound for about two weeks. The removal of the entire skin cancer spot left a larger wound to manage. In addition, my dad had stitches. It was a little stressful at first, because I was concerned about disturbing the stitches. My dad was such a great patient. He always demonstrated the patience of Job in the Bible. God healed the stitches, and that is the end of that story for now.

During my dad's recovery, the caregivers really helped me to manage the wound. Their good advice supported me, along with the instructions from the doctor. I was glad that I also had the patience to get through this process. I was really excited when it was time for the stitches to be removed.

REFLECTION: When is the last time you got weary caring for your loved one? What kept you going?

Reflect, and then write your thoughts in a journal or on a "My Reflections" page in this book.

PRAYER: Lord, thank you for sustaining me on this journey. Let me not grow weary. In the name of Jesus, amen.

My Reflections

_____

_____

_____

_____

_____

_____

_____

_____

_____

_____

_____

_____

_____

_____

_____

_____

_____

_____

_____

_____

_____

CHAPTER 26
Be Mindful of What You Are Saving

When my dad moved in with Kendrick and me, it made sense to me to work toward cleaning out his house. The grass still needed to be cut. I still had to worry about the safety of the house. I transferred the mail, even before my father moved in with me. I was already thinking ahead about selling the house as well. I had heard stories about how much money it was going to take to care for my dad, especially if and when his Alzheimer's disease progressed into more advanced stages.

Well, I can say that cleaning out the house was more stressful than I could have imagined. I was still working and serving as a Local Pastor. I started with the big stuff like the furniture and worked my way down to the paper and little things.

Think about 30 years of stuff in a house with four bedrooms, a garage, an attic, and a shed in the backyard. On some days, it was overwhelming. And I can't begin to talk about the paper. There was paper in the file cabinets. There was paper in the garage. There was paper in the shed. There was paper in boxes. There was paper in closets. I gained greater insight into the struggle that my father was having with his brain function.

And the decision-making process wasn't easy. It was too much. It was emotional. It appeared to be never-ending. The only decision I was clear about when I finished was that I wanted to get my house cleaned out immediately. I have been actively working on decluttering my house since my experience with cleaning out my dad's house.

> **Luke 12:15–21 reads, "Then he said to them, 'Watch out! Be on your guard against all kinds of greed; a man's life does not consist in the abundance of his possessions.' And he told them this parable. 'The ground of a certain rich man produced a good crop. He thought to himself, "What shall I do? I have no place to store my crops." Then he said, "This is what I'll do. I will tear down my barns and build bigger ones, and there I will store all my grain and my goods. And I'll say to myself, 'You have plenty of good things laid up for many years. Take life easy, eat, drink and be merry.'"" But God said to him, "You fool! This very night your life will be demanded from you. Then who will get what you have prepared for yourself?" 'This is how it will be with anyone who stores up things for himself but is not rich toward God.'"**

It actually took me about a year. First, I gave away all the big furniture. I called Kevin and asked him what he wanted. I felt bad at one point, because I gave my dad's bedroom set away. Later, Dad asked if he could have his bed out of his house. What was I going to do? Yes, I admit that sometimes I moved too fast. Kendrick D., my son, told me that maybe Dad would forget about his request, since he was experiencing memory loss. However, he didn't forget. He didn't like the bed in his room at my house. So, I ended up buying him a new bed.

It was a lesson learned. I had to figure out how to balance my own anxiety to get this project done with what made sense. Oh, that sounds good now. At the time, I just wanted to get it all over with as fast as possible. I went through papers. I sorted. I gave stuff away. I had a shredding company bring a truck to the house. I called College Hunks, who are movers, to come to the house several times. Some of the workers knew me personally. I made piles. I went to Goodwill. It was a lot of work. I didn't think I would ever get to the end, but about a year later, I finally did.

REFLECTION: How could removing clutter support you on your caregiving journey? What physical and emotional clutter needs to be removed? Reflect, and then write your thoughts in a journal or on a "My Reflections" page in this book.

PRAYER: God, I know that you are a God of order. Teach me how to keep clutter out of the various areas of my life. Allow me to experience the freedom and peace created inside as a result of decluttering. In the name of Jesus, amen.

My Reflections

CHAPTER 27
Enjoy the Journey

I don't think there is anything funnier than what I've learned by traveling with loved ones who require care. I have taken several trips with my husband (who is disabled) and my father (who is suffering from Alzheimer's disease). In 2019, we went to Williamsburg, Virginia, for my husband's birthday. This is a ritual for my husband. That year I had also reserved rooms for my children to join us for the weekend. I was able to get two of the three sons, one daughter-in-law, one girlfriend, and two grandchildren. That was a huge accomplishment in itself.

A learning moment. My husband, Dad, and I arrived on a Friday evening. By Saturday morning when we went to breakfast, I realized that my husband and Dad just wanted to eat and watch television, just like they do at home. They couldn't wait to get back to the hotel after breakfast. Fortunately, I was able to take advantage of my free time and drove to several places in Williamsburg that I like to visit. I'm learning to make the best of any situation. It may take me a little longer sometimes, but eventually I figure out how to make things work for me.

A funny moment. On that Saturday afternoon, the others came into town in time for dinner. It was a buffet. I went to get my father some food and help my husband with his plate. When I got back, my dad was gone. Jason, my son, told me that Pappap (referring to his grandfather) had gone to the restroom. Then Corey, another son, told me that Pappap had followed Jasmine, Corey's wife, to get to the restroom. However, Jasmine was now back in my sight.

Now, we were out of town and the place was packed. Hundreds of people were in the restaurant, walking all over the place in every direction. Did I mention that my dad is suffering from Alzheimer's disease? I panicked. Corey went to the men's room with me to see if Dad was still in there. Fortunately, he was. It was one of those moments when all you can do is laugh. Of course, my dad stayed in the restroom for a long, long time. That is his usual routine at home. I think he forgets that he is finished, and starts the process all over again. All I could do was wait.

After my dad came out, I got him back to his seat. Then he decided he was not going to eat any food. Food was everywhere. One could have whatever one's heart desired. What could I do? Nothing. I think my dad just wanted to get back to the hotel room. I am realizing more and more just how taxing it is for a person with Alzheimer's disease to have to go with the flow. And I'm sure many are not as cooperative and easygoing as my dad. I am grateful. And I was grateful that the boys and their families made the effort to travel that distance to be with their dad.

Ecclesiastes 2:24–25 reads, "A man can do nothing better than to eat and drink and find satisfaction in his work. This too, I see, is from the hand of God, for without him, who can eat

or find enjoyment?"

Psalm 39:5 reads, "You have made my days a mere handbreadth; the span of my years is as nothing before you. Each man's life is but a breath."

All we can do is enjoy the journey. We all know that life is short and tomorrow is not promised. All experiences will someday be memories. As I write these words, I am also taking the time to chuckle.

REFLECTION: What experiences have caused you to laugh? What experiences have taught you a lesson? Reflect, and then write your thoughts in a journal or on a "My Reflections" page in this book.

PRAYER: Lord, thank you for the gift of laughter. I'm sure I've caused you to laugh at me. Thank you for allowing me to laugh at myself. In the name of Jesus, amen.

REACHING UP FOR COMFORT
My Reflections

_____

_____

_____

_____

_____

_____

_____

_____

_____

_____

_____

_____

_____

_____

_____

_____

_____

_____

_____

_____

CHAPTER 28
What's Next?

T his is a question that only you can answer for yourself. As for me, I am still in the middle of caregiving. As I said in the beginning, you could be at any point in the caregiving journey. If you have just finished your caregiving assignment, then realize that there may be more caregiving assignments to come. Perhaps you really don't want to think about having to do this all over again.

Unfortunately, caregiving needs sometimes come unexpectedly. It has also been my observation that many people are not preparing for the life transitions around aging or loss of health. In other words, I don't believe that many people are preparing to be caregivers. I also don't believe that many people are preparing for their own caregiving needs. If we live long enough, we will need some type of caregiving support. No matter where you are in the process, I leave you with these three summary themes gathered them from the previous chapters.

Trust in God. This is a life experience that you will not be able to get through on your own. If you are not a Christian, I would suggest talking to someone about the Christian faith and what it means to believe in God, the Father, the Son, and Holy Spirit.

Get some support. Most of the time we focus on our financial needs and those things that are tangible. In reality, we need various types of support on the caregiving journey. You will need physical, emotional, financial, and spiritual support. Don't get stuck on those areas where you are not getting the support you expected. Research the options you have available. Sometimes a stranger will be your greatest support.

Take care of yourself. We hear this all the time, but it takes courage and energy to really put this into practice. There always seems to be time for everyone's needs but your own. If you want to continue to care for someone, you have to make yourself a priority. It is not uncommon for a caregiver to die before the loved one being cared for.

Remember. This is not meant to be everything you need for the caregiving journey. Writing this was a very therapeutic process for me, but I hope someone can gain some benefit from where I've already been. In some ways, it is just another way of telling you what you probably already know. Life is short. Try to make things as easy as possible and enjoy the journey.

About the Author

Karen Weaver supports Christ-centered women navigating career and life transitions, and helps them achieve their goals through her company, Crosswalk Coaching and Consulting, LLC. She also serves as a consultant, mentor, speaker, and retreat designer/facilitator. She is a credentialed coach through the International Coach Federation.

She earned a bachelor's degree from Georgetown University, a graduate degree from Bowie State University and two graduate degrees from Wesley Theological Seminary. She enjoyed a 40-year career in the public and private sectors including service at a federal agency, a university and three private industry companies. She also served as a Local Pastor in The United Methodist Church for approximately five years.

Karen, her husband Kendrick, and their family live in the Maryland. She serves as a caregiver to her husband and father.

My Reflections

_____

_____

_____

_____

_____

_____

_____

_____

_____

_____

_____

_____

_____

_____

_____

_____

_____

_____

_____

_____

For more information about Karen's coaching business, please visit her website at www.crosswalkcoaching.com.

Or you may email her at karen@crosswalkcoaching.com.

Made in the USA
Middletown, DE
14 June 2021